T3-BNH-778

# Public Opinion, the President, and Foreign Policy

## *Four Case Studies from the Formative Years*

**Doris A. Graber**

*University of Illinois
at Chicago Circle*

HOLT, RINEHART AND WINSTON, INC.
*New York · Chicago · San Francisco · Atlanta ·
Dallas · Montreal · Toronto · London*

For Tom,
Unfailing Source of Encouragement

This book has been prepared under the auspices of the Center for the Study of American Foreign and Military Policy at the University of Chicago.

Copyright © 1968 by Holt, Rinehart and Winston, Inc.
Library of Congress Catalog Card Number: 68–26991

**2708550**

Printed in the United States of America
1  2  3  4  5  6  7  8  9

# Foreword

All systems of government derive their legitimacy from a myth, be it the monarch governing by the grace of God, an aristocracy governing by dint of superior endowment with wisdom and virtue, or an elected government governing with the consent of the people. These myths, in an ascending order of probability, are exposed to empirical refutation. When Charles II and Louis XVI lost their heads, the justification of monarchy through the divine right of kings lost some of its plausibility. After an upstart from Corsica had swept the aristocracies of Europe from power, it became difficult to believe in the natural superiority of aristocratic rule. Witnessing the decisive influence that elites exempt from democratic control exert upon the policies of democratic governments, one cannot help but doubt the literal truth of the proposition that this is a government of the people, by the people, for the people.

Yet, while the legitimacy of democratic government is exposed to empirical refutation, it is also susceptible to empirical confirmation. Whether or not a government governs with the consent of the governed, whether or not its policies reflect the preferences of the majority of the people is not a matter of theological dogma or metaphysical propositions, but can, at least within certain limits, be ascertained by empirical investigation. It goes without saying that such an investigation raises fundamental issues of a philosophical and theoretical nature, which the contemporary theory of public opinion mistakenly deems to have been settled. For instance, is there such a thing as public opinion with regard to policy formation antedating the formation of policy itself? Or, is not such a public opinion the result of the government's commitment to pursue a certain policy or of vocal opposition to it? In other words, is public opinion the spontaneous expression of popular preferences or is it rather the derivative manifestation of the preferences of the government or of

iii

some counter-elite in opposition to the government? Whatever the outcome of such an empirical investigation may be, it is certain that the relationship between public opinion and policy formation is much more complex and ambiguous than the folklore of democratic government would have us believe.

To elucidate these issues, the empirical investigation of American foreign policy appears particularly promising. For the apparent contradictions between the assumptions of democratic theory and the conventions of democratic folklore, on the one hand, and the practice of policy formation, on the other, are nowhere more striking than here. From the very beginning, the conduct of American foreign policy has continuously been characterized by conflict between the executive branch, on the one hand, and Congress and the people at large, on the other. The latter have time and again accused the former of the usurpation of constitutional powers that belong to them, and the former has reproached the latter for their obstruction. Sometimes the President has pursued a foreign policy in open defiance of public opinion, as Washington did in 1793 when he declared the neutrality of the United States in the War of the First Coalition. Sometimes the President has tried to rally public opinion in support of his foreign policy, as Wilson did when he stumped the country on behalf of the ratification of the Covenant of the League of Nations. Sometimes the President has pared down his foreign policies to the measure acceptable to public opinion, as Franklin D. Roosevelt did in the years preceding the Second World War. Sometimes, the policies of the President coincided with the preferences of public opinion, as was the case during the Eisenhower Administration.

Can any general conclusions be drawn from these conflicts, divergencies, and coincidences? If there is an answer to this question, it can only be the result of the empirical investigation of the actual conduct of American foreign policy and its relations to public opinion. It is the great merit of this book that it raises these issues, which are vital for American democracy in general and for the responsible conduct of American foreign policy in particular. By doing so, it not only sheds new light upon the history of American diplomacy, but also contributes to the clarification and revitalization of certain principles of democratic government.

HANS J. MORGENTHAU

# Preface

The complexities of political behavior can best be explored by using the vantage points of many social sciences. History supplies the patterns and perspectives of the past. Political science analyzes these patterns and distills principles of political interaction from them. Sociology furnishes insights into the cultural settings that shape the minds and personalities of political actors. Psychology traces the why's and wherefore's of individual reaction patterns. A rounded view of political reality requires the perspectives of all these disciplines. Hence data for this book have been collected and combined from all the relevant social sciences.

Unfortunately, in a study of long-dead individuals from the pre-Gallup age, polling data and depth interviews are unobtainable. Although the unavailability of these prized modern research tools is regrettable, there is a weighty compensation for their lack—the rich historical record, researched and analyzed by many different scholars, whose approaches complement each other and whose prejudices, hopefully, cancel each other out. Perceptive analysis of this wealth of data avoids some of the shortcomings of findings that are based on polls and interviews. The historical record reveals a political actor's reactions over a long time span, diminishing the distortions of fleeting moods and of particularized reactions to the personality of the interviewer. Contemporary historical data are voluminous enough for the formative years of American politics, especially in an age of prolific correspondence, to disclose which ideas were typical of each President and which were passing fancies, politically motivated adaptations, or responses to atypical circumstances.

A concerted effort has been made in this book to exclude what seemed to be unrepresentative deviations from the norm or to mark them clearly as exceptional occurrences. Allowances also have been made for the fact that subjective editing of human errors and failures begins the moment a political actor records, verbally or in writing, what has happened. "Success," as President Kennedy was fond of saying, "has a thousand fathers,

v

but defeat is an orphan." Autobiographical history must be read in light of this human foible.

The bulk of the research effort which has gone into this book has yielded negative data—an absence of specific concern with public opinion. This is an important finding, even though it is discouraging to the researcher who spends countless hours examining in full all the formal and informal writings of key participants in the decision-making process, as well as contemporary interpretations and the analyses of historians and political scientists. But even when the record sheds little direct light on the President's concept of public opinion, it clarifies his personality, his social relationships, and the social and political philosophies and conditions of his time. Reconstruction of the President's decision-making activities benefits from the fullness of this background of the puzzle of history.

The data presented in this book have been selected in the light of modern decision-making theories. They are not intended as a full historical account, but focus rather on the narrow perspective of one man—the President. It is his world that is featured, his definition of public opinion which prevails. If momentous events occurred beyond his knowledge, they were excluded. If publics clamored for attention but he was unaware of it, their claims have been mentioned only in passing. The influence of public opinion on the foreign policy activities of congressmen, secretaries of state, and other major decision makers has been included only from the perspective of the impact of these actors on the President. Since Presidents are the final decision makers in foreign policy, the picture of public opinion influence on foreign policy that emerges when the focus is on the President is not unduly narrow.

How can one tell what comes to a President's attention and what interpretations and values he places upon it? Beyond a careful analysis of the record, in light of the President's personality, philosophy, and past actions, one has to depend on scholarly wisdom and intuitive capabilities. This, of course, is slippery ground. Conclusions rest on impressionistic and often incomplete data and on the risky assumption that Presidents act fairly consistently within the framework of their personalities, early socialization, and later experiences. Little room is left for "out of character" acts and events. Such acts and events are embarrassing when they do not fit into the analyst's conceptual framework. They may distort it when the framework is altered to make room for exceptions that should have been excluded from the norm. It is small consolation to know that no absolute proof of accuracy is possible, beyond the reassurance that comes from the supporting interpretations of other scholars who have used the same data for related purposes. Even depth interviews by trained psychologists involve large elements of subjective interpretation, akin to the diagnostic criteria used in this book.

The cases that constitute the empirical portions of this study share the assets and liabilities of all case studies. They illuminate abstract theories through concrete, colorful examples. They are concisely focused in time and range of observation. Yet they are unique, limited in type, time, and number. In this book, only one major decision of each President is put under the political microscope. Although a scanning of other major decisions bears out the conclusions, generalizations from one case study about a President's political behavior require the proverbial grain of salt.

Even when one considers the four case studies as a group that is representative of presidential decision making, one is still in the marshes of uncertainty. All the cases involve relatively unique occurrences in American history. What they say about the game of international politics played for major stakes may not hold true when the game is played penny ante. How valid the conclusions are for decision making under less dramatic circumstances remains to be tested. A few of the events reported in this book support a hunch that opinions of specialized publics may be more influential in minor decisions than in major ones, and that concern with the general public recedes into the background when prosaic issues are involved. Moreover, public opinion may be more crucial at the earlier predecisional phases than at the later ones examined in this book. It may reach a high crest of potency when preliminary decisions take place in a forum readily accessible to public pressures, such as Congress at election time. Public opinion may also be more crucial in the various implementing decisions that follow a trend-setting major decision by the President.

While the policies studied here are similar in that all concern major interests and that all occurred at an early period of American history, they are quite diverse in other respects. These variations broaden the scope of the conclusions. The case studies involve four Presidents with vastly different personalities and with different conceptions and styles of leadership. They encompass periods of both congressional quiescence and hostility. In Madison's case, they entail heavy congressional influence on policy making, while the remainder of the decisions illustrate presidential paramountcy. The cases deal with Presidents who faced much hostility from the out-party and Presidents who had little out-party competition. They include periods of intense intraparty factionalism and periods of intraparty calm. This diversity illuminates the bearing that various environmental political factors have on the role assigned to public opinion in foreign policy decisions.

The cases also demonstrate the use of public opinion in three major types of foreign policies, to borrow a distinction developed by Roger Hilsman (in *Journal of Conflict Resolution*, 3, 1959, p. 376). The Louisiana Purchase and, possibly, Adams' mission to France involved a crisis policy —a reaction to an external event requiring speedy decision. The War of

1812 was a program policy—one developing over time, requiring various implementing steps. Successive economic coercion policies and military mobilization measures were steps building up to the final decision. The Monroe Doctrine is an example of the third type of policy—an anticipatory policy requiring statements about how the United States would react to foreseeable future contingencies. Differences and similarities in the use of public opinion in these various types of decisions indicate the adaptations that may be expected when policy types differ.

A comparison of the political theories of the four Presidents with their actions permits some estimates about the ability and willingness of political actors to bring words and deeds into accord. But more than that, it sheds light on the relative importance of the pressures of the presidency compared to preinaugural role perceptions. If Presidents with different theories abandon them and act in similar ways, it may be concluded that theories give way to the pressures of the job. Again, the examples in this book are not numerous enough to make unqualified generalizations. Still, one can take some comfort from the fact that the four Presidents studied here constitute more than 10 percent of the incumbents of the American presidency. Generalizations that may seem too bold when numbers alone are counted may become quite respectable when one computes percentages that relate the size of the sample to its total population.

Acknowledgments are never short enough to suit the reader, nor long enough to include the names of all people who, in small or large ways, have contributed their brain and brawn to a book. My thanks go to all who have helped me in any way whatever. Among those who undertook important research tasks, Peter Knauss, formerly of Northwestern University, and Thomas Graber of the University of Chicago deserve special mention for their diligence, enthusiasm, and resourcefulness. Professor Robert Remini of the University of Illinois at Chicago Circle gave the manuscript the benefit of his intimate knowledge of early American Presidents. His numerous suggestions have improved the historical precision of the book and sharpened the presentation. Professor Hans Morgenthau, Director of the Center for the Study of American Foreign and Military Policy at the University of Chicago, has played the role of intellectual godfather of the book. His critique of initial outlines fixed the scope and focus of the study, and his advice and encouragement throughout the long writing period helped keep it on course.

D.A.G.

*Evanston, Illinois*
*August 1968*

# Contents

# 1

# The Problem:
# The Opinion-Policy
# Relationship

> . . . What power should be assigned to the mass of free men
> and citizens, who are not rich and have no personal merit . . . ?
> There is still a danger in allowing them to share the great
> offices of state, for their folly will lead them into error, and
> their dishonesty into crime. But there is a danger also in not
> letting them share, for a state in which many poor men are ex-
> cluded from office will necessarily be full of enemies.
> ARISTOTLE, *Politics*

# 1

It is a sacred axiom of the democratic creed that government must heed public opinion in formulating public policy. But although we have treasured this article of faith for centuries and regard it as one of the most sacred cows grazing in democratic ideological pastures, we have very few precise notions of what it means in practice. This lack of precise knowledge about the role of public opinion in governmental decision making in our American democracy has tempted me to go back to the days of the founders of our nation to try to discover what they had in mind when they spoke of government in accordance with public opinion.

## Men and Decisions

I proceeded on the assumption that the founding fathers, as the first American statesmen who had to practice the new preachments of national government guided by public opinion, were more likely than later practitioners to analyze their political assumptions critically and more apt to search diligently for political techniques to carry them out. Moreover, they lived in a historical period in which public interest in governmental policies was at a peak because most Americans felt that political events had a direct impact on their lives and livelihood. If ever there was a public opinion to listen to, to work with, and to struggle against, this was the time. It was also a time when the nation was still small enough so that a relatively high percentage of citizens could be in direct communication with their representatives.

What I have tried to discern from the study of men and decisions at the start of our nation can be put in the form of three questions. First, why did the founders of the nation who were practicing politicians deem it essential to consider public opinion in making policy decisions? Did they merely re-echo a cry of the times, because it happened to be a political fashion? Did they preach it out of conviction that *vox populi* was truly *vox Dei*,[1] wiser than the voice of any single ruler or ruling group? Or were there

---

[1]The phrase was used as early as 798 A.D. in a letter to Charlemagne. See Francis G. Wilson, *A Theory of Public Opinion*. Chicago: Henry Regnery Company, 1962, p. 20. Walter Lippmann contends that the phrase was an attempt to transfer the divine attributes of kings to the people. See his *The Phantom Public*. New York: The Macmillan Company, 1927, pp. 57–58.

3

practical reasons for giving sway to public opinion and practical limitations on the scope to be allowed to it?

The second question is, given the need of worshiping at the altars of public opinion, what was the scope of influence that they believed must be given to public opinion? This query opens a host of quantitative as well as qualitative issues about the role of public opinion. For instance, should public opinion guide only the overall direction of policy? Should it be influential in its details—or, phrased differently, is consensus on the ends of policy enough or must there be consensus on the means too? How many voices constitute "consensus"? If there are many trends of opinion and none is held by a majority of citizens, which opinion deserves to be called "public" and to guide policy? Assuming that a majority can be discerned, should public opinion be the same as majority opinion? Or are there qualitative criteria that could make the voices of the minority more commanding than those of the majority? In any given decision should public opinion be the deciding factor, the most important single factor, or merely one of various equally important factors? Are there certain issues in which it is better to "let sleeping dogs lie" and not inform the public at all if policy makers can get away with secrecy? Do answers vary with the issues and with the pressures of the times?

The third question to be considered is what were the mechanics by which public officials tried to ascertain what the public wanted? Public opinion is not like a Greek chorus speaking in unison and requiring only that public officials keep their ears open in the market place and in the halls of the legislature. Government officials hear many voices or no voices at all, and what these voices say is often dissonant, indiscernible, or inaudible. Depending on when and where the politician puts his proverbial ear to the ground what he hears varies between geographical areas, economic groups, adherents of different parties, and even from day to day. In this Babel of voices, how can one know which truly speak for the "public"? It is difficult enough to ascertain a "yes" or "no" command after policy alternatives have been formulated, but how do conscientious public officials gain access to policy suggestions that may have been generated at the grass roots level and talked about in the citizens' parlor and in public places? What answers did the founders give to these questions? What practical solutions did they devise?

I shall examine questions such as these first by looking at the theories expressed by the founders in their writings, and second by scrutinizing their actions to see whether they tried to put their theories into practice. One must square words with deeds to judge whether a man's theories are merely false fronts behind which he hides his unwillingness or inability to make his deeds conform to his promises. If a man is willing to practice what he preaches, a comparison of words with deeds can show how feasible the theories are under the circumstances and what means are tried to carry them out.[2] Of course, neither expressed intent nor overt action may correspond to the actor's real thinking or subconscious motivation. But until we possess better yard-sticks of motivation measurement, verbal expressions, put in their situational context and checked against action, are our best guides to the relationship between theory and practice.[3]

The Presidents whose decisions we shall analyze are pictured as representatives of the thinking of their age as well as distinct personalities. Each constitutes a unique amalgam of personal traits, circumstances, and social climate. Yet each typifies the *Weltanschauung* of his contemporaries because a common social heritage marks men as indelibly as does their biological inheritance. Just as one could draw a picture of Thomas Jefferson with pig-tailed wig, lace-filled jabot and tight knee breeches and label it "a typical eighteenth century country squire," so could one label an account of Jefferson's activities and writings as a representative intellectual portrait of a member of the governing elite of eighteenth century America. This is why the ideas, ideals, and modes of action of Adams, Jefferson, Madison, and Monroe are more than unique occurrences. They are typical experiences of representative American Presidents, and as such deserve

[2]A recent study of decision making claims that case histories show great divergence between practice and theory. The theory pictures decision making as "a sequence of independent choices made by executives . . . with the assistance of top staff and through consultation with their subordinates, these men . . . carry out decision-making functions . . . through the rational process of defining a problem, identifying the alternatives, selecting the most appropriate and acceptable alternatives, translating it into a course of action, and initiating the implementing activities." The practice is far less rational. William J. Gore, *Administrative Decision Making.* New York: John Wiley & Sons, Inc., 1964, pp. 132–133.

[3]For some doubts on whether a person changes his behavior when his beliefs change see Leon Festinger, "Behavioral Support for Opinion Change," *Public Opinion Quarterly,* vol. 28, 1964, pp. 404–17. For contrary views see Anthony G. Greenwald, "Effects of Prior Commitment on Behavior Change after a Persuasive Communication," *Public Opinion Quarterly,* vol. 29, 1965, pp. 595–601. Also see the interesting observations on "attitude toward an object" and "attitude toward a situation" and their relation to behavioral change in Milton Rokeach, "Attitude Change and Behavioral Change," *Public Opinion Quarterly,* vol. 30, 1966, pp. 529–550. Hadley Cantril contends that "opinions upon which concrete judgments and actions are based, often appear to go contrary to opinions abstractly held, since the latter are purely intellectual data that either call for no concrete action or offer no possibility of concrete action." See "Opinion Trends in World War II: Some Guides to Interpretation," *Public Opinion Quarterly,* vol. 12, 1948, p. 41.

study as models of executive decision making. They are broadly relevant for both their time and ours. Basic social processes, like decision making in various forms of government, have changed very little. The social scientist "deals with a field in which there is (in a sense analogous to that of the physical sciences) nothing new to discover." Nonetheless, "certain older wisdom has to be taught again and again in new language . . ." and it must be applied to new conditions.[4]

Turning to the specific subjects selected for this study—four early Presidents and four major foreign policy decisions in their administrations—a few words ought to be said in explanation. I have already given my reasons for choosing founding fathers. These were men who were consciously setting up a new system of government. They carefully selected the theories on which it ought to be based and then tried to devise techniques to implement these theories. This makes it more likely that they wrestled intellectually and practically with their choice of theory and with problems of application. Since they cast the mold in which the stream of American politics flows today, their theories and practices have become the bedrock of present American politics. An understanding of these theories and practices is important to an understanding of the role of modern public opinion in American politics.

The study focuses on the opinion-policy relationship, as seen from the presidency's perch. It does not seek to describe, except incidentally, how people form their opinions about foreign policy and how they try to bring them to bear on the decision makers. Rather, the focus is just the opposite. The main question is: "What did important decision makers think about the role of public opinion in foreign policy formulation, and what conscious use did they make of this opinion as they heard and interpreted it?" For in the end, it is the leaders' appraisal of what public opinion is and what role it must play that determines the nature of the public opinion ingredient in public policy. It is important to discover which voices, out of the cacophony of the public chorus, leaders pick as *the* public, and what scope they assign to public opinion in the decision-making process.

The cases chosen for examination involve four major controversial foreign policy decisions. Chronologically, they are Adams' decision to resume negotiations with France in 1800 in order to avoid war with her; Jefferson's decision to purchase Louisiana in 1803 despite doubts about the constitutionality of the purchase; Madison's policy of leading the country into war in 1812 at the risk of breaking up the Union; and Monroe's espousal of the hemispheric security principle in 1823, which became famous as the Mon-

[4]Leslie Fiedler in Eugene Burdick, *et al., American Voting Behavior.* New York: The Free Press, 1959, p. 189.

roe Doctrine. All four cases share certain features that made them particularly suitable for this study. They involved controversial and much publicized issues. This meant that they aroused expressions of public opinion and conflicting pressures on the government. Presidents were forced to consider public opinion because it was vocal and because their policies could not succeed without public support.

Each of the four policies culminated in a single decisive action. This makes it easier to analyze how various considerations that went into the final decision interacted, and what role public opinion factors played in the crucial period immediately preceding the decision. The crucial predecisional period is relatively short in all four cases, ranging from four months in the case of the Monroe Doctrine to eleven months in the Adams decision. The time span of a few months makes it feasible to examine the decision-making process with a fair degree of depth while retaining some breadth of perspective in order to avoid the distortions of myopic examinations. Another important factor in choosing the four cases is the comparative wealth of material that is now available for studying decision making during the early days of our country. All our protagonists were prolific writers and vocal political philosophers, and their formal writings as well as their voluminous correspondence have been published in full. The written records of their associates and of politically influential people of the period are equally voluminous.[5] In addition to ample primary sources, numerous biographies and research studies of the period provide a rich harvest of information relevant to public opinion, foreign policy decision making, and the intellectual climate of the times.

Why choose examples from foreign policy? The reasons are several. In the American governmental system, foreign policy, more than most aspects of domestic policy, tends to be formulated by a limited number of people. Most of these people are gathered closely around the President, who has a guiding role in foreign policy formulation. This was especially true during the early years of the nation, when the State Department was quite small and easily supervised by the President, and when congressional influence on foreign policy formulation was comparatively slight.[6] It is therefore easier

[5]Although the sources are comparatively ample, many uncertainties remain. Short of a complete recording of every detail of life, such uncertainties are unavoidable. Eye witnesses to decision making in the White House disagree about happenings that all of them witnessed, even shortly after the event. Compare, for example, the various accounts of participants in the Kennedy Administration.

[6]It has remained slight. See James A. Robinson, *Congress and Foreign Policy Making*, rev. ed. Homewood, Ill.: The Dorsey Press, 1967, *passim*. Also see James S. Young, *The Washington Community, 1800–1828*. New York: Columbia University Press, 1966, p. 214.

in foreign policy than in other affairs to track down the process of decision making and to determine what influences played a substantial part in these decisions.

The Presidents selected for this study considered themselves experts in this field. John Adams had labored in the vineyards of diplomacy for nine years before he became President. Thomas Jefferson had served for eight years, including three as Secretary of State. James Madison had been Secretary of State for eight years, and James Monroe had a total of twenty years of diplomatic experience including three years as Secretary of State. With this background, the Presidents felt qualified to speak authoritatively on foreign affairs. They were not likely to seek advice from other sources out of a feeling of ignorance or insecurity. Rather, when they sought advice to supplement their own ideas, their choice of advisors was apt to be dictated by their political theories and practical experiences.

At this point perhaps one should raise the question of whether data from foreign policy formulation are representative of the role that public opinion can and does play in public policy formulation in general? Is *foreign* policy formulation a unique case? Such, indeed, it was deemed to be by philosophers such as Locke and Montesquieu who considered the "federative power"—the power to deal with foreign affairs—as separate from ordinary legislative powers, and not subject to direct popular control. Nonetheless, the notion that foreign policy matters should be excluded from popular control has been rejected in theory as well as in practice in the United States since the eighteenth century. Other parts of the democratic Western world followed suit in the nineteenth century. The reasons were theoretical as well as practical. It seemed contrary to the essence of democracy to exclude popular influence from one of the most crucial areas of public policy making—crucial in the sense of influencing the life and welfare of the individual. In the days of the citizen army and the fully mobilized nation it was particularly important to gain wide public support for a nation's leaders and their foreign policies. Besides, where could one reasonably draw the line between domestic and foreign policy? Diplomatic negotiations might be conducted without public knowledge and involvement, but most foreign policies adopted in the wake of diplomatic negotiations involve public participation on a minor if not a major scale.[7]

One can, therefore, claim a wide basis of approval in the United States and elsewhere for the belief that popular influence is as essential in foreign

[7]On this point see Leon D. Epstein, "Democracy and Foreign Policy" in William N. Chambers and Robert H. Salisbury, eds., *Democracy in the Mid-Twentieth Century: Problems and Prospects.* St. Louis: Washington University Press, 1960, pp. 126–127, 129.

policy formulation as it is in other types of policy formulation.[8] It can thus indicate the type of role that public opinion can perform (with variations) in policy formulation in general. In many respects it provides an exceptionally good model. The difficulties of forming intelligent opinions and bringing them to bear on foreign policies in a constructive manner are greater in magnitude, although not different in nature than the difficulties in other fields. This serves to highlight the problems and expose their facets more readily.

Without quarreling with the principle that the public should have a voice in foreign affairs, one often hears the complaint that public opinion on foreign policy is inferior in quality and quantity to public opinion on other matters. It is said that the general public neither knows, understands, nor cares as much about foreign matters as it does about domestic ones. Consequently, there are fewer opinion-holders in the country, and opinions are less varied and less intense; they are usually less strongly felt and less esteemed in the halls of government by those who are charged with carrying out foreign policy. These contentions do not stand up under closer examination. Public concern about governmental policies has generally been in proportion to the public's awareness that a certain policy would help or hurt it greatly. Under ordinary circumstances about 10 to 20 percent of twentieth century Americans are interested in political issues. At times of crisis this figure often rises to 70 or 80 percent.[9] It does not matter whether the policy involves foreign or domestic matters. In our days of uneasy perching on the rim of the thermonuclear abyss, the public is so acutely interested in the war and peace aspects of foreign affairs that presidential elections regularly hinge on foreign policies more than on any domestic issue. So it was in the early days of the Republic when survival of the nation likewise depended on the turn of foreign affairs. The man in the street was acutely aware that foreign policies had an immediate and profound effect on his personal security.

As regards public knowledge, foreign affairs may be slightly different from domestic matters, although the difference is not great in many

[8]For supporting views see Leonard S. Stein, "Consistency of Public Opinion on Foreign Policy," Ph.D. dissertation, University of Chicago, 1962, pp. 2 ff., as well as sources cited there. Stein quotes Elihu Root's remark in "A Requisite for the Success of Popular Democracy" in the opening issue of *Foreign Affairs,* 1922–1923, p. 4. Root states that "Public opinion will be increasingly not merely the ultimate judge but an immediate and active force in negotiation." For a contrary view see Quincy Wright, *The Study of International Relations.* New York: Appleton-Century-Crofts, 1955, pp. 177–178.

[9]These figures are taken from Bernard Berelson, "Democratic Theory and Public Opinion" in Bernard Berelson, Paul Lazarsfeld, and William McPhee, *Voting.* Chicago: University of Chicago Press, 1954, p. 323.

instances. In sheer complexity, determination of the economic effects of public land policies, setting up a national banking system, or providing for research into debilitating diseases is as difficult for the general public to understand as decisions about the war-making propensities of a particular country. Even in matters closer to the experience of the average man the difference in understanding is relatively slight. The farmer may know the benefits he will derive from higher prices for his corn or cattle, but he may fail to see that in a generally inflationary economy his real income drops, even though his cash income rises.

In amount of information available to the public for inspection, the files on public land policies or national banks, or medical research, may contain fewer "restricted information" folders than the military records of a certain country. But in practice, considering the type of information that is digestible for the average person, the respective amounts of usable information probably vary little. A skilled public official who undertakes the task of boiling down masses of policy considerations into a few relatively simple policy alternatives that the public can judge generally finds it not much more difficult to do this in foreign affairs than in the domestic field.

The same holds true of the respect which public officials have for the public's views on complex issues, or the more complex aspects of simpler issues. Public officials probably question the degree of informedness of public opinion, regardless of whether the issue is domestic or foreign policy. Their doubts may be greater in foreign than in domestic affairs. Yet on simple issues or the basic lines of policy in complex affairs public understanding can be as good in the foreign field as in the domestic.

As far as pressure on public officials goes, there is no substantive difference. While interest groups likely to be concerned with a certain domestic policy are more easily predicted and more plentiful—for instance farmers will usually have opinions on farm policies—there will always be interest groups who, for various selfish and unselfish reasons, will try to influence public action in foreign affairs. This is especially true in times of international unrest, and at the start of a nation when foreign policies are crucial to the individual's welfare and he knows it. At such times expressions of public opinion are plentiful, varied, and intense and public officials are subjected to strong pressures to advocate or follow a specific course of action.

There have been attempts to muzzle vigorous expression of opinions on foreign affairs on the grounds that in times of crisis the nation must speak with one voice in foreign affairs. Otherwise popular division might give aid and comfort to its enemies and undermine its strength to deal with them. But these attempts have rarely been successful. Despite a number of notable exceptions such as the widely detested Sedition Act of 1798 and later sequels, the nation's leaders have, on the whole, upheld the right of free debate on foreign policy issues regardless of the propaganda advantage that foreign countries might reap from the mere fact of debate. People exercise the right although it often runs afoul of statutory provisions. Thus in foreign as in domestic affairs the pressures of conflicting opinions on government have never been at a standstill. Nor has the American government ever been able to take public support of foreign policies for granted, even in times of military danger. Always, public opinion had to be wooed and won over.

Last, but not least, among the reasons for selecting foreign policy cases is the fact that the role of public opinion in foreign policy formulation is a highly important contemporary issue. We hear public officials disclaim responsibility for unwise policies on the grounds that public opinion guided the decision. Thus Franklin Roosevelt blamed American unpreparedness for entering into World War II on the refusal of public opinion to support him in earlier rearmament measures. The ineffectiveness of America's China policy during the years when Chiang Kai-shek still controlled mainland China and in the more recent period of nonrecognition of Chinese Communist rule of the mainland is laid at the doorstep of the public which allegedly would not permit more aid for General Chiang and would not tolerate recognition of Chairman Mao.

When the public is blamed for causing wrong decisions that its leaders claim they recognized as wrong, one wonders about the wisdom of allowing public opinion such a sway. One also wonders how well the leaders interpreted public opinion and how well they performed the functions of public opinion leadership. One then goes back to the basic question of what the role of public opinion ought to be in a democracy designed to bring about the greatest good for the people.

# 2

# The Political Climate in Eighteenth Century America

Proud, O Demus, thy sway
Thee, as Tyrant and King,
All men fear and obey
Yet, O yet, 'tis a thing
Easy, to lead thee astray.
ARISTOPHANES, *The Knights*

A people cannot be well governed in opposition to their primary notions of right, even though these may be in some points erroneous.
JOHN STUART MILL, *Representative Government*

# 2

## The Gospel of the "Common Man"

The idea that public opinion should guide public policy was not original with the American founding fathers. It was part and parcel of the package of the Enlightenment ideas that became the foundation for popular government in western Europe and its satellites.[1] Political philosophers had become dissatisfied with the rule of crowned individuals, and small warrior, priest, or merchant groups. They believed that government could never operate for the best interests of the people, as they thought it should, unless the people had an important part in it. Power was the corrupting force that made the individual ruler or small ruling group evil. Its evil effects had to be mitigated by splitting up power among large numbers of the people so that selfish interest groups would be checked by other interest groups. It was argued that governmental power could be exercised legitimately only by public participation and consent. Consent had to be refreshed more or less continuously as new and important issues of public policy arose, and as the individual identities of the people changed.

Before philosophers could argue convincingly that power should be transferred from the chosen few to a new and larger group of people, it had to be shown that this new group was as capable and as moral as the old group, and that the transfer of power would be beneficial to those who were dissatisfied with the old order. Enlightenment philosophers devoted themselves to this task with zest.

The average man was pictured as intelligent, good, and highly moral, or at least as capable of becoming all these things with proper education. Since he was not stupid and in need of guidance by an elite of superior talents, as had been argued before, rulers were a luxury, not a necessity. When the people submitted to a ruler it was a voluntary surrender of the decision-making powers to a common decision maker. Thereafter, people expected to be consulted about the precise policies that the ruler wished to undertake on their behalf. If the ruler did not live up to his contract of consulting the people about policies, they might refuse obedience to him. Moreover, rulers

[1]For a discussion of the impact of Enlightenment ideas on American political leaders see Merle Curti, *The Growth of American Thought.* New York: Harper & Row, Publishers, 1943, p. 103. Also helpful are Richard Hofstadter, *The American Political Tradition.* New York: Alfred A. Knopf, 1948, pp. 3–43; and Louis Hartz, *The Liberal Tradition in America.* New York: Harcourt, Brace & World, Inc., 1955, pp. 55–86.

needed this guidance from the people to keep their policies moral and in the public interest. Only the people knew what they wanted; only the people had an infallible sense of goodness; and only the people were free from the corruption that had perpetually tainted kings and ruling groups.[2]

## The Gospel as Propaganda

Since the new gospel of the common man was to be used as a propaganda sledge to shatter the old governmental order, it was designed to be forceful rather than accurate.[3] The image of the totally stupid, disinterested, immoral common man had to be overcome by an equally distorted image of the paragon of virtue and intelligence. Later attempts at retrenchment and qualification were bound to be resented by a public who admired the flattering image that the philosophers had drawn. As Carl Degler puts it in a slightly different context:

> The assertions of the Declaration of Independence that all men are created equal have been sneered at as idealistic, refuted as manifestly inaccurate and denied as preposterous. Nonetheless, they have been capable of calling forth a deep emotional response from Americans. Like so much else in the declaration, this sentence is actually the distillation of a cherished popular sentiment into a ringing phrase.[4]

It was for this reason that the battle waged by nineteenth century sages to prove that the eighteenth century "truths" were partial fallacies was lost. By the twentieth century the mass of people, including many intellectuals, were convinced that these concepts were true.[5] A few critics, like Walter Lippmann,[6] were unwelcome voices in the wilderness, drowned out by the

[2]Carl J. Friedrich, *The New Image of the Common Man*. Boston: Beacon Press, 1950, p. 9; and Carl Becker, *The Declaration of Independence: A Study in the History of Political Ideas*. New York: Alfred A. Knopf, 1942, p. 69.

[3]Hans Morgenthau comments: "It was as the main moral, intellectual, and political weapon of the rising middle classes that rationalistic philosophy became the foundation for political theory and practice." See his *Scientific Man versus Power Politics*. Chicago: University of Chicago Press, 1946, p. 19.

[4]Carl N. Degler, *Out of Our Past: The Forces That Shaped Modern America*. New York: Harper & Row, Publishers, 1959, p. 98.

[5]See Becker, p. 233, and Friedrich, p. 15.

[6]These concepts are evident throughout his writings. See especially *The Phantom Public*. New York: The Macmillan Company, 1927, pp. 22–53; *Public Opinion*. New York: The Macmillan Company, 1922; and *The Public Philosophy*. Boston: Little, Brown, and Company, 1955, pp. 18–20. V. O. Key claims that Mr. Lippmann destroyed a "straw man." "Whether these beliefs had ever been held save in the autointoxication of political oratory directed to the average man may be doubted." V. O. Key, Jr., *Public Opinion and American Democracy*. New York: Alfred A. Knopf, 1961, p. 5.

soothing words of the politicians who knew the value of public flattery, especially at election time. Those who wished to attack the theory did so at the peril of being called undemocratic, aristocratic, fascist, or worse.

Exaggeration for propaganda purposes made the theory a vulnerable one; it also accounts for most of its difficulties of application. Even in the eighteenth century those who dealt with the public knew that it was not omniscient and pure. The discoveries of modern psychologists, sociologists, and political scientists along the same lines are not as novel as some would claim, although they are more solidly based on scientific evidence. But although eighteenth century political leaders knew better, they had to continue to express the theory in its broad and propagandist form for fear of losing it entirely. At the same time, they had to adapt its uses to the facts of life. Opponents of the theory seized upon its exaggerated statements as proof of falsity that required abandonment of the theory rather than a mere toning down.

## The Need for Consent

Quite aside from new theories about the legitimate source of political power and policy guidance, the men of the Enlightenment realized that government without the consent or acquiescence of the governed can be exceedingly difficult and unstable. The French Revolution and the American Revolution, as well as prior English revolutions, had shown that a dissatisfied public can rebel against the actions of its rulers and force them to take their discontents into account.[7]

How could public consent or acquiescence be obtained initially and maintained subsequently? One way was the theory of the social contract. It was argued that people were bound to obey the policies of government because they had consented to them. The individual's consent was given directly through participation in policy-making assemblies or indirectly through election of representatives to such assemblies. The representatives were the human vehicles that brought the opinions of their constituents to bear on the policy-making process. The individual whose views had been consulted directly or indirectly was pledged to support the policy that emerged from consultation, even if it did not fully comply with his desires.

But it became apparent at an early state of popular government that large numbers of people often did not acquiesce in governmental decisions even though they had presumably consented through their chosen representatives. They reserved the right to accept or reject governmental deci-

[7] I am leaving aside a number of practical reasons that are important, yet tangential to our purposes. For instance, a politician bent on reelection, or in need of support for some of his policies, may find it essential to cater to public opinion. Or his ego may demand applause, and the easiest way to get it may be by following the mandate of the crowd.

sions according to their mood of the hour. Government leaders, therefore, were forced to consider public views on a day-to-day basis. Their question was not "Have the people consented through their representatives?" but "Will a substantial portion of the public be overtly hostile to this or that policy? Will it support it effectively, or will it oppose it effectively? If disabling opposition can be anticipated what, if anything, can be done to forestall it?"

To answer these questions it was necessary to know techniques for gauging that part of public opinion that was apt to have an influence on any given policy. It was essential to know how to guide this opinion, how to suppress it, to shape it, even to create it. And it was necessary to do this in an age when the public had been encouraged to express its views by the heady theories of its competence to do so. Inhibitions to revolt against established authority had been broken down by the practice of successful revolutions and the glorification of the rebels. Knowledge and literacy were spreading fast, making ever larger numbers of people feel qualified to judge affairs of state. These were the problems that the founding fathers faced.[8]

## A Daily Diet of Politics

Turning from the general tenor of the age to the specific social milieu of the founders of the United States, what sort of climate of public opinion shaped their theories and influenced their practices?[9] It was, by modern standards, a lusty, brawling age, with strong opinions wielded to bludgeon others into acceptance. Criticism of public policies was no barren intellectual exercise undertaken with resignation in the feeling that not much would be changed anyhow. Rather, there were alternative policies that seemed to have a chance for adoption and over which people could therefore get excited. With sufficient popular pressure, the alternatives might be adopted. Par-

[8]Richard S. Eells, in "Public Opinion in American Statecraft," *Public Opinion Quarterly*, vol. 6, 1942, p. 397, claims that: "Although throughout the history of political philosophy public opinion has been recognized as a great political power, it was only during periods of revolution, either by bloodshed or ballot, that this potential power became kinetic. It was not until the first quarter of the nineteenth century that public opinion was regarded as possibly an active factor during the ordinary course of social events." This is contrary to the findings of this study, which show that even in the eighteenth century public opinion was taken into consideration, short of revolutionary action or threats of election retaliation.

[9]The political and social atmosphere in Washington is described in detail in James Sterling Young, *The Washington Community, 1800–1828*. New York: Columbia University Press, 1966.

tisans of various policies had little tolerance for conflicting views. The times were too uncertain for that.

Politics was a subject of daily excited and exciting conversation. Two friends could scarcely meet on the street without discussing some aspect of it. Liberty, equality, and the rights of man, support for the French or the English, neutrality and commercial rights, were topics of heated talks at the taverns, the inns, the courthouses, and the coffee houses. Half the male population would meet there on Saturdays to gossip and talk politics. With no television to distract them national politics would be debated after local gossip had run out. Since all sorts of travelers stopped at taverns—people of good education did not have their separate "first-class" hotels—the common rooms at the inns became excellent places to learn the facts of political life and to acquire reasonably sound opinions. Often the conversations were so heated, partly from spirit and partly from spirits, that the participants came to blows.

Just belonging to the wrong group was sufficient to invite attack. For instance, when the French ship *L'Ambuscade* arrived in New York in 1793, an anti-French crowd threatened to fight its crew if it ventured out into the streets of New York. Pro-French Americans promised to aid the visitors. In the hot arguments that ensued, many a blow was traded among pro-French and pro-British Americans. The pro-French group then hoisted a crimson silk liberty cap at the Tontine Coffee House and as many as five hundred men guarded it daily to keep the British faction from tearing it down. The sentiment that went along with these sophomoric pranks was exhilarating. Brawling over visiting sailors, French or British, became a popular spectator and participant sport that spurred interest in politics. A cause for which one gets beaten up, or beats up a fellow citizen, becomes as personal and immediate as a bloody nose.

Even without brawls, the strong individual involvement of large numbers of citizens was quite apparent everywhere. Pro-French men wore tri-colored French cockades in their hats and women wore cockades and liberty caps. The old titles "Sir" and "Mister," "Doctor" and "Reverend," were shunned as relics of a bygone aristocratic age. Instead people addressed each other as "Citizen" and "Citess" in the French manner. Newspapers, court proceedings, marriage and death notices, all bore the new titles. Nearly every Republican household sported its flaming liberty cups.

The pro-British faction gave equally visible proof of its allegiance. It ridiculed the antics of the pro-French, but retaliated in kind. It called the French "murderers, red-capped villains, infidel tyrants, sans culottes, and filthy agents of liberty." The pro-French reply was that George III was a "monster, a king of sea robbers," and the English were "the bloody, savage islanders."[10] Federalist pamphlets bore such descriptive titles as "The

[10]See John B. McMaster, *History of the People of the United States*, vol. 2. New York: D. Appleton and Co., 1885, pp. 316–318.

Antigallican; or The Lover of His Own Country, in a Series of Papers, Partly heretofore Published and Partly New, Wherein French Influence and False Patriotism are Fully and Fairly Displayed." Copies of European anti-French pamphlets were also available with such titles as "Cannibals Progress" or "Bloody Buoy."

Most news from abroad reached the port cities through foreign ships. Large crowds used to gather at the harbor when these ships put into port, vivid testimony of the eagerness of the people to learn what was going on in the world. Inland the same would happen when mailriders came to town. People who expected letters or newspapers could hardly wait until the mailbags were opened.[11] Whatever news was received was shared with all those who had gathered around. With crowds of people assembled, it was easy to whip up an emotional response, be it fear, rage, or joy. When there was no news, as happened frequently for months on end, rumors would circulate and often grow to inflammatory proportions. There was little the government could do to quiet them because it, too, lacked news. A three-months blackout of official news was not at all unusual. Then people would listen to sea captains who had been in Europe or the West Indies, or had contacted people who had been there. The resulting scraps of news were pieced together into an impressionistic mosaic, which was usually unreliable, but rarely unemotional.

## Political Gatherings

Popular interest in political affairs was also stirred by the "civic feasts," huge public indoor or outdoor banquets that were occasions to whip up public enthusiasm for political causes. Genêt, the French ambassador, was greeted with a succession of such civic feasts in 1793 on his triumphal tour from Charleston Harbor to the nation's capital. In his honor, halls or meadows were decorated with French emblems and anti-British slogans. People ate "civic cakes" and drank toasts to France. Those who were not present could read the glowing reports of the feasts in the local papers. The papers also printed the many new songs composed in honor of Genêt, songs that show that pro-French Americans believed that American liberty depended on the success of the French experiment. A typical song warned:

> Should France from her lofty station,
> From the throne of fair Freedom, be hurl'd,
> 'Tis done with every other nation,
> And Liberty's lost to the world.

[11]Personal correspondence among political leaders in various parts of the country was exceedingly important in spreading a common body of news and political ideas. See Eells, p. 396 ff.

The chorus then responded:

> Liberty! Liberty! Be thy name adored forever;
> Tyrants, beware, your tottering thrones must fall;
> One interest links the free together,
> And Freedom's sons are Frenchmen all.[12]

At night time, after the civic feast, lanterns would be hoisted to the top of the ever-present liberty pole. In Boston, one side of a huge lantern displayed in honor of Genêt showed the ruins of the Bastille, the other a prostrate British lion. Beneath the lion was the written wish that he might never rise again unless he did so in support of the liberties of mankind. In Charleston, pro-French Americans celebrated Bastille Day by dragging the British flag through the filth of the streets and burning it in front of the British consul's door.

Theater performances were also turned into political occasions. After the publication of the XYZ dispatches in 1798, during the Adams administration "the Federalists, highly elated . . . turned the play-house into a political engine of great power."[13] Night after night excited Federalists packed the theater for the express purpose of shouting themselves hoarse over newly composed patriotic songs such as the stirring "Hail Columbia" and a new version of the "President's March," which urged the crowd:

> Firm united let us be,
> Rallying round our liberty;
> As a band of brothers join'd,
> Peace and safety we shall find.[14]

When Republicans asked the band to play pro-French tunes, the request was drowned "amid a storm of hisses and groans." This was no time to "grate the public ear with those Gallic murder-shouts."[15] Republicans then bribed the musicians so that they would not play Federal tunes. In response, the irate crowd pelted the musicians and broke their instruments. The next day, Federalist newspapers urged that the crowd should boycott the theater until the managers promised to play the "President's March." In turn, Republicans threatened to keep away from all performances if the theaters would yield to the demands of the pro-British faction. Thus the battles of the theater ebbed and flowed, keeping the political pot boiling by night, and the press full of acid accounts by day.

For citizens with a penchant for more active politicking, there were influential political societies to join. These societies existed in most cities and towns throughout the United States. The pro-French Democratic so-

[12]McMaster, vol. 2, p. 102.
[13]McMaster, vol. 2, p. 379.
[14]McMaster, vol. 2, p. 378.
[15]McMaster, vol. 2, p. 377.

cieties were particularly strong. With the avowed purpose of defending
liberty and protecting the rights of man, they scrutinized every governmental act. If it seemed in conflict with their ideals, they denounced it
and campaigned against it in Congress and among the public.[16]

Even the churches were centers of political discussion. During the
family's regular Sunday attendance at church, the ministers would not hesitate to urge support of particular policies, no matter how partisan. Many
preachers held forth against the Godless French and all the atrocities they
had allegedly committed, much in the fashion in which modern clergymen
hold forth against communism. Pro-French feelings were akin to sin; devout
Christians must not harbor them nor ally their country with the French
devils. Some of these sermons were published, often adorned with skull
and crossbones to make the connotation of deathly evil more graphic. Bearing the mark of approval of a citizen's own clergyman—a respected authority figure—they were apt to be highly influential for those whose opinions had not already been formed.

## Popular Political Language:    Form and Substance

The church itself, or the surrounding property, was often covered with
political broadsides, or pamphlets were handed to the faithful, with no opposition from the church, as they were leaving the services. Many of these
pamphlets and broadsides were lusty stirs to emotion and opinion. The
language was to the point, colorful, coarse, and suited to the rough and
bawdy life of a developing nation. By hitting at a low common denominator
it had the vaudeville mass appeal, which much of today's bowdlerized
press lacks.

In fact, such crude language seems to be a trademark of developing
nations in general. It tends to be outgrown, just as youngsters outgrow the
blunt language of the playground, the poolroom, and the locker room—
at least during their more formal public contacts. Yet the toning down of
the language of politics seems to be both cause and reflection of the toning down of political involvement among the people. The no-holds-barred
slugging of political combat is far more interesting and understandable for
the man in the street than the polite, antiseptic language of much of the
present-day political dialogue. The average man is bored by the "double-
speak" and "double think" of the language of diplomacy and politics, which

[16]For a discussion of their activities, see Eugene P. Link, *Democratic Republican Societies*, 1790–1800. New York: Columbia University Press, 1942,
pp. 50–53, 74–75. Link believes that much of the pro-British and pro-French
feeling was based on related economic issues such as taxation and debt funding
policies.

makes it difficult to understand what goes on and also difficult to become emotionally involved. All this contributes to the very real feeling that he no longer understands politics and has no real share in it, and that his government's consultation with him is merely a matter of form. It also substantiates the superior attitude of the "expert" who feels that the man on the street lacks information, understanding, and comprehension.

Not only was the language of early politics rough, but the contents of pamphlets and papers were sensationalist. Often they were deliberately false, libelous, and even treasonable. The press did not feel any compunction to abstain from undermining the government or its policies. Frequently, undermining was its chief purpose. Whatever could serve to do this, was acceptable and accepted. This is why the Federalists eventually felt compelled to stop political criticism by the passage of the Sedition Act. A free press might be essential, but it could be disastrous if the springs of public information were deliberately poisoned because the press was controlled by men who wished to destroy the government. The antidote of truth might come too late to save the nation. Jefferson, violent and voluble critic of the Sedition Act, when faced with a vituperative press was forced to resort to similar measures of suppression later on. It seemed impossible to conduct a sound foreign policy if "wrong" opinion, inspired by traitors, was allowed free sway. There were even suspicions, many of them well founded, that stories in the American press were planted by foreign agents. Among others, Benjamin Franklin Bache, editor of the *Aurora*, was suspected of being in the pay of the French directory.

The fear that people might very easily be subverted to an overthrow of the government was very real and seemingly justified. Precisely how much influence popular political writing and political actions had on individual opinions is hard to measure. We have no public opinion polls that tell us the numerical distribution of opinions, and the intensity with which they were held. But it really does not matter. What does matter is that there was sufficient smoke to make the decision makers think that a large fire was burning. They took inciting pamphlets and hostile or favorable crowd action as evidence of strong political interests with which they had to reckon in their policy formulation. This is all that matters for the purposes of our discussion. The factors that go into policy formulation at any particular time are never objective facts—if, indeed, there is such a thing—but the facts as perceived, rightly or wrongly, by the decision makers.

## Serious Political Writings

Besides the writing for the masses, there was exceptionally good political writing for the well-educated—what we would now call the "opinion elite"—whose views were valued and whose leadership impact was prized.

In fact, the years immediately preceding independence and immediately following have properly been called the Golden Age of American political writing. The authors were writing about contemporary issues for an interested and critical public that expected to make use of the principles expounded to them. These were no mere academic exercises or professorial monologues. These were battles fought with the pen, rather than the sword, and the combatants carefully sharpened their pens for the encounters. A convincing argument could win the battle of opinion and vanquish political foes, foreign as well as domestic.

Many important political treatises appeared as serials in the newspapers before publication in pamphlet form. The best examples are the *Federalist* papers, which appeared first in the *New York Independent Journal* and the *New York Packet*, and were widely reprinted by sympathetic papers throughout the country. This very common practice of reprinting gave wide circulation to the views of those who had a press outlet. It helped to overcome the dearth of political news in most of the local papers in outlying regions of the country. It also gave to the country what amounted, in essence, to a nationwide circulation of prominent opinions. The intelligentsia, especially, thus read the same things and formed opinions that could be discussed with ease among the well-educated in all parts of the country.[17]

Since there was much interest in the daily press, prominent politicians on the state and national level, in and out of office, decided from an early day to use it for political explanation and rebuttal. Again, the *Federalist*, written by Hamilton, Madison, and Jay to win acceptance of the new federal constitution, is the most familiar example. Madison and Hamilton also wrote extensively on Washington's proclamation of neutrality. John Quincy Adams wrote about Genêt and neutral rights and duties; Charles Pinckney wrote on impressment, expatriation, and neutral rights. The Jay treaty was attacked and defended by many prominent men, often under the transparent guise of pen names. It was popular sport to guess who guided the pen of "Camillus, Atticus, Cato, or Gracchus—Americanus, Columbus or John Doe."

Many of the famous and less famous authors of these treatises were lawyers who dissected and exposed the issues carefully. This gave the intelligent public an excellent chance to examine all viewpoints, pro and con, and make up its own mind. Since it was not difficult to know whose brain was behind the stories, the identities of prominent authors lent interest and

[17]The majority of papers were in Federalist hands because the Federalists had more money to support them than did the Republicans. The New York *Minerva* was kept from financial collapse by gifts from Federalist merchants. Federalists also sent extra copies of Federalist newspapers as gifts to areas in which these papers would not normally circulate. (See Link, pp. 189–192.)

authority to their writings. In the mid-twentieth century, the tune has changed. Reader appeal has suffered through attempts to be overly fair and impartial. High officials within the government still leak stories to the press. But these stories usually appear under the byline of a commentator, or are disguised as "high sources within the State Department," or "usually reliable sources," or a "spokesman for the administration." Only rarely can the public penetrate this screen of anonymity to know what flesh and blood spokesman is behind it. When it does, public interest in political affairs mounts.

## The Role of the Press

From what I have described thus far it is clear that the early American press, unlike most modern American papers, did not view itself as an impartial medium for the spread of news. As far as political news was concerned it was the purpose of papers and pamphlets to win converts for a cause. This might be the cause of the government or the cause of the opposition, in general, or an attack or defense of particular policies and men. The *Aurora* and Philip Freneau's *National Gazette,* the "Republican" newspapers, were considered Jefferson's and Madison's mouthpieces. They were written expressly to sustain pro-French feelings, support and make converts for the Republican viewpoint, and to discredit the opposition with no holds barred. In fact, Jefferson believed that it was the social responsibility of the press to criticize the government. It must do this, not as a mouthpiece of the whole people, but as a mouthpiece of enlightened partisan critics. William Cobbett's *Peter Porcupine's Gazette* and John Fenno's *Gazette of the United States* were considered the "Federalist" newspapers, mouthpieces for Hamilton, and a match for the *Aurora* in diatribe and scandal. Cobbett had founded the *Gazette* chiefly to carry on pro-British propaganda.[18]

Because the press was so frankly partisan, politically sophisticated citizens took its advice with the proverbial grain of salt.[19] This was especially true of the advice of papers of the "wrong" political persuasion. Thus, while the press probably stirred greater political interest and emotion among all its readers than do most American papers today, its substance of advice was heeded less than it is now. This does not mean that the press lacked influ-

[18]Margaret Woodbury, "Public Opinion in Philadelphia, 1789–1801," *Smith College Studies in History,* vols. 1 and 2 (1919–1920), p. 13.

[19]The tradition of distrust of the press lingers on. Even today, people trust the electronic media far more than the press. See Wilbur Schramm, ed., *The Process and Effects of Mass Communication.* Urbana: University of Illinois Press, 1954, p. 82.

ence in shaping political opinions. It guided the direction of discussion and furnished many of the verbal brickbats which were tossed back and forth.

Bernard C. Cohen, in his recent study of *The Press and Foreign Policy,* describes this guiding role of the press in a modern setting:

> For most of the foreign policy audience, the really effective political map of the world—that is to say, their *operational* map of the world—is drawn by the reporter and editor, not by the cartographer. (Latin America, for instance, takes up a lot of space on the cartographer's map, but it scarcely exists on the political map delineated by most newspapers in the United States.) And if we do not see a story in the newspapers (or catch it on radio or television), it effectively has not happened so far as we are concerned. . . .
>
> This is to say, then, that the press is significantly more than a purveyor of information and opinion. It may not be successful much of the time in telling people what to think, but it is stunningly successful in telling its readers what to think *about.*[20]

This was precisely the role of the early press. Its advice might not be heeded, but it selected the topics for discussion. And it performed this task for a politically important audience. Newspapers were widely read, especially in the cities where copies were passed from hand to hand. Allan Nevins claims that "All who voted read the press" and that this fact made the press tremendously important.[21] Among the politically influential readers were not only ordinary voters, but all the opinion leaders such as editors, clergymen, local politicians, and members of the national government. Although they often held newspapers in contempt, public officials had to rely on them for much of their information on foreign as well as domestic affairs, given the scarcity of news sources. Often it was difficult to separate fact from rumor or opinion. Like it or not, what public officials read in the papers influenced their direction of thought and even their opinions to some degree. Papers published in the capital were particularly important. When New York was the seat of government, members of Congress and the executive branch including Washington, Madison, Adams, and Jefferson, read the New York *Packet,* however crude and coarse it might have been. Freneau daily sent Washington three copies of the *National Gazette.* Washington abhorred the paper, but he read it nonetheless. He spent many an hour discussing its articles with his friends and advisors —unintended testimony to its influence.

Because the press was so clearly partisan, political leaders of the time did not equate the views of the press with the views of the people, as is done so often today when studies of public opinion are nothing more than

[20]Bernard C. Cohen, *The Press and Foreign Policy.* Princeton: Princeton University Press, 1963, p. 13.

[21]Allan Nevins, *American Press Opinion: Washington to Coolidge.* Boston: D. C. Heath, 1928, p. 6.

studies of press opinion.[22] The views of the press were deemed to be the personal views of the writers whose essays were published, or the views of the paper's editors or sponsors. Although not an image of public opinion, they could be taken as an indication of the influences to which the public would be subjected and which might be reflected in future public opinion. Adams, for instance, felt that it was the prolonged influence of editorial attacks which prejudiced the public against his reelection. In 1809 he wrote to a friend:

> The causes of my retirement are to be found in the writings of Freneau, Markoe, Ned Church, Andrew Brown, Paine, Callender, Hamilton, Cobbett, and John Ward Fenno and many others. . . . Without a complete collection of all these libels, no faithful history of the last twenty years can ever be written nor any adequate account given of the causes of my retirement from public life.[23]

## Mass Political Action

Considering the many stimuli which aroused political passions among all segments of the people, it is not surprising that people did more than cheer or chide their government. Mass action supporting or opposing foreign and domestic policies was common. Action in support of the government was welcome. For instance, when Congress voted in 1794 to fortify American port cities along the Atlantic coast, the government was pleased when people from all walks of life joined voluntary work brigades to build the fortifications and to help in enforcing neutrality and embargo policies against would-be violators. Some came as individuals, others as members of patriotic societies or trade groups. The grocers, the bakers, the sawyers, and the sailmakers came, as did the students, the lawyers, and the schoolmasters.

On other occasions, citizens raised thousands of dollars to pay for fortifications and to build new ships for the navy. On June 29, 1798, Stephen Higginson reported from Boston that "We have opened a subscription for a loan of money to government to build a ship or any other more pressing service, which will amount to $150,000 I expect, or more . . . ." He thought much more than this would be available. "I think that half a million of dollars may be at once subscribed here, should the affairs of our country require it . . . perhaps a million."[24] This was at a time

---

[22]On this point see Cohen, p. 234.

[23]Charles Francis Adams, *The Works of John Adams*, vol. 9. Boston: Little, Brown and Co., 1856, p. 612.

[24]George Gibbs, *Memoirs of the Administrations of Washington and John Adams, Edited from the Papers of Oliver Wolcott, Secretary of the Treasury*, vol. 2. New York: W. Von Norden, 1846, p. 69.

when total revenues of the government were estimated slightly over $8 million and expenditures had been budgeted at a shade less than $7 million.

But the other side of the coin is not so pleasant. Mass interest is good as long as the public supports the government. But when sizeable numbers of people actively oppose government policies, the government and the country may encounter serious difficulties. This was the problem Washington faced when he issued the Neutrality Proclamation. Despite the proclamation, and despite severe penalties for violators, large groups of citizens persisted in partisan action. "During these months of unbridled political passion the danger was ever present that some irresponsible persons might plunge the country into war," a war that it was not prepared to fight.[25] Not even Washington's stature and public image could convince them to abide by the official policy. As a result, the government was greatly embarrassed on many occasions and the neutrality policy was brought to the brink of failure.

For example, Citizen Genêt, the French ambassador, who arrived in the United States barely ahead of the official declaration of neutrality, was able to buy two sailing vessels from sympathetic Americans. He also found an American crew willing to sail them, and use them to attack British merchant ships. When captured ships were brought into American ports, sympathetic local officials closed their eyes so that French consuls could sit as admiralty judges and condemn the prizes.

Jefferson, the Secretary of State, was soon faced with a long protest memorandum from the British minister who complained that ships fitted out and manned by Americans were attacking British ships for the benefit of France. British ships had been condemned as prizes by French admiralty courts operating in the United States. To these serious charges, which certainly could lead to a break in friendly relations between the two countries, Jefferson could reply little beyond a promise that the matter would be investigated and seized ships would be restored whenever possible. But he could have little faith in his own promises when, simultaneously, riotous Republicans paraded along Philadelphia's streets denouncing neutrality, cursing Washington, and threatening that they would force the government to declare war on England.

Another graphic example of popular defiance of foreign policy came in the wake of the Jay Treaty of 1794, which settled long-standing irritating problems in United States-British relations. The treaty was so unsatisfactory in many respects that the administration, fearing popular outcry against it, had first tried to keep it secret. But it was no use. Even before the treaty was ratified contraband copies were circulated. Less than three days after the Senate had approved the treaty, Benjamin Franklin Bache

[25]Thomas A. Bailey, *A Diplomatic History of the American People*, 5th ed. New York: Appleton-Century-Crofts, 1955, p. 73.

published an abstract in the *Aurora* and followed it with publication of the full treaty in pamphlet form.

The popular reaction was heated. Anti-treaty meetings were held all over the country with prominent citizens participating. At Boston the Selectmen summoned a town meeting to consider the treaty. More than 1500 men crowded into Faneuil Hall. Since they were angry at the British, the outcome of the meeting was a foregone conclusion. When the question was put: "Do the citizens of this town approve the treaty?" not a single hand went up. A committee of 15 men then drafted a 20-point protest and sent it to Washington. Other public meetings were not so peaceful.

At New York, Hamilton and Rufus King drew up an address and published it in the local papers saying they could not find anything hideous about the treaty They urged people to discuss it calmly. But at a meeting at city hall, there was so much shouting and hissing and hooting, that no discussion could be held. Attempts to restore order failed. Later on that day Hamilton, who had tried to defend the treaty at the meeting, was stoned by an angry crowd. Anyone bold enough to publicly defend the treaty did so at the risk of physical harm.

At Philadelphia a large crowd carried the treaty atop a pole to the residence of the British minister, smashed his windows, and burned the treaty on his doorstep. Throughout the country copies of the treaty were burned by the hangmen. John Jay was hanged in effigy. At the Fourth of July meetings that year, toast after toast was drunk to the destruction of the treaty. Speakers waived copies of the treaty, tossed them to the ground, and invited their listeners to "kick this damned treaty to hell!"[26]

While these events showed the embarrassments to which public opposition to government action could lead, they also showed that public anger, no matter how fierce, does not usually last. Gradually the opposition died down, and those who saw merit in the treaty were allowed to come to its defense. Hamilton defended it in a series of essays; Washington chided its opponents as selfish and shortsighted. Ultimately, the Senate ratified the treaty by a vote of 20 to 10, after striking out its most obnoxious clauses. The House, last hope of the treaty's opponents, passed the required appropriations following an impassioned address by Fisher Ames that the nation could be ruined if there was no treaty with Britain. This turn of events provided some encouragement for statesmen who felt it necessary to pursue an unpopular course in foreign policy. At least there was some hope that the public would ultimately come around to the statesmen's view.

Even when public acts did not overtly hamper the government's policies, they often had bad side effects. Consider again the example of Citizen Genêt, traveling in the United States after the President had declared the country's neutrality. His public reception certainly contradicted official

[26]McMaster, vol. 2, pp. 225–226.

policy. Genêt was given a tumultuous welcome. Along his route men on horseback waited for his entourage, and when he was in sight they carried the news to the nearest town. Once he was in town the bells would ring, as if for a conquering hero, and large, cheering crowds would come out by the hundreds to hail the visiting ambassador. He would be escorted to the best inn by a crowd shouting itself hoarse with pro-French cheers. At the inn he would be welcomed with flowery public addresses and a sumptuous meal. No wonder he began to think that the French cause was highly popular in the United States and that the government's neutral attitude did not represent the people.

By May 16, 1793, Genêt reached Philadelphia. Here too, the scene to which he had become accustomed was reenacted. Thousands came out to welcome him, and Republican groups deluged him with formal welcome addresses. By contrast, Washington's studied, cool, and formal reception the next day seemed completely out of tune with everything that had gone on before. Genêt felt offended; he felt that the people were with him and, he reasoned, therefore opposed to the government. He felt encouraged to violate the neutrality laws and to report to his own government that the people of the United States did not believe in the neutrality policy. This policy could therefore safely be ignored because it was doomed to fall in short order. A few years later, an American envoy to France was to be reminded of the unfortunate impression created in France. When Pinckney threatened to break off negotiations with France because the terms were insulting to the United States, he was told by a French negotiator that it was "a rupture you had better avoid; for we know well that there is in America a great and flourishing party firmly devoted to our cause."[27]

## Intragovernmental Opposition

The idea that each citizen might weigh the policy of the government and support or defy it as his conscience dictated, reached all the way up into the highest circles of government. Monroe, Washington's minister to France, defied the spirit of the neutrality policy and virtually placed the United States at the side of France against Britain. This not only undermined the policy, but it also made it difficult for Jay, the minister to England, to carry out his assigned mission.[28]

Jefferson's actions are another example of sabotage of public policy in high places. Although he was Washington's Secretary of State, Jefferson felt justified to subtly undermine the neutrality policy because he believed a pro-French policy would be better. When a French privateer, the *Petit Democrat,* was about to leave the port of Philadelphia, Jefferson did noth-

[27]McMaster, vol. 2, p. 374.
[28]Bailey, p. 79.

ing more than plead with Genêt to prevent her departure. Although Genêt gave no firm promise that the vessel would not sail, Jefferson ignored the requests of Knox and Hamilton that troops should throw up a battery on nearby Mud Island and sink the ship if it left the harbor. The *Petit Democrat*, as was to be expected, sneaked out to sea to prey on British ships. Washington chided his Secretary of State, but the damage—or benefit, depending on one's point of view—was done.[29]

In our day, under similar circumstances, we would expect the ambassador to France or the Secretary of State to resign if they disapproved of the policies of their chief.[30] But in the early days, close to independence struggles, strong and even violent opposition was still widely acceptable as a mark of patriotism. Defying established authority to carry out what one believed was best for the country was a sacred patriotic duty. The rewards were success for the nation and the praise of one's countrymen. The penalties were loss of respect, loss of one's job, and, in extreme cases, the accusation of treason and punishment for it.

State authorities, likewise, felt no compunctions about undermining a President's policies if they deemed them wrong. This was not surprising in an era when states were jockeying to have the nation's foreign policies represent their particular interests, and when a sense of broad national interest was largely lacking. Nor were state officials wrong in suspecting favoritism toward certain sections. Eastern seaboard interests were only too willing to sacrifice the interests of westerners in return for advantages for themselves. The reverse was also true.[31]

State legislatures frequently discussed foreign policies and passed approving or disapproving resolutions. Often the entire state administration was hostile. This was true in Pennsylvania where top state officials, from the governor on down to the commanders of the state militia, were strongly pro-French during the Washington Administration. Defiance was veiled or open. State legislatures passed resolutions declaring national policies beyond the constitutional powers of the national government and null and void in their application to the states.[32] Half the states talked of nullification and even secession in one form or other during the first quarter century of the nation. There was little the national government could do about this. As long as it lacked the power to enforce its decisions its only alternative lay in persuasion and propagandizing on behalf of its point of view.

[29]McMaster, vol. 2, p. 113.

[30]However, we have some examples where this did not take place, such as Vice-President Wallace's disagreements with Franklin Roosevelt about U. S. relations with the Soviet Union and General McArthur's difficulties with President Truman during the Korean War.

[31]Bailey, p. 48.

[32]For examples see McMaster, vol. 5, p. 474.

Washington had scant recourse against governors who developed an acute blindness to events in the ports of their state, after the President had ordered them to seize privateers. Nor could he cope with tactics of sly sabotage. For instance, Governor Moultrie of South Carolina allowed the *Vanqueur* to fit out in Charleston harbor and sail as a privateer. When taken to task, he sent two slow sailing vessels after her in a mock attempt at capture. At the expected news that they had failed to retrieve the *Vanqueur*, the Governor with tongue in cheek expressed great regret.[33]

State courts were defiant too. For instance, French admiralty courts had made prizes of British ships contrary to American law, and in violation of the declared policy of the country. But when the British owners sued in the courts of Pennsylvania for a return of their ships, the courts dismissed the claim on the spurious grounds that the matter involved was a political affair, not a judicial one.[34] When an American citizen, Gideon Henfield, had been arrested and indicted for serving as a French privateer, the jury, despite undisputed evidence of violation of the neutrality laws, declared Henfield innocent. The spectators at the trial shouted their approval. There was little the national government could do about such open defiance of its laws, as long as local public officials and the local citizenry were in accord in their opposition to national policies.

## Means to Influence Public Opinion

From what has been said thus far, it is clear that Americans formed strong opinions about foreign policies and that these opinions could and did become a serious obstacle to the conduct of foreign policy. This makes it of interest to know what means were available to the government to ride the tiger of public opinion in the days before the press conference, the fireside chat, and the television program beamed to millions. We have already mentioned the use of the press to appeal to the emotions of the reading public and the use of more reasoned pamphlets that tried to make an intellectual case for certain policies in an age in which rationalism was rated highly.

Besides the press, there were the annual messages of the President, which could be used as official pronouncements to inform and influence the public as well as Congress. They announced policies that had been adopted and defended their adoption. In addition, they discussed the political situation that would influence future policy formulation. The slant of the discussion could prepare the public mind for the types of policies to follow. It could serve as an opinion scaffold, set out early so that public

[33]McMaster, vol. 2, p. 107.
[34]McMaster, vol. 2, p. 108.

opinion might crystallize around it in a manner broadly in accord with contemplated government action. Speeches could also be used as trial balloons, sent up to see whether they would attract public applause or sniping.

Washington had initiated the practice of delivering his messages regularly at the start of each session, rather than "from time to time" as indicated in the Constitution. Congress then framed a formal answer (generally, an approval) and delivered it in full body to the President at his house. This gave the impression that the representatives of the people were united behind the leadership of the President. Such apparent unity was particularly important in a period when representatives were primarily defenders of state interests against other states and against the national government, which was trying to moderate the interests of the various states.

Aside from the use of the press, messages and speeches, leaks of information and suppression of news were practiced early. For instance, an insolent letter addressed by Genêt to Washington was leaked to the public. This helped to stem the tide of public approval of France and helped in making the Neutrality Proclamation more popular. The same technique, well timed, was used by Adams when he released the XYZ correspondence to show the perfidy of France in soliciting bribes from American diplomats. Prior to ratification of the Jay treaty, the government suppressed information when its disclosure jeopardized ratification. Such secrecy, in the words of a modern commentator, "in the name of the national interest has social sanction, while secrecy for the sake of narrow political advantage is always under attack from the press."[35]

Other means of influencing public opinion were presidential answers to public addresses and petitions presented to the President. These gave Presidents a chance to lecture to special interest groups on a subject matter to which they had already given their consideration. Presidents could also use their personal influence directly with selected individuals or indirectly by influencing their own friends. In addition, there were the more tangible rewards such as public office, public contracts, and political benefits during election time for the "right" word and action.


## John Q., Property Holder

Thus far we have talked about the various factors that influenced the formation of strong public opinion on foreign policy, and about the prac-

[35]Cohen, p. 200. Few, however, would openly go as far as President Kennedy's Assistant Secretary of Defense, Arthur Sylvester, who spoke of "the inherent right of the government to lie to save itself when faced with nuclear disaster." (See p. 198, speech to the Deadline Club in New York, December 6, 1962, following the Cuban missile crisis.)

tical reasons that forced government leaders to take notice of publicly expressed opinion. But we have said nothing about the theory that the public
should be an advisor to government, which must seek its advice regarding
the proper substance of policies. Eighteenth century political leaders did
pay homage to the theory that the people must have a voice in government.
But who were the "people"?

Contrary to the notions of many European Enlightenment philosophers, the "people," for governmental purposes, did not include everybody. It included "substantial" citizens, those who owned property and
paid taxes and therefore had a real stake in good government. What a boon
this was to politically timid souls! It made it possible for them to believe
that it was quite democratic if only a small part of the citizenry was consulted on public matters. In fact, this was well understood, without the necessity to specify it, just as much as it was well understood that children,
women, criminals, and similar "incompetents" were not entitled to
vote.

That this was a widely accepted view is evident from the fact that government nearly everywhere was government of the propertied classes. In
none of the earlier legislatures was representation based on population.
It was based on tax payers, freeholders, amount of taxes paid by local sub-
divisions, and often on correct religious beliefs. Only those who paid taxes,
owned or rented property, or had a certain income could vote. Most high
public offices were barred to the person who did not own property. Moreover, people generally voted for members of the lower house of the legislature only. The legislature then did the rest. It elected governors, judges,
and other public officials. Thus the early "people" were a limited group
with limited functions. For most of the period under consideration there
was distrust of the poor man and faith in the social conscience of the "better"
people who, through their votes and opinions, would act as trustees for
all.[36]

[36]As suffrage was broadened in the 1820s and 1830s it was assumed that
those who could vote, automatically held sound opinions on public issues and
that these opinions deserved consideration. Perhaps this was a wrong assumption.
Even granting that the people can make wise choices in picking their representatives, the factual knowledge required to decide most public issues is infinitely
greater. It does not permit the type of intuitive choice that is possible, often
with good results, in selecting a human representative. Nor is it true that the
choice of a representative automatically involves an intelligent appraisal of public issues—for the very reason that issues present a far more difficult problem of
understanding, analysis, and interest capture than a choice of personalities.
Many people have experience and knowledge about choosing people, but lack
experience and ability to analyze issues of public policy.

## The Role of the Chief Executive in Decision Making

What were the prevailing views of decision making at the top executive level in the early days of the Republic? Whose advice was the President supposed to heed in the formulation of his policies? Was his personal role that of a mouthpiece for some collectivity such as the "people," a party, or a section of the nation? Or was he the compromiser who would weigh various conflicting views and come up with a compromise that would please the greatest number of people? Or was he a leader charged with formulating his own opinions after consultation with other members of his government and representatives of the public?

Answering the last question first, there is no doubt that the early years of the nation were an age of strong leadership. Despite the antipower outlook that pervaded American culture, Presidents, beginning with Washington, felt that their conscience, tempered by the advice of their associates, must be their main guide.[37] The admiration for the strong leader who defies the public to do what he deems proper was well-expressed by John Adams when he praised Washington for signing the Jay Treaty. Although the spirit of violent opposition "was manifested in all the chief towns of the seaboard, and undoubtedly animated the population everywhere," and although "some hopes were entertained that the President might yet be induced, by earnest remonstrances, to withhold his signature," Washington would not budge from his decision. "No more enduring memorial of a statesman's firmness is to be found in history."[38]

Among the factors that predisposed early political leaders to rely heavily on their own judgments, especially in foreign affairs, was the fact that most of them had had extensive political and diplomatic experiences that gave them confidence in their ability to understand problems of foreign policy as well or better than most people in the country. Besides, during their tours of foreign duty, they had become used to making decisions on their own because communication with the home government was intolerably slow. For instance, it took more than five months before the American peace commissioners in London received their government's instructions about the important peace treaty with England. Four different copies of the treaty had been sent aboard four different sailing vessels to make sure the text would reach its destination with the utmost speed and security. No wonder that on many lesser matters American diplomats acted on their own without awaiting instructions, thereby acquiring the habit of independent decision making. Besides, many of them felt that their own judgment was far su-

[37]Young, pp. 60–63 discusses the moral problems posed by an antipower attitude of power holders.
[38]Adams, vol. 1, p. 481.

perior to the judgment of a distant President and Congress who could not possibly know all the current factors which deserved consideration in a foreign policy decision. Soundness of decision was more important than compliance with the instructions of one's political masters.

One of the earliest traditions developed by the executive branch was the practice of calling the Cabinet for consultations. The Constitution, of course, does not provide the President with a formal council of advisors. But it does authorize him "to require the opinion, in writing, of the principal officers of each of the executive departments upon any subject relating to the duties of their respective offices."

On the strength of this provision, Washington set the precedent of calling his secretaries together for informal discussions of affairs of state with no obligation, on the President's part, to accept the advice tendered to him. For instance, when news reached the United States that its ally, France, had become involved in war with Spain and England, Washington immediately summoned his Cabinet and asked them sixteen questions. Some involved legal issues: Were the treaties with the kingdom of France still binding when she had become a republic? Did the treaty of alliance apply to an offensive as well as a defensive war? Other questions required an appraisal of the actual situation, such as whether France was fighting an offensive or a defensive war. Then there were questions on policy methods and substance: Should he assemble Congress to ask it to participate in the deliberations? Should he declare neutrality? Should he forbid American citizens to meddle in the war? As an immediate matter, should he receive Citizen Genêt, the new minister from the French republic who had landed ten days earlier at Charleston and was on his way to Philadelphia?

Consulting the Cabinet had several advantages. These men were readily available and well informed on governmental matters. More than half of them had served in Congress.[39] They could advise quickly. For instance, Washington had asked the Cabinet's advice about the neutrality policy on April 18, 1793. Four days later, on April 22, he felt that he had sufficient information on hand to be able to announce his decision. Since the various departments were directly involved in the conduct of domestic and foreign affairs, they had information that the President needed for policy making. Secretaries were effective exponents for vantage points from which decisions had to be considered. They also could judge better than the President the likely effects of certain policies on the affairs entrusted to their departments. Besides, they needed to be informed on all those policy decisions that required their active participation. Overlapping of interests was the rule and made a joint meeting of all the department heads valuable. Foreign policy, for instance, was not only the concern of the State Department and the military departments. The treasury, too, was

[39]Young, pp. 176–177.

greatly interested whenever foreign policies required spending of money or involved foreign economic policies. Thus when Genêt arrived in the United States and asked for money to buy war provisions for his country, Hamilton was chosen to "scotch" his request by telling him that the treasury was empty.

The House and Senate, too, were involved in executing foreign as well as domestic policy decisions. In the field of foreign affairs the Constitution requires Senate approval for treaties. For matters involving appropriations both houses have to concur. Presidents learned early not to take congressional cooperation for granted. For this reason, they felt forced to consult with members of both houses about many proposed foreign policies. But in foreign policy making such consultations were not a matter of principle; they were a matter of practical politics. Presidents from Washington's day on believed that they were far better qualified than Congress to make foreign policy decisions and that it was unwise to involve Congress deeply in the foreign policy–decision process. This is why Washington refused the request of the House of Representatives to be fully informed on details of the Jay Treaty negotiations. The House could consider the product, but only after negotiations were finished and all preliminary decisions had been made. Congressional debates might be interesting because of the various viewpoints expressed, but they were no substitute for the President's own decision-making faculties in what was deemed to be strictly executive business.

The acrimony with which foreign policies were discussed once they reached Congress enhanced the impression that Congress was not temperamentally fit to deliberate calmly and coolly. After Adams had delivered a message to Congress in 1797 on American policy toward France, Congressmen debated so viciously that some arguments ended in duels. They accused each other of heads as empty as Newton's vacuum, and it was said of one that anyone who bought him at his true value and sold him at the price he set on himself, would become a wealthy man. William Smith's efforts to increase American defenses were ridiculed with a ditty:

> Twelve motions Smith in one day made,
> Yet the mountain brought forth but a mouse;
> The next motion he makes, let us pray,
> He may move himself out of the House.[40]

There was also the widespread belief of Americans from all walks of life that the President, rather than Congress, represented the interests of the general public. Congressional leaders, if they did not speak solely for themselves, spoke for sectional and local points of view, rather than the views of the nation. It was up to the President and the men around him,

[40]McMaster, vol. 2, p. 330.

as officials beholden to all the people, to formulate the policy that was best for the country as a whole.

This does not mean that the views of individual congressional leaders were not heeded. Many of the outstanding men of the period served in Congress or in their state legislatures. Service in the legislative body enhanced the weight placed on their advice, but it did not give weight to their advice per se. The President consulted them as individuals because he valued their advice in light of prior personal relationships or because of their position and policy-relevant experiences.

Selection of the inner circle of advisors was deemed a personal matter for each President to be made as he saw fit. In the pages that follow we shall try to identify the chief members of these inner circles who advised Adams, Jefferson, Madison and Monroe in the foreign policy decisions on which this study focuses. We shall also try to discover the scope of their influence, although this is a hazardous intellectual exercise. No scholar, not even a psychoanalyst, can determine with precision the myriad interacting influences that go into a public figure's decision making. Not even the man himself knows. Even if we have his diary and his letters available in which he tries to reconstruct the influences that swayed him, we cannot say with certainty: "This is the way it happened." We are forced to guess and hope that our guesses are blessed with more clairvoyance than we have any right to expect.

# 3

# John Adams' Theory
# of Public Opinion

... A good decision is based on knowledge and not on numbers. . . .

PLATO, *The Dialogues of Plato*

... The rulers well know that the general will is always on the side which is most favourable to the public interest, that is to say, most equitable; so that it is needful only to act justly, to be certain of following the general will.

ROUSSEAU, *A Discourse on Political Economy*

# 3

## The Realist-Idealist Battle

Ambivalence is the striking feature of John Adams' theory of public opinion. He wanted to believe, and did believe, that the average man was capable of understanding political affairs and making sound political decisions. Yet he was also convinced, from his experiences with the political acts of misguided publics, that the people could be wicked and unwise. Page Smith, his biographer, talks of:

> the classic conflict in him between realism and idealism. He dared to dream bold and magnificent dreams, yet, unlike many dreamers, he was so solidly planted in the real world that he was always acutely conscious of the gap between the hoped-for and that which might be achieved in an imperfect universe.[1]

John Adams, the idealist, dreamed of a republic in which a well-educated citizenry participated intelligently in the making of public decisions. Citizens and government officials alike, would put the public good above private advantage. John Adams, the realist, remembered that citizens could easily become a "rude and insolent rabble"[2] bent on destruction of symbols of authority, oblivious to the needs of the nation, and interested only in their own selfish concerns of the moment.

One cannot really say that he ever struck a middle ground between the two points of view. Rather, he alternated between them, partly conditioned by his general moods, which rose and fell precipitously, and partly depending on the purposes that called forth an expression of opinion. Nor can one call him wrong on either view. For men, as theologian Reinhold Niebuhr points out, are both "the children of light and the children of darkness" with capacity for justice coupled with the strong inclination to do injustice.[3]

Much of Adams' optimism about public capacity was expressed in his writings, which were intended to tell the British why the American colonists had a right to disobey British laws and why they had the right to gov-

[1]Page Smith, *John Adams*, vol. 1. New York: Doubleday, 1962, p. 273.

[2]Smith, vol. 1, p. 159.

[3]Reinhold Niebuhr, *The Children of Light and The Children of Darkness*. New York: Scribners, 1949, p. xi. The framers of the Constitution based the entire system of checks and balances and the mixture of democratic and aristocratic elements in the American constitutional structure on similar feelings of ambivalence about the capacity and intentions of average Americans.

ern themselves. His pessimism came to the fore in private correspondence at times of particular disillusionment. These were times when his own views of right and wrong conflicted with the views expressed around him or when he was arguing against what he considered an excess of popular control in government.

## New England Heritage

What factors in Adams' background help to explain his views about public opinion?[4] Looking at the ideal picture first, his upbringing in the New England town of Braintree must have been a strong influence in convincing him of the ability of the average citizen to run his own affairs, and his eagerness to do so. His parents and their friends who visited were much interested in political life, not only on the local level, but in world affairs as well. As Page Smith pointed out:

> What distinguished it (the village of Braintree) from the villages of the Old World . . . was the extraordinary engagement of the inhabitants of Braintree and her sister communities with the world that reached far beyond the boundaries of the town. . . .[5]

From an early age on, John's father took him to town meetings. To an impressionable youngster, it must have seemed as if the grown men assembled at the town meeting certainly were concerned with the public good, knew the needs of the town, and could make wise decisions. When at a later age he realized how narrow the horizons of Braintree had been, this did not destroy the powerful image of citizens gathering together to intelligently decide the political affairs of the community.

John also learned early that public affairs were everybody's affairs. Citizens were expected to spend considerable time and effort, without pay, on the town's business. There were many public jobs to be done and everybody took their turn in performing them, regardless of whether or not these jobs interfered with their personal time schedules. John's own father was a lieutenant in the town's militia, a selectman of the town assembly, as well as a deacon in the church. John Adams came to believe that demands for public service brought out the best qualities in men. They produced "strength, hardiness, activity, courage, fortitude, and enterprise;

[4]This discussion is based on the assumption that a man's political views are determined by his personality and background, as well as by the current political stimuli that reach him. As Cournot says: "The springs of politics are the passionate movements of the human heart." Quoted in Bertrand de Jouvenel, "Political Science and Prevision", *American Political Science Review*, vol. 59 (1965), p. 37.

[5]Smith, vol. 1, p. 3.

the manly, noble, and sublime qualities in human nature in abundance."[6] Modern psychology supports Adams' views.

Adams' experiences between 1770 and 1778 as a member of the Massachusetts legislature, the Revolutionary Provincial Congress, and the first and second Continental Congresses impressed him with the political ability of his friends. Certainly these people whose governing talents the British authorities had ignored were able to manage their own political affairs. Besides, the work of government was not as difficult as an outsider might think. Many of his fellow legislators were not well-trained at all, but did a very creditable job nonetheless. Did not this prove that the average citizen was capable of running his own affairs? "Government was a plain, simple, intelligible thing, founded in nature and reason, and quite comprehensible by common sense."[7]

Religion, too, reinforced John Adams' belief that the average man owed a duty of service that he must perform in accordance with the dictates of his own conscience, rather than someone else's ideas. When Adams followed his conscience in an unpopular cause—like the defense of Captain Preston, an English soldier, against murder charges growing out of the Boston massacre—he expected to reap his reward from heaven. For a man of Puritan stock with hell fire and damnation vividly in mind, divine approval was important. Much of Adams' stern courage and the courage of his friends to resist the temptations of this world may have been due to even sterner fears of eternal punishment at the end of a brief sojourn on earth.

But fear was not the only motivation for doing one's duty. Adams and others raised in the Puritan tradition of New England felt that each individual had been chosen by God to play an important part in the world. Therefore, the political acts of each and every individual were important. How different from the feeling of the average man today! When political participation is no longer a sacred duty, the temptation to neglect it becomes well-nigh irresistible if there is neither financial gain, nor prestige and power as a reward. Why should modern man participate in government when his individual acts do not seem to matter? The voice of democratic duty, lacking the megaphone of divine command, is feeble indeed. The feeling that each man is chosen by God and watched by God to make sure that he performs his mission to the fullest and thereby earns eternal salvation gave men of Adams' time an extra impetus toward public service. Even if the community took no note of them, or did not appreciate them, God was watching.

If God ordained that each must have a share in government, this meant

[6]Letter to Mercy Warren, Smith, vol. 1, p. 233.
[7]Charles Francis Adams, *The Works of John Adams*, vol. 3. Boston: Little, Brown, 1856, p. 454.

that each possessed the mental capacity to make political decisions and the moral capacity to know what was right and wrong. *Vox populi* was *vox Dei* because the people's instincts were moral. The single ruler might ignore moral principle and do the opportune. But the people as a group would be incapable of Machiavellian machinations. If God ordained that the individual citizen must take an active part in politics, it also followed that the ruler must listen to the voice of the people. And well he might. People with their unerring instinct about what was just, coupled with knowledge of what would hurt or help them, could certainly judge the propriety of policies. Public debates must "become researches into the grounds and nature and ends of government, and the means of preserving the good and demolishing the evil. . . ."[8]

Adams' college years, his span of time as a teacher, his early training in the law, and his early years of diplomatic service in France provided him with an environment that would perpetuate the notion that human beings are intelligent, interested, and capable of guiding their public affairs. At Harvard, as at many other colleges in the United States, students followed essentially the same curriculum. Their backgrounds of information —a thorough grounding in the classics and in the writings of English and French philosophers—were thus almost identical. Besides, most of them came from a similar social, religious, and ethnic milieu. They shared their basic values and their outlook on life. "They were thus a community of scholars in the deepest sense, for they shared the intellectual experiences of their college generation, and they could converse."[9] Moreover, they were a community of scholars living in an exciting age when man was beginning to master nature. The scientific method was coming into its own, and the promises of mastery over his physical environment made man optimistic that human reason could also guide his destiny in society. This impression continued strong, as the young Adams read voraciously and as he learned to mold young minds as a school master—although he at times despaired of the ability and willingness of the young to learn. It continued in his conversations with his law tutors and in the animated, intelligent discussions in the salons of France.

## Early Political Experiences

Adams' early political experiences seemed further proof of the ability of the people to perceive their political problems and act on them, regardless of personal sacrifices. The possible break with the mother country was widely and intelligently discussed among all classes of people. While mem-

[8]Adams, vol. 3, p. 463.
[9]Smith, vol. 1, p. 21.

bers of the Continental Congress—the old elite, drawn to the old system that had benefited them—were hesitant about declaring independence, the mass of the colonists seemed eager for it. Adams, who was firmly convinced that the colonies must break away from the mother country, felt much heartened by the evidence that many of his countrymen, even simple men in the street, felt likewise. Agreement with what Adams deemed correct opinion proved their wisdom.

Adams' involvement in the independence struggle heightened his respect for public opinion. He wrote a series of papers to defend the views of the colonists and affirm their right to independence. With a lawyer's instinct for amassing favorable evidence and shaping it into a verbal spear, Adams used natural rights philosophy to make his point that the people have the right to resist tyranny and determine their own fate. Supporting points were stressed and put in their best light, contradictory evidence was omitted. As happens with many an orator, Adams did his job so well that he partly convinced himself. He had to, for Adams was never a hypocrite. He had to accept these views as his own creed or his conscience would not let him rest.

Among the points that he stressed, and about which he partly convinced himself, was the rationality of man. If the average American was not rational, if he could not decide for himself what was good for him and what was abstractly good because it was morally sound, then he had no right revolting against divinely appointed kings whose education and training had prepared them to rule. The king's duty to listen to his subjects, which Adams stressed, sprang from the fact that his subjects were capable of making wise decisions.

The rationality of man was also the logical basis for the claim that subjects must have representation in a legislative body and that this representation must be a direct, explicit relationship. Adams was not satisfied with the concept of representation, which claimed that a citizen had a sufficient voice in government if his special interest had a spokesman, but he had not selected the spokesman. It was not enough that the interests of the colonists were "virtually" represented, just as the interests of Birmingham and Manchester were virtually represented in the English Parliament. In order to be bound by the action of Parliament the citizen had to have a direct voice in its election.

The Stamp Act and similar measures were invalid as long as the citizens of the colonies had not agreed to them. Adams argued that his fellow Harvard man, John Hancock, could not be punished for smuggling wine ashore from the sloop *Liberty* since he was not bound by a law of Parliament to which he had not given consent through his own representative. The corollary that Adams deduced from this argument was that citizens must be capable of understanding the consequences of legislation. Otherwise, how could it be claimed that their consent was important?

## The Value of Education

The magic potion that transformed the stupid subjects of an earlier age into intelligent citizens was education. Education, Adams confidently wrote to his wife, Abigail, made "a greater difference between man and man than nature has made between man and brute. The virtues and powers to which men may be trained, by early education and constant discipline, are truly sublime and astonishing. . . ."[10] Self-government, when the people were uneducated was "as unnatural, irrational, and impracticable as it would be over the elephants, lions, tigers, panthers, wolves, and bears, in the royal menagerie at Versailles . . . all madness."[11] But when they were educated it was a different matter altogether. In an age when the mind of man, trained and prepared by education, seemed to conquer nature at an exhilarating pace, education seemed a nostrum for all defects of the human character.

This was Adams, the optimist. But what of his darker moods? In the face of examples of mass stupidity, of disagreement with his own beliefs, or to counter writings which, he believed, exaggerated the capacities of the common man, Adams would argue the cause of man's stupidity and avarice.[12]

In *Discourses on Davila,* written when he was Vice-President, he refuted Jefferson and others who had argued that people only need more education to fit themselves for self-government. He argued that progress of science, art, and letters had not lessened the passions of the human heart. "Bad men increase in knowledge as fast as good men; and science, arts, taste, sense, and letters are employed for the purposes of injustice and tyranny as well as those of law and liberty; for corruption as well as virtue."[13] In fact, too much knowledge among the people would make it difficult to govern. When Benjamin Rush said that universal education would make all people capable of enlightened government, Adams contended that education would mean more people with firm opinions about what was right and wrong in government. People would argue and disagree and nothing would be achieved.

[10]Smith, vol. 1, p. 220.

[11]Adams, vol. 10, p. 52.

[12]John R. Howe, *The Changing Political Thought of John Adams.* Princeton: Princeton University Press, 1966, p. xv. Howe contends that a close "correspondence developed between the satisfactions of his own life . . . and his outlook on American society." When the people faulted him, he faulted the people. (Also see pp. 106–131.)

[13]Smith, vol. 2, p. 800; Adams, vol. 1, p. 462.

## The Stupidity of the People

There were several lasting experiences that gave Adams a jaundiced view of human nature. High among them was his experience with mob action in his own New England. His grandson, Charles Francis Adams, reports that Adams was particularly upset by mob action against the officials charged with the enforcement of the Stamp Acts:

> These events, and the principles which they contributed to form and establish in his mind, gave a tone to his character, and had an overruling influence on the subsequent history of his life. He saw that the end of all popular movements of violence was destruction, and that they were ill adapted, under any circumstances whatever, to the furtherance of justice.[14]

The burning of the library of the Hutchinson family was an unpardonable act of mass stupidity. The "rude and insolent rabble," Adams claimed, with sound psychological insight, were acting in "resentment for private wrongs" and out of jealousy of the political influence and social prominence of the Hutchinsons. He condemned the rioters for acting in pursuance of private prejudices and passions. He believed that they were knowingly putting their private interest above the public interest. As rational human beings they were bound to know what the public interest demanded.

Adams was also distressed by public demands for war during Washington's presidency. What rationality was there in people who wanted to go to war without an army, without a navy, with the new government deeply in debt and certainly not able to fight? He wrote to Abigail that public opinion was incapable of making a sound choice between alternative courses. "The public opinion is a chaos, a Proteus—anything, everything, and nothing. Yet all sides trumpet and dogmatize about the public opinion."[15] He felt that people, urged on by bad counsel, were rushing toward a disastrous war that would lead to debt, corruption, civil conflict, and possibly to absolute government. Even New England men went along, although it should have been quite obvious to them that war would ruin them. It seemed nothing could be done to stop people. Only disaster would teach them. Adams wrote, "The spirit, principles, and system of rational liberty to all nations is my toast; but I see no tendency to anything but anarchy, licentiousness, and despotism. Mankind will not learn wisdom from experience."[16] The majority of the House were in favor of war, "and there is no doubt they represent the people in the southern States and a large number in the northern. *Vox populi, vox Dei*, they say, and so it is sometimes; but it is some-

[14]Adams, vol. 1, p. 72.
[15]Adams, vol. 1, p. 468.
[16]Smith, vol. 2, p. 855.

times the voice of Mahomet, of Caesar, of Catiline, the Pope, and the Devil."[17]

Watching the war spirit grow in the country and being unable to check it was very hard for Adams. He wrote to his son, John Quincy Adams, that it had been fashionable to charge wars to kings, but it seemed that " 'le peuple souverain' is as inflammable and as proud, and at the same time less systematic, uniform and united, so that it is not easy for them to avoid wars." The Washington Administration had tried to avoid war, but people were "continually committing some intemperance or indiscretion or other, tending to defeat all our precautions."[18]

The same people who clamored for war were opposed to any increases in the budget to provide the money for waging it. Adams wrote to his wife:

> It grieves me to the heart to see an increase of our debts and taxes, and it vexes me to see men opposing even these augmentations, who are every day pushing for measures that must involve us in war, and ten times greater expenses. But the inconsistencies and absurdities of men are no novelties to me.[19]

This was certainly a candid confession that Adams doubted the people's ability to make sound decisions in foreign affairs.

### Congressional Stupidity

Not only were the people stupid, but Congress was little better:

> We have had an incessant struggle all the winter to restrain the intemperate ardor of the people out of doors and their too accurate representatives in both houses. Too many of our good federalists are carried away at times by their passions, and the popular torrent, to concur in motions and countenance sentiments inconsistent with our neutrality and tending directly to war.[20]

Congress had voted for the nonintercourse bill, which prohibited all commerce with Great Britain and which would have brought certain and disastrous war with England. Only Adams' deciding vote in the Senate defeated the dangerous law.

While Adams had served in Europe, he had already been annoyed about congressional stupidity. Congress had delayed paying interest on money loaned by Dutch bankers, endangering the shaky credit rating of the country. Adams knew that the Netherlands was the only place to get

[17]John Adams, *Letters of John Adams to His Wife*, vol. 2. Boston: Little, Brown, 1841, p. 155.

[18]*Letters of John Adams*, vol. 2, p. 162.

[19]*Letters of John Adams*, vol. 2, p. 150.

[20]*Letters of John Adams*, vol. 2, p. 149.

money. If the United States spoiled its credit rating there, it would not be able to raise money elsewhere.

Adams was also alarmed at news that a strong faction in Congress wished to do without ministers to European courts because it was morbidly afraid of foreign influence. These men feared that European ambassadors sent to the United States would plot to embroil the United States in European troubles. Moreover, their high living standards would corrupt Americans. Such provincialism, harmful to the nation, infuriated Adams. Were these the men who knew what was "best" for the country? Popular representatives, the demigods of Enlightenment philosophy, surely were cursed with clay feet.

Even the Committee on Foreign Affairs, which had been charged with conducting the nation's foreign policy under the Confederation, seemed utterly naive and incapable of understanding the finer points of diplomacy. The French representative had been able to convince the Committee on Foreign Affairs in 1781 that Adams, who was then in France, should take no action without clearing it first with the Count de Vergennes, the French foreign minister. Adams was instructed accordingly. The instructions appalled him and he was ready to resign.[21] How blind could the committee be! It was crystal clear to him that it was in France's interest to support the United States and that the United States could therefore insist on being an equal partner. It did not have to kowtow to the French and seek their advice and consent before acting. When Congress would not listen, Adams decided to defy his orders. His conscience required that he should do what was right, regardless of his instructions from popularly elected officials.

Similarly, in 1785, during his mission to England, Adams became convinced that American foreign policy could not succeed without a show of strength. He wrote to Congress, urging legislation that would discriminate against English commerce. Such laws could be used as a bargaining point to force the British to respect American demands. Moreover, a policy of firmness would also impress the French and Dutch and make it easier to negotiate with them. But Congress would not listen to his advice, proof again that the people at home, including Congress, lacked all understanding of the finer points of diplomacy.

Nor was there much hope that they would learn from their own history or the history of other people. There were many lessons in history, but "moral reflections, wise maxims, religious terrors have little effect upon

[21]While it seems clear to present day historians that the French were primarily pursuing their self-interest, this was not so clear at the time. As Page Smith asks rhetorically (Smith, vol. 2, p. 547), "What better hand could there have been to guide the American novices through the troubled waters of European diplomacy than the wise and experienced Foreign Minister of the United States' great ally? So, in fact, it seemed to many honest men."

nations when they contradict a present passion, prejudice, imagination, enthusiasm or caprice." Adams had long been convinced "that neither philosophy, nor religion, nor morality, nor wisdom, nor interest will ever govern nations or parties against their vanity, their pride, their resentment or revenge, or their avarice or ambition." This, he claimed, "is not melancholy but experience."[22]

## Who Were the "Public"?

Thus Adams vacillated between praise and condemnation of the public's political abilities. Turning from the general to the more specific, when Adams spoke of the right of the public to have a voice in politics, what specific people were included in this "ghostly sociological entity"?[23] Clearly, it was not every Tom, Dick, and Harry who loafed in the town square and hung out at the tavern. Adams had a thorough contempt for the uneducated, propertyless man who was the raw material for the ugly collectivity, which Adams called the rabble or the mass or the mob—shiftless, ignorant, vulgar, and incapable to rule.[24]

As mentioned, his experiences with Boston mobs had given him a very personal taste of mob violence. His knowledge of conditions in France reinforced the example of mob rule at its worst. When the educated elite had been destroyed and government was turned over to the rabble, murder and destruction reigned. It was worse, indeed far worse, than the rule of despotic kings, however imbecile and cruel. If historical examples of the horrors of mob rule were needed, Roman history provided its share. When the Gracchi had given the vote to the propertyless Roman mobs, these mobs had used the vote to confiscate the property of the rich and distribute it to the poor. Rousseau was mistaken when he believed that virtue resided in man in his natural state. He did not know the sordid and depraved lives of savages, motivated only by the instincts of survival. He did not understand that unmitigated selfishness of the many threatened the rights of the individual: ". . . that the desires of the majority of the people are often for injustice and inhumanity against the minority, is demonstrated by every page of the history of the whole world."[25]

[22]Smith, vol. 2, pp. 721–722.

[23]A description coined by V. O. Key in *Public Opinion and American Democracy* New York: Alfred A. Knopf, 1961, p. 15.

[24]Adams, vol. 2, p. 458. The word "mob" came from the Latin *mobile vulgus*, the fickle crowd, and aptly describes a mass of people with unstable views. (See Francis G. Wilson, *A Theory of Public Opinion*. Chicago: Regnery Co., 1962, p. 152.)

[25]Adams, vol. 6, p. 48.

> They [the mass] can neither act, judge, think, or will, as a body poli-
> tic or corporation . . . . All kinds of experience show, that great numbers
> of individuals do oppress great numbers of other individuals; that par-
> ties often, if not always, oppress other parties; and majorities almost
> universally minorities.[26] . . . . There have been examples of self-denial,
> and will be again; but such exalted virtue never yet existed in any large
> body of men, and lasted long.[27]

While "in theory, . . . the only moral foundation of government is, the
consent of the people"[28] in practice, this did not mean all of the people,
but only certain kinds of people. For:

> men in general, in every society, who are wholly destitute of property,
> are also too little acquainted with public affairs to form a right judgment,
> and too dependent upon other men to have a will of their own . . . .
> very few men who have no property, have any judgment of their own.
> They talk and vote as they are directed by some man of property, who
> has attached their minds to his interest.[29]

The voice of the servant would echo the voice of the master. To John
Adams, as to most of his contemporaries, *vox populi*, could only be *vox
Dei* if it was the voice of "substantial" people.

Since Adams believed firmly that self-interest was the prime motivat-
ing force in man, it followed that only the man who owned property was
interested in public order and the welfare of his country. He had a stake
in orderly government because government was primarily a protective agen-
cy for the life and property of the individual. The poor with nothing to
protect stood little to gain from government. The idea was not that the poor
man was incapable of judgment. Rather, he formed no opinions because
he had no stake in society. If he formed opinions he did so on the spur of
the moment, as member of a mob. Or his opinions were nothing but a
blurred shadow of his master's opinions.

There was also the Puritan notion that property was a sign of God's
blessing bestowed on the worthy. Poverty was a sign of improvidence and
sin. The property owner was the "substantial" good citizen. The poor man
showed that he was lazy, for God helped those who helped themselves.

The idea that property ownership makes the individual knowledgeable
and interested in government was supported by Adams' personal experiences at home and abroad. Men with property constituted a civic elite.
They were more likely to have formal education, more likely than the

[26]Adams, vol. 6, p. 7.
[27]Adams, vol. 6, p. 61.
[28]Adams, vol. 9, p. 375.
[29]Adams, vol. 9, p. 376.

hand-to-mouth classes to have time to participate actively in public affairs.[30] In Europe, where Adams spent so many of his younger years, only the rich participated in government and were interested in it. The poor, the servant class, obviously did not care. They were creatures of the day, plodding and taking their pleasures where and when they could find them. They were the model for the propertyless mobs who merely echoed their masters' voices, if they had any views at all. Even modern research supports the idea that a small amount of property is ordinarily a prerequisite for an interest in politics. The totally deprived tend to be the totally apathetic.

With the characteristic faith in human perfectibility, so common in the age of Enlightenment, Adams believed that acquisition of property, even though the amount might be small, would immediately transform the shiftless man into a prudent one. "If the multitude is possessed of . . . real estate, the multitude . . . will take care of the liberty, virtue, and interest of the multitude, in all acts of government."[31] Therefore property ownership must be made easy, as was true in his native Massachusetts. However, an occasional exception was permissible, as in Massachusetts, where a man was allowed to vote even without a forty-shilling freehold if he was of good character and well known in the community.

## The Temptations of the Rich

Nor must the belief that property is the basis of sound opinion be carried too far. There were bound to be occasions when even property owners succumbed to the evil instincts which were the bane of humanity. There was "so much rascality, so much venality and corruption, so much avarice and ambition, such a rage for profit and commerce among all ranks and degrees of men even in America" that men like Adams might doubt whether there was virtue enough to support a republican form of government.[32]

An excessive amount of property, moreover, could easily corrupt the rich man so that he would then seek to acquire ever more property, even at the expense of the public welfare. The spirit of commerce above all, "corrupts the morals of families." It keeps them from being ready and happy to "sacrifice their private pleasures, passions and interests, nay, their private friendships and dearest connections, when they stand in competition with the rights of society."[33] Adams felt that this had been true of the

[30]These concepts began to change in the 1830s and 1840s. See Merle Curti, *The Growth of American Thought*. New York: Harper & Row, Publishers, 1943, p. 295 ff.

[31]Adams, vol. 9, p. 377.

[32]Smith, vol. 1, p. 233.

[33]Smith, vol. 1, p. 234.

Southern representatives in the Continental Congress. These plutocrats, whose social ease he envied, had been lukewarm about breaking the ties with England because a republican government might endanger their genteel way of life. Later, during the Revolutionary War, Adams was disgusted with evidence of profiteering among the merchants and tradesmen who were supplying the needs of the Revolutionary army. What better proof could there be of the venality of men than watching the petty ways in which they sought to enrich themselves at the expense of their country!

Wealth and position were particularly dangerous when newly acquired. Decent fellows, once you made them army officers, tended to become undemocratic, rank conscious, jealous of those above them, intolerant of their inferiors, ever fearful that others might aspire to their rank. The newly rich would be more venal as leaders and could be controlled through the promise of private gain. Many of these people entered public service, not as a sacrifice, but as a money making venture. The badge of office became nothing but a hunting license for private gain.

An excess of property was not the only corrupting influence. There were men's evil instincts, forever to be fought, and not always successfully. "Although reason ought always to govern individuals, it certainly never did since the Fall, and never will, till the Milennium."[34] Those who deemed man capable of consistently enlightened behavior were mistaken. "All projects of government, formed upon a supposition of continual vigilance, sagacity, and virtue, firmness of the people, when possessed of the exercise of power, are cheats and delusions."[35]

There also was the danger of party spirit. By 1768, long before his skirmishes with Republicans, Adams confided to his diary that ". . . I had learned enough to show me, in all their dismal colors, the deceptions to which the people in their passions are liable, and the total suppression of equity and humanity in the human breast, when thoroughly heated and hardened by party spirit."[36]

Another worry was that even "substantial" people would not have enough fortitude to stick with their convictions in the face of opposition by people of superior background and training. "The aristocratical part of mankind ever did and ever will, over-awe the people, and carry what votes they please, in general."[37] Nor would the people be able to resist the call of

[34]Adams, vol. 6, p. 115. (See also Howe, pp. 18–19, for a discussion of Adams' views on human passion.)

[35]See also Gilbert Chinard's evaluation in *Honest John Adams*. Boston: Little, Brown, 1933, p. viii. "There were, in his opinion, no special virtues and no special wisdom in the people, not any more than in the aristocratic or ruling classes. Both were formed of the same clay."

[36]Adams, vol. 2, p. 214.

[37]Adams, vol. 6, p. 37.

flattery. Candidates without scruples would lie outrageously and deceive an ever gullible public:

> . . . What is horrible to think of, that candidate, or that agent, who has the fewest scruples; who will propagate lies and slanders with most confidence and secrecy; who will wheedle, flatter, and cajole; who will debauch the people by treats, feasts, and diversions, with the least hesitation; and bribe with the most impudent front, which can consist with hypocritical concealment, will draw in fools and worm out enemies the fastest. Unsullied honor, sterling integrity, real virtue, will stand a very unequal chance.[38] [For] . . . the people will not bear a contemptuous look or disrespectful word; nay, if the style of your homage, flattery, and adoration, is not as hyperbolical as the popular enthusiasm dictates, it is construed into disaffection . . . .[39]

Given the average property owner, uncorrupted by an excessive desire for property, how far could he be trusted in his political judgment? Adams believed that at best the average man could judge broad issues of the time, such as independence versus continued allegiance to Britain, neutrality versus involvement in the wars of Europe, support for legal procedures versus mob justice in the marketplace, and so forth. He could also judge what specific policies would be economically advantageous or disadvantageous to him, at least in the short run. And he had sufficient knowledge, unless deliberately misled, to know which of his fellow citizens were capable of representing him wisely in the common councils:

> A man who can read will find in his Bible, in his common sermon books that common people have by them, and even in the Almanac, and the newspapers, rules and observations that will enlarge his range of thought, and enable him the better to judge who has, and who has not that integrity of heart and that compass of knowledge and understanding which forms the statesman.[40]

When men erred in these decisions—and error was any opinion contrary to the truth, as seen by Adams—such error was due to the misleading influence of inner passions or outer guidance.

### The Channels of Public Opinion

What were the channels of communication that led from the knowledgeable citizen to his government? For Adams, there was no single source. A public official could discern the people's opinion from talking with a

[38]Adams, vol. 6, pp. 51–52.
[39]Adams, vol. 6, p. 89.
[40]Adams, vol. 2, p. 131.

number of "substantial" citizens who in turn had talked to others at their firesides, places of business, or at the public meeting places.[41] Or he could judge people's opinion from their actions. If they answered the call to arms, if they volunteered their services for building fortifications, if they adopted resolutions in town meetings in support of governmental policies, this was proof of the public will. Besides, there was always the assumption that acquiescence in the policy of the government was a form of active support.

However, Adams did not believe that all acts of mass disobedience expressed popular disapproval of governmental policies. Any clever orator, any daring, ruthless, unprincipled agitator could gather a crowd around himself and sway it to action. The public attracted to this type of gathering was not John Adams' public who must be heeded. John Adams' public, if it gathered at all, did so with passions tempered by a sense of justice and patriotism. It acted with dignity and decorum using its powers of reason, rather than its fists.

For Adams, the press was not worthy of respect as a vehicle of the public voice. The press was suspect as a mouthpiece of special interest groups. It was motivated by partisan considerations, by the interests of venal American politicians, and, not infrequently, by the interests of foreign powers. For instance, Adams suspected foreign influence in the violent press reaction to his conciliatory policy toward France:

> And by whom were these [accounts] written? As I was informed, by MacDonald, the Scottish-British commissioner for adjusting the claims of British creditors, and by William Smith, the British agent for claimants before that board of commissioners, of whom MacDonald was one. . . . It was given out that John Ward Fenno [editor of the Federalist *United States Gazette*] was the writer of the most important . . . *but the pen was not his.*[42]

What, then, was the role of the other reputedly great mirror of public opinion, the legislature? Did Adams believe that it reflected the thoughts of the public, that each representative was a spokesman for the desires of his constituents? Ideally, yes, for a popular assembly should, as far as possible, "be in miniature an exact portrait of the people at large. It should think, feel, reason, and act like them. . . . Equal interests among the people should have equal interests in it."[43] And it should be reelected annually

[41] For a description of how his predecessor, George Washington, solicited reports on public opinions and reactions from friends and acquaintances throughout the country, see Leonard White, *The Federalists*. New York: The Macmillan Company, 1948, pp. 110–114.

[42] Adams, vol. 9, p. 248.

[43] Quoted in Smith, vol. 1, p. 246.

to keep in touch with the people and to check the over-ambitious who might be corrupted by overlong enjoyment of political power.

But in practice, Adams believed, things were far different. He had seen legislative bodies in action and knew that many a legislator was more interested in preserving and enhancing his own political status within the legislative body than in furthering the interest of the nation in general, and of his constituents in particular. Legislators were:

> liable to all the vices, follies, and frailties of an individual; subject to fits of humor, starts of passion, flights of enthusiasm, partialities, or prejudice, and consequently productive of hasty results and absurd judgments. . . . Corruption in almost all free governments has begun in the legislature.[44]

Even if the voice of the legislature echoed what many people were saying, one could not be sure that it was echoing the proper public. For legislators, like people in general, were often misled by agents of special interests and could not distinguish the true voice of the enlightened public from the chorus of the misguided. Only an expert leader could make the distinction. Only he could tell which public voices demanded the proper course of action and deserved to be heeded.

The implication in this approach was that there is only one right course for a nation's policies and only one version of the national interest. There could be no "honest" differences of opinion and hence no legitimate room for political parties of divergent views. A politically experienced leader knew what was right because his conscience told him so, unequivocally. It was his duty to mobilize support behind the right course if it was not forthcoming spontaneously. If the course was wrong, he would fail in the long run to gain support for it. His policies would fail and his political career would be at an end. If it was right, there would always be voices among the public to support it, sooner or later.

## The Influence of Public Opinion

This leads us to a discussion of Adams' views on the influence that must be assigned to public opinion. As a basic proposition, one can say that Adams believed that the public had a right to express its political opinions, and that political leaders had a duty to listen to the public, to answer petitions and addresses, and to keep their doors open to visitors who might wish to make personal pleas for their opinions. But there the obligation ended. Leaders did not have to solicit opinions. And, regardless of how overwhelming the "popular mandate" might appear, it was the duty of government officials to reach their own conclusions on the basis of their own

[44]Adams, vol. 9, p. 302.

past experience, supplemented by the advice of available "experts." "Experts" were those people in and out of government who possessed special information about the problems at hand and whose judgment the decision makers valued and trusted.

This did not mean that public opinion could be ignored. Quite the contrary. The experience of the Revolution had taught Adams the practical importance of keeping in touch with the feelings of the crowd. Not only democratic theory, but the necessity to stay in office made it vital to know the demands of vocal segments of the population and to guide them. A French king out of touch with his public would lose his head. The London mobs demonstrating in the streets would force the will of Parliament. And American colonists, irate about the actions of the British government, would dump tea into Boston harbor, destroy the royal Governor's mansion, and go to war with the mother country. These were the masses that must be reckoned with somehow. Either their violence must be gratified to the detriment of the nation, or leaders, with their fingers on the public pulse, must note when the heartbeat was quickening and head off violent eruptions before they occurred.

The methods of squaring public policies with mass pressures varied with the circumstances. If it was possible through political methods to reduce or squash opposition and increase support for policies preferred by governmental leaders, so much the better. If not, the policy might have to be altered or even abandoned if its success depended on popular support, or if opposition could ruin its effectiveness.

Since public reaction was most likely to become a factor in the success of major policies—such as war or peace, carrying on trade or embargoing it, paying increased wartime taxes or evading them—these were the policies in which public reaction had to be weighed most carefully and in which it was most apt to be influential. Again, this was expediency and not principle. Adams could take a major step like the reopening of peaceful negotiations with France in almost complete secrecy because no public support was required. On the other hand, relatively minor questions (like the adjustment of a boundary line) could present major problems in the control of public sentiment. Thus it did not matter in determining the weight to be assigned to public opinion whether issues were substantial or minor, complex or simple, or whether they affected part of the population with greater impact than other parts. What mattered was the likely impact of public pressure on the course of action.

## The Importance of Leadership

Just how much influence a vocal public would have depended heavily on the quality of its leadership, as matched against the strength and skill of governmental leaders. On this subject, Adams held very strong beliefs. One cannot fully understand his ideas about the role of public opinion in decision making without comprehending his ideas about the role of leadership in popular government. Adams believed that popular government was bound to fail without good leadership. A political leader was great by virtue of his ability to draw out the best in the people who acknowledged him as their leader and who had chosen him because he was better educated, better informed, and could better control his passions. It was his duty "to make the character of his people, to extinguish among them the follies and vices that he sees, and to create in them the virtues and abilities which he sees wanting."[45] A leader was a man who could discern the universal truths. He was a man with a highly developed sense of responsibility to do the right thing, who led in the right direction. The public, in turn, owed him the duty to follow his leadership.

The good leader was beholden to no one. He did his best to secure public support for his policies. But if the public did not support the right course, the leader must swim against the stream, come what may. Adams had known such a man during his childhood in Braintree and had made him the idol on which he patterned his own life. As Page Smith remarks: "To be nobody's man, to owe nothing except to God and his own conscience was his early determination and lifelong aim."[46] Looking back on his life from the vantage point of nearly seventy years, Adams felt he had achieved his aim. He reminisced that he had resolved in his youth that:

> I never would deceive the people, nor conceal from them any essential truth, nor, especially, make myself subservient to any of their crimes, follies, or eccentricities. These rules, to the utmost of my capacity and power, I have invariably and religiously observed to this day.[47]

Adams believed that public leaders, like he and his colleagues, belonged to a trained and responsible upper class that was sensitive to the needs of the people.[48] Such a class was absolutely essential to a well run state. "A society can no more subsist without gentlemen than an army without officers."[49] Only a small group of people, most of them well-to-do, would ever put the ideal of service to their country above the desire for private gain. This intellectual elite had the duty to lead:

[45]Smith, vol. 1, p. 233.

[46]Smith, vol. 1, p. 7.

[47]Adams, vol. 2, p. 214.

[48]The notion of a governing elite is deeply imbedded in the English tradition. See Carl J. Friedrich, *The New Image of the Common Man.* Boston: Beacon Press, 1950, p. xxiv ff.

[49]Smith, vol. 2, p. 819.

> This natural aristocracy among mankind . . . is a fact essential to be considered in the institution of government. It forms a body of men which contains the greatest collection of virtues and abilities in a free government, is the brightest ornament and glory of the nation, and may always be made the greatest blessing of society if it be judiciously managed in the constitution.[50]

Besides, members of the elite were the only kind of people who could anticipate problems before they arose and devise policies to cope with them —something the public could never be expected to do. A policy that could not be formulated until the public had actually expressed its opinion could never anticipate new conditions. It could react only to the initiative of others. It could thus not cope with the many instances in which it was important to seize an opportunity, as Adams realized in his own dealings with France.

Adams vigorously opposed the then popular idea that all people were equally capable of leadership. On February 4, 1794, he wrote to his cousin, Sam Adams:

> By the law of nature, all men are men, and not angels—men, and not lions—men, and not whales—men, and not eagles—that is, they are all of the same species; and this is the most that the equality of nature amounts to. But man differs by nature from man, almost as much as man from beast. The equality of nature is moral and political only, and means that all men are independent. But a physical inequality, an intellectual inequality, of the most serious kind, is established unchangeably by the Author of nature; and society has a right to establish any other inequalities it may judge necessary for its good.[51]

To Dr. Price, Adams complained that "Too many Americans, pant for equality of persons and property. The impracticability of this, God Almighty has decreed, and the advocates for liberty who attempt it will surely suffer for it."[52]

However, the leadership elite was not a closed class. It was open to those from the lower classes who were able enough to enter it and who had received the necessary training. Ability and training were the key. No man had the right to lead simply as a matter of birth, be it high or low. The public business required an aristocracy of demonstrated ability, rather than leadership based on heredity and station in life.

Adams feared that an abdication of the leadership functions by the elite would bring second-rate leaders or the radical masses to the fore, people who would ". . . obtain an influence, by noise not sense, by mean-

[50]Smith, vol. 2, p. 696.
[51]Adams, vol. 1, p. 462.
[52]Adams, vol. 1, pp. 453–454.

ness not greatness, by ignorance not learning, by contracted hearts not large souls."[53] When the majority of the delegates to the Pennsylvania constitutional convention were Radical Democrats, he complained that the conservative, moderate, well-educated elite had abdicated its duty of leadership, probably because it had interfered with its personal affairs. The type of leader that had come to the fore was the spineless puppet of the public who would dance to their whims and perform sensational political tricks just to curry favor with the people.

Adams practiced his conception of leadership throughout his life. When he was only thirty-five years old and still hankering for public acceptance, he was asked to defend Captain Preston who was accused of murdering Americans during the Boston massacre. The popular press and Paul Revere's engravings had inflamed public feelings. They had pictured wounded and dying Americans shot down in cold blood on the order of a petty English officer. Bostonians were convinced that Captain Preston was guilty. What patriotic American would defend such a man? Only a British agent or a completely mercenary sheister would do so. Along with his fee and British plaudits he would earn the contempt of his countrymen.

Yet Adams took the case with little hesitation. He felt that it was his duty to resist the public clamor and defend an unpopular accused person, even at the risk of personal unpopularity and, perhaps, the danger of mob attack against his person, his family, and his property. It takes little away from the strength of character displayed by this decision to point out that Adams also knew that the trial would receive wide public attention in England and other parts of the Empire and might spread his reputation for personal courage. Besides, it would serve to demonstrate that supposedly benighted colonists would deal like sophisticated civilized Englishmen with their prisoners, regardless of public passion.

Nor does it lessen Adams' stature to point out, as Page Smith does, that Adams enjoyed the pose of the martyr to a degree and even exaggerated his martyrdom. As Smith puts it: "Self-righteousness, to be fully enjoyed, needs a feeling of isolation, of lonely defiance. The greater the outcry, the more overwhelming the opposition, the greater sense of the righteousness."[54] The fact remains that Adams chose personal, immediate unpopularity in his own bailiwick over distant benefits and vague spiritual satisfaction. Against impressive odds, he stuck to what he believed to be the proper role of the opinion leader.

The leadership that came forward in the wake of the Revolution sustained Adams' faith that America could produce a leadership elite to guide the country along the proper course and to inspire the people to follow. The new political chiefs—many of them drawn from the same intellectual

[53]Smith, vol. 1, p. 242.
[54]Smith, vol. 1, p. 122.

stratum as Adams—appeared to be men of capacity, spirit, and zeal with the ideal of service to the community. In the British tradition they considered unselfish and unpaid service to the people as the mark of the gentlemen's code and burden. James Truslow Adams mused about his illustrious ancestors and their contemporaries:

> As we look over the list of the early leaders of the republic, Washington, John Adams, Hamilton, and others, we discern that they were all men who insisted upon being themselves and who refused to truckle to the people. [It would not always be thus.] With each succeeding generation, the growing demand of the people that its elected officials shall not lead but merely register the popular will has steadily undermined the independence of those who derive their power from popular election. The persistent refusal of the Adamses to sacrifice the integrity of their own intellectual and moral standards and values for the sake of winning public office or popular favor is another of the measuring rods by which we may measure the divergence of American life from its starting point.[55]

The influence of the frontier and Jacksonian ideals lowered the prestige of public office. Adams' ideas about the type of leadership one could expect were no longer valid.[56]

## The Public's Right to Information

In addition to the duty to make public policy and to create a supportive public opinion climate for it, if necessary, did popular leaders owe a duty of information to the people? Unlike populist democrats of a later age, Adams' answer would be a qualified *yes*.[57] The obligation of the good citizen to take an interest in government and to be educated implied that he must be well-informed about government. Much of this information and education must come from the elite, in and out of government. Works such as Adams' "A Dissertation on Canon and Feudal Law," published in the Boston *Gazette*, were written to trace for his fellow citizens the rise of freedom in human society and to suggest how freedom could be preserved and extended in their own society. His "A Defense of the Constitutions of Government of the United States, 1787" was intended to teach

[55]James Truslow Adams, *The Adams Family*. Boston: Little, Brown, 1930, p. 95.

[56]In some respects, in the twentieth century we are getting back to government by a well-educated elite—private school, ivy league trained, widely traveled, rich and worldly-wise. Such are the Roosevelts, Kennedys, Stevensons, Lodges, Deweys, Rockefellers, and their kind.

[57]For a contemporary discussion of the duty of wide publicity, see Edward A. Shils, *The Torment of Secrecy*. Glencoe, Ill.: The Free Press, 1956, p. 41 ff,

his countrymen the canons of good government. It was to counteract such works as Paine's *Common Sense,* Macaulay's *History,* Burgh's *Political Disquisitions,* and Turgot's *Letters,* which, Adams believed, were misinforming the public.

But the duty to inform was subordinate to the duty to govern successfully. Information had to be tailored to its audience whenever this could improve the governmental process. Thus, news about prospective policies was always presented in a form designed to elicit the average citizen's support. This explains the one-sidedness and hortatory style of Adams' regular messages to Congress. To his ministers, Adams would offer alternative courses of action because he wanted their advice and they had to know the alternatives to counsel him properly. But to Congress and the public he presented only one course—the one that he deemed best. He did not wish to encourage public debates. The flow of information between President and Congress was to be strictly a one-way street: down to Congress and the public, with governmental leaders waiting, not for a dialogue, but for an affirmation.

If information was likely to be harmful, either because it might arouse the wrong kind of public reaction or because its disclosure would hinder successful execution of policy, Adams believed that it must be suppressed. He had no hesitancy at all about such suppression. The fact that the opposition would usually manage to ferret out suppressed information and put a hostile interpretation on it strengthened Adams' conviction that the flow of information must be carefully guarded lest it do harm or be put to wrong use. Good government for the nation and survival in a world of grasping enemies were far more important than the people's privilege to be fully informed.

# 4

# John Adams Practices
# What He Preaches

A man of conscience and known ability should insist on full freedom to act as he in his own judgment deems best; and should not consent to serve on any other terms. . . .

JOHN STUART MILL, *Representative Government*

Tis a misfortune to be at such a pass, that the best test of truth is the multitude of believers, in a crowd, where the number of fools so much exceeds the wise.

MONTAIGNE, *Essays*

# 4

When John Adams became President, he put his public opinion theories to the test and found them workable. He solicited expert advice before making decisions; he tried to convince the public to support his decisions; but he insisted that the ultimate responsibility for decision making must be his. He refused to change his opinions for any reason other than a genuine change of his own mind or irresistible pressure. "John Adams," he told his wife, "must be an intrepid to encounter the open assaults of France, and the secret plots of England, in concert with all his treacherous friends and open enemies in his own country."[1] Public clamor, if it was wrong, must be ignored if this could be done without dire consequences.

## Franco-American Relations

The most crucial foreign policy decisions that Adams had to make during his presidency involved America's relations with France. France, embroiled in war with England, wanted the United States to become her ally in repayment for France's aid during the Revolutionary War. But Washington was afraid of becoming involved in war at the side of France and launched the young nation on a policy of neutrality instead. Adams concurred that neutrality was the correct course and pledged himself to it.

Since America's neutrality bestowed commercial benefits on both France and England, both belligerents were angry at the aid granted to their adversary. Both vented their anger by attacking American seamen and ships, and by hampering American commerce through confiscation and restrictive import and export legislation. Washington had been able to settle many of the points of friction with England through the Jay Treaty. Although the treaty was highly unpopular in the United States, Anglo-American relations became relatively cordial thereafter.[2] Now it fell to Adams to make a settlement with the French.

The French, partly encouraged by strongly expressed pro-French sentiments among some Americans, asked abandonment of neutrality as the

[1]Charles Francis Adams, *The Works of John Adams*, vol. 1. Boston: Little, Brown, 1856, pp. 494–495.

[2]See Bradford Perkins, *The First Rapprochement: England and the United States, 1795–1805*. Philadelphia: University of Pennsylvania Press, 1955, p. 93 ff.

price for settling grievances. This price Adams was unwilling to pay. But how else could he swing a bargain? Adams held no trump cards because the French were strong enough to take by force whatever favors the United States might offer as bargaining inducements. The French also knew that the United States urgently needed some sort of a settlement, since the status quo was intolerable for a nation that depended on foreign commerce for much of its livelihood. Already ship insurance rates had risen prohibitively. For instance, the insurance for a round trip to the island of Jamaica and back to the United States amounted to forty percent of the value of the ship and its cargo.[3]

A policy of threats of violence seemed the only choice—threats that the United States would retaliate against French attacks and threats that she might join the war on the side of the enemies of France. Such threats, if the United States carried through with them, would be a real danger for France. The hitch was that Adams wanted to use the threats as threats only, but did not want to be forced to carry them through. War would lose what he intended to preserve—the advantages of neutrality—and would force the United States to spend its human and material treasures on war, rather than building the internal strength of the country.

So here was Adams' challenge—negotiate with the threat of war or measures short of war as a lever, without actually getting into the war. This exercise in delicate brinkmanship was made doubly difficult by the fact that Adams could foresee strong popular outbursts against his policies including threats of secession, open cooperation with foreign agents, and open defiance of governmental measures. The President somehow would have to keep unity or acquiescence at home, so that he could present a united front abroad. He would have to threaten France with violence while trying to settle differences with her on an honorable basis by "amicable negotiation" as pledged in his inaugural address.[4]

### The French Rebuff Adams' Mission

The events selected for a detailed case study of the role of public opinion in foreign policy making occurred in the period from March 8, 1798 to February 25, 1799. Adams had sent a three-man mission to France in 1797 to settle mutual grievances. The mission was composed of Republican Elbridge Gerry and Federalists John Marshall and Charles Pinckney. For many months no word was received about the progress of negotiations.

[3]Edward Channing, A History of the United States, vol. 4. New York: The Macmillan Co., 1929, p. 184.

[4]James D. Richardson, ed., Messages and Papers of the Presidents, vol. 1. New York: National Bureau of Literature, 1917, p. 231.

Meanwhile, public anxiety about Franco-American relations remained high. Initially, the French had refused to even discuss normalizing relations until their demands had been accepted first. There had been a change of heart when they agreed to receive the Gerry-Pinckney-Marshall team, but no one could be sure that it was either permanent or complete. During the long wait Adams had supported a policy of arming the country, believing that negotiations must be conducted from strength.[5] Military preparations ought to make the French wonder whether the American threats were empty after all.

When news from France finally arrived on March 5, 1798, it was worse than Adams had ever dreamed it would be. Pinckney and Marshall had abandoned negotiations as hopeless. Gerry was continuing talks on a private basis because his republicanism had given him a preferred position with French Foreign Minister Talleyrand. Not only had the French refused to come to terms on any of the disputed points and grievances, but they had even refused to receive the Americans officially unless the way was greased first with a substantial monetary settlement. Three agents, cloak and dagger fashion, had visited the Americans and asked for a bribe of £50,000 sterling for the French Directory. Adams knew that such settlements were not unusual. The British had considered paying £450,000 sterling to ease their peace negotiations with France in 1797 until further naval victories made such a deal unnecessary. Portugal had purchased peace for a reputed price of £1,000,000. But the United States had neither the money nor the desire to participate in the diplomacy of bribery. Besides, paying money to France might be deemed a violation of American neutrality towards Britain. Paying off one enemy would mean purchasing trouble with the other.

Disclosure of the proposition was bound to anger the Francophobes in the United States and silence the Francophiles. Popular pressure for war with France might be strong. Faced with these problems, Adams turned to his cabinet for suggestions:

> Will it be advisable to present immediately to Congress the whole of the communications from our minister in France . . . under an injunction of secrecy as to that particular [Talleyrand's demand for the bribe]? Ought the President, then, to recommend, in his message, an immediate declaration of war?[6]

The Cabinet advised that there should be no immediate declaration of war, but split on whether or not the bribe demand should be disclosed to Congress. Adams, supported by Treasury Secretary Wolcott, decided to withhold the most inflammatory news from Congress. He merely informed Congress that he "perceived no ground of expectation that the objects of

[5]See his message to Congress (November 1798) in Richardson, vol. 1, p. 251.
[6]Adams, vol. 8, p. 568.

their mission can be accomplished on terms compatible with the safety, the honor, or the essential interests of the nation."[7] He asked for strong measures to prepare the nation for the war, which might become inevitable.

The news that the mission had failed aroused the anger of the Francophiles. They accused the President of bad faith in the negotiations. "How hot this Judas Iscariot of our country is for war with the French Republic!"[8] They called his message a War-Hawk's cry and circulated petitions opposing his defensive measures. They believed that the President had yielded to pressure by pro-British partisans and that the mission had merely been eyewash to soothe the pro-French partisans. ". . . What wonder that our Government lies prostrate at the feet of England, when the chief automaton is made to respond to the wishes of a profligate and unprincipled Creole!" Excitement mounted in Congress and pro-French Congressmen asked to see the dispatches from France so that they might read with their own eyes what had transpired. The pro-British faction who had heard rumors that the envoys had been insulted, joined in the request hoping to use it for their own advantage.[9]

Adams had not meant to release the dispatches because he feared that they might arouse the pro-British faction to fever pitch and force his hand to declare war on France. Premature disclosure might endanger the safe return of his envoys. But stung by criticism of double dealing, he restrained himself no longer. He sent the dispatches to Congress with the letters "X," "Y," and "Z" substituted for the names of the three French officials who had asked for the bribe. Adams requested that the dispatches "may be considered in confidence until the members of Congress are fully possessed of their contents and shall have had opportunity to deliberate on the consequences of their publication." After that time, he added, "I submit them to your wisdom."[10] This left it up to Congress to decide what the consequences would be if this information were released to the public. Adams was not sure what they would be. As Secretary Wolcott phrased it in a letter written to Hamilton on April 5, 1798: "The disclosure was, I suppose necessary, though I regret the necessity. The dose will kill or cure, and I wish I was not uncertain which. . . ."[11]

---

[7]Richardson, vol. 1, p. 264.

[8]This quotation and the next are from the January 24, 1797 issue of the *Massachusetts Mercury*, as cited in John B. McMaster, *History of the People of the United States*, vol. 2. New York: D. Appleton, 1885, p. 316. Although they antedate the period of our case history, they are representative of newspaper comments in 1798.

[9]They had opposed the disclosure of the Jay Treaty papers.

[10]Richardson, vol. 1, p. 265.

[11]George Gibbs, *Memoirs of the Administrations of Washington and John Adams, Edited from the Papers of Oliver Wolcott, Secretary of the Treasury*, vol. 2. New York: W. Von Norden, 1846, p. 44.

In Congress, Republicans voted to suppress circulation of the correspondence. But the pro-British faction could not have had a better find. They immediately arranged for publication and circulation of 50,000 copies of the dispatches among loud cries that the United States had been terribly insulted. Insults were bound to be fiercely resented by patriotic citizens of a young nation unsure of its reputation and painfully proud and eager to guard it. If anything could swing Francophiles into the opposition camp it was the charge of official French insults.

As the Federalists had predicted, the effect of the dispatches was fantastic. Charles Francis Adams, the grandson of the President, later wrote that the publication of the papers was:

> like the falling of a spark into a powder magazine. Among the friends of France who had, down to this moment with praise-worthy constancy, adhered to their allies . . . the news spread utter dismay. . . . The huge rising wave of national feeling [promised to carry the Federalists] for a long way in triumph on its crest. . . . There was but one voice to be heard, and that was in denunciation of the arrogance and profligacy of France, and in warm approbation of every measure calculated to uphold the dignity and honor of the United States.[12]

## The Impact of the XYZ Episode

What followed must have been a rare pleasure for Adams. For the first time in his presidency—and for the last time—he seemed genuinely popular. Applause greeted him wherever he went, a delightful change from the cool reception to which he was used. Addresses and memorials began to pour into the White House from merchants, city councils, individual citizens, and youth groups. Delegations who came to present these messages wore four-inch-wide black American cockades in the hatband. French cockades began to disappear, as did liberty poles. When the President greeted 1200 young men at the White House on May 7, he too was sporting a black cockade. The fashion spread, especially among the young, and there were many street fights and even duels fought between those who wore the emblem and those who ridiculed it or tried to tear it off.

A wave of emotional patriotism swept the country. In the theatres, patriotic tunes were played night after night to cheering, waving audiences. Hecklers were shouted down. One of the many songs set to the tune of "Yankee Doodle" proclaimed:

> The President, with good intent,
> Three envoys sent to Paris,
> But Cing Têtes would not with 'em treat,
> Of honor France so bare is.

[12]Adams, vol. 1, p. 519.

Thro' X and Y, and Madame Sly
They made demand for money;
For, as we're told, the French love gold
As stinging bees love honey.

Bold Adams did in '76
Our Independence sign, sir,
And he will not give up a jot,
Tho' all the world combine, sir.

Americans, then fly to arms,
And learn the way to use 'em.
If each man fight to 'fend his rights,
The French can't long abuse 'em.

The refrain to this ditty threatened that if Frenchmen came to enforce their demands, Yankee Doodle Dandy would "spank 'em hard and handy."[13] Details of the XYZ episode were submitted to the public in prose, verse, and even in a play called "The Politicians; or, A State of Things."

Two weeks after the publication of the dispatches the Republican newspaper, the *Aurora,* was close to financial collapse because subscriptions and advertising had fallen off badly.[14] Republicans might be perfectly willing to accede to the demands of France, but they did not want to yield to threats, insults, and blackmail. Many of them, although they still loved France, gave unstinted support to Adams and his policies.

Along the Atlantic border many towns started public subscriptions to build armed ships for loan to the government. Boston raised $125,000 in a short time and started building two frigates. New York, Portland, Portsmouth, Charleston, Salem, Norwich, Philadelphia, and Baltimore followed. Money was collected to build shore defenses. Citizens volunteered their labor. All this was proof that they were willing to do more than talk and shout. They were willing to pay with money and labor and, ultimately, blood.

Even Congress was cooperative. It speedily passed the defensive measures that the President had requested. Republican opposition in Congress disintegrated and even the number of Republicans diminished. Four southern Congressmen left for home.[15]

But all was not bliss. The cries for alliance with France had been stilled for the moment, although Adams knew that his foes were only temporarily subdued and wounded. Instead there was what seemed like an overwhelming popular mandate for war with France and alliance with

[13]McMaster, vol. 2, pp. 384–385.
[14]Paul Leicester Ford, ed., *Writings of Thomas Jefferson,* vol. 8. New York: Putnam's, 1894, p. 412.
[15]Ford, vol. 8, p. 412.

Britain. Adams had supplied his Cabinet and his party with the ammunition to kill his neutrality policy. He found himself walking a narrower,
slicker tightrope than ever. Like Maréchal Villars at the court of Louis
XIV, he might well have pleaded: "Defend me from my friends; I can
defend myself from my enemies."

The pro-British faction, riding its crest of popularity, managed to steer
much defensive legislation through Congress, in fact more than the President had asked. Congress enlarged the navy and created a cabinet-level
navy department. It provided for better coastal defenses. It levied new
taxes to pay for all these military expenses and approved a $5,000,000
loan. It also voted that all treaties with France were void, and authorized
hostilities equivalent to war. A declaration of war was stalled in the House
by a narrow margin only.[16] Articles urging war appeared in the *Gazette
of the United States*. The atmosphere grew so tense and bitter that Federalists managed to push through Congress the notorious Sedition Act to
muzzle their opposition.

Later, the President complained that he had hardly been consulted in
all these measures. What was worse, he disagreed with many of them, as
did some members of his Cabinet.[17] However, at the time, he made no
attempts to dissuade Congress from passing these laws.[18]

Adams felt that increased ground forces were pointless when battles
would be fought on the water only. "At present there is no more prospect
of seeing a French army here, than there is in Heaven" he wrote to War
Secretary McHenry on October 22, 1798.[19] Only the navy required enlargement. He suspected that Alexander Hamilton, conservative proponent
of strong government, wanted a large army so that it would be available
to squelch domestic violence.[20] Increasing taxes for the army "at a time
when so many tax laws, already enacted, were unexecuted in so many
States, and when insurrections and rebellions had already been excited in
Pennsylvania, on account of taxes, appeared to me altogether desperate,
altogether delirious."[21] He agreed with Wolcott that "nothing, however,
is more certain than that the army is unpopular, even in the Southern

[16]Manning J. Dauer, *The Adams Federalists*. Baltimore: The Johns Hopkins Press, 1953, pp. 168–170.

[17]Gibbs, vol. 2, p. 317.

[18]Stephen G. Kurtz, *The Presidency of John Adams*. Philadelphia: University of Pennsylvania Press, 1957, p. 322.

[19]Adams, vol. 8, p. 613.

[20]Adams, vol. 1, pp. 523–527.

[21]Adams, vol. 9, p. 291. Anson E. Morse, *The Federalist Party in Massachusetts to 1800*. Princeton: University Library, 1909, p. 176, says the heavy
taxes lost far more votes for the Federalists than the Alien and Sedition acts.

States. . . . the state of idleness to which they are necessarily condemned, tends to corrupt their principles. . . ."[22]

As for the Sedition Act:

> . . . as they [the Alien and Sedition Acts] were then considered as war measures, and intended altogether against the advocates of the French and peace with France, I was apprehensive that a hurricane of clamor would be raised against them, as in truth there was, even more fierce and violent than I had anticipated.[23]

He did not wish to arouse his public opposition, if he could help it, even though "I knew there was need enough of both."[24]

### France Makes Overtures for Peace

When summer came, political passions cooled as Congressmen went home and people went about the chores of summer. Adams' mind turned from politics to problems of his own hearth in "one of the most gloomy seasons" of his life. "Mrs. Adams lay stretched on the bed of illness for a long time flickering between life and death; and even when issuing from the trial" it was difficult to dispel "the uneasiness her frail condition could not but waken."[25] The President was in no mood for political controversy. He wrote to Wolcott: "The long continued dangerous sickness of my best friend, and her still precarious destiny, have thrown my mind into a state of depression, agitation, and anxiety, which will not admit of a full discussion of the various points on which you and I appear to differ in opinion."[26]

In the midst of these strains came reports from France indicating that the Directory had changed its mind and was willing to renew negotiations. What Adams had hoped for without a basis for hope, had come to pass. His long-time friend, Elbridge Gerry, a member of the original XYZ mission who had stayed in France as a private citizen when the other members left, arrived in the United States in October 1798, with a tale that corroborated what Adams had heard from other sources—the French were willing to negotiate.[27] The same story had come to him second-hand from General Washington who had talked with Dr. George Logan, a Pennsylvania Quaker, on his return from France from a private mission to seek peace for his country. Joel Barlow, an American residing in France for

[22]Gibbs, vol. 2, p. 317.
[23]Adams, vol. 9, p. 291.
[24]Adams, vol. 9, p. 291.
[25]Adams, vol. 1, p. 531.
[26]Adams, vol. 8, p. 602.
[27]Adams, vol. 1, pp. 532—533; vol. 7, pp. 677–680.

many years, had conveyed a similar message, which Washington had forwarded to Adams.

What convinced Adams more than anything else was:

> a letter from Talleyrand himself, giving declaration, in the name of his government, that any minister pleni-potentiary from the United States shall be received according to the condition at the close of my message to Congress, on the 21st of June last. . . . Barlow's letter had . . . very little weight in determining me to this measure [renewal of negotiations].[28]

The letter had been forwarded by William Vans Murray, the American minister at the Hague. Murray had received it from M. Pichon, secretary of the French legation at the Hague and an expert on American affairs, who had evidently been assigned to the Hague so that he might conduct informal negotiations. Murray assigned a motive to Talleyrand which made sense to Adams—self-interest. The French were eager to resume negotiations because they feared American collaboration or even alliance with Britain against France. At the time, French fortunes of war were at a low ebb. The French fleet had been destroyed at the Battle of the Nile on August 1, 1798.

Other letters had preceded the Talleyrand letter, all in the same vein. Secretary of State Pickering had decoded the Murray correspondence at the State Department. Adams, who had urged Pickering to "keep their contents within his own bosom,"[29] confided to the Secretary that the letters from the start had "made a great impression on me."[30]

## A Recalcitrant Cabinet

Adams was convinced that a renewed attempt to negotiate with France would be worthwhile.[31] The problem was how to sell this idea to his political advisors. He was afraid that his Cabinet would oppose, despite the news from France. His ministers seemed bent on keeping anti-French sentiment alive and steering the country to the brink of war with France. They seemed convinced that this was the proper foreign policy for the United States. Besides, they felt that a Federalist victory in the forthcoming elections depended on rallying the country around an aggressive foreign policy.[32] Renewing the mission to France would strengthen the Republicans because it would be a feather in their cap.

[28]Adams, vol. 8, p. 625; vol. 9, pp. 241–242.
[29]Adams, vol. 8, p. 677.
[30]Adams, vol. 8, pp. 614–615.
[31]Adams, vol. 8, pp. 621–622.
[32]C. R. King, ed., *Life and Correspondence of Rufus King*, vol. 2. New York: Putnam's, 1895, pp. 352–353.

A letter, dispatched from Quincy on October 20, 1798, to the Secretary of State, received no reply. In it Adams had asked the opinions of the department heads "whether any further proposals of negotiation can be made with safety." Would such a proposal be beneficial at home or abroad "by uniting minds more in our favor?" Should he nominate:

> a minister to the French republic, who may be ready to embark for France, as soon as he, or the President, shall receive from the Directory satisfactory assurances that he shall be received and entitled to all the prerogatives and privileges of the general law of nations, and that a minister of equal rank and powers shall be appointed and commissioned to treat with him?[33]

Should the Gerry dispatches from France be submitted to Congress to give the members an idea of Talleyrand's changing position? Or would it "be expedient for the President to recommend to the consideration of Congress a declaration of war against France"?[34]

When Adams arrived in Philadelphia a month later for the opening of Congress, he found out why there had been no reply to his letter. The cabinet, alarmed at the chance of renewed negotiations, had met with some of the leading generals and had prepared a message for Congress that would tie the President's hands. It was so belligerent in tone that it would preclude further negotiations. Wolcott handed the draft to the President.

The President made no changes, except for one crucial paragraph. Wolcott's draft stated that sending another minister would be "*an act of humiliation to which the United States ought not to submit without extreme necessity. No such necessity exists. It must, therefore, be left with France, if she be indeed desirous of accommodation, to take the requisite steps.*"[35] Such a statement would bar Adams from sending another minister unless France sent one first—an unlikely contingency. Over the objections of the cabinet, Adams changed the paragraph to read "But to send another minister without more determinate assurances that he would be received would be an act of humiliation to which the United States ought not to submit."[36] This left him free to send another American mission, provided the proper assurances were received, without waiting for French overtures to send a mission of their own first.

Adams also asked Congress to increase military preparations in accordance with his belief that a policy of strength would improve the chance for negotiations and would improve America's position in such negotia-

[33]Adams, vol. 8, p. 609.
[34]Adams, vol. 8, p. 609.
[35]Adams, vol. 1, p. 536 (Italics in original).
[36]Richardson, vol. 1, p. 273; Adams, vol. 1, p. 537.

tions. "An efficient preparation for war can alone insure peace."[37] The message delivered, the President left a few days later for Quincy.

There matters stood. Federalists in the Cabinet and in Congress, taking their cue from Alexander Hamilton, tried to push the country closer to war. They even met to see if they could pilot a declaration of war through Congress but found they lacked the necessary majority. The President, on the other hand, contrary to the views and desires of the Hamilton faction of his party, was convinced that the road to negotiations was open once more. He must find an opportunity to embark upon it without losing face, if this was possible.

### Adams Takes the Public's Pulse

Adams believed that most of the people would approve renewed negotiations. It was his Cabinet and the Hamilton faction of his party, not he, who were out of tune with the people. If the war-like stance of Congress was approved by the public, why had Congress been flooded with thousands of petitions asking disbanding of the army and repeal of the Alien and Sedition laws?[38] Why had there been "the insurrection in Pennsylvania, the universal and perpetual inflammatory publications against the land tax, stamp tax, coach tax, excise law, and eight percent loan . . . the circular letters of members of Congress from the middle and southern States . . . the French cockades, ostentatiously exhibited against the American cockades . . ."?[39] Why had there been printed and spoken appeals for peace by "the venerable patriarchs, Pendleton and Wythe of Virginia" evidence of "serious and solid importance, indicative of public opinion"? Was it not ample proof of the public's feeling that "General Heath came out with an address to the public in Massachusetts, declaring that every man he met was decidedly for peace"? Was it not true that Governor M'Kean of Pennsylvania had won his election with a majority of 30,000 votes because he had declared himself "decidedly against a war with France"?[40] By contrast, the fall elections had gone poorly for the Federalists in Maryland where they had expected otherwise.[41] Besides "these symptons of the popular bias" there were "conversations, of which I was .informed, at taverns and insurance offices, threatening violence to the

[37]Richardson, vol. 1, p. 273.

[38]Manning J. Dauer, *The Adams Federalists*. Baltimore: The Johns Hopkins Press, 1953, pp. 228–229.

[39]Adams, vol. 9, p. 279.

[40]Adams, vol. 9, p. 280. Kurtz, p. 364, agrees that the Pennsylvania elections were won and lost on the issue of war and increased taxes, and not on local issues.

[41]Gibbs, vol. 2, p. 111.

President." There were "French cockades that were everywhere paraded before my eyes, in opposition to the black cockade." There were numerous "declarations and oaths . . . that if we went to war with France, and the French should come here, they would join them against the Federalists and the English."[42] No, the Hamiltonians were certainly wrong, when they declared that pro-French feelings were on the wane. They had mistaken minority sentiments for majority views. Adams felt that no "great alteration in public opinion had . . . taken place."[43]

Adams ascribed the revival of pro-French feelings, a few months after the XYZ episode to:

> the state of our presses . . . popular eloquence of the editors of the opposition papers; that scoffing, scorning wit, and that caustic malignity of soul, which appeared so remarkably in all the writings of Thomas Paine and Callender . . . the members of the Senate and House who were decided against the administration. . . .[44]

Besides, there had been some leaks about France's willingness to reopen negotiations. Logan and Barlow had not kept quiet, which dismayed Adams because he did not like to have his hands tied.[45] Early in 1799, the Richmond *Examiner* published the entire Talleyrand-Pichon correspondence, along with relevant diplomatic dispatches. There was some suspicion that the *Examiner* had received its information through a direct leak by the French government which hoped to incite the public in this manner to urge the government to begin new negotiations.[46] Murray had warned the President that the French would try to play on divisions among the American people to force his hand into negotiations, and that the renewal of negotiations must be seriously weighed for that reason. The French "will try every art to impress upon the public mind in America" their willingness to negotiate, so "that two opinions might yet rise in the United States. . . ."[47] If it became known that the President had refused to explore a reasonable opportunity for peace, he would lose public support.

Even assuming that the country was united against France, one could never be sure when a fickle public would turn. Popular passions were like a straw fire—quickly blazing and quickly cooled. Adams confided his doubts to Rufus King in a letter dated October 16, 1798: "Our country seems to be, as we used to say in 1774, unanimous and firm. They are much more

[42]Gibbs, vol. 2, p. 111.

[43]Adams, vol. 9, p. 278. See also John R. Howe, *The Changing Political Thought of John Adams.* Princeton: Princeton University Press, 1966, pp. 205–206.

[44]Adams, vol. 9, p. 278.

[45]Adams, vol. 8, p. 615.

[46]Gibbs, vol. 2, pp. 240–249.

[47]Adams, vol. 8, p. 682.

so now than they were then. New York and Pennsylvania were always a little *chancelantes*, but they will be kept tolerably steady. There are strong pillars in both." But one could never depend on public steadiness. "But, watchman, what of the night? Where is all tending? I am weary of conjectures. Will princes ever be more wise, or people more temperate or united, or aristocrats more willing to acknowledge a superior?"[48] Other Federalists shared these doubts. It might be true that "French principles are very much out of fashion. . . ." But this could change quickly because "still the leaders are indefatigable, are more industrious and violent as their party lessen and lose ground."[49]

Because of the conflicting pro-French and pro-English pressures and the difficulty of predicting public reactions accurately, Adams delayed as long as he dared before announcing his decision. Finally, delay was no longer possible. Had it continued, "the two parties in the United States would have broken out into a civil war."[50] Or:

> I might have been drawn by the force of public opinion, or the influence of the legislature, into an alliance with England; but it would have been against my own judgment and inclination because it should tie up our hand for making peace whenever we pleased. . . . We want no alliance; we are equal to all our own necessary wars.[51]

## Renewal of Negotiations

John Adams did what he deemed right. On February 18, 1799, he sent the Talleyrand-Pichon correspondence to the Senate. On the strength of it he asked approval for the nomination of yet another minister to France. He took this step completely on his own, without even informing his cabinet.[52] He felt that they knew his position well enough. Had he confronted them with his decision first, they might have tried to delay him or stop him. Pickering had stalled earlier, in January 1799, when Adams had asked him to draw up a model consular convention and treaty with France. Pickering had made excuses and delays while trying to convince Adams that renewed dealings with France would be a mistake.

The reaction in the press and in the Senate seemed to bear out Adams'

[48]Adams, vol. 8, p. 606.
[49]Gibbs, vol. 2, p. 108.
[50]Adams, vol. 9, p. 294.
[51]Adams, vol. 9, p. 268.
[52]In a letter to his wife, a few days later, he wrote that he had deliberately kept the decision completely to himself. See Stephen G. Kurtz, "The French Mission of 1799–1800: Concluding Chapter in the Statecraft of John Adams," *Political Science Quarterly*, vol. 80 (1965), p. 547.
[53]Dauer, p. 232.

hunch that there was substantial support among influential groups of people for renewing negotiations with France. Among the popular papers, only *Porcupine's Gazette* and the *Gazette of the United States* disapproved of the mission. *Porcupine's Gazette* simply denied that the President had suggested resumption of negotiations.[53] Aside from insisting, on Hamilton's advice, that two additional members be named to the mission, the Senate did not forcefully oppose Adams' suggestion. Wolcott claimed that Senate approval was grudging, given "to unite all opinions, at least of the federalists." He believed that it was couched "in such terms as when critically analyzed would amount to no approbation at all . . ."[54] But what Wolcott deemed a grudging expression of party acquiescence, Adams interpreted as consent. Both were right; there were important members of government like Pickering, Fisher Ames, Cabot, and Sedgwick who denounced the mission, and others who approved it. Prominent among those who approved were John Marshall, Henry Lee, Harrison Otis, Governor Davis of North Carolina, Patrick Henry, Benjamin Stoddart, and Charles Lee of the cabinet.

Regardless of how political leaders felt, the majority of the vocal public seemed to be on Adams' side. As Pickering put it disappointedly in a letter to George Washington on October 24, 1799:

> Among the most enlightened citizens and truest friends to our country, but one opinion prevails. All deprecate the French mission, as fraught with irreparable mischiefs. *Once* I would have relied on the good sense of the people for a remedy of the mischiefs when assailing us; but my opinion of that good sense is vastly abated. A large proportion seems more ready to embrace falsehood than truth.[55]

He agreed with Wolcott that "in general, the people are ignorant, strongly prejudiced against the measures of government, vindictive in their resentments, and, I fear, incapable of being influenced except by their fears of punishment."[56] Henry Knox, who approved of the mission, put the public in a more favorable light. He wrote to Adams from Boston, on March 5, 1799:

> I have no doubt (uninformed as the public are) that their entire reliance on your superior knowledge of the state of Europe, and wisdom to embrace every proper occasion, will be perfectly satisfactory to ninety-nine persons out of a hundred . . . the great body of the federal interest, confide implicitly in your knowledge and virtue . . . in every division of opinion they will adhere and cling to you in preference to all others.[57]

[54]Gibbs, vol. 2, p. 314.
[55]Gibbs, vol. 2, p. 280.
[56]Gibbs, vol. 2, p. 240.
[57]Adams, vol. 8, pp. 626–627.

The mission brought home the hoped-for treaty. John Adams considered it the "most disinterested and meritorious action of my life" and asked that his gravestone bear the inscription, "Here lies John Adams, who took upon himself the responsibility of peace with France in the year 1800!"[58]

Whether or not he felt that he was purchasing the treaty at the price of reelection is not certain. There are some indications that he believed that his policy toward France might be more of a help than hindrance in reelection. First of all, despite strong opposition on the part of many Federalists, his party renominated him. This could be interpreted as faith in his ability to win. Second, he felt that his policy would appeal to the middle-roaders, those who were lukewarm towards both France and England. He believed that the majority of people would align with such a moderate position, rather than with the radical extremes. He may have been right. The Federalist party did well in New York, Massachusetts and throughout the entire South in the election of 1800. Virginia and North Carolina elected more Federalists to office than ever before.[59]

But Adams' popular support was not strong enough to overcome the opposition engendered by his political enemies. Without the support of the Hamilton faction he could not win. When the Federalists later blamed the loss of the election on the mission to France, rather than on defections within their own party ranks, Adams did not flinch. If he was to be sacrificed for doing what he deemed right, so be it. The picture of the martyr for a cause was not at all unpleasing to his Puritan mind. As he had written earlier to his wife, "I never in my life, that I know of, sacrificed my principles or duty to popularity or reputation. I hope I am now too old ever to do it."[60]

## The United States Strategic Position, 1798–1799

What factors influenced Adams in making his decisions? One cannot say for sure, for the well springs of action are hidden even to the actor. But one can sketch the circumstances and use the actor's personality traits and convictions as an imperfect, yet broadly accurate reading lens through which to view the events, as he may have viewed them.

Strategically, the United States was a small and underdeveloped country in 1798, still recuperating from the effects of its War of Independence.

[58]Adams, vol. 10, p. 113.

[59]Adams, vol. 10, pp. 115–118; Kurtz, *Presidency*, pp. 352 and 394, writes that Adams did better in electoral votes in 1800 than in 1796, except for the state of New York, and that this supported Adams' views of the public's feelings.

[60]Charles Francis Adams, ed., *Letters of John Adams to his Wife*, vol. 2. Boston: Little, Brown, 1841, p. 121.

It was struggling along with a new form of government, which faced much individual and sectional opposition. By contrast, France and England were the most powerful nations in the world, experienced in war and peace operations and with vast military and economic resources. Neither one would have been averse to annexing part or all of the United States to its colonial empire. Other European nations, standing in the wings, were also ready to pounce on any weak colonial region. Militarily, the United States was a third-rate power. It had a volunteer army, small for the size of the country, and difficult to keep together as Washington could attest. The navy in 1798 consisted of 15 ships, with a dozen more on order. It was good enough to win in individual combat with pirates and other marauders, but certainly no match for the British or French fleet. Moreover, the country was extremely vulnerable to attack once its enemies had crossed the ocean. It had a vast, sparsely settled coastline to defend, which made it practically impossible to prevent a landing of foreign armies. In light of these strategic conditions, how did the President appraise the foreign policy situation?

Adams, like Washington, felt that a small and weak country, which had the good fortune to be at some distance from the perpetual wars of Europe, must try its level best to maintain a neutral stance.

> Our system [of foreign policy] was, to form treaties of commerce . . . but by no means to form any political or military connections with any power in Europe, or engage in any hostilities against any, unless driven to them by necessity to support our independence and honor, or our just and necessary interests.[61]

There was little to be gained from joining the wars of European powers, and much to be lost. With such uneven odds, neutrality was the only logical choice. Temperamentally such a policy suited Adams—and temperament is a significant factor at the pinnacle of government. But American policy might have been different if Adams had not been repelled by the excesses of the French Revolution. Adams was no Anglophile either, for good political as well as personal reasons. During his years of diplomatic service in England, he had been snubbed quite frequently. His pleas to Prime Minister Pitt and the cabinet were listened to, but rarely answered. An impatient man, Adams was angry and resentful.

But there were other considerations. Alliance with a major European power would hamper America's freedom of action. The United States might be unable to pursue its national interests in a completely single-hearted manner. If she became involved in hostilities, the costs and efforts would retard internal development. Interruption of foreign trade would

---

[61]Adams, vol. 9, p. 243. Kurtz, "French Mission," p. 551, believes that one major purpose of the Murray mission was Adams' desire to stop the agitation for closer cooperation with England which Federalists in Congress favored.

bring about a collapse of the fiscal system, which depended on tariff revenues. Raids by one of the belligerents would stop, and trading privileges
might increase. But this would be balanced by increased raids by the other
and decreased trading privileges. As a neutral, the United States might be
able to play off one belligerent against another and gain concessions from
both. How reminiscent such arguments must sound to new nations today,
who are trying to preserve their neutrality for essentially similar reasons.

Like many of the developing nations today, the United States also faced
the problem of keeping its people together at a time when the sense of national unity and common interests was still weak. The hatreds of war
might lead to the dissolution of the union. What Arthur P. Whitaker has
said of the West was true for the entire country. "Neither unionism nor
disunionism was deeply rooted . . . at the end of the century. Patriotism
ebbed and flowed with almost every act of the federal government and
every turn of international affairs."[62]

In addition, many of the nation's prominent military and political
leaders were in the pay of foreign powers whose interests, they felt, corresponded with those of the United States. These men were not likely to
take up arms against their employers, should the fledgling national government request this. George Rogers Clark, a hero of the Revolutionary
War, had sold his services to France to aid her in recovering Louisiana
from Spain. Ira Allen of Vermont was pledged to collaborate with the
French in their plans to attack Canada. Aaron Burr was involved in intrigues to establish an independent republic in Canada. General James
Wilkinson, ranking officer of the regular army after the death of General
Wayne, was in the pay of Spain. Senator William Blount of Tennessee
had been expelled from the Senate on July 8, 1797, for collaborating with
the British minister to the United States, concerning British plans for the
Louisiana territory.[63]

While the union might not survive the strains of war, Adams believed
it could continue to withstand the strains of ordinary political division.
Foreign policy especially had been a hotly debated issue from the beginning of the country. The Federalists favored neutrality or war with France
and looked upon Great Britain as the world's last hope for sane and responsible government. The Republicans, when war broke out between
England and France on February 1, 1793, felt that England was once

[62]Arthur P. Whitaker, *The Mississippi Question, 1795–1803.* New York:
Appleton-Century-Crofts, 1934, p. 25. Kurtz, "French Mission," p. 549, says
that "although historical investigation has uncovered little that suggests preparation for armed rebellion on the part of Republican leaders in 1798 or 1799, Federalist escatology insisted upon it. . . . Hamilton was convinced that Virginians
contemplated armed revolt. . . ."

[63]Dauer, pp. 172–173.

more fighting against freedom. George III was trying to suppress liberty in France, as he had tried to suppress it in the United States. Jefferson claimed that "The liberty of the whole earth was depending on the issue of the contest."[64] An alliance with France against Britain was essential. Adams, by contrast, was not too worried about these partisan divisions in peace time. "As to our being a divided people, all nations are divided. France is divided; so are Holland, England, Italy, and Germany. There will ever be parties and divisions in all nations; but our people will support their government . . . not to expect divisions in a free country, would be an absurdity."[65] But it would be unwise to put the loyalty of the extremists on both sides under too great a strain. For this, as well as all the other reasons mentioned, the middle road policy of neutrality and conciliation seemed wisest.

## The President Sets Guidelines for Policy

Adams reached his decisions about the broad outlines of American foreign policy on his own. There is no record to show that he discussed the validity of his basic assumptions with anyone. He would consult with others about specific diplomatic actions required by the march of events. But he would not seek their advice on the general outlines of policy.

It was easier for Adams, than for modern Presidents, to act as his own Secretary of State in making basic foreign policy decisions. The State Department was still small enough and its transactions few enough so that Adams could read nearly all dispatches in person. He apparently did this.[66] On the basis of this information, and his past experience in foreign affairs, he was able to come to his own conclusions with confidence. In fact, Adams often knew more than his Secretary of State about foreign affairs because a number of correspondents wrote directly to him or visited him, bypassing the State Department. He had no corps of secretaries to predigest correspondence and to determine what he ought and ought not to read. There was thus in this period none of the subtle shaping of policy that goes on in today's State Department, where lower level officials reduce the flood of incoming information to a manageable stream to the top. Such editing invariably imparts a distinct flavor to the final policy.

The appointment of the Murray mission is a telling example. The President had convinced himself that negotiations with France had to be resumed, and decided to go ahead with them regardless of the objections

[64]Andrew A. Lipscomb, ed., *The Writings of Thomas Jefferson*, vol. 9. Washington: Thomas Jefferson Memorial Association, 1905, p. 10.

[65]Adams, vol. 8, p. 548.

[66]The early State Department is described by Leonard D. White, *The Federalists*. New York: Macmillan, 1948, pp. 183–188.

of his formal advisors. His justification is characteristic in what it contains, what it omits, and in the order of reasons. "If, with all this information [official and unofficial correspondence on French intentions], I had refused to institute a negotiation . . . I should have been degraded in my own estimation as a man of honor; I should have disgraced the nation I represented, in their own opinion and in the judgment of all Europe."[67]

There is little reason to believe that the President's basic outlook was materially influenced, even unconsciously, by individuals inside or outside the government. For he conceived of leadership ". . . not primarily as the response to popular pressures but as a lonely search for the path that the leader's superior knowledge and understanding indicated as the right one."[68] There was no danger of a solipsistic conception of right. Natural law philosophy taught the existence of a higher, correct law that the wise individual could discover through reason.[69] Nor was Adams influenced by considerations of party politics in the sense that he might wish to pursue policies agreeable to members of his party individually, or of benefit to his party at the polls. He felt that the President "is bound by his honor and his conscience, by his oath to the Constitution, as well as his responsibility to the public opinion of the nation, to act his own mature and unbiased judgment, though unfortunately, it may be in direct contradiction to the advice of all his ministers. This was my situation in more than one instance."[70]

As for party spirit, it was a wicked thing and the President must guard against it in himself as well as others. ". . . Party spirit will convert white into black and right into wrong, we have, I fear, very corrupt individuals in this country, independent of the common spirit of party."[71] Party spirit would lead people to say things that they did not mean. Adams had little use for such intellectual dishonesty. On February 19, 1799, he wrote to General Washington in disgust: "There is not much sincerity in the cant about peace; those who snivel for it now, were hot for war against Britain a few months ago, and would be now, if they saw a chance. In elective governments, peace or war are alike embraced by parties, when they think they can employ either for electioneering purposes."[72] He felt that Dr. Logan's ostensibly private peace mission to France, of which he highly disapproved, had been inspired by political purposes of the Republican party. He asked Pickering: "Is this constitutional, for a party of opposition to

[67]Adams, vol. 9, p. 246.

[68]Page Smith, *John Adams*, vol. 2. Garden City, N. Y.: Doubleday, 1962, p. 1030.

[69]Francis G. Wilson, *A Theory of Public Opinion*. Chicago: Regnery, 1962, p. 24.

[70]Adams, vol. 9, p. 270.

[71]*Letters of John Adams*, vol. 2, pp. 133–134.

[72]Adams, vol. 8, p. 626.

send embassies to foreign nations to obtain their interference in elections?"
He thought the Republican party was looking "to do or obtain something
which might give opportunity for the 'true [pro-French] American character to blaze forth in the approaching elections.' "[73]

Adams, furthermore, did not feel that he must kowtow to his party
because his personal political popularity was relatively small. In a letter
to Attorney General Charles Lee, written from Quincy, March 29, 1799,
he threw down the gauntlet to would-be opponents:

> If anyone entertains the idea, that because I am a President of three
> votes only, I am in the power of a party, they shall find that I am no more
> so than the Constitution forces upon me. If combinations of senators,
> generals, and heads of departments shall be formed, such as I cannot re-
> sist, and measures are demanded of me that I cannot adopt, my remedy
> is plain and certain. I will try my own strength at resistance first, how-
> ever. This is free, and *entre nous*.[74]

What this "remedy" was, is not quite clear, though the implications seemed
to be that Adams would refuse to knuckle under.

However, in practice he was not quite so uncompromising. He did back
down at times on matters of lesser importance to him, when he felt that
his hand was forced. Thus he appointed Alexander Hamilton as Inspector
General of the army against his own wishes because *not* to do so would
have sacrificed his important plan of creating a sound defensive force.
General Washington had warned Secretary of War McHenry that he would
resign if Hamilton did not receive the appointment. Washington's resignation would have been a severe blow to rearmament.[75]

Adams was also willing to base his selection of army officers on partisan
considerations. He appointed a number of Republicans as officers in the
army to gain bipartisan support for his military policies. He felt that it was
particularly important to give appointments to Republicans from Pennsylvania and New York to gain the support of these middle states. He even
expected to nominate Aaron Burr and Peter Muhlenberg of Pennsylvania
as brigadier generals to win them over to his cause. However, strong objections by the Hamiltonians and General Washington stopped him on
this score. All of this shows that Adams was willing to engage in party politics to accomplish his purposes, but not if matters of major importance

[73]Adams, vol. 8, p. 615.

[74]Adams, vol. 8, p. 629. The phrase "President of three votes only" refers to
his selection by a three vote electoral college margin.

[75]Adams, vol. 8. pp. 601–602; Octavius Pickering, *The Life and Times of
Timothy Pickering*, vol. 3. Boston: Little, Brown, 1867, p. 463; and Bernard C.
Steiner, *Life and Correspondence of James McHenry*. Cleveland: Burrows
Brothers, 1907, pp. 338–339. Washington, likewise, had backed down on lesser
matters (See White, pp. 110–111).

were involved. Then he stuck to his principles, regardless of party considerations.

## The Cabinet as Presidential Advisor

While Adams made up his own mind on the major outlines of policy, he did consult with others on the specific steps to be taken in day-to-day diplomacy. We must now try to discern who his advisors were in these day-to-day decisions. Unfortunately, no Adams diary is available for the period of his presidency. This makes it difficult to construct a day-by-day account of the people who came to see him and their possible influence on him. But from other records (mostly letters by him, to him, and by his contemporaries) we know that Adams spent much of the time period of our case history—between March 8, 1798 and February 25, 1799—at Braintree. This meant that his personal contacts were mostly of the home village variety—close friends and neighbors, his family, and the correspondents who wrote him directly from abroad. Among the latter, Elbridge Gerry, although a Republican, and Adams' son, John Quincy Adams, seem to have been the most influential as regards Franco-American relations. This was true primarily because they mirrored his own views and counseled him in the manner in which he wished to be counseled. Moreover, he trusted them while distrusting most others so that the barriers of distrust closed his mind off from much of the advice tendered to him.

His long periods at Braintree meant that the affairs of state had to be transacted largely by mail. His Cabinet members were unhappy about this procedure because an exchange of letters took at least two weeks. But Adams thought it quite adequate, especially since delays made it easier for him to remain independent in his decisions. When he did not wish to act, he could stall without having to feel personal pressure by his aides. As for our inquiry, it benefits from the written communications because these give us a record of Adams' dealings with members of his cabinet.

Adams felt duty-bound to follow Washington's precedent and the constitutional mandate to consult members of his Cabinet about prospective governmental actions and ask for their suggestions in writing. Pickering acknowledges this: "In most matters we are consulted."[76] But the Constitution says nothing about the obligation of a president to accept the advice tendered to him. Adams felt under no obligation to heed his secretaries' suggestions except if they constituted "an apparent compliment to his own understanding."[77]

Whether his secretaries' advice would have fallen on more receptive

[76]Henry Cabot Lodge, *Life and Letters of George Cabot*. Boston: Little, Brown, 1878, p. 249.

[77]Gibbs, vol. 1, p. 476.

ears had they been his personal friends and close confidantes is a matter for conjecture. We do know that they were neither. Adams inherited his Cabinet from his predecessor and made no changes until the last year of his administration when the rift between him and his main secretaries became too great to be tolerated. In the intervening years he made do with what he had, knowing full well how difficult it was to staff the administrative departments with capable people, let alone congenial ones. Already as Vice-President, Adams had complained to his wife about the difficulty of finding good men to fill Cabinet posts:

> . . . Where shall be found good men and true to fill the offices of government? . . . It is very difficult to find gentlemen who are willing to accept of public trusts, and, at the same time, capable of discharging them. . . . The expenses of living at the seat of government are so exorbitant, so far beyond all proportion to the salaries, and the sure reward of integrity in the discharge of public functions is such obloquy, contempt, and insult, that no man of any feeling is willing to renounce his home, forsake his property and profession, for the sake of removing to Philadelphia, where he is almost sure of disgrace and ruin.[78]

Even Washington had found it impossible to get the men he really wanted. As a result, the Cabinet was top heavy with mediocrities. Any attempt to represent various sections of the country or choose men by other political criteria was completely out of the question. Pickering had been appointed as Secretary of State by President Washington after three other choices had turned the job down. Adams commented about his former Secretary of State:

> Mr. Pickering would have made a good collector of the customs; but, he was not so well qualified for a Secretary of State. He was so devoted an Idolator of Hamilton, that he could not judge impartially of the sentiments and opinions of the President of the United States.[79]

McHenry, the Secretary of War, had also been a fourth choice, after three others had declined the office. Charles Lee, the Attorney General, had been picked by Washington after his brother, Henry Lee, had suggested him when five others had been considered and found unavailable. He was virtually unknown at the time, although he later had a distinguished legal career. Wolcott had entered government service as an auditor for the Treasury Department when Hamilton headed it. He was a mediocre Secretary of the Treasury, and little more than a mouthpiece for Hamilton.

The types of questions that Adams asked of his Cabinet members are revealing. All of them indicated the policies he had in mind and merely

---

[78]*Letters of John Adams*, vol. 2, pp. 188–189.

[79]John Adams, *John Adams–William Cunningham Correspondence*. Boston: E. M. Cunningham, 1823, p. 40.

asked for reactions to these policies. They did not leave his ministers free to suggest their own solutions. For instance, in January 1798, when lack of word from the mission dispatched to France in the previous fall aroused fears of its failure, Adams asked the Cabinet for suggestions. If his misgivings were right,

> in what manner should the first intelligence be announced to Congress; by message, or speech? What measures should be recommended to Congress? Shall an immediate declaration of war be recommended or suggested? . . . Will it . . . be advisable to recommend an embargo? . . . What will policy dictate to be said to England . . . ? Will it not be soundest policy, even in case of a declaration of war on both sides, between France and the United States, for us to be totally silent to England, and wait for her overtures? Will it not be imprudent in us to connect ourselves with Britain, in any manner that may impede us in embracing the first favorable moment or opportunity to make a separate peace? What aids or benefits can we expect from England by any stipulations with her, which her interest will not impel her to extend to us without any? On the brink of the dangerous precipice on which she stands, will not shaking hands with her necessitate us to fall with her, if she falls?[80]

Adams knew what alternatives he wished to explore, and he asked for suggestions on his ideas. He did not ask for fresh ideas or innovations and he would not have liked it had he received them.

### The Cabinet Evaluates Public Opinion

Among the considerations that went into his decisions and that he wanted his secretaries to explore for him was the response that certain policies might elicit from the public. What he wanted to know was his cabinet's appraisal of the likely reaction of the public to the policies he might choose. Such an estimate of latent opinion, then as now, would have as much influence, or possibly more, on policy decisions than expressed opinions after a policy course had already been chosen. Adams did not feel that his Cabinet represented public opinion, or that Cabinet members could interpret public opinion better than he. Quite the contrary.[81] But since public opposition could be a real obstacle to carrying out his plans, and public approval could be a real help, it was wise to explore public reactions as fully as possible.

Thus the first foreign policy question asked of his secretaries at the start of his administration was "Whether the refusal to receive Mr. Pinckney

[80]Adams, vol. 2, pp. 561–562.
[81]Adams, vol. 2, pp. 601–602.

[sent as American representative to France] and the rude orders to quit Paris and the territory of the Republic with such circumstances of indignity, insult, and hostility, as we have been informed of, are bars to all further measures of negotiation. Or, in other words, will a fresh mission to Paris be too great a humiliation of the American people in their own sense and that of the world?"[82] A strong ground swell of public indignation might lead to anti-French action that would force the President's hand. The rest of the questions suggested specific terms of negotiation, indicating that Adams expected his secretaries to answer his first question in the negative. He was right. Secretary Wolcott was of the opinion that many Americans were not at all insulted by the expulsion of Pinckney because they felt that his rank had been too low to expect that he would be received. He cited a newspaper article from a recent issue of the *Aurora* in support of his views. He also informed the President that

> there is still a party blindly devoted to French attachments; in the southern states the slaves are numerous, and this description of men universally consider the French as friends and deliverers; the influence and popularity of the general government is inconsiderable in the western [portions of the country].[83]

All these seemed good reasons to go slow on a declaration of war. Secretary of State Pickering likewise advised the President that the people were eager to continue negotiations. Secretary of War McHenry and Attorney General Lee concurred in this view.

Even when the President did not expressly ask for an appraisal of public opinion it was often supplied. The Cabinet, too, realized the importance of public opinion for the execution of public policies. For instance, in January 1798, when Adams asked the Cabinet for suggestions in case the mission to France failed, Secretary of the Treasury Wolcott based his proposals in part on an appraisal of public opinion. He thought that the people were averse to war, and a portion of them especially averse to war with France. For this reason, an express declaration of war was inadvisable because popular opposition might make such a policy impossible. Instead, Wolcott recommended strong measures to put the country on a war footing.[84]

When Adams asked his secretaries about their appraisal of public opinion he apparently solicited a personal answer. He never suggested in his requests for advice that his secretaries should consult others either inside or outside the government to help them formulate broadly based views. He was aware, of course, that three out of four members of his Cabinet

[82]Adams, vol. 2, p. 540.
[83]Gibbs, vol. 1, pp. 505, 507.
[84]Adams, vol. 2, p. 562.

regularly went beyond government circles and turned to Hamilton for advice. Often they relayed Hamilton's advice verbatim so that Hamilton became, in influence at least, a member of the innermost advising circle. It is not clear whether Adams knew that Hamilton was always much concerned with public opinion. But it was Hamilton who after the release of the XYZ dispatches warned Secretary of State Pickering against a policy of war with France and an alliance with England because public opinion was unready. Hamilton wrote Pickering that: "Public opinion is not prepared for it . . . in case of offers from France, satisfactory to us, the public faith might be embarrassed by the calls of the people for accommodation and peace."[85] On another occasion Hamilton advised Wolcott that he must learn to be "pliant" to avoid policies which would outstrip public opinion.[86]

## The Influence of Prominent Men and Media of Mass Expression

Since the leadership elite of the day was a fairly small group, well known to each other, and in fairly constant contact, Adams knew that the opinions of other prominent men were also reflected in the advice given to him by his Cabinet. For foreign policy problems were well known and extensively discussed even by those who were not members of the President's official family. Correspondence among political figures of the time shows a keen awareness of the necessity to consider the views of the public. Letters from various parts of the country reported the state of public feeling and the information contained in these letters reached the ears of the President either directly or indirectly through his Cabinet and through his friends. The authors of the letters relied on impressions from their personal contacts or often made a point of attending public gatherings, or soliciting the advice of their own circle of friends.

General Washington, for instance, was interested in the state of public sentiment during the spring of 1798, after publication of the XYZ correspondence. On May 28, 1798, he asked Edward Carrington, a friend of his, about the feelings of the people in central Virginia. "The present dangerous crisis of public affairs, makes me anxious to know the sentiments of our citizens in different parts of this commonwealth [Virginia]."[87] In return, he relayed other information he already possessed about public opinion:

[85]John C. Hamilton, *Works,* vol. 6. New York: J. C. Hamilton, 1850–1851 p. 278.

[86]Hamilton, vol. 6, p. 229.

[87]John C. Fitzpatrick, ed., *The Writings of George Washington,* vol. 36. Washington: Government Printing Office, 1941, p. 275.

Several counties above the Blue Ridge have come forward with warm addresses, and strong professions of support. From Norfolk two meetings, one *good* the other *bad,* have their proceedings detailed in the Gazettes. Meetings have taken place in a few of the middle Counties, with unpromising results. . . .[88]

Two and one-half weeks later, on June 13, 1798, he asked James Lloyd in a letter "What are the sentiments of the people of Kentucky? Or has there been any reverberation yet?" He felt encouraged by news from other parts of the country. "It is very consoling to perceive such expressions of the spirited feelings of the Yeomanry and other description of the people of this Country as appears in the Addresses, going from all quarters, to the President of the United States, and to Congress; and it is peculiar (sic) pleasing to find that *this* Spirit pervades the western parts of the Atlantic States." He expressed hope that popular approval might lessen opposition to the President. "Much is it to be wished that, this unanimity might effect a change in the conduct, even if it should produce no conviction in the minds, of *some* of the leaders of the opposition."[89]

On July 4, 1798, Washington wrote directly to the President that he felt that public expression of opposition to France and support of the Government would discourage the French from attacking the United States. He could not believe that the French "will attempt to invade this Country, after such a uniform and unequivocal expression of the sense of the *People*, in all parts, to oppose them with their lives and fortunes."[90]

Among others whose appraisals of public opinion were relayed to the President either directly or indirectly were Chief Justice Oliver Ellsworth, who reported on sentiments in New England and New York and Supreme Court Justice James Iredell who reported from Richmond, Virginia.[91] There was also Joseph Hopkinson, one of Wolcott's correspondents, who wrote to Wolcott in the spring of 1798: "The people here are driving at their private occupations, and seem plunged in the mire of commercial avarice. They attend to nothing else; they seem to consider themselves as having no kind of connection with the affairs of the nation, and no interest in it."[92] Fisher Ames, the Federalist leader in Congress, lamented "the stupor which every public falls into, when for want of an impression from government, it is left to the anarchy of its own opinions."[93] Ames and other Federalists felt that the President was not doing enough to stir public opinion. On April 22, 1798, Ames advised Wolcott—and, indirectly, the Presi-

[88]Fitzpatrick, vol. 36, p. 273.
[89]Fitzpatrick, vol. 36, pp. 288–289.
[90]Fitzpatrick, vol. 36, p. 313.
[91]Gibbs, vol. 1, pp. 523, 542.
[92]Gibbs, vol. 2, p. 49.
[93]Gibbs, vol. 1, p. 498.

dent—that "the time requires the government to do what I know it cannot and will not, that is, give a strong impulse to the public mind; that it should lead, and the people would cheerfully follow . . . the people are open to right impressions, but they are not yet enough roused to give them to government. . . ." The President, it seemed to Ames, was reluctant to exercise his prerogative of public opinion leadership because he feared the political consequences in an election year. "Cowardice will cry peace; it has been the popular cry. The elections are approaching."[94]

As a result of the efforts of political leaders in different parts of the country, Adams could feel that he was aware of the state of public opinion in many sections throughout the United States. Besides, he had direct expressions of public opinion in the form of addresses and reports of mass meetings to supplement the assessments supplied by his personal contacts. After the Senate had ordered publication of the XYZ dispatches, addresses of support for Adams' policy had swelled into a flood as the days passed. They came from all the major cities, from hundreds of small towns, from men of means and positions, and from young men in the colleges and in militia companies—young men who would have to do the fighting if war became inevitable.

## Reliability of Presidential Sources of Information

How sound Adams' sources of information were is a different question. In the first place, the personal assessments relayed to Adams were based on haphazard sampling and impressions by people of varying political shrewdness and predispositions. Nearly all of them were members of his own party and many of them had a political axe to grind.[95] They gathered information on public opinion to support their personal advice to the President. They were not impartial poll takers interested in as objective a picture as could possibly be obtained. A modern public.opinion analyst, fully aware of the crudeness of even modern methods, would shudder at the investigators and the sample employed. But he would probably have to admit that the political savvy of many of the investigators compensated to a large degree for the crudeness of their tools and their lack of awareness of scientific sampling methods, and even their partiality.

The validity of taking mass meetings, letters and petitions to the President, and press opinion as indicative of public sentiment throughout the

[94]Gibbs, vol. 2, p. 47.

[95]Some may have been as eager to guard their political future as vice-presidential hopeful Robert F. Kennedy who quipped at a White House meeting in August 1964, "I refuse to participate [in the discussion] on the ground that it may eliminate me." (New York Times, August 3, 1964.)

country would raise scholarly eyebrows even more. It has always been easy for a few determined and skillful agitators to gather a crowd that purports to speak for the community. At times such meetings do reflect strong public feelings; at others, they express feelings held only weakly by an indifferent public. At times they are an echo for small groups of individuals whose views are not shared by the community at all. It takes skillful analysis to determine which holds true in any given case. Political leaders generally are unwilling and often unable to determine how representative expressions of mass opinions are. They tend to choose the interpretation that suits their purposes best.

Adams was no exception. He took favorable mass meetings as an expression of nation-wide support for him. He praised those who sent him laudatory messages for their insight and patriotism. He wrote to Washington during the summer of 1798 that: "The approbatory addresses are very precious to me, as they discover more union among the States, and greater unanimity among the people, than was expected."[96] His heart was gladdened by favorable press stories. Here was the "good" public, the intelligent, patriotic people, expressing itself.

Manifestations of adverse public opinions through these very same media were condemned as isolated expressions of the rabble, misled by dishonest leaders, and not worthy of consideration by the President. Hostile newspapers deserved nothing but contempt because they were "employed with great industry to poison the minds of the people."[97] He charged derisively that: "It is impossible that newspapers can say the truth. They would be out of their element. I regard them no more than the Gossamer that idles in the wanton summer air."[98]

## The Role of the Vice-President and Congress

In the history of the American presidency there have been a number of instances in which the Vice-President has become an informal member of the Cabinet during its deliberations on foreign policy. There was some precedent for this during the Washington Administration when Adams had been drawn into Cabinet discussions on several occasions. But Adams did not continue the practice because "party violence soon rendered it impracticable or at least useless. . . ."[99]

He was not opposed in principle to consulting members of the opposition party. "I did not think that the rumbling noise of party calumny

[96]Adams, vol. 2, p. 573.
[97]*Letters of John Adams*, vol. 2, p. 119.
[98]*John Adams–William Cunningham*, p. 82.
[99]Adams, vol. 9, p. 285.

ought to discourage me from consulting men whom I knew to be attached to the interest of the nation, and whose experience, genius, learning, and travels had eminently qualified them to give advice."[100] However, with Vice-President and President belonging to different parties and totally opposed in their ideas about the issues of the day, it seemed pointless to draw the Vice-President into consultations. Adams did not feel that he needed an official Republican spokesman within the administration, a position which Jefferson could have filled very well indeed.

Nor did Adams deem it necessary to consult Congress. Congress, like the public, was merely another obstacle to be overcome. It had to be humored when its support was essential. And it had to be cajoled through messages to play its proper part. But it was not necessary to ask the opinion of Congress as a body, not even the opinion of the Senate. In the field of foreign affairs the framers of the Constitution had expressly bypassed the lower House when they provided for Senate approval of treaties.[101] Adams shared their belief that the lower House, although most directly controlled by the people, was not particularly well-equipped to cope with difficult foreign policy problems. It was not even representative of public feelings, much of the time. As Wolcott phrased it in an appraisal of the fifth Congress: "The present House of Representatives will afford a better copy of the public opinion than the last, but still the likeness will not be a good one."[102]

A good illustration of Adams' feelings about the advice of Congress are the events that followed after he had requested Senate approval of his nomination of Murray for another mission to France. Senators Bingham, Read, Sedgwick, Ross, and Stockton were commissioned by their confrères to see the President to discuss the proposed nomination with him.

The President agreed to receive them. But when they arrived, he put them in, what he deemed, their proper place, with this greeting: "Gentlemen, I am glad to see you, as friends, and members of the Senate; but, as a committee, interfering, as I think you are, with my executive duties, I cannot consent to receive you, and I protest against all such interference.

[100]Adams, vol. 9, p. 285.

[101]For a discussion of the framers' views of the role of Congress see Holbert N. Carroll, *The House of Representatives and Foreign Affairs*. Pittsburgh: University of Pittsburgh Press, 1959, pp. 5–14. Also see Howe, pp. 94–96, for Adams' disdain for Congress.

[102]Gibbs, vol. 1, p. 500. The view that legislative bodies did not necessarily represent public opinion, was also shared by others. Washington, for instance, wrote to Patrick Henry, on January 15, 1799 (Fitzpatrick, vol. 37, p. 88) that he believed that the people of Virginia approved of Adams' policies even though the Virginia legislature was controlled by an anti-Federalist group who claimed to speak for the entire state.

I have a duty to execute, and so have you. I know, and shall do mine, and want neither your opinion nor aid in its execution. . . ." When a member of the committee, during the interview, questioned the wisdom of sending a minister to France instead of asking France to send one to the United States, the President "said with warmth, 'here you are all wrong, gentlemen. I know more of diplomatic forms than all of you. It was in France that we received the insult, and in France I am determined that we shall receive the reparation.'—Obviously he felt no need to consult the Senate to learn anything from them."[103] Although his exact words may have been misquoted, since they were recollected many years after they were spoken, the meaning is clear. Adams would brook no advice, even from the Senate. It could take or leave his proposals, but he was not willing to let it make proposals of its own. He felt that "the unity, consistency, promptitude, secrecy, and activity of the whole executive authority are so essential in any republican system, that without them there can be no peace, order, liberty, or prosperity in society" and that anarchy would be produced, "whenever popular assemblies meddle with executive power."[104] He did not intend to permit such meddling.

However, he was willing to make concessions to Congress on his own terms whenever he felt that this was important in keeping Congress receptive to support his policies. He might delay an unpopular request, or go along with an undesirable policy, in order to smooth the way for a program for which he cared deeply. After all, a little political flexibility was absolutely essential for a President who wished to do a good job. It was alright, as long as principles were only bent, not broken.

### The Uses of Supportive Public Opinion

While Adams sought no help from the public in establishing the proper course for foreign affairs, he used public expressions of support to bolster his chosen policies. He cited favorable public opinion in his letters and speeches as proof that he had embarked upon proper action. After all, the people in their wisdom had concurred. This should be enough to silence opposition from friends and enemies alike. For instance, when Adams feared congressional disapproval of the Murray mission he was hopeful that the pressure of public opinion would give Congress a pause. Of course, it would have to be the "right" opinion in favor of the mission. Hence he decided to withhold news of his plan until the last minute to avoid mobilization of the "wrong" opinion. Had he released the news earlier, "a clamor [would have been] raised and a prejudice propagated against the measure that would probably excite the Senate to put the negative on the

[103]Pickering, vol. 3, pp. 440–444.
[104]Smith, vol. 2, pp. 922–923.

whole plan."[105] If he waited, things would be different. Once the announcement was made the President expected

> that the British Faction would excite a clamor, and that some of the senators, representatives, and heads of departments would make no exertions to discountenance it, if they did not secretly or openly encourage it, yet I was so perfectly convinced of the national sense, and that the Senate felt it so strongly, that they would not dare to negative it, even if the majority had disliked it, which I very well knew they did not. I thought a clamor after the fact would be much less dangerous than a clamor before it.[106]

A policy of withholding news to avoid public opinion complications and releasing it to encourage public opinion support was deemed appropriate. Senators would heed public opinion for the same reasons that made the President listen to public reactions. They feared public disobedience, rebellions, and possibly loss of office at the next election—the latter more of a bugaboo to senators than to President Adams.

Adams was also keenly aware of the effect that expressions of public opinion might have abroad. Dissension at home would weaken the government's hand and might encourage foreign agents to split opinions even further. For this reason, his messages to Congress always stressed that the people were behind the government. For instance, in the message of December 8, 1798, he said ". . . a manly sense of national honor, dignity, and independence has appeared which, if encouraged and invigorated by every branch of the government, will enable us to view undismayed the enterprises of any foreign power and become the sure foundation of national prosperity and glory."[107] This would inform the French as well as prod Congress, about the need to have a united nation and keep it united.

He used official replies to citizens' petitions to drive home this same point. For instance, he wrote to the legislature of New Hampshire on June 29, 1798, that

> the increasing union among the people and their legislatures is as encouraging as it is agreeable . . . . As far as my information extends, the opposition to the Federal government in all the other states is too small to merit the name of division. It is a difference of sentiment on public measures, not an alienation of affection to their country.[108]

More positive still, six weeks later, he informed the people of Cincinnati that "it may be asserted with confidence, that at no period of the existence of the United States have evidences of the unanimity of the people been given, so decided as on the present question with France."[109]

[105]Adams, vol. 9, p. 272.
[106]Adams, vol. 9, p. 272.
[107]Richardson, vol. 1, pp. 271–272.
[108]Adams, vol. 9, p. 203.
[109]Adams, vol. 9, p. 216.

These messages were used to good advantage abroad. William Vans Murray, the American ambassador at the Hague, who had received copies of them, wrote in July: "I circulate them here, and they open the eyes of even the willful as to the long-told tale and inveterate error, that the people and the Executive are at variance."[110] In his talks with Monsieur Pichon, the French diplomat charged with making peace feelers, he repeatedly stressed that the people were united behind the government and approved its defense policies.[111]

Since public reaction was so closely watched abroad, Adams was worried that after the Murray mission had been announced the Republican enthusiasm for negotiations would hurt the chances of getting a good treaty. He wrote to George Washington: "I wish the babyish and womanly blubbering for peace may not necessitate the conclusion of a treaty that will not be just nor very honorable. I do not intend, however, that they shall."[112]

If it was possible to withhold information to prevent public expression of opinion from embarrassing the government, Adams approved of curbs on public information. For instance, while he was still Vice-President during the Washington Administration he deplored excessive publicity. He wrote to his wife:

> I write you little concerning public affairs, because you will have every thing in print. How a government can go on, publishing all their negotiations with foreign nations I know not. To me it appears as dangerous and pernicious as it is novel. . . . Errors are unavoidable when the people in crowds out of doors undertake to receive ambassadors (Genêt), and to dictate to their supreme executive.[113]

He felt no compunctions about withholding information, even from Congress. For instance, as President he tried to suppress information on Gerry's relations with Talleyrand because he feared it would arouse anti-French feelings. He did not agree with his predecessor that: "*concealment* is a species of misinformation; and misrepresentation and false alarms found the groundwork of opposition."[114]

Adams never believed that the public must be informed as a matter of principle. In transactions that required secrecy and speed he had no hesitation at all about making decisions without telling anyone. When there

[110]Adams, vol. 8, p. 677.

[111]Adams, vol. 8, p. 681.

[112]Adams, vol. 8, pp. 625–626.

[113]*Letters of John Adams*, vol. 2, pp. 132–133.

[114]Fitzpatrick, vol. 37, p. 126. Washington apparently thought more of the people's wisdom than Adams. He wrote to James Lloyd, February 11, 1799 (p. 129), "I wish, however, they [Gerry-Talleyrand communications] were in every man's hand, for I am persuaded the great mass of our Citizens require only to understand matters rightly, to form the right decisions."

was no need to create public or congressional support for contemplated policies, Adams would save the announcement of his decision for his annual message to Congress. If public opinion could not be used in some way to improve governmental activities there seemed no point in alerting the public at the earliest possible moment. Adams did not even release foreign policy news to counteract a hostile press or hostile speeches as long as they did not endanger policy execution. The fact that hostile publicity might have adverse effects on the fortunes of his party was not sufficient inducement to mobilize public opinion, as it has been for many a later President. Others might wish to use public opinion on foreign policy as merely another pawn in the game of party politics. To Adams, foreign policy was the king of the chessmen of politics, never to be manipulated for the sake of lesser figures.

## Public Opinion Manipulation

But what could be done if an unfavorable public opinion had already emerged or was likely to emerge and hinder governmental policies? The solution to this type of situation lay in the use of what would now be called public relations work. Adams and other contemporary politicians realized the importance of associating controversial policies with widely respected names. After the decision had been made to recruit an army to present a strong military posture to France, the prestige of General Washington's name was deemed highly useful in overcoming public opposition. Therefore Adams appealed to George Washington: "We must have your name, if you will, in any case, permit us to use it. There will be more efficacy in it than in many an army."[115] Earlier Hamilton, ever conscious of public opinion, had already thought of using Washington's name for a public relations tour. He suggested in the spring of 1798 that Washington should travel through Virginia and North Carolina. Wherever he went there would be public dinners and addresses in his honor. Washington could answer the toasts and addresses with speeches in support of the government's foreign policies. This would throw Washington's prestige behind the Adams administration. Washington declined. He judged the likely results of such a tour by his own adverse reaction to emotional appeals to sway him. The tour would be fruitless because its object would be too obvious. His motives would be misconstrued and more harm than good would result.[116]

Similarly, Adams asked Jefferson and Madison to undertake the first mission which he dispatched to France. "If the mission should be unsuc-

---

[115]Adams, vol. 8, p. 573.

[116]Fitzpatrick, vol. 36, p. 271. Also see White, pp. 112–114, on Washington's objections to pressure tactics.

cessful, his [Jefferson's] report, upon his return, would unite and brace the public mind to those exertions the case might require."[117]

There were additional reasons for seeking Jefferson's or Madison's participation. Not only were they prominent and widely respected political leaders, but they represented the opposition. Adams realized that he would need the support of Republicans, as well as Federalists to present France with a picture of a strong and united nation that could demand a favorable settlement of grievances. A bipartisan commission was the answer. Moreover, the commission should represent all sections of the country so that all would feel they had had a share in the negotiations:

> It is, in the present critical and singular circumstances, of great importance to engage the confidence of the great portions of the Union in the characters employed, and the measures which may be adopted. I have, therefore, thought it expedient to nominate persons of talents and integrity, long known and intrusted in the three great divisions of the Union. . . .[118]

Even Wolcott, who was opposed to including Republicans on official missions lest it boost the Republican party and offend ardent Federalists, conceded that a bipartisan mission "will convince the people completely, that the government is at least as solicitous to avoid war with France, as it was to avoid it with Great Britain. . . . In case of failure [of the mission], it will contribute to the important end of uniting opinion at home."[119]

More direct techniques of public opinion manipulation included organization of mass meetings, preparation of public addresses, and publication of pro-government articles in the press, along with ordinary conversations designed to keep the political pot boiling. Adams did not feel that a President should participate directly in such ventures. Like Washington, he wanted to remain above emotional partisan strife and preserve the decorum of the new office so that its prestige would enhance its strength. But he was grateful when members of his party did the job for him. Among those who did were Hamilton and George Cabot. Both men felt that it was "necessary that the country should be roused . . . if the people do not support the government . . . all is lost."[120] Keeping people aroused was a more or less continuous task. "Popular gales sometimes blow hard, but they don't blow long."[121] To keep people in tune with their government, Cabot wrote letters to his friends, urging them to work through

[117]Adams, vol. 8, p. 534; the quotation is from Henry Knox, but Adams had voiced similar sentiments.

[118]United States Congress, *American State Papers*, Class I, vol. 2. Washington: Gales and Seaton, 1832, p. 19.

[119]Gibbs, vol. 1, p. 510.

[120]Gibbs, vol. 1, p. 482.

[121]Gibbs, vol. 1, p. 490.

community leaders "because certain facts . . . ought to be imparted to those whose influence in the community will contribute greatly to preserve its interest and its honour . . . at this time, when our political affairs are fast verging to a great and unavoidable crisis."[122] Earlier he had advised that

> . . . the public mind should be informed and prepared as fast as possible, for the efforts we may be called to make. The country should be roused without being inflamed; and by a dispassionate attention to the public dangers, should be reconciled to additional taxes, and should strengthen the government by additional confidence in the measures it may adopt. What these will be, no man can foretell . . . on the other hand, the Jacobin plan will be to enfeeble and divide the public sentiment, that nothing may be done. . . .[123]

General Washington urged men like Patrick Henry to run for public office so that there would be more friends of the government in official positions capable of leading public opinion in the proper direction.[124] As Gabriel Almond has noted: "Who mobilizes elites, mobilizes the public."[125]

The press was also used to circulate the "right opinions" and vigorously attack the wrong ones. Broadsides were printed and widely distributed, even in churches. George Cabot wrote: "we keep our presses going . . . proving to the people the absolute propriety of what is done." Optimistically, he concluded, "my expectations are strong that the business will prosper, and that the body of the people will be brought to a good temperament, so that the measures of government will be zealously supported by a majority, and duly acquiesced in by all."[126]

In the same letter, Cabot gave instructions for effective public relations. In preparing the public for additional taxes "let great care be taken to show that they are unavoidable, and that we are called to part with a little, as the only possible means of saving the remainder, and with it our liberty and independence."[127] Other themes to be stressed to rally the nation behind its official leaders were complaints that the nation had been insulted, that outlets for trade were barred by foreign powers, and that there was danger of attack on American soil.

In the wake of conversations and newspaper articles, rallies were often organized by political leaders to inspire public sentiment even more and draft rousing resolutions and addresses to be presented to the President. When there were opposition rallies, leaders made arrangements to invade

[122]Gibbs, vol. 1, p. 520.

[123]Gibbs, vol. 1, p. 522.

[124]Fitzpatrick, vol. 37, pp. 88; vol. 36, p. 273.

[125]Gabriel A. Almond, *The American People and Foreign Policy.* New York: Praeger, 1960, p. 138.

[126]Gibbs, vol. 2, p. 48.

[127]Gibbs, vol. 2, p. 48.

them to temper or spike the efforts of the assembly, or even to take the meeting over completely.

At times there were lengthy public debates preceding the adoption of an address. Both Federalists and Republicans participated in these debates in front of an eager audience that often included the most influential people in the area. Adams was not much enamored with this manner of conducting the public business. But he conceded that

> . . . in the ordinary course of affairs, interpositions of popular meetings, to overawe those to whom the management of public affairs were confided, will seldom be warranted by discretion, or found compatible with the good order of society; but at a period like this, there is no method more infallible to determine the question, whether the people are or are not united. Upon no occasion in the history of America has this mode of discovering and ascertaining the public opinion been so universally resorted to.[128]

Adams' personal preference was for mass meetings in which a single speaker would set the proper tone for discussion. For this reason he approved of the declaration of national days of humiliation, fasting and prayer in which the seriousness of the political crisis would be brought before the minds of the assembled people. He hoped that the sermons of sympathetic clergymen would stir the people to support the government's defensive measures. When such a prayer day had been proclaimed for May 9, 1798, he commented: ". . . at a time of crisis there is nothing upon this earth more sublime and affecting than the idea of a great nation all on their knees at once before their God. . . . it can scarcely fail to have a favorable effect on their morals in general, or to inspire them with warlike virtues in particular."[129]

Still another productive propaganda device was the publication of the President's speeches in the papers and their distribution as handbills throughout the country. Adams had a fine sense of the sort of comments that would arouse people to follow his lead. He could transform political issues into basic moral terms of right and wrong, justice and injustice, making it easy for the people to become involved and choose sides. For instance, he delivered a stirring speech to a special session of Congress in mid-May 1797, to prepare the country to support increased defensive

[128]Adams, vol. 9, pp. 215–216.

[129]Adams, vol. 9, p. 291. Not all days of fasting and prayer were favorable to the cause of the government. When Adams dispatched Pinckney, Marshall, and Gerry to come to terms with France, pro-British preachers declared fast days and predicted that God would curse the land and people if they gave any comfort to the murderers and regicides in France. When yellow fever broke out in the ports from which the envoys had sailed, the preachers claimed that this proved their predictions of doom.

measures. The speech was widely circulated with good results. Washington felt that it would "mediately or immediately, bring . . . about . . . an unequivocal expression of the public mind."[130] In this speech Adams had charged that the French had treated us "neither as allies nor as friends, nor as a sovereign state." Their negotiations with Monroe had been "studiously marked with indignities toward the Government of the United States" and their refusal to receive Pinckney had amounted to "the denial of a right." The French had tried to use discord within the United States to their own advantage. They had tried "to separate the people of the United States from the Government, to persuade them that they have different affections, principles, and interests" from their popularly elected officials. And then came the rousing punch line. The attempts to play on the division between the people "ought to be repelled with a decision which shall convince France and the world that we are not a degraded people, humiliated under a colonial spirit of fear and sense of inferiority, fitted to be the miserable instruments of foreign influence, and regardless of national honor, character, and interest." The rousing note of defiance was then muted by the promise that "I shall institute a fresh attempt at negotiation, and shall not fail to promote and accelerate an accommodation on terms compatible with the rights, duties, interest, and honor of the nation." For "neither the honor nor the interest of the United States . . . forbid the repetition of advances for securing these . . . objects with France."[131]

Because Adams' messages seemed to arouse the people to support his policies, Adams' friends urged him to employ his talents in answering the addresses sent to him by people throughout the country. Adams hesitated at first, but then he complied. And he managed to strike the right note again in uniting people behind his leadership. A letter to Wolcott credited to these answers "the great success of the President, in awakening the country from the fatal stupor into which it had sunk . . . the good effect of these open declarations cannot be overrated. They have excited right feelings everywhere, and have silenced clamour."[132] Federalists were "unbounded in their applause of the manly, just, spirited, and instructive sentiments expressed by the President in his answers to the addresses."[133]

## Some Conjectures

Adams' enemies would not have been quite so optimistic in appraising the degree of public support that the President could muster by his own

[130]Gibbs, vol. 1, p. 539.
[131]Richardson, vol. 1, pp. 234–236.
[132]Gibbs, vol. 2, pp. 53–54; see also p. 69.
[133]Gibbs, vol. 2, p. 53.

and his party's appeals to the public. There was plenty of opposition left, much of it quite vocal and often vicious. But it stopped short of the one thing the President feared—massive disobedience of government policies and revolt against the established authorities. Adams, with the aid of his friends, had to labor hard to keep the public—Hamilton's "great beast" —appeased tnrough astute management of public information and occasional concessions to public whims. But Adams always managed to keep on top of the beast.

What he would have done in the face of mass violence or disobedience is hard to say, although one may guess that he would have yielded to the inevitable. He hinted as much on several occasions when he spoke of the danger of public pressure, which might have forced him into war against his better judgment.[134] For Adams, the idealist was also a realist when idealism seemed no longer feasible. Just as he considered the facts of the international situation in making his policies, without worrying what ought to be or what he would have liked to see, so he took public reaction as merely one more factor that must be taken into consideration in shaping a workable policy. He would seek to manipulate public opinion to gain support for his policies, if he could, within the scope of what he considered proper presidential etiquette. He would defy public wrath as long as public opposition was at a level at which it was no bar to action, or if it concerned a matter in which the public could not take action. And he would yield, if he had to, but not until he had tried to the utmost of his ability to defy a misguided public.

What would have happened if Adams had accepted the advice that he rejected? This is an intriguing question, especially for political scientists who should speculate whether a change of political techniques in a given situation would have served better to bring about the desired result. In some respects, such an inquiry is reminiscent of a recent television show that featured a panel of scholars in lively speculations about what would have happened if certain historical events had taken slightly different turns. Of course, none of the scholars could agree on the precise results that certain variations would have caused, but all their answers seemed very plausible.

When we try to assess the value of the public suggestions that Adams received but scorned, we are in the same boat as the television scholars. We can have a lot of fun guessing, but we have no proof to back up our conjectures. In a complex, fluid political situation there is no such thing as 20–20 hindsight vision. We may know what actually happened better than the participants. But the minute we begin to tamper with any of the major factors in the picture, we cannot validly assume that the remainder of the factors would have remained constant. The most we can do is to

[134]See p. 77, above.

look at the alternative proposals that were brought to the fore and venture an appraisal of whether, under the circumstances, they presented a logical alternative that might have furthered the welfare of the nation. Moreover, "welfare of the nation" must be broadly interpreted to include a number of policy objectives that historians would deem to be in accord with traditional American foreign policy aims.

While, in the light of hindsight, neutrality does seem to have been the preferred course, a siding with England against France would have been a defensible choice. With this choice one could picture the United States allied to a victorious Britain, and rewarded with parts of the French colonial empire in America. The XYZ reaction showed that the country could rally in opposition to France when properly stirred. Entering the war on the French side would have been equally justifiable—to repay an old debt, reap trade advantages, and join Britain's American possessions to the United States after victory.

The point here is not to play the game, but merely to indicate that the facts of 1798–1799 (even from the perspective of the twentieth century) do not point out a single "best" policy. They lend no support for any theories that claim a priori that decision making is done better outside the White House than within and that the President should be an agent, rather than a leader. They do not tell which voices the President should have heeded—those of his public, or Jefferson's public, or Hamilton's public. No *vox populi* has an obvious monopoly of being the *vox Dei*. Rather, there are many public voices, all or none of which may be blessed with divine intuition. It is the difficult task of each President to choose the particular altar of public opinion at which to conduct his worship.

# 5

# Jefferson Rationalizes
# His Premises

There is a schematic and formalist way of thinking which pro-
ceeds without the cooperation of life and without direct intuition. It is a kind of cultural utopianism. We fall into it
whenever we admit, without antecedent revision, certain principles of an intellectual, moral, political, esthetic, or religious
nature, and, making the immediate assumption that they are
valid, insist on the acceptance of their consequences.

JOSE ORTEGA Y GASSET, *The Modern Theme*

Ill fares the land, to hastening ills a prey,
Where wealth accumulates, and men decay;
Princes and lords may flourish or may fade;
A breath can make them, as a breath has made;
But a bold peasantry, their country's pride,
When once destroy'd, can never be supplied.

OLIVER GOLDSMITH, "The Deserted Village"

# 5

## A World View Tailored to a Vision

> We hold these truths to be self-evident, that all men are created equal, that they are endowed by their creator with certain unalienable Rights, that among these are Life, Liberty, and the pursuit of Happiness. That to secure these rights, Governments are instituted among Men, deriving their just powers from the consent of the governed, that whenever any Form of Government becomes destructive of these ends, it is the right of the People to alter or abolish it, and to institute new Government, laying its foundation on such principles and organizing its powers in such form, as to them shall seem most likely to effect their Safety and Happiness.

These ringing phrases of the Declaration of Independence epitomize Thomas Jefferson's creed about the political capacity of man and his right to have his opinions control his government. Although these words were written as an impassioned propaganda tract to justify the break with the Mother country to the colonists, its truths were, indeed, "self-evident" enough to make them solid, widely accepted, and acceptable arguments for revolution. These were the truths on which Jefferson and his contemporaries had been nourished and which, to them, were the premises on which their political theories were based.

Jefferson never bothered to examine these premises. He took them for granted. Page Smith, John Adams' biographer, believes that:

> He lived by a set of liberal stereotypes (noble ones to be sure) which could not be easily reconciled with the reality of a disorderly world; perhaps sensing this, he refrained from any systematic examination of the precepts which he professed.[1]

Page Smith felt that "the result was a lack of tension in his thought, a liberal blandness. His writings, personal or political, were not studded with the paradoxes and ambiguities which mark real life."[2] Yet this may not have been so much an unwillingness to examine his premises, as an inability to see the need for such an examination. Jefferson was unaware that these premises did not conform to reality. Had he fathomed the discrepancy, he would not have tolerated it, for he was averse to abstract philosophizing remote from the realities of life.

[1]Page Smith, *John Adams*, vol. 2. Garden City, N. Y.: Doubleday, p. 672.
[2]Smith, vol. 2, p. 672.

Jefferson's somewhat sheltered background kept him from seeing the rough edges of life during his formative years. He was born on a Virginia plantation, son of the owner; his father's friends were people of the same genteel social background. The Negro slaves who performed the heavy labor were not considered social equals. Jefferson never regarded them as "people" in the same sense in which he thought about whites as people. Their intellectual inadequacies therefore did not strike him as inadequacies common to human beings in general

In his early youth, Jefferson was privately educated in the classical tradition. He read the literature of the Enlightenment and imbibed the concepts of human liberty and dignity later expressed so eloquently in the Declaration of Independence. His college days were spent at William and Mary College in Virginia. There, too, his classmates and associates were "sons of the middle gentry of Virginia and in many respects . . . its sturdiest stock."[3] His social companions then and later, after he had entered upon a five-year legal apprenticeship with George Wythe, were men "deeply versed in law and government, which were their chief occupations other than the running of their plantations; steeped in classical literature; most of them disliking and mistrusting an industrial and commercial society."[4]

Jefferson matched the pattern well. Almost immediately after his admission to the bar, he began the typical mixture of government and private service. Successively he became a justice of the peace, a member of the Virginia House of Burgesses, steadily reelected until he entered the Continental Congress in 1775 at the age of thirty-two, with six years of legislative experience already behind him. By that time, he had abandoned his law practice and turned instead to his plantation duties as his private vocation. After two years of service in the Continental Congress, he returned to the Virginia legislature to help revise the constitution and laws of his beloved state. In 1779, still in his middle thirties, he began the first of two terms as governor of the Old Dominion. Service in the state and national legislature followed. Then came his long apprenticeship in foreign affairs, beginning with a tour of duty in France in 1784, and culminating in his appointment as Secretary of State during President Washington's first term. The vice-presidency in 1796 and presidency four years later topped a life-time service to the nation which brought him into contact, correspondence, and conversation with the most knowledgeable, public spirited, and progressive men of his time.

His own personal experiences and contacts with the intellectual elite of his day thus conformed in large measure to the preconceptions about

[3]Nathan Schachner, *Thomas Jefferson*. New York: Appleton-Century-Crofts, 1951, p. 30.

[4]James Truslow Adams, *The Living Jefferson*. New York: Scribner's, 1936, p. 34.

human capabilities that he had formed as a result of his readings. In addition, his temperament made him a rationalizer, and Nature had endowed him with a very thin-skinned disposition. He hated to be wrong, hated to be criticized. As he confided to Abigail Adams:

> I do not love difficulties. I am fond of quiet, willing to do my duty, but irritable by slander and apt to be forced by it to abandon my post.[5]

When criticism came, either overtly or in the form of opinions that did not fit into his preconceived conceptual scheme, Jefferson did one of two things. He either resigned from the exposed position—as he had done when under fire as Governor, when Secretary of State, and as he had longed to do during his presidency whenever the storm of abuse rose too high for him—or he interpreted disagreement out of existence. Somehow he often was able to adapt all evidence to make it fit into his conceptual scheme and thereby erase all possible conflict. For example, in reading Montesquieu, "Jefferson absorbed those sections which agreed with or factually confirmed his own natural predilections and omitted, or contradicted, those which did not."[6] Thus, if Jefferson had doubts about man's capacity for self-government, he probably did not allow himself to become conscious of them. Moreover, he was given to round and sonorous pronouncements that pleased his sense of phrase making and convinced him, as much as his readers, that what was so beautifully expressed, was true. Madison, after Jefferson's death, commented on this "habit in Mr. Jefferson as in others of great genius of expressing in strong and round terms, impressions of the moment."[7] Dumas Malone's biography of Jefferson gives a more prosaic explanation: "Mr. Jefferson, who was so much on his guard in public, blew off steam in private to relieve the pressure."[8] Be that as it may, throughout his life Jefferson clung to the sweeping principles that he enunciated so eloquently in the Declaration of Independence.

## In Praise of the Farmer

But who were the "people" who had the right to alter or abolish their government and to decide the principles which were most likely to assure their safety and happiness? On this, Jefferson had very definite ideas. The people whose opinions counted were the sturdy yeomanry, independent farmers of the type Jefferson knew in his native Virginia. Excluded were

[5]Paul Leicester Ford, ed., *Writings of Thomas Jefferson,* vol. 4. New York: Putnam's, 1894, p. 100.

[6]Schachner, p. 77.

[7]Gaillard Hunt, ed., *Writings of James Madison,* vol. 9. New York: Putnam's, 1910, p. 479.

[8]Dumas Malone, *Thomas Jefferson as Political Leader.* Berkeley: University of California Press, 1963, p. 64.

the aristocracy and the mobs of great cities. Excluded, too, were Negroes who "are inferior to the whites in the endowments both of body and mind."[9] The aristocracy Jefferson characterized as "founded on wealth and birth, without either virtue or talents . . . a mischievous ingredient in government . . . provision should be made to prevent its ascendency."[10] Aristocrats were power hungry and organized government for their own aggrandizement only. Kings, oligarchies, and religious hierarchies by force and cunning stripped the masses of their inherent natural rights.

At the other extreme, the poor propertyless masses, whom Jefferson often disparaged as "mobs . . . debased by ignorance, poverty, and vice,"[11] were not much better than the aristocracy. Jefferson felt an almost pathological horror for "the industrial artisans and mechanics, who, to his imagination, inevitably swarmed in the rabbit warrens of·large cities."[12]

> Dependence begets subservience and venality, suffocates the germ of virtue, and prepares fit tools for the designs of ambition. . . . The mobs of great cities add just so much to the support of pure government, as sores do to the strength of the human body.[13]

Jefferson put his trust into the small land owners who managed their own estates. They alone were free and intelligent enough to value their heritage of liberty. Of them he wrote:

> Those who labour in the earth are the chosen people of God . . . whose breasts he has made his peculiar deposit for substantial and genuine virtue. . . . Corruption of morals in the mass of cultivators is a phenomenon of which no age nor nation has furnished an example.[14]

By contrast:

> I consider the class of artificers as the panders of vice and the instruments by which the liberties of a country are generally overturned.[15]

[9]Andrew A. Lipscomb, ed., *The Writings of Thomas Jefferson*, vol. 2. Washington: Thomas Jefferson Memorial Association, 1905, p. 201. Jefferson was willing to change his mind on this point, should later evidence prove him wrong. Commenting on the ability of Benjamin Banneker, a free Negro, he wrote to Condorcet on August 30, 1791, "I shall be delighted to see these instances of moral eminence so multiplied as to prove that the want of talents observed in them is merely the effect of their degraded condition, and not proceeding from any difference in the structure of the parts on which intellect depends." Paul Leicester Ford, ed., *The Works of Thomas Jefferson*, vol. 6. New York: Putnam's, 1904, pp. 310–312.

[10]Lipscomb, vol. 13, p. 396.
[11]Lipscomb, vol. 13, p. 402.
[12]Schachner, p. 230.
[13]Lipscomb, vol. 2, pp. 229–30.
[14]Lipscomb, vol. 2, p. 229.
[15]Lipscomb, vol. 5, p. 94.

This, too, was an elitist concept, although different from that of John Adams. Virtue and the ability to have sound opinions about public affairs were the monopoly of a class shared by all in that class. The children of light were the American farmers; the children of darkness were aristocrats and city dwellers. Unlike Adams, Jefferson did not discern a duality in man with the capacity for good and evil and for wisdom and folly joined within a single human breast.

While Jefferson probably would not have stressed property ownership as a requirement for political sagacity, the two went together for him.[16] All the respectable citizens he knew owned property. When he proposed a new constitution for Virginia in 1776, he made suffrage dependent on property ownership. At the same time, he made it easy for people to qualify. The minimum acreage was so small that most freemen had no difficulty in meeting the requirement. Furthermore, every adult who did not possess fifty acres of land was entitled to a grant of fifty acres from the lands held by the state. Still, property was important to give a man a very personal stake in the conduct of government. He wrote to Madison that provisions should be made in the United States "that as few as possible shall be without a little portion of land."[17] He argued that: "The purse of the people is the real seat of sensibility. It is to be drawn upon largely, and they will then listen to truth which could not excite them through any other organ."[18]

## The Role of Education

Yet property ownership by itself was not enough. Laws could only be "wisely formed, and honestly administered, in proportion as those who form and administer them are wise and honest."[19] Every citizen needed a modicum of education to hold sound opinions about the public business. For this reason, Jefferson, from the start of his career, was very much interested in legislation to assure public education. For his own state of Virginia he drafted general education bills that provided for a completely free system of tax supported elementary schools for all boys and girls, other than slaves. "I think by far the most important bill in our whole code [the new constitution of the state of Virginia] is that for the diffusion of knowledge among the people. No other sure foundation can be

[16]Charles A. Beard claims that cheap land was the chief basis of Jefferson's political philosophy. *The Economic Origins of Jeffersonian Democracy.* New York: Macmillan, 1936, Chapter 14.

[17]Schachner, p. 292.

[18]Lipscomb, vol. 10, p. 60.

[19]Ford, *Works*, vol. 2, p. 415.

devised, for the preservation of freedom and happiness. . . ."[20] Jefferson praised a new Spanish constitution for disfranchising every citizen who could not read and write. "This is new, and is the fruitful germ of the improvement of everything good, and the correction of everything imperfect in the present constitution. This will give you an enlightened people, and an energetic public opinion which will control and enchain the aristocratic spirit of the government."[21] "Enlighten the people generally," he opined,

> and tyranny and oppressions of body and mind will vanish like evil spirits at the dawn of day. Although I do not, with some enthusiasts, believe that the human condition will ever advance to such a state of perfection as that there shall no longer be pain or vice in the world, yet I believe it susceptible of much improvement, and most of all, in matters of government and religion; and that the diffusion of knowledge among the people is to be the instrument by which it is to be effected.[22]

Although it would take time and effort, the human condition could be permanently improved up to a point. The upper limit varied depending on a people's innate qualities and historical experience.

However, not all citizens needed an extensive education. Jefferson believed that there were differences in ability, and that political leaders—those whom nature had endowed with superior virtue and ability—required more education than the masses of the people whose political duties would be light. Since ability and money did not always go hand in hand, it was in the public interest to provide free education for the most gifted children whose parents lacked money to educate them properly. For this reason, Jefferson planned for Virginia a system of grammar schools open (through scholarships) to gifted boys regardless of means. The most promising youngster from each county was to be sent to college free of charge. "The impulse," as Max Beloff points out, "was civic and political, not egalitarian."[23] Society must educate the best minds because it needs them, not because each individual has an inherent right to education.

Nor was Jefferson the absolute equalitarian that he has often been reputed to be. To John Adams, Jefferson confided his thoughts about natural inequalities:

> I agree with you that there is a natural aristocracy among men. The grounds of this are virtue and talents. . . . The natural aristocracy I consider as the most precious gift of nature, for the instruction, the trusts, and government of society. And, indeed, it would have been inconsistent in creation to have formed man for the social state, and not to have pro-

[20]Lipscomb, vol. 5, p. 396.

[21]Lipscomb, vol. 14, p. 130.

[22]Lipscomb, vol. 14, pp. 491–92.

[23]Max Beloff, *Thomas Jefferson and American Democracy*. London: Hodder and Stoughton, 1948, p. 79.

vided virtue and wisdom enough to manage the concerns of the society. [To this he added the question:] May we not even say, that that form of government is the best, which provides the most effectually for a pure selection of these natural aristoi into the offices of government?[24]

Although the people of Virginia had disagreed with him, he felt no expense of money was too much for public education to make the masses better citizens. While still hopeful of adoption of his education provisions he had written to his friend and mentor, George Wythe:

> Let our countrymen know, that the people alone can protect us against these evils [monarchy], and that the tax which will be paid for this purpose, is not more than a thousandth's part of what will be paid to kings, priests and nobles, who will rise up among us if we leave the people in ignorance.[25]

Public education would render

> the people the safe, as they are the ultimate, guardians of their own liberty. . . . Apprizing them of the past, will enable them to judge of the future. . . . Every government degenerates when trusted to the rulers of the people alone. The people themselves therefore are its only safe depositories. And to render even them safe, their minds must be improved to a certain degree.[26]

This doctrine that all must have a chance for education because an educated public is essential for the success of democratic government was shared by Washington and Hamilton, as well as by most of Jefferson's fellow Republicans.[27]

But the seeds of education for citizenship must be sowed on well-conditioned soil. With a keen appreciation for the difficulties involved in acculturating a people to democratic practices, Jefferson warned his friend, the Marquis de Lafayette, that no people could be prepared for liberty overnight:

> More than a generation will be requisite, under the administration of reasonable laws favoring the progress of knowledge in the general mass of the people, and their habituation to an independent security of person and property, before they will be capable of estimating the value of freedom, and the necessity of a sacred adherence to the principles on which it rests for preservation.[28]

---

[24]Lipscomb, vol. 13, p. 396. Also see Beloff, who feels that the scheme of an aristocracy of talent was an eighteenth century attempt to combine majority rule with protection of minority rights (p. 255).

[25]Lipscomb, vol. 5, p. 397.

[26]Lipscomb, vol. 2, pp. 206–207.

[27]Merle Curti, *The Growth of American Thought.* New York: Harper & Row, Publishers, 1943, pp. 135–137.

[28]Lipscomb, vol. 14, p. 25.

He cautioned that "with an unprepared people" liberty would become "a tyranny still, of the many, the few, or the one."[29] He worried that people who came to the United States from Europe might never be able to throw off their early experiences and become good citizens:

> They will bring with them the principles of the governments they leave, imbibed in their early youth; or, if able to throw them off, it will be an exchange for an unbounded licentiousness, passing, as is usual from one extreme to another. It would be a miracle were they to stop precisely at the point of temperate liberty. These principles, with their language, they will transmit to their children.[30]

Even with proper conditioning, people from all walks of life often absorbed democratic doctrines incompletely. Jefferson himself could express disbelief and exasperation about the attitudes of free Americans towards slavery. "What a stupendous, what an incomprehensible machine is man!" He can

> . . . endure toil, famine, stripes, imprisonment and death itself in vindication of his own liberty, and the next moment be deaf to all those motives whose power supported him thro' his trial, and inflict on his fellow men a bondage, one hour of which is fraught with more misery than ages of that which he rose in rebellion to oppose.[31]

Yet Jefferson did not castigate them for it. Neither, of course, did he dispense with the services of his own slaves. Although he deplored slavery and advocated that it should end, he was a slave owner throughout his entire life.

While Jefferson had great faith in an educated public, he realized that its political judgments were not always right. The existence of opposition parties proved to him that people obviously made political mistakes and persisted in wrong views. "In every free and deliberating society, there must, from the nature of man, be opposite parties, and violent dissensions and discords; and one of these, for the most part, must prevail over the other for a longer or shorter time."[32] But there was always the expectation that the popular misjudgments would be only temporary:

> . . . A little patience, and we shall see the reign of witches pass over, the spells dissolved, and the people recovering their true sight . . . restoring this government to its true principles.[33]

[29]Lipscomb, vol. 14, p. 25.
[30]Ford, *Works*, vol. 3, pp. 487–488.
[31]Ford, *Works*, vol. 5, pp. 71–72.
[32]Ford, *Works*, vol. 2, pp. 206–207.
[33]Ford, *Works*, vol. 8, p. 432.

The people "may be led astray for a moment, but will soon correct themselves." At worst,

> the people are the only censors of their governors; and even their errors will tend to keep these to the true principles of their institution. To punish these errors too severely would be to suppress the only safeguard of the public liberty.[34]

In a choice between the dangers of popular error and the dangers of governmental suppression, the former were infinitely preferable.[35]

## Truth Through Free Speech and Press

Jefferson believed that free access to information and unhampered discussion would, ultimately, lead to the right course of action. Supply the people with facts, and, in time, they will hold the proper opinions. Thus he could proclaim with confidence in his First Inaugural Address: "If there be any among us who would wish to dissolve this Union or to change its republican form, let them stand undisturbed as monuments of the safety with which error of opinion may be tolerated where reason is left free to combat it."[36] This was a familiar and persistent theme in his thoughts. His preamble for "A Bill for Establishing Religious Freedom" had proclaimed that:

> Truth . . . will prevail if left to herself. . . . She is the proper and sufficient antagonist to error, and has nothing to fear from the conflict unless by human interposition disarmed of her natural weapons, free argument and debate. . . .[37]

And his *Notes on Virginia* declared:

> Reason and free inquiry are the only effectual agents against error. . . . If it be restrained now, the present corruptions will be protected, and new ones encouraged. . . . It is error which needs the support of government. Truth can stand by itself.[38]

Because he felt so strongly that free information would ultimately result in proper opinions on the part of the people, he always was very concerned about freedom of the press. To Edward Carrington he wrote:

[34]Lipscomb, vol. 6, p. 57.

[35]For a fuller discussion see Adrienne Koch, *The Philosophy of Thomas Jefferson.* New York: Columbia University Press, 1943, p. 150.

[36]Lipscomb, vol. 3, p. 319.

[37]Ford, *Works*, vol. 2, p. 441.

[38]Lipscomb, vol. 2, pp. 221–222.

> The basis of our governments being the opinion of the people, the very first object should be to keep that right; and were it left to me to decide whether we should have a government without newspapers or newspapers without a government, I should not hesitate a moment to prefer the latter.

He feared, that once people "become inattentive to the public affairs, you and I, and Congress and Assemblies, judges and governors shall all become wolves."[39] This was hyperbole of course, because the newspapers he had seen until that time warranted no such confidence. They shed only a limited amount of light, and that was generally filtered through the distorting prism of party bias. Still, newspapers were the only means of mass information except for the circular letters on current issues sent by some congressmen to their constituents.

Later in life, Jefferson was more disillusioned about the value of the press. He wrote to a friend that he deplored "the putrid state into which our newspapers have passed, and the malignity, the vulgarity, and mendacious spirit of those who write for them." He spoke of the "abyss of degradation into which we have fallen," and expressed fears that papers were "rapidly depraving the public taste, and lessening its relish for sound food. As vehicles of information, and a curb on our functionaries, they have rendered themselves useless, by forfeiting all title to belief."[40] He stopped reading all but local news because newspapers were "so false and so intemperate that they disturb tranquility, without giving information."[41] But even then he did not advocate suppression of the press. As he had recommended in his Second Inaugural Address:

> . . . The press, confined to truth, needs no other legal restraint; the public judgment will correct false reasonings and opinions, on a full hearing of all parties; and no other definite line can be drawn between the inestimable liberty of the press and its demoralizing licentiousness. If there be still improprieties which this rule would not restrain, its supplement must be sought in the censorship of public opinion.[42]

As late as 1823, after his tolerance of a venal, mendacious press had been strained beyond the breaking point on a number of occasions, he was to write to the Marquis de Lafayette:

> . . . The only security of all is in a free press. The force of public opinion cannot be resisted when permitted freely to be expressed. The agita-

[39]Ford, *Works*, vol. 5, p. 253.

[40]Leonard W. Levy, *Jefferson and Civil Liberties, the Darker Side*. Cambridge: The Belknap Press of Harvard University Press, 1963, p. 67.

[41]Schachner, p. 890.

[42]Lipscomb, vol. 3, pp. 381–382.

tion it produces must be submitted to. It is necessary to keep the waters pure.[43]

## The Limits of Public Capacity

Though Jefferson believed in the right of the public to determine the basic form of government which "to them shall seem most likely to effect their Safety and Happiness,"[44] and to run their local affairs, he did not feel that the general public was well qualified to judge what policies would serve the national interest best. In the first place, the public could not interpret political news in the press unless it was written in a simple way so that the people would be able to comprehend the meaning. For instance the people had been deceived by publication of the XYZ letters. While he hoped that "The unquestionable republicanism of the American mind will break through the mist under which it has been clouded, and will oblige its agents to reform the principles and practices of their administration," he was afraid this might not take place unless the facts in the situation were simplified. ". . . These communications are too voluminous for them and beyond their reach. A recapitulation is now wanting of the whole story, stating everything according to what we may now suppose to have been the truth, short, simple and leveled to every capacity."[45]

When he was President, he struck a long passage concerning the Sedition Act from his second annual message with the notation that it was omitted "because it was thought better that the message should be clear of everything which the public might be made to misunderstand."[46]

Second, the formation of public opinion was apt to be unduly slow. Understanding of the XYZ affair might lag too long. He wrote to James Madison on January 30, 1799:

> But it is on the progress of public opinion we are to depend for rectifying the proceedings of the next Congress. The only question is whether this will not carry things beyond the reach of rectification.[47]

Although he had full confidence that the public would ultimately see the light of truth, truth might come too late to save the country from the consequences of erroneous policies.

Third, Jefferson was concerned about public lethargy. In times of crisis people and their representatives would take an interest in public affairs,

[43]Lipscomb, vol. 15, p. 491.
[44]Declaration of Independence.
[45]Lipscomb, vol. 10, pp. 83–87.
[46]Schachner, p. 694.
[47]Lipscomb, vol. 10, p. 94.

form opinions, and exert themselves on behalf of the common welfare. But this attitude would not last. In time, "rulers will become corrupt, our people careless. . . . They will be forgotten . . . but in the sole faculty of making money, and will never think of uniting to effect a due respect for their rights."[48] Jefferson had good reason for questioning public perseverance in self-government. He knew how difficult it had been after the Revolutionary War to keep enough delegates in Congress to conduct important public business. Protests sent to delinquent states whose representatives remained absent, had been of little avail.[49] He knew how quickly, after the Revolution, the public ardor had died down.[50] He was fully aware of the difficulty to sustain public willingness to pay for the necessary expenses of government. Talk of concern with public affairs was cheap; but when financial nerves were touched, or sustained effort required, many a solid citizen disappeared from sight.

One other aspect of the public's capacity, which Jefferson repeatedly questioned, was the people's ability to select good representatives for public assemblies. Jefferson had served in a number of these assemblies and had been shocked by the poor performance of the delegates. He never developed his experiences into a theory that would concede that the public competence was limited. However, in drafting a new constitution for the state of Virginia he incorporated plans for an indirectly elected upper house. When he was challenged about the wisdom of this decision, he defended it by a strong attack on the abilities of the people. His curtness, in part, was his typical response to any attack on his ideas, always painful to his ego. But it also reflected his feelings about the public's capabilities. In defending his plan Jefferson wrote: "I have ever observed that a choice by the people themselves is not generally distinguished for its wisdom. This first secretion from them is usually crude and heterogeneous." On the other hand, ". . . give to those so chosen by the people a second choice themselves, and they generally will choose wise men." The Senate, he felt should "get the wisest men chosen, and to make them perfectly independent when chosen."[51] Why the representatives who were "crude and heterogeneous" would be so much smarter than the people in their own selection of an upper house, Jefferson did not say. Had he commented, he might have enunciated some sort of an elitist concept contrary to his political premises. This he did not care to do.

Nor did Jefferson want the senators to be dependent on the people. He preferred a single term for them so that they would not be tempted to court popular favor while in office. But, "I could submit tho' not so willingly

[48]Lipscomb, vol. 2, p. 225.
[49]Ford, *Writings*, vol. 3, pp. 396–406.
[50]Schachner, p. 406.
[51]Schachner, pp. 122–123.

to an appointment for life or to anything rather than a mere creation by and dependence on the people."[52] Again, he did not carry his reasoning through to the logical conclusion that he believed in limitations on popular control of government. Similarly, he expressed doubts about the U. S. Constitution because, as he confided to Madison, "I think a house chosen by them [people] will be very illy qualified to legislate for the Union, for foreign nations. . . ."[53] Yet he complained

> that our governments have much less republicanism than ought to have been expected; . . . the people have less regular control over their agents, than their rights and interests require.

Governments, he asserted,

> . . . are more or less republican, as they have more or less of the element of popular election and control in their composition; and believing, as I do, that the mass of the citizens is the safest depository of their own rights and especially that the evils flowing from the duperies of the people are less injurious than those from the egotism of their agents, I am a friend to that composition of government which has in it the most of this ingredient.[54]

Adrienne Koch, biographer of Jefferson's intellectual development, attributes such intellectual inconsistencies to "political relativism." In support, she quotes from a letter to Dupont de Nemours in which Jefferson explained why he had retained some Federalist practices which he had earlier condemned. "What is practicable must often controul what is pure theory: and the habits of the governed determine in a great degree what is practicable."[55] Jefferson was a man of action. When his theories ran afoul of effective governmental practices, the theories must be ignored. But ignoring them for a time did not mean that they must be abandoned. Jefferson, like most human beings, could live quite comfortably in two separate mental worlds—one of the wishful mind, the other of sobering experience. The multifarious experiences of his life could not be fitted into the rigidities of a completely logical and consistent philosophical scheme.

## Channels of Opinion Expression

Since Jefferson had no systematic comprehensive philosophy of government, one must piece together his ideas about how the voice of the

[52]Schachner, pp. 122–123.
[53]Ford, *Works*, vol. 5, p. 370.
[54]Lipscomb, vol. 15, p. 23.
[55]Ford, *Works*, vol. 9, p. 344.

public would make itself heard in a democracy. Only two channels are indicated, one nonviolent and the other violent. As a nonviolent channel, Jefferson repeatedly mentioned memorials and petitions by the public to the executive department or to the national and state legislatures as evidences of public desires and opinions. This emphasis is somewhat surprising since he frequently acknowledged that such expressions of opinion rarely originated with the masses. Rather, they were inspired and drafted by prominent individuals in and out of government.

On many occasions, Jefferson himself had drafted petitions and resolutions or urged his friends, especially Madison, to draft them. The resolutions would then be submitted anonymously directly to legislative assemblies or to some nonofficial gatherings for the adoption of their membership. One could, of course, argue that the discussions which preceded adoption of the messages during public meetings constituted an endorsement of the sense of the message and therefore a public expression of opinion.

On the other hand, as Jefferson well knew, large groups of people often will endorse a complete statement of political purposes, especially if it is written in rousing form, without fully comprehending its meaning, or its relationship to their own interests. Skilled politicians have little trouble in winning public endorsement to lend prestige to their personal desires. The "planted" opinion, which then is reiterated to governmental officials, is not really an expression of public opinion flowing directly from the average man to his government. But this Jefferson chose to overlook with characteristic failure to square his theories with the facts of political life which he knew so well.

The other channel for public opinion that Jefferson singled out for repeated mention was the expression of opinion through rebellion. (Civil disobedience would be the modern equivalent.) To Jefferson, rebellion was the voice of the people par excellence. He never conceded that rebellions might be inspired by a small number of selfish individuals for their own purposes, or that rebellions could degenerate into mouthpieces of a small, unrepresentative elite as had happened during the French Revolution. To him, willingness to fight and die for the slogans of the rebellion indicated a strong public opinion in support of these slogans. When unrest was reported in the eastern United States in the winter of 1787, Jefferson was not displeased. Revolution, he contended, "prevents the degeneracy of government, and nourishes a general attention to the public affairs. I hold it, that a little rebellion, now and then, is a good thing, and as necessary in the political world as storms in the physical."[56] To his friend, Colonel Smith, he exclaimed:

> God forbid we should ever be twenty years without such a rebellion. The people cannot be all, and always, well informed. The part which is

[56]Lipscomb, vol. 6, p. 65.

wrong will be discontented, in proportion to the importance of the facts they misconceive. If they remain quiet under such misconceptions, it is lethargy, the forerunner of death to the public liberty. . . .[57]

And then he mused:

> . . . What country can preserve its liberties, if its rulers are not warned from time to time, that this people preserve the spirit of resistance? Let them take arms.[58]

The remedy, as he saw it, was "to set them [the rebels] right as to tacts, pardon and pacify them. What signify a few lives lost in a century or two? The tree of liberty must be refreshed from time to time, with the blood of patriots and tyrants. It is its natural manure."[59] Such views were no mere whimsy. Nearly a year earlier he had voiced similar sentiments to Dr. Ezra Stiles of Yale University. "If the happiness of the mass of the people can be secured at the expense of a little tempest now and then, or even of a little blood, it will be a precious purchase."[60] He realized that it was hard for responsible government officials to stand by and watch what seemed like anarchy.

> A consciousness of those in power that their administration of the public affairs has been honest, may, perhaps, produce too great a degree of indignation. . . . They may conclude too hastily, that nature has formed man insusceptible of any other government than that of force, a conclusion not founded in truth or experience.[61]

But weigh this turbulence "against the oppressions of monarchy, and it becomes nothing."[62] Rebellions are "a medicine necessary for the sound health of government."[63] This was Jefferson, the philosopher, then on the sidelines of government, not charged with the responsibility of assuring public order. Things would look different from the perch of power.

## The Press as a Propaganda Tool

While petitions and revolutions revealed public sentiments, Jefferson never felt that the newspapers were mouthpieces of public opinion. They were a vehicle for the submission of private views to the public. As such, Jefferson believed that they were very important in providing the background for opinion formation. This is why he was so much disturbed when

[57]Lipscomb, vol. 6, pp. 372–373.
[58]Lipscomb, vol. 6, p. 373.
[59]Lipscomb, vol. 6, p. 373.
[60]Lipscomb, vol. 6, p. 25.
[61]Lipscomb, vol. 6, p. 64.
[62]Lipscomb, vol. 6, p. 65.
[63]Ford, *Works*, vol. 5, p. 256.

he believed during the Washington Administration that all influential papers in the country were controlled by the opposition party. The people, he feared, would hear one side of the political story only and would be swayed in that direction because they would not have the antidote of the opposition view. He was very eager to start an opposition paper—so eager, in fact, that he was willing to subsidize it with public funds.

In 1791, he offered to Philip Freneau, a writer known for his caustic tongue and pen and his strong republicanism, the clerkship for foreign languages in the State Department. The idea was that Freneau would use his free time to publish a Republican journal, and that Jefferson would see to it that there would be plenty of free time. Jefferson was willing to give him "the perusal of all my letters of foreign intelligence and all foreign newspapers." In addition to supplying Freneau with this inside information, invaluable for one determined to attack the government, Jefferson promised to subsidize the paper by using it for "the publication of all proclamations and other public notices within my department, and the printing of the laws."[64] In Jefferson's defense of this partisan use of public funds, it must be noted that the chief Federalist paper, also a pure party organ, was subsidized through official Treasury Department advertising.

It was Jefferson, too, who was instrumental in setting up a presidential newspaper in Washington. He persuaded Samuel Harrison Smith of Philadelphia to start the *National Intelligencer* in Washington in October, 1800. Although the paper was privately run, it was subsidized by public printing contracts and was considered by its readers the mouthpiece of the President.

Whenever a public crisis arose in which Jefferson felt that the viewpoints of the Republicans were not properly represented, he was almost frantic in his pleas to his friends to use the press to denounce the opposition. "The engine is the press. Every man must lay his purse and pen under contribution. . . ."[65] When Hamilton as "Pacificus" was denouncing Jefferson and France for Genêt's misguided unneutral acts, Jefferson called on Madison to take up the defense in the papers. "Nobody answers him, and his doctrines will therefore be taken for confessed. For God's sake, my dear Sir, take up your pen, select the most striking heresies and cut him to pieces in the face of the public. There is nobody else who can and will enter the lists against him."[66] Apparently it was necessary to give guidance to the public in detecting falsehoods. Papers, pamphlets, handbills had to be distributed as widely as possible to expose the lies and distortions published by the opposition. Unaided, the people would be duped by the clever political arguments presented by Hamilton:

[64]Schachner, p. 442.
[65]Ford, *Works*, vol. 9, p. 34.
[66]Ford, *Works*, vol. 7, p. 436.

. . . The delusion of the people is necessary to the dominant party. . . .
There is no length to which it may not be pushed by a party in possession
of the revenues and the legal authorities of the US. . . .[67]

That such reasoning impugned the ability of the public to know what was
good for it, to distinguish truth from falsehood and to make the proper
political decisions did not faze Jefferson.

## The Authority of the Public

When one searches for an answer to the question of how far governmental leaders must be guided by public opinion, one runs into the conflicting statements so characteristic of Jefferson's political views. On the
one hand, Jefferson believed that people should be allowed to decide
matters as fundamental as the adoption of the Constitution, and serious
matters of foreign and domestic policy. When the people wanted a bill of
rights, although the experts denied the necessity of such a document, such
a bill had to be added because "the general voice has legitimated" the
request.[68] When the public rejected Jefferson's ideas about the term of
the President and preferred a different scheme, it was to be heeded and
the experts to be slighted. The people had

> . . . not, however, authorized me to consider as a real defect, what I
> thought and still think one, the perpetual reeligibility of the president.
> But three States out of eleven, having declared against this, we must
> suppose we are wrong, according to the fundamental law of every society,
> the *lex majoris partis*, to which we are bound to submit.[69]

On the other hand, when pressed to define the scope of popular guidance
of government, he limited it to the election of qualified legislators and executive officials and to judging facts as jurors in the public courts. He recommended that the people

> . . . should exercise in person every function which their qualifications en-
> able them to exercise, consistently with the order and security of society
> . . . we now find them equal to the election of those who shall be invested
> with their executive and legislative powers, and to act themselves in the
> judiciary, as judges in questions of fact. . . .[70]

Somewhat later he elaborated:

[67]Ford, *Works*, vol. 8, pp. 443–447.
[68]Lipscomb, vol. 7, p. 323.
[69]Lipscomb, vol. 7, pp. 323–324.
[70]Lipscomb, vol. 14, p. 47.

> . . . With us, the people (by which is meant the mass of individuals composing the society) being competent to judge of the facts occurring in ordinary life, they have retained the functions of judges of facts, under the name of jurors; but being unqualified for the management of affairs requiring intelligence above the common level, yet competent judges of human character, they chose, for their management, representatives, some by themselves. . . . Action by the citizens in person, in affairs within their reach and competence, and in all others by representatives, chosen immediately, and removable by themselves, constitutes the essence of a republic. . . .[71]

A similar ambivalence marks his views about the duty of public officials to heed the mandate of the public. He believed that the natural right of the people to govern themselves included the right to make mistakes. It was the duty of public officials to heed the people, even when the people directed them to wrong action. "Government being founded on opinion, the opinion of the public, even when it is wrong, ought to be respected to a certain degree."[72] For example, Jefferson was chagrined that his countrymen did not share his aversion to a merchant marine. Nevertheless he informed John Jay, who had asked him about the creation of such a marine, that the United States

> . . . are not free to decide this question on principles of theory only. Our people are decided in the opinion, that it is necessary for us to take a share in the occupation of the ocean. . . . I think it a duty in those entrusted with the administration of their affairs, to conform themselves to the decided choice of their constituents; and that therefore, we should, in every instance, preserve an equality of right to them in the transportation of commodities. . . .[73]

This held true even though he deemed the consequences of such a policy to be seriously disadvantageous for the United States:

> But what will be the consequence? Frequent wars without a doubt. Their property will be violated on the sea, and in foreign ports, their persons will be insulted, imprisoned, et cetera, for pretended debts, contracts, crimes, contraband, et cetera, et cetera. These insults must be resented, even if we had no feelings, yet to prevent their eternal repetition; or, in other words, our commerce on the ocean and in other countries, must be paid for by frequent war.[74]

If one engages in the risky sport of looking for hidden motives in a statement, such as this, one can perhaps detect Jefferson's ability to make a virtue out of necessity. He knew that certain policies could not be car-

[71]Lipscomb, vol. 14, pp. 488; 490.
[72]Ford, *Works*, vol. 6, p. 194.
[73]Lipscomb, vol. 5, pp. 94–95.
[74]Lipscomb, vol. 5, pp. 94–95.

ried out in the face of strong public opposition. In those instances it was certainly the better part of valor to let the public have its way and claim that the government had bowed to it as a matter of principle, rather than as a matter of necessity.

Such an interpretation makes it easier to reconcile his views about the duty of public officials to follow public guidance, with his admonition that they must guide public opinion and his advocacy and practice of all sorts of opinion manipulation to change adverse public opinion and bring it in line with the views of political leaders. In fact, Jefferson was so intent on rescuing the public from wrong opinions that he even was willing to appeal to the baser instincts. For this purpose, he collected gossip and salacious materials. Visitors to Monticello reported that he proudly showed them a six volume, privately printed edition of scandalous memoirs of court life in France and England to corroborate his assaults on monarchs and aristocrats.[75] To counteract Federalist influence, he kept a meticulous record about the foibles of leading Federalists, including any utterance which might expose them as undemocratic.[76] He also tolerated the character assassination practiced by the Republican editors, whom he subsidized, to destroy the reputation and credibility of his political foes. Again, this did not conform to his theories of the rationality of man who, presumably, would not ordinarily yield to an appeal to baser instincts and curiosities. It did not jibe with his or posterity's prim notions of proprieties. But Jefferson knew that this type of appeal, better than most others, would arouse public interest and sustain attention. Hence, like many upright men in political life, he used it.

## The Plight of Leadership

Jefferson's willingness to manipulate public opinion reveals the importance which he assigned to it in the decision-making process. Obviously, what the public thought was important, since it could force the government to go along with its mandate. But the public was not always right. The fact that Jefferson considered it permissible to consciously mold public opinions indicates that he believed in the right and ability of political leaders to decide what was proper and then, through the use of persuasion tactics, sway the public along with the leadership's decision.

It is implicit in his writings that those who become highly placed public officials, and who are not blinded by narrow, factional interests know better than the people what decisions are proper. Their function is to explain their policies to the people, but not in order to allow them a true choice.

[75]Ford, *Works*, vol. 1, p. 12.
[76]Schachner, p. 932.

Rather, the function is to persuade the people to go along with the leadership. Once the people have been persuaded, their approval of the administration's policies indicates their good sense. If the people cannot be swayed, this indicates that public officials have done an ineffective job of persuasion, or that the people have been temporarily duped.

For himself, Jefferson did not want to take the risks of public opinion leadership. He did not relish the idea of being charged with responsibility for public policies when he might have to follow the mandates of the public even if he deemed them wrong. When Washington offered him the position of Secretary of State he wrote in his letter of reply:

> . . . I should enter on it with gloomy forebodings from the criticisms and censures of a public, just indeed in their intentions, but sometimes misinformed and misled, and always too respectable to be neglected. I cannot but foresee the possibility that this may end disagreeably for me, who, having no motive to public service but the public satisfaction, would certainly retire the moment that satisfaction should appear to languish.[77]

Yet, he was willing to preach to others to take disappointments in stride and be content with doing the bidding of the public, pending their conversion to sounder views. Charles Clay, a candidate for representative in Congress, must know

> . . . that the ground of liberty is to be gained by inches, that we must be contented to secure what we can get, from time to time, and eternally press forward for what is yet to get. It takes time to persuade men to do even what is for their own good.[78]

Perhaps one reason why Jefferson felt especially reluctant to take public office was his acute awareness that he had difficulties in public speaking and lacked mass appeal which was so essential for a successful political leader. Of the office of Secretary of State he wrote, "I cannot be insensible of my inequality to it."[79] He had a morbid fear of getting involved in debate. Although he wrote exceedingly well, he rarely engaged in the pamphleteering or any other controversial writing in which his confrères were so adept. However, he would reply to petitions and memoranda sent to him. While he admittedly was "averse to receive addresses, yet unable to prevent them," he told Attorney General Lincoln that:

> I have generally endeavored to turn them to some account, by making them the occasion, by way of answer, of sowing useful truths and principles among the people, which might germinate and become rooted among their political tenets.[80]

[77]Lipscomb, vol. 8, pp. 1–2.
[78]Lipscomb, vol. 8, p. 4.
[79]Lipscomb, vol. 8, p. 4.
[80]Henry S. Randall, *The Life of Thomas Jefferson.* New York: Derby and Jackson, 1858, p. 2.

When he delivered his messages to Congress, they were so inaudible that hardly anyone knew what the President had said. Acute awareness of his distaste for the rough and tumble of political life made him feel that he was not particularly well qualified to deal directly with the public. As a leader who shrank from giving voice to his thought in order to convince his listeners he would, if he followed his theories, have to follow the mandate of the public regardless of where it would lead him. This, obviously was not a prospect to be relished.[81] Yet the alternative of engaging in public debate was equally chilling. For Jefferson, the apostle of the rights of the masses "loathed crowds, loved privacy, and built his house upon a mountain."[82]

## The People's Role in Foreign Policy Making

Jefferson's writings, as well as his public acts, convey the distinct impression that he considered the people far more competent to decide matters of domestic policy than matters of foreign policy. He insisted that foreign affairs were strictly the province of the national government with no state interference brooked, even though state governments were in close touch with the people and able to mirror their views better. When he thought he could do so with impugnity, he ignored public opposition to his foreign policies. Thus he would not listen to the protests of shipowners, seamen and merchants during the Embargo of 1807. He claimed he was acting for their benefit and blamed all dissent on the machinations of the Federalist party. Just like the Communist party in a later age, the Federalist party made a perfect scapegoat on which to blame unrest and dissent. With a kernel of truth at the core, one could not easily judge whether or not the danger had been inflated unduly.

Jefferson also claimed the right to make foreign policy in secret and to withhold information from the public if this was in the interest of good policies. All this reveals his strong inclination to keep foreign policy decisions largely an executive matter. As the next chapter illustrates, this is precisely what he did once he became President. But even earlier, as Secretary of State, he favored secrecy. When in August of 1793, the Cabinet discussed whether or not to publish the facts surrounding the Genêt episode, Jefferson voted for suppression of the news. His reasoning was that

[81]Malone notes that even as a writer Jefferson rarely spoke directly to the public. The Declaration of Independence was a manifesto of Congress. His other famous papers were mostly legislative acts and diplomatic papers. He did not write for the newspapers during the violent controversies of the 1790s. He exercised direct influence, especially in party matters, chiefly through private letters. In these he communicated largely with political leaders, not with average citizens. (Malone, p. 4.)

[82]Malone, p. 5.

publication of the facts would enable Genêt to appeal directly to the American people. He did not trust the people to be able to see through whatever claims Genêt might make.[83] By contrast, in a matter of domestic policy, he had been highly critical of the secrecy observed by the Constitutional Convention in 1787. He wrote John Adams that he had no sympathy with the delegates' attempts to ease their work through secrecy.

> I am sorry they began their deliberations by so abominable a precedent. . . . Nothing can justify this example but the innocence of their intentions, and ignorance of the value of public discussions.[84]

While the public was not particularly qualified to judge foreign policy matters, references to public opinion could be used by policy makers to implement foreign policy making. For instance, minority legislators could allege a necessity to consult with the people to win a delay in policy formulation. Jefferson suggested this tactic in 1798 when he hoped to gain time to arouse opposition to the administration's anti-French policies.[85] As a member of an opposition party which disagreed with the foreign policy decisions of the party in power, Jefferson was also fully aware of the use which could be made of public opinion to persuade the administration to alter its policies. If public opinion could be roused in favor of a policy opposed by the administration, it then could be cited as a mandate for the adoption of this policy. The same tactic could be used against a hostile Congress and a recalcitrant foreign power. In 1805, when he wanted to purchase Florida, he brought pressure on Spain and on Congress by stirring up public sentiment with a message indicating war with Spain over Florida was imminent. This gave punch to his secret request to Congress for $2,000,000 to purchase Florida even though the secret message revealed that the war scare had been exaggerated.[86] Similarly, on several occasions Jefferson justified policies which otherwise seemed improper on legal or even moral grounds by citing public support for these policies. For instance, during the crisis occasioned by the Burr conspiracy of 1807, Jefferson assured General Wilkinson that arrests of persons against whom the evidence was scanty, were permissible since the public had approved them.[87] He also believed that *post hoc* public approval would lift the cloud of illegality from the Louisiana Purchase.

At times, public opposition could be stirred to undermine established policies. Sectional differences were great and it was easy to show that policies that seemed advantageous to one section of the country might ob-

[83]Lipscomb, vol. 1, pp. 381–382.
[84]Lipscomb, vol. 6, pp. 285–289.
[85]Ford, *Works*, vol. 8, pp. 386–388.
[86]Ford, *Works*, vol. 10, pp. 198–205.
[87]For a full discussion see Levy, pp. 84–86.

viously be wrong for another section of the country. For long, it was quite easy to play on the pro-French sentiments of the Southerners, for instance, as against the pro-English sentiments of the northern part of the country. At other times the task was far more difficult. It required great political skill to overcome an adverse nationwide sentiment. For example, in the summer of 1793 Jefferson conceded that "the desire of neutrality is universal. The towns are . . . declaring their firm adherence to their president." For this reason

> it would place the republicans in a very unfav[ora]ble point of view with the people to be cavilling about small points of propriety; and would betray a wish to find fault with the President in an instance where he will be approved by the great body of the people who consider the substance of the measure only, not the small criticisms to which it is liable.

In the light of these circumstances, Jefferson advocated that:

> It will be true wisdom in the Republican party to approve unequivocally of a state of neutrality, to avoid little cavils about who shall declare it, to abandon G[enêt] entirely, with expressions of strong friendship and adherence to his nation and confidence that he has acted against their sense. In this way we shall keep the people on our side by keeping ourselves in the right.[88]

Finesse, rather than blunt action, was the order of the day. Similarly, during the XYZ agitation he turned down a proposal that riots against governmental policy should be encouraged. "Nothing could be so fatal." Astutely gauging the public temper, he concluded:

> Anything like force would check the progress of the public opinion and rally them round the government. This is not the kind of opposition the American people will permit.[89]

Deist though he was, Jefferson was willing to resort to religious appeals to sway the public mind to lend the prestige of public support to foreign policies. When the British closed the port of Boston in 1775, he joined with a group of friends to urge a day of "fasting, humiliation and prayer" to impress the public with the seriousness of the occasion.[90] What Congressman Randolph later called "an allowable trick of political warfare" seemed highly effective to Jefferson. He wrote:

> The effect of the day thro' the whole colony was like a shock of electricity, arousing every man and placing him erect and solidly on his centre.[91]

[88]Schachner, pp. 505–506.
[89]Ford, *Works*, vol. 9, p. 46.
[90]Ford, *Works*, vol. 1, p. 12.
[91]Ford, *Works*, vol. 1, p. 13.

Nevertheless, in later life he declined to repeat the tactic because it offended his sense of propriety.

How can one sum up a man whose record in words and deeds does not speak unequivocally? Leonard Levy, in his analysis of Jefferson's theories and practices on civil liberties, talks of Jefferson's "darker side." What he means is that Jefferson proclaimed a very libertarian creed when out of office yet did not practice it when in office.[92] Levy, along with a condemnation of Jefferson's illiberal practices, implies that there is something dark or evil in a man's not living up to his philosophies. Yet this disregards the human fact that men do not use their theories as blueprints for action. It is their biographers and analysts who superimpose the action on the philosophy and demand "the beautiful consistency of cloistered philosophy."[93] Jefferson, as most decent men, desired the ideal and preached what he considered ideal—a government guided by the opinions of its citizens. As the case history of the Louisiana Purchase in the next chapter demonstrates, when he acted contrary to these ideals, or even when some of his pronouncements contradicted these ideals, he often was not aware of the contradiction or managed to shut it out of his mind. "It may well be that compartments in his mind opened and shut automatically without too great an intercommunication among them."[94] He coped with the needs of the moment on an *ad hoc* basis. The pressures of political life were so acute that he did not take time to reflect whether his words and deeds were consistent. One wonders whether the analyst who looks to consistency as the hallmark of the life of great and little men is not looking for a chimera that never existed and never can exist, except when the facts of life, by sheer coincidence, match the philosophies.

[92]Saul Padover, *Thomas Jefferson and the Foundations of American Freedom.* Princeton: D. Van Nostrand Co., 1965, p. 28, has leaped to Jefferson's defense. "To dwell on this as the 'darker side' is to distort the whole spirit of the man and the meaning of the history of his time. It is like painting a man's warts rather than his face."

[93]Merrill D. Peterson, *The Jefferson Image in the American Mind.* New York: Oxford University Press, 1960, p. 115.

[94]Schachner, p. 261.

# 6

## The Louisiana Purchase:
## An Exercise
## in Presidential Secretiveness

Thus to be independent of public opinion is the first formal
condition of achieving anything great or rational whether in
life or in science. Great achievement is assured, however, of
subsequent recognition and grateful acceptance by public opinion, which in due course will make it one of its own prejudices.

HEGEL, *The Philosophy of Right*

Great souls care little for small morals.

NAPOLEON

# 6

## Western Demands for River Rights

In 1786 a letter was widely circulated in the United States. It was read at musters, town meetings, and court openings. In agonized biblical language it broadcast the plight of the Westerners:

> Shall we be bondsmen of the Spaniards, as the children of Israel were bondsmen of the Egyptians? Shall one part of the Americans be slaves and another freemen?. . . .

Westerners were complaining about the strictures that Spain imposed on the vital trade on the Mississippi River. But they had a remedy in mind. "Twenty thousand troops can easily be raised west of the Alleghenies and the Appalachians to drive the Spaniards from their settlements at the mouth of the river." And then the threat:

> If this is not countenanced in the East, we will throw off our allegiance and seek elsewhere for help. Nor will we seek in vain, for even now Great Britain stands with open arms to receive us.[1]

It is doubtful that Jefferson ever saw this letter, although one copy was addressed to the legislature of the state of Virginia. For he was in France when it made the rounds. But he knew well the sentiments whereof it spoke and shared them, at least as far as the right of Americans to use the mouth of the Mississippi River was concerned. This he deemed a "natural right" inherent in the geographical position of an up-river state to use the river and its shores to carry, land, and deposit merchandise for transshipment.[2] In that same year he had written to a friend that "the navigation of the Mississippi we must have."[3] As Secretary of State, a few years later, he drafted instructions for the American chargé d'affaires at Madrid to negotiate for full rights to the use of the river.[4] Thus, when he reached the presidency he was deeply conscious that the right to ship their products down river and to the sea was sacred to Westerners. He was determined to make that right secure, because he deemed it essential for the future growth of the United States and because he knew that Westerners would

[1]John Bach McMaster, *History of the People of the United States*, vol. 1. New York: D. Appleton, 1885, p. 383.

[2]Samuel F. Bemis, ed., *The American Secretaries of State and Their Diplomacy*, vol. 2. New York: Alfred A. Knopf, 1927, p. 51.

[3]Paul Leicester Ford, ed., *The Works of Thomas Jefferson*, vol. 5. New York: Putnam's, 1904, p. 73.

[4]Ford, vol. 6, pp. 111–114.

resort to force in or out of the union to retain that right. In the process he proved that "he could be as hard-boiled, as practical and as cynical, if you will, when the occasion arose, as any veteran diplomat of the Old World."[5] He also displayed a wide gap between his proclaimed political theories and his official practices.

When Jefferson became President, the mouth of the Mississippi River was in Spanish hands. As the letter indicates, this had caused problems with the Spaniards in the past. Difficulties continued even after Pinckney's Treaty of 1795 had guaranteed the right of free navigation of the Mississippi River and the use of some of its port facilities. The United States had always been able to settle disputes through diplomatic negotiations or, failing that, Westerners had been able to send their goods down-river in defiance of Spanish authorities. Therefore, Jefferson was not too worried about Spanish control as such, as long as it was not used to America's disadvantage. He felt that the United States must "not press too soon on the Spaniards. Those countries cannot be in better hands." The only danger would be that the Spaniards would be "too feeble to hold them till our population can be sufficiently advanced to gain it from them piece by piece."[6] In the hands of Spain the area was safe for the time being. The time being was that relatively brief period that it would take for the United States to become strong enough to force the Spaniards to relinquish the territory.

### From the Frying Pan into the Fire

What Jefferson had feared came to pass in 1801. In that year rumors began to circulate in the United States that Spain had ceded the Louisiana Territory including the mouth of the Mississippi River to France. Instead of weak Spain, with the control of Louisiana slipping from her fingers, the United States would henceforth have a powerful and aggressive neighbor tightly squeezing her jugular vein of commerce. Jefferson warned:

> There is on the globe one single spot, the possessor of which is our natural and habitual enemy. It is New Orleans, through which the produce of three-eighths of our territory must pass to market, and from its fertility it will ere long yield more than half of our whole produce, and contain more than half of our inhabitants.[7]

[5]Nathan Schachner, *Thomas Jefferson*, vol. 1. New York: Appleton-Century-Crofts, 1951, p. 407.

[6]Ford, vol. 5, pp. 73–76.

[7]Henry S. Randall, *The Life of Thomas Jefferson*, vol. 3. New York: Derby and Jackson, 1858, p. 6.

Recent events in Santo Domingo boded ill for the future. There the French had imprisoned American merchants and sea captains, expelled American residents, and seized American goods. Promptly, Jefferson ordered Madison, his Secretary of State, to instruct the American ministers in Europe to investigate the rumors. No instructions were given about what should be done if the rumors proved correct. Jefferson merely wanted to know and, for the present, hoped that rumors of the cession would not alarm the people in the back country. If they suspected that France was to be their new neighbor, they might fear that the river would be effectively and permanently closed to them. In that case, they were willing to go to war. Jefferson was not.

Early in 1802 confirmation came from both England and France that Louisiana had been retroceded to France. Jefferson was alarmed—"displeased" may be the better word. Studied alarm marked the letter which he sent to France. He informed Robert Livingston, the American representative in Paris, that "a French take-over in Louisiana will cost France, and perhaps not very long hence, a war which will annihilate her on the ocean."[8] Then he threatened:

> The day that France takes possession of New Orleans . . . seals the union of two nations who in conjunction can maintain exclusive possession of the ocean. From that moment we must marry ourselves to the British fleet and nation.[9]

Although the threat conveyed extreme concern, especially since it came from a confirmed Anglophobe, Jefferson did not consider the situation serious enough to inform Congress or the country. Above all he wanted to keep his hands untied by domestic complications. Once he had made what he deemed a proper settlement, it would be time enough to tell the public. Therefore, for domestic consumption, he maintained what Leonard Levy has called an "almost sphinx-like silence until a year later, when he needed money for his diplomacy."[10]

Unfortunately, other events, which could not be concealed from the public, ruffled the waters of domestic quiet. On July 14, 1802, the Spanish Intendant at New Orleans, Don Juan Ventura Morales, closed the

[8]The message was given by Jefferson to Dupont de Nemours, April 25, 1802. Andrew A. Lipscomb, ed., *The Writings of Thomas Jefferson*, vol. 10. Washington: Thomas Jefferson Memorial Association, 1905, p. 317.

[9]Paul Leicester Ford, ed., *The Writings of Thomas Jefferson*, vol. 8. New York: Putnam's, 1894, p. 145.

[10]Leonard W. Levy, *Jefferson and Civil Liberties, The Darker Side*. Cambridge: The Belknap Press of Harvard University Press, 1963, p. 96. A motion in Congress in January 1803 to ask the President for information about the cession was defeated. United States Congress, *Annals of Congress*, 7th Congress, 2d session, pp. 314–366.

mouth of the Mississippi River to American traffic. Henceforth, goods were to be allowed passage only on express permission from Madrid. The western countryside was thrown into an uproar. As Madison explained it: "The Mississippi to them is everything. It is the Hudson, the Delaware, the Potomac, and all the navigable rivers of the Atlantic formed into one stream."[11] Western legislatures passed angry resolutions asking that battle-ready troops be sent to the Southwest and that the United States go to war with Spain. If not with Spain, it should certainly fight the minute the French moved into New Orleans.

Jefferson was worried that the unrest might force him to take stronger action than he deemed proper. It might even lead Westerners to take foreign policy into their own hands by attacking Spanish territory. Peaceful diplomacy might then become impossible. Gravely, he informed Monroe that: "The agitation of the public mind on occasion of the late suspension of our right of deposit at N. Orleans is extreme."[12] He tried to alleviate the problem through talks with the Spanish and French ministers in Washington. By the end of November he had obtained a renewal of commercial rights in New Orleans. At the same time, he initiated negotiations through his representatives in France to effect a permanent settlement which would guarantee American rights to the navigation of the mouths of the crucial southern rivers.

## A Mission to Mollify the West

Unfortunately, Westerners remained disturbed. "The measures we have been pursuing being invisible, do not satisfy their minds. Something sensible therefore has become necessary. . . ."[13]

The "sensible" thing he decided on to quiet the West and keep it from forcing him into war was a mission by James Monroe, lately Governor of Virginia, to France. Monroe, unlike Livingston, was well-known and popular in the West. If the news spread that he had been sent to France to make a settlement that would assure commercial rights in Louisiana, Westerners would feel that their interests were well represented. This would keep them quiet until some sort of diplomatic settlement could be made. Jefferson did not really expect that Monroe would be able to accomplish anything more than Livingston could. In fact, he was dubious that any settlement at all could be reached rapidly. "I did not expect he (Napoleon)

[11]Alcee Fortier, A History of Louisiana vol. 2, New York: Manzi, Joyant, 1904, p. 250. See Jefferson's letter to Pinckney, January 10, 1803 (Annals, 7th Congress, 2d session, pp. 1062–1063).

[12]Ford, Works, vol. 9, p. 418.

[13]Ford, Works, vol. 9, pp. 418–421. See also the speech by Senator Ross of Pennsylvania (Annals, 7th Congress, 2d session, pp. 83–89, 93–95).

would yield till a war took place between France and England, and my hope was to palliate and endure. . . ."[14] But:

> This measure [sending Monroe] being a visible one, and the person named peculiarly proper with the Western country, crushed at once and put an end to all further attempts on the Legislature. From that moment all has become quiet. . . .[15]

Jefferson felt that his plan was an immediate success. On January 13, 1803, before Monroe had embarked for France, he noted that:

> The measure has already silenced the federalists here. Congress will no longer be agitated by them; and the country will become calm as fast as the information extends over it.[16]

## Congressional Scrutiny and Support

Jefferson's problems with the Western settlers were not his only public opinion difficulties. His annual message to Congress on December 15, 1802, had been what Hamilton dubbed a "lullaby message."[17] Jefferson had tried to soft pedal the impending problems with France so that Congress, for partisan reasons or out of conviction, would not embarrass the negotiations and force his hand. Although he had pleaded many times that the people must have full access to information and that Congress must be allowed full debating rights on foreign affairs, Jefferson now preferred to proceed in secrecy. In spite of his promise to Congress a year earlier that: "nothing shall be wanting on my part to inform as far as in my power the legislative judgment," he deliberately withheld information from Congress to allow himself greater freedom of action, even though his party enjoyed comfortable majorities in both houses.[18] He passed over the Louisiana problem with the single, innocuous comment that the cession, if carried into effect will

> . . . make a change in the aspect of our foreign relations which will doubtless have just weight in any deliberations of the Legislature connected with that subject.[19]

[14]Ford, *Works*, vol. 10, p. 71.
[15]Lipscomb, vol. 10, p. 353.
[16]Lipscomb, vol. 10, p. 345.
[17]Randall, vol. 3, p. 27.
[18]James D. Richardson, *Messages and Papers of the Presidents*, vol. 1, New York: Bureau of National Literature, 1917, pp. 331–332 (First Annual Message, December 8, 1801). There were 69 Republicans and 36 Federalists in the House and 18 Republicans and 14 Federalists in the Senate.
[19]Richardson, vol. 1, p. 343 (Second Annual Message, December 15, 1802).

So eager was he to avoid a discussion of foreign policy, that he had not even mentioned to his Cabinet the possibility of including foreign affairs at length in his address to Congress and the nation. Ordinarily he always indicated the areas of greatest concern and then asked his Cabinet for suggestions for the message.

But his precautions were to no avail. His own party, under the leadership of John Randolph of Roanoke, asked for the documents pertaining to the closure of the Mississippi and the right of American deposit at New Orleans. Five days later Jefferson sent the papers.[20] Even this constituted a deliberate delay, because the papers were at hand and contained nothing that was not already familiar to most congressmen. Much of it had previously appeared in the press. The House then went into secret session and promptly vindicated Jefferson's conduct in the whole affair by a vote of 50 to 25. Giving him *carte blanche*, it declared that it was "relying, with perfect confidence, on the vigilance and wisdom of the Executive" and would "wait the issue of such measures as that department of the Government shall have pursued for asserting the rights and vindicating the injuries of the United States."[21] Undoubtedly, the House was influenced by the news that Spanish authorities had once more rescinded the closure of New Orleans. Two months later (on February 25, 1803) the Senate, after a lengthy and spirited debate, passed a resolution that also approved Jefferson's Western diplomacy and gave him full powers as well as money to use the armed forces if the "unauthorized" closure of New Orleans continued.[22]

Congress had thus put its weight officially behind the President. He could claim full support from the majority of the representatives of the people. However, congressional action had not been without difficulties. The Federalists in Congress, to embarrass Jefferson (at least that is what he thought), had passed a number of very belligerent resolutions designed to increase pro-war sentiments. They had declared that the right of deposit was an undoubted right of United States citizens; that Spain's closure of the Mississippi was an act of aggression hostile to the honor and interests of the United States; that 50,000 militia should be called out immediately to fight for the right of deposit, and $5,000,000 should be appropriated for the expedition, if necessary. Spain, the Federalists claimed, was insulting the United States everywhere:

> They insult our national flag upon every sea where they meet it; they seize our merchantmen; they plunder our merchants of their property;

[20]*Annals,* 7th Congress, 2d session, p. 281; *American State Papers, Foreign Relations,* vol. 2, Washington: Gales and Seaton, 1832, p. 469.

[21]*Annals,* 7th Congress, 2d session, pp. 339–342.

[22]*Annals,* 7th Congress, 2d session, pp. 255–256.

they abuse our seamen; shackle them with chains, and consign them to dungeons; and yet honorable gentlemen cry out peace, peace, when there is no peace. If this be peace, God give us war![23]

Jefferson granted that Westerners had valid reasons for pressuring for war. "In the western country it is natural, and grounded on honest motives." But things were different in the East, especially when Federalists were involved:

> In the sea ports, it proceeds from a desire for war which increases the mercantile lottery; in the Federalists generally, and especially those of Congress the object is to force us into war if possible, in order to derange our finances, or if this cannot be done, to attach the western country to them, as their best friends, and thus get again into power.[24]

In fact, at times he even charged that Western agitation was largely inspired by Federalists whose "inflammatory proceedings" were designed to instigate "the Western country to force on a war between us and the owners of New Orleans."[25] This was not true, but Jefferson habitually impugned the motives and wisdom of the opposition. One had to be wicked, stupid, or misguided to fail to see the proper policy course. Yet he himself had acknowledged the gravity of the situation when he claimed that the future destinies of our country hang on the event of this negotiation. . . ."[26] He described "the use of the Mississippi so indispensable, that we cannot hesitate one moment to hazard our existence for its maintenance."[27] But now he felt pressured by the public and he disliked it. Still, he responded to the pressure. Pushed by Westerners, harried by Federalists, and pulled by his own desires for westward expansion of the Union, he redoubled his efforts for a peaceful diplomatic solution to the problem.[28]

[23]*Annals*, 7th Congress, 2d session, p. 110.

[24]Ford, *Works*, vol. 9, p. 418. Also see *Annals*, 7th Congress, 2d session, p. 224.

[25]Schachner, vol. 2, p. 727. Also see letter to Monroe, January 1803 (Ford, *Works*, vol. 9, pp. 416–417). Republicans in Congress contended that three-fourths of the people opposed war (*Annals*, 7th Congress, 2d session, pp. 133–135).

[26]Ford, *Works*, vol. 9, p. 443.

[27]Ford, *Works*. vol. 9, p. 437.

[28]Adams claims that public clamor in the West made Jefferson think that his alternatives were the purchase of Louisiana or war. This is the story that General Smith of Maryland, at Jefferson's behest, told a secret session of Congress (January 11, 1803) when he asked for a $2,000,000 appropriation for the purchase. Henry Adams, *History of the United States*, book 1. New York: Albert and Charles Boni, 1930, pp. 432–433.

## Jefferson's Contingency Plans

What was it that the President hoped to obtain through the negotiations in France? In the instructions to Livingston and Monroe[29] prepared in the wake of Cabinet conferences, but apparently based primarily on Jefferson's own ideas,[30] Jefferson suggested that his emissaries should buy the Southern territory east of the Mississippi River. The river as such should be free for navigation from its source to its mouth to nationals of both countries. If France was unwilling to part with that much territory, or was unable to convey title to that much, the envoys were to try to purchase all or part of the Island of New Orleans. In addition they were then to seek the rights of deposit and free navigation of all rivers emptying into the Gulf of Mexico along its northern shore. Failing this minimum request, which would provide the vital access to the ocean, the envoys were to try a game of force; they were to talk to the British representatives in Paris about the possibility of an alliance with Britain. In the impending war between Britain and France, Louisiana would be a prize. The threat of such an alliance, or the fact if that became necessary, was intended to convince the French that the United States would seek by force what it could not obtain by negotiations. It is not clear whether Jefferson really intended to use force if the French proved intransigent. He had confided to Livingston that public pressure was irresistible:

> Such, indeed, has been the impulse given to the public mind by these events [debates in Western legislatures and in the press], that every branch of the Government has felt the obligation of taking the measures most likely, not only to re-establish our present rights, but to promote arrangements by which they may be enlarged, and more effectually secured.[31]

Failure of the negotiations could only spell war:

> If we cannot by a purchase of the country insure to ourselves a course of perpetual peace and friendship with all nations, then as war cannot be distant, it behooves us immediately to be preparing for that course. . . .[32]

But Jefferson did not intend to use force immediately. To his diary he confided: "Leave us in peace till Congress meets, and prevent war till Spring."[33]

[29]*American State Papers, Foreign Relations,* vol. 2, pp. 540–544. The instructions were signed by Madison (March 2, 1803).

[30]Randall contends that "the policy which secured the purchase of Louisiana was purely original" with the President. "Not a distant hint—not even an analogous idea—was received from any other quarter." (Randall, vol. 3, p. 50.)

[31]*American State Papers, Foreign Relations,* vol. 2, p. 529.

[32]Ford, *Writings,* vol. 8, p. 191.

[33]Ford, *Works,* vol. 1, p. 372.

In June of 1803 startling news reached Washington. Instead of scaling down American demands as Jefferson had feared, Napoleon had offered the whole vastness of Louisiana to the United States. Reverses in the French campaigns in the island of Santo Domingo and danger of renewed war with Britain had convinced him that his hold on Louisiana was precarious, and without Santo Domingo not very profitable for France. If he tried to hold on to Louisiana he might very likely lose it. Why not then offer it to the Americans for a price? Even the price was fantastically reasonable—$16,000,000 for the entire area. Small wonder that the American ministers jumped at the bargain, albeit with trepidations.

The news that the American envoys had agreed to purchase the entire Louisiana territory, as well as New Orleans, astounded Jefferson. "He had offered to buy an island for a dockyard and a place of deposit. He was offered a magnificent domain."[34] Yet he was not completely overjoyed. He realized, of course, the tremendous bargain that the United States had struck. But, at the same time, he realized some of the many difficulties that lay in his way in bringing the bargain to fruition. He dealt with them, not by an appeal to the country or consultation with a wide circle of advisors, but by individual decision and consultation with the Cabinet.

He summoned the Cabinet in mid-July to discuss the various problems raised by the French offer. The Cabinet agreed on the main decisions, that the purchase should be made and Congress summoned for October 17, for a special session, to ratify the decision, and to pass implementing legislation.[35] Since the transfer documents had to be signed by October 30, this would leave Congress a scant two weeks to debate—a short enough period, Jefferson hoped, to force speedy action without too much time for deliberation. What he wanted was a rubber stamp for his decisions, not a debilitating debate that might detract from the magnificent bargain. As in the embargo policy a few years later: "He treated Congress as he treated the nation, expecting unquestioning obedience based on faith in him as President."[36]

Objections to the purchase could be raised along several lines. In the first place, and least worrisome of all to Jefferson, there was the fact that the Spanish authorities were objecting to the American purchase of the Louisiana territory. Their objections were well-grounded. The treaty by which they had ceded Louisiana to the French specified that the area was

---

[34]McMaster, vol. 1, p. 628.

[35]Ford, *Works*, vol. 1, pp. 373–375.

[36]Levy, pp. 95–96. Another instance in which the summoning of Congress was deliberately delayed to reduce the time for debate occurred during the Chesapeake-Leopard affair of 1803. The attack took place on June 25, but Congress was not summoned until October 26, ostensibly because Washington's summer climate was too oppressive.

not to be ceded to any other power without the consent of the Spanish King. Napoleon's action was in direct conflict with the agreed stipulation.

Should the United States proceed with the deal and take over the territory, the Spaniards threatened the possibility of war. However, Jefferson deemed the Spaniards too weak to carry out any threats. Nevertheless, he mobilized militia contingents in Ohio, Kentucky, and Tennessee to be ready for possible trouble. He felt certain that the public would support this step. Much more troublesome were the constitutional and political objections to the purchase. Jefferson was convinced that the Constitution did not authorize him to purchase additional territory that would become a part of the Union. Even though his Treasury Secretary, Albert Gallatin, assured him that he possessed the right to make the purchase, he concurred with his Attorney General, Levi Lincoln, who shared his doubts about the constitutionality of the acquisition. But there was a way around these constitutional objections. Jefferson believed that a constitutional amendment could cure the legal defects in the transaction. Other than swallowing his own objections to broadening the powers of the national government, he foresaw little difficulty in securing adoption of such an amendment.

Politically, a number of important issues were raised by the purchase— most of them of much greater concern and portent to the Federalists, however, than to the Republicans. Federalists would argue that a doubling of the territory of the Union would put the power of their own section permanently into eclipse. The influence, and with it the prosperity of New England, would be gone forever. The United States would be dominated by the Virginia dynasties and by the Westerners. The Federalists might threaten that New England would leave the Union. Even though Jefferson anticipated that the purchase would raise the spectre of secession again, he was not seriously worried. These were partisan attacks involving a minority. Aside from verbal sparring they would cause no real difficulties with the public.

He was more concerned with the financial part of the transaction. To a President who had talked of "the emancipation of our posterity from that mortal canker," the national debt, the task of raising enough money to pay an indebtedness of $16,000,000 was embarrassing.[37] He feared that Congress, including members of his own party, would hold his past preachments about governmental economy up to him. There might be resistance to paying the purchase price.

## We Shall Not Be Disavowed

But after consultation with members of his Cabinet he threw all hesitation to the wind. If he presented the country with a *fait accompli*, the

[37]Richardson, vol. 1, p. 345 (Second Annual Message, December 15, 1802).

people would agree to whatever implementing steps were necessary. The prize was too great to be a stickler for detail. The challenge was too vast to risk losing it on the shoals of public debate. As he advised Congress:

> The Constitution has made no provision for our holding foreign territory, still less for incorporating foreign nations into our Union. The executive in seizing the fugitive occurrence which so much advances the good of their country, have done an act beyond the Constitution. The Legislature in casting behind them metaphysical subtleties, and risking themselves like faithful servants, must ratify and pay for it, and throw themselves on their country for doing for them unauthorized what we know they would have done for themselves had they been in a situation to do it. It is the case of a guardian, investing the money of his ward in purchasing an important adjacent territory; and saying to him when of age, I did this for your good; I pretend no right to bind you: you may disavow me, and I must get out of the scrape as I can: I thought it my duty to risk myself for you.[38]

After the deed was done, one would admit that it had been *ultra vires* and throw oneself onto the mercy of the country. He felt that ". . . we shall not be disavowed by the nation, and their active indemnity will confirm and not weaken the Constitution, by more strongly marking out its lines."[39]

These were not novel sentiments for Jefferson. He had expressed similar views earlier, using somewhat different reasoning. When President Washington had asked him in 1793 whether the treaties with France were binding on the United States and would force the United States to come to the assistance of France, even to its own detriment, Jefferson had answered: ". . . If performance becomes *self-destructive* to the party, the law of self-preservation overrules the laws of obligation in others."[40] He claimed that "the head and the heart of every rational and honest man" were "the true fountain of evidence" for his theories. "He will never read there the permission to annul his obligations for a time, or forever, whenever they become dangerous, useless, or disagreeable. . . ."

> To ignore one's obligations, or legal or political scruples, the danger must be imminent and the degree great. Of these, nations are to be judges for themselves.

He concluded:

> But the tribunal of our consciences remains, and that also of the opinion of the world. These will revise a sentence we pass in our own

[38]Lipscomb, vol. 10, p. 411 (Letter to Senator Breckinridge, August 12, 1803).
[39]Lipscomb, vol. 10, p. 411.
[40]Lipscomb, vol. 3, p. 228.

case, and as we respect these, we must see that in judging ourselves we
have honestly done the part of the impartial and rigorous judges.[41]

Call this the law of expediency if you will. It is also the law by which
great deeds are done, and the philosophy shared by great statesmen.[42]

And so the decision was made, much in the manner in which a kindly,
absolute monarch would have made it, surrounded by a bevy of admiring
yes-men advisors. Circumstances had thrust within reach of the President
an objective that to him furthered the national interest, and he seized it
with few qualms. To him, it also seemed that all right-thinking people in
the country would be behind his decision and that the opposition would
be largely partisan and inconsequential.

## Navigating Past Congressional Shoals

His next job would be to overcome the congressional hurdle. This is
what he considered Congress primarily, not a forum for discussion and
airing of the viewpoints of the general public, but an arena of politics
where· opponents try to obstruct the government while the friends of the
Administration try to carry through its program.[43] Given this view, the
primary task was to scale the hurdle as easily as possible. He hoped that
a short discussion period would do the trick:

> . . . It will be desirable for Congress to do what is necessary *in silence*.
> I find but one opinion as to the necessity of shutting up the country for
> some time.[44]

Foreign events made it especially important to minimize congressional
discussion. News had come from France that Napoleon had second thoughts
about the sale of the territory. If Congress would raise too many objections, or if there should be a delay in meeting the ratification date, it
was quite possible that the unpredictable Corsican would withdraw his
offer. This, Jefferson did not want to risk. Congress must do what needs

[41]Lipscomb, vol. 3, pp. 228–229.

[42]Also note his rationalization to John Adams when he suggested an agreement with other European powers for joint action against the Barbary pirates:
"I know it goes beyond our powers, and beyond the powers of Congress too;
but it is so evidently for the good of all the States, that I should not be
afraid to risk myself on it. . . ." (Lipscomb, vol. 10, p. 42.) Also see his
letter to J. Calvin (Lipscomb, vol. 12, p. 418).

[43]Selection by a congressional caucus and prior service in Congress meant that
the President could count on having some reliable supporters in Congress. However, there was little party discipline and aversion to submit to executive guidance. See James S. Young, *The Washington Community, 1800–1828.* New
York: Columbia University Press, 1966, pp. 162–163.

[44]Lipscomb, vol. 10, p. 417 (Letter to Levi Lincoln, August 1803).

to be done "with as little debate as possible, and particularly so far as respects the constitutional difficulty."[45]

In his special message to Congress in which he urged ratification of the Louisiana Treaty, Jefferson did not mention anything about the constitutional qualms he had. It would be dangerous to do this under the circumstances. Besides, his friends did not seem to share his objections. Tongue in cheek he had conceded, "If, however, our friends shall think differently, certainly I shall acquiesce with satisfaction. . . ."[46] He had urged his supporters in Congress, in advance of the session, to ignore the constitutional issues and explained to them the reasons for this precaution.[47] However, he was unable to make this point stick. The constitutional issues were discussed fully in Congress. Republicans followed their Chief's lead largely and blinked their eyes at the difficulties. As the Federalists had done when they were in power, the Republicans now were ready and willing to sign on the dotted line with not many questions asked. Senator John Taylor of Virginia admitted that the treaty was "a violation of the constitution." But, borrowing Jefferson's phraseology, he pleaded: "I will, like an attorney who exceeds the authority delegated to him by his client, vote to ratify it, and then throw myself on the people for pardon."[48] It was the Federalists' turn now, in typical opposition style, to raise every possible issue to deter the action of the party in power. But the final vote along party lines sustained the Administration. Three days after the opening of the session, the Senate ratified the treaty by a 24–7 vote. The House took four days for its stamp of approval. All the while,

> Jefferson was following the proceeding with the keenest interest and anxiety. Overtly, he could do nothing; but he tried to hold the sagging lines intact, and sought indirectly to bolster the faithful and overcome the recalcitrants.[49]

By October 28, congressional action on the Louisiana Purchase was completed. Less than two months later, on December 2, 1803, the French Tricolor, after flying over the territory a mere twenty days, was lowered once more to make way for the "Stars and Stripes Forever."

One of the most momentous decisions in American history had been made, a decision often likened to the adoption of the Constitution and to the Declaration of Independence. What role did public opinion play?.

[45]Ford, vol. 10, p. 10 (Letter to Nicholas, September 1803).

[46]Lipscomb, vol. 10, p. 420 (Letter to Nicholas, September 1803).

[47]Jefferson was the first President to select certain members of Congress as his agents to prepare the ground for his program. Ralph V. Harlow, *The History of Legislative Methods in the Period Before 1825*. New Haven: Yale University Press, 1917, pp. 175–177, 192. See also Young, pp. 128–129.

[48]Schachner, vol. 2, pp. 750–751.

[49]Schachner, vol. 2, p. 752.

How much did Jefferson, the man of the people, the apostle of free policy choice for the masses, consult the public in this fateful venture?

## The President's Advisors

The record shows that it was essentially a one-man show, played behind curtains of secrecy. Perhaps a "three-ring performance" would be a better image. As Jefferson described the technique:

> Our government, although, in theory, subject to be directed by the unadvised will of the President, is, and from its origin has been, a very different thing in practice. . . . All matters of importance or difficulty are submitted to all the heads of departments comprising the cabinet; sometimes by the President's consulting them separately and successively as they happen to call on him; but in the gravest cases by calling them together, discussing the subject maturely, and finally taking the vote, on which the President counts himself but as one: so that in all important cases the Executive is, in fact, a Directory, which certainly the President might control, but of this there was never an example either in the first or the present administration.[50]

Although it was Jefferson's conception of government that he had the power to make foreign policy decisions unaided, he felt bound by tradition and his own inclinations to consult with the Cabinet on all occasions. He had instructed them that all communications to and from them were to pass across his desk, giving him a chance to alter the course of action if necessary. While he occasionally consulted with individual Cabinet members, especially in matters of particular interest to their department, in all serious matters (even in a crisis like the peace-time attack on the American frigate *Chesapeake* when the Cabinet could not meet for over a week) he delayed action until all had been heard from.[51] This did not necessarily mean that he would always take their advice or agree with their appraisal of public reaction to present and future policies. However, there are many instances on record in which he changed his opinion in the light of Cabinet discussion, or when he altered the methods which he had selected to accomplish his objectives.[52]

There were five members in the Cabinet. James Madison who held the State Department post and Albert Gallatin, head of the Treasury Department, were by all odds the outstanding members. By native ability, by

[50]Schachner, vol. 2, p. 842.

[51]McMaster, vol. 3, p. 262.

[52]For notes on what transpired, see various notations throughout his *Anas*. Henry Adams, ed., *The Writings of Albert Gallatin*, vol. 1. Philadelphia: J. B. Lippincott, 1789, p. 84.

experience, and by their closeness in thought to Jefferson's own views they earned their position as his prime advisors. Levi Lincoln, a Massachusetts lawyer who had served for a time in Congress, became Jefferson's Attorney General. Since there was relatively little work for him to do he did not reside in Washington, and his participation in Cabinet decisions was minimal. For the War Department Jefferson had picked another New Englander, Henry Dearborn of Maine. Henry Adams in his history of the Jefferson Administration comments about Dearborn and Lincoln:

> Neither Dearborn nor Lincoln was so strong, either in political or social connections or in force of character, as greatly to affect the course of the Cabinet, and both were too honest to thwart it.[53]

The last member of the Cabinet, and the least noteworthy, was Secretary of the Navy Robert Smith of Maryland. He had taken the job, as a reluctant choice, after several other candidates had refused to serve in a post that was marked for near-extinction. Since he was to preside over the dissolution of a defense force that Jefferson considered unnecessary and a danger to the Republic, Jefferson had not hesitated to pick a man whose qualifications for the position were second-rate. His performance matched the qualifications. This left Madison and Gallatin as the chief lights of the Cabinet. Since both were fully loyal to their chief, admiring his qualities and his decisions and sharing many of his predilections and political views, their advice, on most occasions, went along the same lines as Jefferson would have chosen anyway. For this reason it was not difficult for him to claim that the political decisions made by his administration were, in general, decisions fully supported by the entire Cabinet.[54]

Jefferson also deemed it good politics to take congressional leaders into his confidence, although he did not consider it a duty to seek their advice. He made it a practice to dine regularly with small groups of congressional leaders of his own party, as well as that of the opposition. He never mixed the two. In his own party he would meet with men such as William Giles of Virginia, John Randolph of Roanoke, Samuel Smith and Joseph H. Nicholson of Maryland, as well as the Speaker of the House, the able but not too bright Carolinian, Nathaniel Macon. Senate leaders who enjoyed his confidence were John Breckinridge of Kentucky, Dewitt Clinton of New York, and James Jackson of Georgia. He would summon these leaders to give them a confidential preview of political events and solicit their support in getting his measures through Congress. In January of 1803, to give him the financial freedom to negotiate for purchase of territory from France, he took a few congressional leaders into his confidence. One of them was Samuel Smith of Maryland who was in-

---

[53]Adams, *History*, Book 1, p. 220.
[54]Randall, vol. 2, p. 655.

structed on how to engineer the necessary votes for the required sum. When the Smith resolution for granting the appropriation was referred to a committee headed by Joseph H. Nicholson, the committee was privately informed what the real purpose of the appropriation was.[55]

On the whole, Jefferson did not trust members of Congress too highly. He feared that they would not be able to keep a secret and he did not believe in their discretion. Hence, a news blackout seemed advisable:

> Were the members of that body [Congress] to come together while the excitement was at its height, the consequences might be serious. It would, indeed, be hard to prevent a declaration of war, or at least some act of defiance that would hopelessly embarrass the tame and peaceful negotiation soon to begin. . . .[56]

This is the way McMaster describes Jefferson's reaction to the Congress, albeit on a different occasion (the British assault on the *Chesapeake*). Jefferson's sentiments were the same throughout the Louisiana negotiations, however.

So were the sentiments of Congress, especially the opposition. Representative Barent Gardenier of New York gave eloquent voice to congressional disappointment during foreign policy debates on Jefferson's embargo policies:

> Darkness and mystery overshadow this House and this whole nation. We know nothing, we are permitted to know nothing. We sit here as mere automata; we legislate without knowing, nay, sir, without wishing to know, why or wherefore. We are told what we are to do, and . . . do it. . . . Sir, the gentlemen of this House . . . are disposed to do all that men can do for their country. But we wish to know what we are doing—the tendency of the measures we are called upon to adopt. If the motives and the principles of the Administration are honest and patriotic, we would support them with a fervor which none could surpass. But, sir, we are kept in total darkness. We are . . . execrated because we do not approve of measures the origin and tendency of which are carefully concealed from us! We are denounced because we have no confidence in the Executive, at the moment the Executive refuses to discover to us—even this House, nay, sir, this nation, its actual condition.[57]

Opposition leaders who were wined and dined by the President included James Bayard of Delaware and Roger Griswold and Samuel Dana, both of Connecticut. On the Senate side there was Gouverneur Morris of

[55]*Annals*, 7th Congress, 2d session, pp. 367, 370–374.

[56]McMaster, vol. 3, p. 263.

[57]*Annals of Congress*, 10th Congress, 1st session, pp. 1655–1657, February 20, 1808. Also see *Annals of Congress*, 7th Congress, 2d session, pp. 315–368 for expressions of disappointment about presidential secretiveness with regard to the Louisiana policy.

New York, Jeremiah Mason of Massachusetts, and James Hillhouse of Connecticut. Jefferson apparently hoped to learn about the feelings and intentions of his congressional opposition from these leaders and may have had some expectations of swaying their opinions. But social lobbying of the opposition was a dubious success:

> Jefferson might just as well have saved his assiduous attentions, for he never converted—except for a very few—the Federalist leaders he wooed with food, drink and flattering conversation.[58]

In addition to congressional leaders, Jefferson at times consulted with close personal friends or important personages who had come to his attention. There is no evidence that he relied heavily on their advice. In the Louisiana affair Dupont de Némours was one of these contacts. The ex-Frenchman, somewhat in the manner of Dr. Logan, had offered his services to smooth negotiations between his former fatherland and his newly adopted country. He had gotten in touch with Jefferson prior to departing for France in 1802, and Jefferson had availed himself of his offer by entrusting him with a number of letters for the American delegation in France. In addition, Jefferson had informed Dupont of the state of negotiations in hopes that the information would be passed on to the French authorities. He had also tried to impress Dupont with the seriousness of the Jefferson Administration in considering war and an alliance with Britain in case France would not come to terms. He hoped that these threats would be relayed to Napoleon and, coming from a person of Dupont's station who had been in direct contact with the President, would carry considerable weight. However, when Dupont considered the instructions excessively harsh and communicated alternative proposals to the President, Jefferson paid little heed to them. Apparently Dupont, like most outsiders, was for Jefferson more a tool of communication, rather than a trusted advisor.

Jefferson also kept in close touch with the leading American diplomats in Europe. Many of the instructions issued to Livingston and to the American ministries were drafted by the President. He read the replies sent by the ministers with great interest and attention. Naturally with his own long experience in the diplomatic service he considered himself an expert in interpreting the events which were going on abroad. He did not deem it necessary to have these events interpreted for him by anyone else, not even his Secretary of State. When he wrote about his impressions of po-

---

[58]Schachner, vol. 2, p. 723. Senator Plumer cites the nomination of William C. C. Claiborne as Governor of Louisiana Territory as one example where presidential dinners silenced opposition within his own party to a man generally deemed unqualified. Everett S. Brown, ed., *William Plumer's Memorandum of Proceedings in the United States Senate, 1803–1807*. New York: Macmillan, 1923, pp. 220–221.

litical events in Europe it was generally in the first person. The impressions were his own thoughts, rather than a repetition of the views of his ministers. In fact, he frequently took issue with the interpretation placed on events by his European representatives.

## A Consensus Seeker

When one tries to discern the criteria by which Jefferson selected the limited number of people whose advice he considered in foreign affairs, one is forced to the conclusion that personal congeniality was the guiding light. Jefferson looked for ability, but beyond this, he wanted advisors who were deferential to him and with whom he could feel personally comfortable. He apparently did not weigh the abilities of his advisors in terms of communicating with the public or in terms of expressing public opinion to him. However, he knew that Madison was facile with his pen; in appraising his qualifications, this had some weight. Also, when he picked Monroe for the mission to France he stressed the fact that Monroe was popular with the people. Such emphasis was an exception made necessary by the fact that the primary purpose for sending Monroe was to pacify the western areas. Monroe's diplomatic qualifications, in this instance, were strictly secondary.

There was no attempt to pick advisors from the opposition party aside from the informal advice tendered to the President when he entertained the leaders of his congressional opposition. In fact, it seemed to Jefferson that public positions should go to members of his own party and that opposition views, being obviously misguided or ill-intentioned, did not deserve formal representation within the government.

However, although his own tastes were for politics in the Southern style, he did have two New England men and one Pennsylvanian in his Cabinet. Whether this was an attempt to strike a sectional balance within the Cabinet is not certain. Jefferson was very eager to have nationwide approval and watched election returns carefully, even in traditional Federalist territory. For instance, he noted that in the spring of 1803 ". . . the spirit of Republicanism . . . repossessed the whole mass of our country from Connecticut southwardly and westwardly." Even in New Hampshire, Massachusetts and Connecticut ". . . we are gaining steadily and sensibly." Except for a few remnants in the northeast and southwest, he prognosticated that the opposition was "dead and buried, and no day of resurrection will ever dawn upon that. . . ."[59] Among other things, this meant to him that his past policies had nationwide public approval. He need not fear difficulties from the public, except in isolated pockets of resistance, in car-

[59]Randall, vol. 3, pp. 68–69 (Letter to Governor Claiborne, May 24, 1803).

rying out the policies of the immediate future. Historian Schachner speaks of his "almost pathetic yearning" for

> . . . a solid backing of approval for his policies and an end to sniping and criticism of himself as man and President. He was like the princess in the fairy tale—the tiniest pea underneath the sevenfold featherbeds was sufficient to disturb his slumbers and harrass his thoughts.[60]

For such a man, and an astute politician, it would have been only natural to discern the broader support and other political advantages that he might reap from giving his Cabinet a national complexion.

## Praise and Opposition Dispassionately Viewed

Jefferson's keen awareness of the power of an aroused public opinion and his occasional efforts to arouse, subdue, or channel it, represent the scope of his accommodation to public opinion in the rough and tumble of political life. Regardless of his theories of popular competence and control, he did not turn to the general public for counsel and guidance in policy formulation. He did not give them the facts they needed to form intelligent opinions, nor did he explain the reasons behind his policies. He rarely appealed to them for support of his policies or for tolerance and forbearance with unexplained sacrifices and silences. Rather, using satisfying circular logic, he assumed that the people wanted "right" policies, and since his policies met that criterion they had popular approval *ipso facto*. This does not mean that he lacked interest in what the people were saying whenever public opinions seemed to have little influence on policy execution.

Desirous to please and sensitive to praise and criticism alike, he eagerly scanned all expressions of public approval or disapproval. Aside from the initial pressure to act to secure an outlet to the sea for Western commerce, there had been little effective agitation in the Louisiana affair. A few letters and memorials to state legislatures and to the national government, and a few laudatory comments in the press constituted the sum total of direct approbation.

The President had kept the negotiations quiet enough to allay public fears. Where fear left off, unconcern and even apathy took over. Jefferson did not complain about public inactivity. He was pleased that the reports he received from public officials in the West, such as Governor Claiborne and General Wilkinson, supported his impression that the people, in general, were quiet.

[60]Schachner, vol. 2, p. 708.

On the negative side there were hostile accounts in the press. But these reports did not bother him as expressions of public opinion. He took them to be mainly partisan attacks on himself when they were not favorable. As he had written General Kosciusko, the Polish war hero, a year before the purchase:

> The people are nearly all united. Their quondam leaders, infuriated with the sense of their impotence, will soon be seen or heard only in the newspapers, which serve as chimneys to carry off noxious vapors and smoke. . . .[61]

And even these noxious vapors were not very poisonous. The expenditure of $16,000,000 for a vast wilderness had aroused the hostile imagination of Federalist editors. "The sale of a wilderness has not usually commanded a price so high," they had commented:

> Weigh it, and there will be four-hundred and thirty-three tons of solid silver. Load it into wagons, and there will be eight-hundred and sixty-six of them. Place the wagons in a line, giving two rods to each, and they will cover a distance of five and one-third miles. Hire a laborer to shovel it into the carts and, though he load sixteen each day, he will not finish the work in two months. Stack it up dollar on dollar, and, supposing nine to make an inch, the pile will be more than three miles high. It would load twenty-five sloops; it would pay an army of twenty-five thousand men forty shillings a week each for twenty-five years; it would, divided among the population of the country, give three dollars for each man, woman, and child.[62]

Although this was highly effective rhetoric that was sure to be read and repeated, Jefferson was no longer worried about the reaction to the cost of his acquisition. He had made arrangements for keeping other governmental expenditures at a new low and his Secretary of the Treasury had informed him that the funds could be made easily available. Besides, Congress had not blinked at the sum. That was assurance enough for him that raising the money would not cause problems with the public.

There also were press accounts that ridiculed the purchase as such. And well they might. Jefferson had bought a territory whose boundaries he did not know and whose interior was largely unexplored. He was keenly aware of this lack of knowledge and immediately upon the acquisition he had begun to study all available records, maps, books, and charts to gain some information about the nature of the new lands. But even with all his efforts his information was very sketchy. Some of it was obviously legend and when he passed it on to Congress as fact he laid himself wide open to the criticism that followed. Reports of a vast mountain of

[61]Richard Hildreth, *The History of the United States,* vol. 5. New York: Harper & Row, Publishers, 1880, p. 451.

[62]McMaster, vol. 2, p. 630.

salt, a thousand miles up the Missouri River, were greeted with scoffs and jeers. "Can the Mountain," one journal asked, "be Lot's wife?"

> What a dreadful glare it must make on a sunshiny day! . . . No trees on it? How strange! There ought to be a salt eagle to perch on the summit, and a salt mammoth to clamber up its side. The President, being a cautious philosopher, has surely been afraid to tell us all; he must have kept much back, else we should have seen some samples from that vale of hasty pudding and that lake of real old Irish usquebaugh that lies at the mountain's base. The stories told 14 years since about the Ohio country are now surpassed. The pumpkin-vines, the whoop snakes, the shoe-and-stocking tree of the Muskingum, are but "pepper-corns" beside the mountain of salt.[63]

While Jefferson winced at such attacks as painful personal slurs, he never once considered them reason enough to alter his policies in the slightest.

In the Louisiana affair it was easy to ignore contrary public opinion because the bulk of the country, including many Federalists, were obviously in accord with the President's actions. Election returns, which he watched so intently, showed that his party was gaining adherents and that the opposition party was not increasing its support. Action in Congress, with few exceptions, had given him comfortable majorities for his entire foreign policy program. He thus could claim that by accepted criteria of public opinion appraisal his program had the support of public opinion—at least in retrospect. For approval was assumed at the decision-making stage, without any effort to measure it. In fact, public discussion at the formative stages, as we have seen, was deliberately discouraged. The public came in when there was little left to do but the shouting—when it could comment, but do little to alter the facts.

Even when the public strongly opposed his policies, as in the embargo that closed down foreign trade a few years later, Jefferson felt that his own opinions, supported by the Cabinet, must prevail. He did not even try to explain his policies to the public or even to Congress beyond explaining that "advantages" could be expected from the embargo. He answered petitions with meaningless generalities, rather than point by point explanations. He was not willing to debate the merits of his policies with his questioners. If the people did not like the embargo, if they tried to evade

[63]McMaster, vol. 2, p. 632. Stories such as these appeared in the *Connecticut Courant,* August 10, 1803 and November 30, 1803; *The New England Repertory,* December 1803; *The Gazette of the United States,* December 23, 1803; *The Boston Gazette,* December 5 and December 29, 1803; *The Herald,* November 30, 1803; *The Spectator,* November 26, 1803; *The Independent Chronicle,* December 5, 1803; and *The National Aegis,* December 7, 1803. See also the *Columbian Centinel,* August 24, 1803, and *The New York Evening Post,* November 12, 1803.

it, and if their appointed officials resorted to subterfuge in order to get around the embargo, he thought that they must be forced to obey. He felt certain that they would see the wisdom of the policy even without presidential explanations and then give him the public support that was only temporarily withheld. About the attack of the British war ship *Leopard* on the American frigate *Chesapeake* in 1807, McMaster comments:

> Never had a more just cause for war been given to any people. Never had a people called more loudly for war. Never was an Administration less inclined to fight or an antagonist more ready to accept that issue.

Yet Jefferson stood his ground.

> . . . He well knew that such outbreaks of wrath were never lasting and that in a few weeks, if no new offense was committed, the brawlers would have begun to count the cost and would soon be as submissive as ever.[64]

Public support would come sooner or later, almost automatically. The inclination of the public to forgive and forget had been demonstrated with comforting regularity.

As stressed before, willingness to ignore public pressure does not mean that Jefferson was unaware of the fact that public desires may set limits to governmental action. He was keenly conscious of this fact. His attempts to manipulate public opinion by withholding inflammatory information, his initiation of the Monroe Mission as a sop to the Westerners to make them believe that their wishes were taken into consideration, and his stress in instructions to his representatives that they should mention to Napoleon the state of the public mind in the United States all show that he knew the power of public opinion in forcing the hand of the government. But his inclination was not to yield to these pressures if he disagreed with them, but to shape them in such a way as to gain support for what he desired to do.

In the Louisiana affair public support seemed so evident that Jefferson did not find it necessary to allude to it to justify his actions. There was no need to waste propaganda ammunition when the battle was already won. But on other occasions, especially when his party was still the minority party (out of government), he frequently stressed public support as justification of the rightness of his policy. At that time, too, he campaigned for public support by instructing his lieutenants to refute the claims of the Federalist Party. "For God's sake, tear them to pieces," or similar injunctions were his favorites. But when he judged the opposition to be weak and inconsequential—a judgment that he did not always make accurately —refutation seemed a waste of effort. Let the opposition die the ignominious, slow death of nonrecognition!

[64]McMaster, vol. 3, p. 262. Also see Claude Bowers, *Jefferson in Power.* Boston: Houghton Mifflin, 1936, pp. 428–432.

## On ne comprend pas français

There is, in Jefferson's feelings about the rights of the people, a curious blind spot about the rights of foreigners. His tender concern for mass wishes did not extend to the wishes of the people of European countries, nor to the people of the province that the United States was about to take over. In all of his writings about Louisiana there is never any concern expressed for the political desires of the people of that state. Jefferson may have shared the chauvinistic self-assurance that prompted Senator Robert Wright of Maryland to proclaim the joy of the people of Louisiana about their new American citizenship with the rhetorical question: "Can they be so unwise as to prefer being the colonists of a distant European Power, to being members of this immense Empire, with all the privileges of American citizens?"[65]

If one is to judge from the flowery expressions of delight of the leading citizens of New Orleans when the country was returned to France, there certainly was very little desire to exchange French citizenship for American citizenship. At this time, a petition addressed to Peter Clement Laussat, the French prefect at New Orleans, proclaimed that:

> France had rendered justice to our sentiments, in believing in the unalterable attachment which we have preserved for her. Thirty-four years of a foreign domination have not weakened in our hearts the sacred love of country, and we return to-day under her banner with as much joy as we had grief when we had to part from it. Happy the colonists of Louisiana who have lived long enough to be witnesses of this reunion . . . which satisfies their dearest wishes.[66]

The planters of Louisiana spoke of how the reunion

> . . . has given our souls the rapture of supreme felicity; it was the object of our most ardent desires. The old men repeat on all sides: "We may die now, we are French," and the young men: "The dawn of happiness is rising for us."[67]

With such ardent protestations of pro-French sentiments ringing in his ears, it is only natural that Laussat refused to believe that the territory had been surrendered by France to the United States:

> The news of the cession to the United States is an impudent and incredible falsehood, and it is only a canard put forth by the party which, at this time of elections and on the expiration of Jefferson's Presidency, has thought, by divulging this news suddenly, to assist the partisans of the President.[68]

[65]*Annals of Congress*, Eighth Congress, 1st session, p. 44.
[66]Fortier, vol. 2, p. 229.
[67]Fortier, vol. 2, p. 231.
[68]Fortier, vol. 2, pp. 234–235.

The people of Louisiana must have been equally as incredulous. Or were they? Sometimes it is exceedingly difficult to know which appraisal of public opinion to believe. Morales, the Spanish Intendant who surrendered Louisiana to the French, reported officially to his superior: "On November 30, at 12 o'clock, took place the transfer of the province. There was not a single demonstration of joy when the French flag was raised, and there were many tears when the Spanish flag was taken down."[69] Yet Governor William C. Claiborne informed President Jefferson that "the flag of our country was raised in this city amidst the acclamations of the inhabitants."[70]

## The Principle: Expediency

The student of the decision-making process in the Louisiana Purchase comes away with the distinct idea that Jefferson used a rule of thumb, rather than a set of principles, in determining how much attention to pay to public opinion. When it seemed necessary and possible to keep the public in the dark it did not matter how important the decisions were for the public welfare. It did not matter whether the facts were easy or difficult to understand. Jefferson would keep quiet and make his own decisions. By the same token, if public disclosures could not be helped, or if they could be used for an ulterior purpose, he would take the public into his confidence and then couch his consideration of the demands of the people into language that made it appear an act of principle, rather than convenience and expedience.

On balance, he seemed to lean toward secrecy. His annual messages to Congress are models of understatement in which the most serious matters were either glossed over entirely or passed off in an innocuous sentence. This was done at a time when his private correspondence and records of his private conversations indicated deep concern about the tremendous significance of the actions under consideration. Thus he could write to Livingston that the entire future of the United States depended upon the success of his negotiations, at the same time that he was almost completely silent about the negotiations in his official and unofficial communications with Congress. Nor did he make any effort to apprize the country of the events that were then in the making. Since rumors about the negotiations, many of them very close to the truth, were circulating throughout the country, he certainly would not have been disclosing secret facts if he had taken the public more into his confidence. But this was not his way. Despite his theories he acted in the tradition of his Federalist predecessors.

[69]Fortier, vol. 2, p. 238.
[70]Fortier, vol. 2, pp. 295–296.

As he frankly admitted, he considered himself the people's trustee who takes care of the affairs of his ward for the ward's best interests, with the full expectation that the ward will approve the action and stand behind it.

In the Louisiana Purchase, Jefferson's stance posed few problems. Little opposition forced itself on his attention. People in general seemed satisfied with the purchase. The Westerners and Southerners, who were most directly concerned with the addition of the new territory, were naturally pleased and not likely to send resolutions of opposition to the President. In fact, since political leaders felt that the opposition could safely be ignored, few resolutions of approval reached the halls of government. This is another sign that most of the resolutions that were sent to the White House and to the state legislatures originated with political leaders, rather than spontaneously with the mythical "average man." When the small group of recognized political leaders did not take the trouble of starting the resolutions, John Q. Citizen did nothing.

In the East, the visible effects of the purchase were nil. War with Spain had not materialized and the Spaniards, despite their threats, had not closed any of their European and colonial ports to American commerce. The spectre of increased taxes had not come true either. In fact, the country on the whole seemed more prosperous than ever before. Why, then, should the average citizen worry about constitutional technicalities or future adverse political consequences?

Such worries were largely left to the men in Congress, and they were debated there in full during Congressional sessions. But the outcome was a foregone conclusion. Jefferson could therefore ignore Congressional opposition safely, especially since it was not likely to bring forth a mass echo among the people. As previous election returns had shown him, he did not even have to worry about adverse electoral consequences of the Louisiana Purchase. In fact, if anything, the purchase improved the popularity of his party in the country. By lessening discontent in the West it had also lessened the chances of immediate secession of the Western states and had cut the foundations from under the Burr Conspiracy to take the Western states out of the Union.

## History's Verdict

In retrospect, one must agree with Jefferson's appraisal of the value of the Louisiana Purchase for the entire country and with the majority of the public who obviously approved of the transaction. They shared Laussat's vision of "The Nile of America, the Mississippi, which flows not through parched deserts of sand, but through the most extensive and the most fertile plains of the new world," which "will soon see its bosom darkened with a thousand ships belonging to all the nations of the earth, and mooring at the quays of another Alexandria."[71] Although the facts would turn out somewhat differently than the dream, the reality was even more fantastic than the vision. The fears and objections of the opposition, in so far as they were genuine and not motivated by narrow partisanship, did not materialize and were obviously invalid. The Purchase did not embroil the country in dangerous foreign complications. It did not increase its size to such a point that it could no longer be governed democratically. It did not bring about the sacrifice of the interest of the Eastern States to the clashing interest of the South and the West, nor did it deplete the population of the East. The debts incurred as a result of the purchase were easily paid off and the financial benefits derived by the country from the new territories more than made up for the outlay. One could indeed agree with Talleyrand's comment to Livingston: ". . . you have made a noble bargain for yourselves, and I suppose you will make the most of it."[72]

Yet one must not jump to the conclusion that the President's decision is always right. His batting average seems better than that of the public, as it ought to be considering that he is a professional in the conduct of foreign affairs. But even professionals make mistakes. It was the public that called the correct shots in the embargo policy when it refused to abide by the regulations and finally forced its abandonment. Who can tell with assurance when the public's voice is wiser than the decisions of the President? No one can, although many make that claim. Jefferson, like his predecessors and successors, chose to place the bets on himself.

[71]Fortier, vol. 2, p. 245.
[72]Adams, *History*, Book 2, p. 44.

# 7

# James Madison,
# Moderation Personified

And as a feast to which all the guests contribute is better than
a banquet furnished by a single man, so a multitude is a better
judge of many things than any individual. . . .

Again, the many are more incorruptible than the few; they
are like the greater quantity of water which is less easily corrupted than a little. The individual is liable to be overcome
by anger or by some other passion, and then his judgement
is necessarily perverted; but it is hardly to be supposed that
a great number of persons would all get into a passion and go
wrong at the same moment.

ARISTOTLE, *Politics*

Moderation is best, and to avoid all extremes.

PLUTARCH, *Lives*

# 7

## Handicaps for Leadership

". . . Jemmy Madison—oh, poor Jemmy!—He is but a withered little apple-john,"[1] so wrote Washington Irving in 1812 about our fourth President. Even to his friends and, later, his biographers, Madison's personality was perplexingly vague. He was a man who carefully concealed whatever emotions and private ideas he might have had. He rarely relaxed his guard, although he could, on occasion, be "a jovial and good humored companion full of anecdote. . . ."[2] We can see him physically but we can barely peer behind the façade. He "always appeared neat and genteel, and in the costume of a well-bred and tasty old-school gentleman." In his clothing he wore

> . . . never any other color than black, his coat being cut in what is termed dress-fashion; his breeches short, with buckles at the knees, black silk stockings, and shoes with strings . . . He wore powder on his hair. . . .[3]

"He was a little man with small features . . . occasionally lit up with a good-natured smile"[4] and "his small bright blue eyes would twinkle most wickedly when lighted up by some whimsical conception or association."[5]

What was the background of this small, impeccably dressed young man that would explain his political views and actions? Madison had the mixed heritage of the Virginia Piedmont gentry. His aristocratic tastes and inclinations were instilled in him early in life. His father was the owner of one of the most extensive plantations in the Piedmont country and the young Madison knew that he would inherit this estate. It would entail the responsibilities of acting as master of a large crew of servants, including many slaves, and as head of an extensive family. He would of necessity become a leader of men. The unquestioned obedience of his subordinates would give him a sense of his own superior judgment and the feeling of belonging to a natural aristocracy of talent, born to lead.

[1]Henry Adams, *History of the United States,* Book 1. New York: Albert and Charles Boni, 1930, p. 189.

[2]Irving Brant, *James Madison,* vol. 4. Indianapolis: The Bobbs-Merrill Co., 1956, p. 47. Brant claims that Madison's ribald humor embarrassed his editors and biographers, who suppressed it and made him appear a dry figure.

[3]Adams, Book 1, p. 189.

[4]Adams, Book 1, p. 190.

[5]Brant, vol. 4, p. 47.

On the other hand, there were strong democratic tendencies in the Piedmont region. Many of the Piedmont families were descendants of northern immigrants who had done well and acquired property, or descendants of poorer whites who had been forced out of the Tidewater region by the blue-blooded aristocracy. Such people were sufficiently close to the laboring classes to have a healthy respect for the common man. They resented many of the practices and laws, especially inheritance laws, of the Tidewater aristocrats. They were near enough to rugged frontier life to know that a man's worth had to be judged by what he could do, rather than by his ancestry.

It is to this mixed heritage that one can probably trace the marriage in Madison's personality of the aristocratic notion of *noblesse oblige* with the disdain for privilege and wealth, the praise of the virtues of the common man, with the attacks on his base nature. It is this mixture that may account for his lifelong stress on a balancing of conflicting forces to reach a golden mean. It explains his sense of duty to listen to the wishes of the people and his insistence that public demands, after they had been tempered through partisan debate, must pass through the purifying filter of the legislature and must then be condoned by the executive.

At age eighteen, Madison enrolled at Princeton University. He had always been deeply religious. His father, an Episcopalian vestryman, had engaged a clergyman of that faith, the Reverend Thomas Marten, to tutor his son prior to entry into college. Madison's mother had been a pious Quaker. With this background it was no surprise that the young Madison should major in subjects closely related to theology. He studied Hebrew, Greek, and ethics. So moralistic was he in demeanor, orientation, and even appearance, that one contemporary likened him to a Roman cardinal.[6] His black clothing heightened this impression. And there was something very sanctimonious about a young man who at twenty-one would admonish a classmate not

> to suffer those impertinent fops that abound in every city to divert you from your business and philosophical amusements. . . . You will make them respect and admire you more by showing your indignation at their follies, and by keeping them at a becoming distance.[7]

His biographers agree that there was little exuberance in Madison, a youth who liked neither sports nor games; who joined his fellow students in only one student club, a debating society; and who spent most nights studying. He was a young man who had but one love affair before he married at forty-three, and who enjoyed neither drink nor smoking to help him pass his lonely hours. Sidney H. Gay says that "he seems never to have been

[6]Adams, Book 1, p. 180.

[7]Sidney Howard Gay, *James Madison*. Cambridge: The Riverside Press, 1884, p. 26.

a young man."[8] And Gaillard Hunt adds that "he sowed no wild oats."[9]

In part, Madison's muted outlook on life may have been the consequence of physical infirmities. Madison was frail and frequently ill and fancied that he was not long for this world. In his early twenties, he wrote to a friend:

> I am too dull and infirm now to look out for extraordinary things in this world, for I think my sensations for many months have intimated to me not to expect a long or healthy life; though it may be better with me after some time; but I hardly expect it and therefore have little spirit or elasticity to set about anything that is difficult in acquiring and useless in possessing after one has exchanged time for eternity.[10]

If one did not expect to live long, one did not build a world for the future. Rather, a man at the edge of death lived his life in small increments, always ready to meet his maker. This type of outlook explains Madison's lack of zest and venturesomeness, the absence of grand plans for the future, the preoccupation with the immediate next step. Even his righteousness in small matters may spring from his fear for survival, although this could be a carping explanation. For he was righteous even when it hurt his career and his pocketbook. In 1777 he lost the election to the Virginia legislature because he refused to treat prospective voters with the customary punch and rum. At a later date he declined an increase in his legislative salary because he was opposed to legislatures voting themselves such increases. He would not even accept free stationery offered by the state to its Solons.

He lost his qualms only when he acted in a public capacity. But even though his public life spanned many decades in the legislative and executive branches—beginning with state public office in 1775, when he was only twenty-four and continuing with few breaks until he reached the presidency at age fifty-eight—the occasions when he shed the shackles of his restrictive conscience and personality were relatively rare. As Secretary of State he acquiesced in the purchase of Louisiana, despite the constitutional questionability, and as President he took parts of Florida with even slimmer legal claim. When adoption of the national constitution by the Virginia legislature was at stake, he scoffed at the idea that the framers had ever intended to deprive slave owners of their property, even though he himself had publicly and privately questioned the continued right to hold slaves.[11] And he openly defied the authority of the national government

[8]Gay, p. 26.

[9]Gaillard Hunt, *The Life of James Madison.* New York: Doubleday & Company, Inc., 1902, p. 23.

[10]Gay, p. 11.

[11]Gaillard Hunt, *The Writings of James Madison,* vol. 5. New York: G. P. Putnam's, 1910, p. 233. Future references to Hunt are to this work except when noted otherwise.

in the Virginia Resolutions of 1798, although earlier and later on he would deny the legality of such a position. "A character that seemed incapable of surprising the world by reckless ambition or lawless acts" could, at times, pay "surprisingly little regard to rules of consistency or caution . . . in pursuit of an object which seemed to him proper in itself."[12]

So here we have Madison: cautious, deliberate, thoughtful, modest, unobtrusive, not given to intemperate outbursts, yet occasionally venturesome —the sort of man who would fill his canvas of life with meticulous marks of the pen inked in black and white and shades of grey, rather than the daring strokes of the paint brush daubed in lustrous colors. And it was with the pen, rather than deeds or oratory, that he left his political creed for posterity.

## A Consistent View of Base Mankind

The most notable and systematic exposition of Madison's political thought is contained in the *Federalist* papers. Madison composed his contributions to these essays when he had nearly fifteen years of experience in government to his credit, and after he had had a refresher course in political theory and practice at the national constitutional convention with the brightest minds and keenest practitioners of the art of politics in attendance. He knew he was writing for an intelligent and critical audience, trying to sell to them ideas that he deemed essential to the survival of the new nation. Considering the time of his life and the importance of the occasion, one cannot doubt that these papers represent the essence of his mature political thinking. His moralistic personality would not have permitted him to prevaricate and deceive in the grand manner.

If more proof is required to show that the *Federalist* papers were not merely propaganda fulminations, one can find it in Madison's private correspondence. His letters throughout his life bear out his thoughts and philosophy with remarkable consistency. Madison himself remarked, near the close of his life, that "there were few, if any, of my contemporaries, thro' the long period, and varied scenes of my political life, to whom a mutability of opinions was less applicable, on the great Constitutional questions which have successively agitated the public mind."[13] The sage of Montpelier, divorced from the cares of public office, said little which does not fit in perfectly with the views of the young father of the constitution and the mature practitioner of politics in the presidential chair.  While

---

[12]Adams, Book 5, p. 310.

[13]Donald O. Dewey, *The Sage of Montpelier: James Madison's Constitutional and Political Thought, 1817–1836.* Chicago: University of Chicago, Ph.D. dissertation, 1960, p. 198.

not wholly devoid of flattery and moralizing, the thoughts expressed in the Federalist papers are evidently a remarkably true image of Madison's views of political behavior, fully intended to provide a workable plan of government, rather than merely a theoretical model.[14]

What were these views about the role that the opinions of the mass of the people could and should play in politics? Madison's thoughts were characterized by what Max Beloff calls "cautious realism and modified pessimism of analysis and prescription."[15] He sought not perfection, but the least imperfection, not the absolute good, but the least evil. When he spoke of the public whose political views must be heeded, he talked broadly about the opinions of "mankind." He spoke of the respect to which the views of each and every individual were entitled. But a belief in universal goodness and intelligence was not the reason. The reason, or reasons, were negative.

Mild-mannered Madison, appalled by mass violence he had witnessed from revolutionary days onward, shocked by land speculations, debtors' pressures, and steals from the public purse, feared and disdained the mass of common people. Human beings, he contended, are generally governed by base and selfish motives, by suspicion, jealousy, desire for aggrandizement, and disinclination to do more than is required by convenience or self-interest or exacted of them by force.[16] Selfishness was particularly pronounced in political affairs. Since it was the chief purpose of government to protect property, and inequalities in property were the chief source of disagreements among people, disputes about governmental policies were fought most vigorously and viciously. *Federalist* No. 37 describes the nature of political battles:

> The history of almost all the great counsels and consultations held among mankind for reconciling their discordant opinions, assuaging their mutual jealousies, and adjusting their respective interests, is a history of factions, contentions, and disappointments, and may be classed among the most dark and degraded pictures which display the infirmities and depravities of human character.[17]

Exceptions merely proved the rule.

> If, in a few scattered instances, a brighter aspect is presented, they serve only as exceptions to admonish us of the general truth; and by their

[14]Dewey attributes exceptional consistency to Madison's thoughts, based on consistency in goals. The goals: preservation of the Constitution and preservation of the federal union.

[15]Max Beloff, *Thomas Jefferson and American Democracy*. London: Hodder and Stoughton, 1948, p. LIII.

[16]Jonathan Elliot, *Debates in the Constitutional Convention*, vol. 2. Washington: Taylor and Maury, 1838, p. 199.

[17]Robert M. Hutchins, ed., "The Federalist" in *Great Books of the Western World*, vol. 43. Chicago: Encyclopedia Britannica, 1952, pp. 120–121.

lustre to darken the gloom of the adverse prospect to which they are contrasted.[18]

Moreover, selfishness was a trait of nations, as well as individuals. National actions, past and future, had to be interpreted in terms of economic motivations. Thus the objective of France's aid to the United States during the American Revolution "was not only the independence, but the commerce and gratitude of America; the commerce to render independence the more useful, the gratitude to render that commerce the more permanent."[19] Given this belief in an all-pervading economic motivation, it is not surprising that Madison should be a strong believer in the effectiveness of policies of economic coercion, such as embargoes and nonintercourse.

Even if property or the "pestilent effects of paper money"[20] did not undermine the confidence between man and man and the morals of the people, human nature was perverse and disputacious enough to embroil men in violent arguments for arguments' sake. "Where no substantial occasion presents itself, the most frivolous and fanciful distinctions have been sufficient to kindle their [men's] unfriendly passions and excite their most violent conflicts."[21]

But one must never seek the remedy for strife in general, and political strife in particular, in suppressing factions, "which are a natural offspring of Freedom"[22] or in denying the ability of people to govern themselves. The foibles of mankind were common to all men. If a choice had to be made between rule according to the whims of a chosen few or rule in tune with the opinions of the mass of people, the latter was infinitely preferable.

Madison explained this rather well in an article written for the *National Gazette* in 1792. He referred to two conflicting views of human nature, which provided the theoretical underpinnings for parties advocating differing views of government. "One of the divisions," condemned by Madison,

> consists of those, who from particular interest, from natural temper, or from habits of life, are more partial to the opulent than to the other classes of society; and having debauched themselves into a persuasion that mankind are incapable of governing themselves, it follows with them, of course, that government can be carried on only by the pageantry of rank, the influence of money and emoluments, and the terror of military force. Men of those sentiments must naturally wish to point the measures of government less to the interest of the many than of a few, and less to the reason of the many than to their weaknesses.[23]

[18]Hutchins, vol. 43, *Federalist* No. 37, pp. 120–121.
[19]Hunt, vol. 1, p. 296.
[20]Hutchins, vol. 43, *Federalist* No. 44, p. 144.
[21]Hutchins, vol. 43, *Federalist* No. 10, p. 50.
[22]Hunt, vol. 4, p. 124.
[23]Hunt, vol. 6, pp. 115–117.

In the views of these anti-republican aristocrats, the masses of men were slavish, dissentious, ignorant, greedy, and incapable of knowing their own interests, let alone the interests of the people as a whole. The other division, the one with which Madison aligned himself,

> consists of those who believing in the doctrine that mankind are capable of governing themselves, and hating hereditary power as an insult to the reason and an outrage to the rights of man, are naturally offended at every public measure that does not appeal to the understanding and to the general interest of the community, or that is not strictly conformable to the principles, and conducive to the preservation of republican government.[24]

Even in the Virginia ratifying convention in 1788, when Madison justified the restraining provisions of the new Virginia constitution by reference to the base nature of human beings, he proclaimed his faith in the public's ability to select their representatives reasonably and conscientiously.[25] With his typically cautious realism, Madison summed up the gist of his views of human character in the *Federalist:* "As there is a degree of depravity in mankind which requires a certain degree of circumspection and distrust, so there are other qualities in human nature which justify a certain portion of esteem and confidence."[26]

Madison believed that the foibles of mankind that impaired its judgment were equally prevalent in all classes. The socioeconomic elite were as corrupt and corruptible as the common people, if not more so. Only the small farmer, the darling of Jefferson's political philosophy, had a better chance than members of other occupations to be a solid pillar of the community. Madison set forth these ideas in a short essay on the "Republican Distribution of Citizens," which he wrote for the *National Gazette* in 1792. Like Jefferson, he argued that

> The class of citizens who provide at once their own food and their own raiment, may be viewed as the most truly independent and happy. They are more: they are the best basis of public liberty, and the strongest bulwark of public safety. It follows, that the greater the proportion of this class to the whole society, the more free, the more independent, and the more happy must be the society itself.[27]

Madison particularly "distrusted the proletarian masses of large cities, the hangers-on of parasitic capitalists, the rootless mobs that have neither the stability nor the independence essential for the responsibilities of citi-

[24]Hunt, vol. 6, p. 118.
[25]Hunt, vol. 2, p. 393.
[26]Hutchins, vol. 43, *Federalist* No. 55, p. 174.
[27]Hunt, vol. 6, pp. 98–99.

zenship."[28] He talked of the vices which "distinguish crowded from thin settlements" and ascribed them to the loose sexual morals which undermined family life in the cities.[29] In his view, " 'Tis not the country that peoples either the Bridewells or the Bedlams. These mansions of wretchedness are tenanted from the distresses and vice of overgrown cities."[30]

Mankind in large aggregates always conjured visions of malevolence in Madison's mind:

> Bodies of men are not less swayed by interest than individuals, and are less controlled by the dread of reproach and the other motives felt by individuals. . . . Hence agrarian laws, and other leveling schemes: Hence the cancelling or evading of debts, and other violations of contracts. We must not shut our eyes to the nature of man, nor to the light of experience.[31]

In 1786 he warned James Monroe against the dangers that would follow from government in accordance with the wishes and opinions of urban majorities. "There is no maxim in my opinion which is more liable to be misapplied . . . than the current one that the interest of the majority is the political standard of right and wrong."[32] In effect, majority rule could only mean the assumption of the vicious principle that force is the measure of right. "Whenever therefore an apparent interest or common passion unites a majority what is to restrain them from unjust violations of the rights and interests of the minority, or of individuals?"[33] The obvious answer was that no inherent restraints within a majority would keep it from ruthlessly pursuing its desires, often to its own ultimate disadvantage. In fact, Madison claimed that the destruction of ancient and modern republics had generally resulted from the hatred and discord growing out of majority tyranny over the rights of minorities. The remedy for the tyranny of majority opinion lay in a system of checks and balances. "We must therefore introduce in our system Provisions against the measures of an interested majority—a check is not only necessary to protect the Executive power, but the minority in the Legislature."[34]

[28]Edward M. Burns, *James Madison: Philosopher of the Constitution.* New Brunswick: Rutgers University Press, 1938, p. 90.

[29]Hunt, vol. 6, p. 66. See Madison's article on "Population and Emigration" in the *National Gazette,* November 21, 1791.

[30]Hunt, vol. 6, pp. 97–98.

[31]Hunt, vol. 4, p. 122.

[32]Hunt, vol. 2, p. 273.

[33]Hunt, vol. 2, p. 367.

[34]Hunt, vol. 3, p. 89. (This statement was made at the Constitutional Convention in Philadelphia, June 4, 1787.)

## Checks and Balances as Safety Valves

Evil tendencies in men, singly or in groups, could be neutralized by pitting interest against interest and power against power. The larger the number of individuals who expressed their clashing selfish interests within a group, the better the chance that the interests of one would find a counterbalance in the interests of another. The result would be a mass opinion, stripped of its crudest excrescences of selfishness. With a rare bow to the benefits of mass-interaction, Madison argued that there was safety in numbers and that, therefore, democracy in the United States was far more secure if it encompassed the nation, rather than individual states only. The larger the area the better the balance of interests would be.

> He believed it essential to play one faction off against another in Machiavellian fashion, and to extend the territorial sphere of government so that the people would be broken up into so many conflicting interests and parties that a common sentiment could hardly ever be felt by a majority.[35]

But intragroup checks and balances were not enough. There had to be intergroup checks and balances as well to keep powerful factions within the polity in general, and within the governmental structure in particular, from riding roughshod over the rights of competing factions. Within the national legislature the Senate, which would represent the interests of the upper classes, should have equal power with the House, which would represent the more numerous laboring classes. In this way the lower class economic interests, despite their greater numerical strength, would be kept in check. The twin dangers of "despotism growing out of anarchy" or "an oligarchy founded on corruption" would be averted.[36] Giving the less numerous Senate equal power with the House did not indicate greater faith in the upper classes, but merely a belief in the necessity of an exact balancing of interest, rather than a balancing of numbers. Democracy was not an equal numbers game. As Madison wrote in 1787:

> In a just and a free Government, therefore, the rights both of property and of persons ought to be effectually guarded. . . . It is nevertheless certain, that there are various ways in which . . . property may oppress liberty; and that the world is filled with examples. . . . On the other hand, the danger to the holders of property cannot be disguised, if they be undefended against a majority without property.[37]

[35]Burns, pp. 63–64. (Also see Hunt, vol. 5, p. 31 and vol. 6, p. 86.)
[36]Hunt, vol. 5, p. 286. (See also Hutchins, vol. 43, *Federalist* No. 52, p. 167.)
[37]Hunt, vol. 4, p. 122. However, Burns comments: "Alexander Hamilton or John Adams could scarcely have made a more candid avowal of aristocratic inclinations." (Burns, p. 65.)

Besides balancing conflicting economic interests, each House would be a check on the excesses of the other since "those charged with the public happiness might betray their trust."[38] All business liable to abuse should be "made to pass thro' separate hands, the one being a check on the other."[39]

That it was concentration of power in any hands rather than a preference for aristocrats that prompted Madison's plans for equal power for the upper Chamber becomes even clearer from a letter written to Jefferson on October 17, 1788. In words foreshadowing Lord Acton's famous dictum, he wrote "Wherever the real power in a Government lies, there is a danger of oppression."[40] It did not make much difference who the rulers were—power corrupted all.

> In Monarchies and Aristocracies oppression proceeds from a want of sympathy and responsibility in the Government towards the people. In popular Governments the danger lies in an undue sympathy among individuals composing a majority, and a want of responsibility in the majority to the minority.[41]

"In our Governments," he warned:

> real power lies in the majority of the Community, and the invasion of private rights is *chiefly* to be apprehended, not from acts of Government contrary to the sense of its constituents, but from acts in which the Government is the mere instrument of the major number of the Constituents.[42]

Therefore, this was the source of oppression which needed to be checked. And then he continued, probably with reference to Shay's rebellion and other instances of civil unrest and mass violence which Jefferson, being abroad, had not witnessed: "This is a truth of great importance, but not yet sufficiently attended to" which "is probably more strongly impressed on my mind by facts, and reflections suggested by them, than on yours which has contemplated abuses of power issuing from a very different quarter."[43] Experience in the United States had taught Madison to fear the masses, while experience in France had taught Jefferson to fear the aristocracy. Although Madison had the highest regard for Jefferson's philosophical capabilities, he put his own experiences up as a match for Jefferson's appraisal of the realities of political life.

[38]Hunt, vol. 3, p. 285.

[39]Hunt, vol. 3, p. 285.

[40]Hunt, vol. 5, p. 271. In the same vein, in the *Federalist* he advised: "The greater the power is, the shorter ought to be its duration." Hutchins, vol. 43, *Federalist* No. 52, p. 167. Acton wrote in 1887: "Power tends to corrupt; absolute power corrupts absolutely."

[41]Hunt, vol. 4, pp. 122–123.

[42]Hunt, vol. 5, p. 271.

[43]Hunt, vol. 5, p. 271.

## An Aristocracy of Intelligence

Nor did Madison share Jefferson's faith in the ability of education to lead to the ultimate perfection of *homo politicus*. The best that he felt that education could accomplish was to make man aware of the deficiencies of the human character and aware of the needs of government to counterbalance these limitations. Since education was not a panacea for the ills of the public mind, Madison was less interested in mass public education than many other public leaders of his time and less willing to strain an already strained public purse to provide for it.[44] However, if public schools were to be established, rich and poor citizens alike ought to be willing to pay for them because all would reap benefits, directly or indirectly:

> Learned Institutions ought to be favorite objects with every free people. They throw that light over the public mind which is the best security against crafty and dangerous encroachments on the public liberty. . . . They multiply the educated individuals from among whom the people may elect a due portion of their public Agents of every description. . . . There can be little ground for objections from any class, to plans of which every class must have its turn of benefits.[45]

This admonition he climaxed with the glowing query: "What spectacle can be more edifying or more seasonable, than that of Liberty and Learning, each leaning on the other for their mutual and surest support?"[46]

Although education would not perfect man's character, it would heighten his intelligence and make him more capable to cope with society's problems. High intelligence sharpened by education was particularly important for those who were to take an active part in government. Madison knew from experience that a certain group of people were more interested in government and more knowledgeable than the general public. To this aristocracy of intelligence which, in his opinion, did not coincide with an aristocracy of means, Madison felt that the ship of state should be entrusted. He wrote to Randolph during the constitutional convention period:

> Whatever respect may be due to the rights of private judgment, and no man feels more of it than I do, there can be no doubt that there are subjects to which the capacities of the bulk of mankind are unequal, and on which they must and will be governed by those with whom they happen to have acquaintance and confidence.[47]

[44]Hunt, vol. 2, pp. 292, 302–303.
[45]Hunt, vol. 9, pp. 105–106.
[46]Hunt, vol. 9, pp. 165–166. See also his letter to Jefferson, on p. 244.
[47]Hunt, vol. 5, pp. 81–82.

He believed that "The proposed Constitution is of this description. The great body of those who are both for and against it must follow the judgment of others, not their own."[48] If the people were not capable of evaluating the proposed constitution, Madison concluded:

> I infer from these considerations, that, if a government be ever adopted in America, it must result from a fortunate coincidence of leading opinions, and a general confidence of the people in those who may recommend it.[49]

## The Legislature as Political Brain

The exponents of "leading opinions" who enjoyed the "general confidence of the people" were the members of the legislature. They were to be the political brain of the people, alike to it in every respect except for greater intelligence. Legislatures presented an aggregation of political talents and intelligence because the public, whatever else its political deficiencies might be, had a knack for selecting the most intelligent citizens as their representatives. "I go," said Madison

> on this great republican principle, that the people will have virtue and intelligence to select men of virtue and wisdom.

To him, this was an essential article of faith for believers in popular government:

> Is there no virtue among us? If there be not—no form of government can render us secure. To suppose that any form of government will secure liberty or happiness sans any virtue in the people, is a chimerical idea.[50]

On the other hand, lack of popular approval did not mean that a man was unworthy.[51] The man who lost an election therefore need not lose esteem for himself, nor ought he lose the esteem of his peers. The public in general could detect unworthiness for office, but it could not always discern high character and capabilities.

Since the legislature was more intelligent and capable than the people, it was not primarily a device for giving more efficient expression to the desires of the majority. Rather, it was a means

[48]Hunt, vol. 5, pp. 81–82.

[49]Hunt, vol. 5, pp. 81–82.

[50]Abbot E. Smith, *James Madison, Builder—A New Estimate of A Memorable Career.* New York: Wilson-Erickson, 1937, p. 139.

[51]See Madison's letter to Randolph on November 2, 1788, in which he remarked that "Popular favor or disfavor, is no criterion of the character." Hunt, vol. 5, p. 297.

to refine and enlarge the public views, by passing them through the medium of a chosen body of citizens, whose wisdom may best discern the true interest of their country, and whose patriotism and love of justice will be least likely to sacrifice it to temporary or partial considerations.[52]

Not only was the legislature a filter which barred evil influences from entering the bloodstream of public law making, but it also purified, strengthened, and even modified those public demands that legislators deemed proper. The results were better laws and better government.[53]

In part, the incapacity of the people to formulate sound opinions on public issues was a problem of excessive numbers for decision making. "Where a multitude of people exercise in person the legislative functions" policies suffer from "their incapacity for regular deliberation and concerted measures."[54] But when the numbers of policy makers were fewer, matters were different. Good policy is made in a representative assembly "which is sufficiently numerous to feel all the passions which actuate a multitude, yet not so numerous as to be incapable of pursuing the object of its passions, by means which reason prescribes."[55] Keeping policy formulation rational rather than emotional was particularly difficult if numbers grew too large. The whisper of the tiny voice of conscience was more easily drowned out in large masses than in smaller assemblies. Moral and religious restraints on violence and injustice "lose their efficacy in proportion to the number combined together."[56] More restrained, and hence better, opinions emerged from small and more select bodies.

Likewise, it was best on the whole if the legislature was insulated from popular passions and pressures, although this must not be carried to the point where "the people would be lost sight of altogether; and the necessary sympathy between them and their rulers and officers, too little felt."[57] Legislators must be exposed to the advice of public opinion leaders. They must know the gist of conflicting press claims, of conflicting petitions, and of conflicting party and sectional opinions. Yet they must not be caught up in the midst of public opinion conflicts. To achieve the necessary detachment Madison urged in the Philadelphia convention that the members of the legislature should have fairly long terms of office. Three years for representatives and nine years for senators would assure

[52]Hutchins, vol. 43, *Federalist* No. 10, p. 52.
[53]Madison also believed that Presidents would be wisely chosen because the popular choice was filtered through representative bodies. See Hunt, vol. 5, pp. 391–392.
[54]Hutchins, vol. 43, *Federalist* No. 48, p. 157.
[55]Hutchins, vol. 43, *Federalist* No. 48, p. 157.
[56]Hutchins, vol. 43, *Federalist* No. 10, p. 51.
[57]Hunt, vol. 3, p. 48.

that the legislature had sufficient firmness and independence, as well as the necessary experience to act for the public good:

> The tendency of a longer period of service would be, to render the [legislative] Body more stable in its policy, and more capable of stemming popular currents taking a wrong direction, till reason and justice could regain their ascendancy. . . .[58]

A relatively permanent legislature which would "seasonable interpose against impetuous councils" would prevent disgust with popular rule that might culminate in a movement towards despotism.[59]

It would have been very much unlike Madison to put a stamp of complete approval on any human institution. His praise for the ability of legislative assemblies to articulate sound public opinion was tempered with repeated warnings that legislators, like other mortals, were selfish, deceitful, and often mistaken in their views. He believed that:

> Representative appointments are sought from three motives. 1. ambition. 2. personal interest. 3. public good. Unhappily the two first are proved by experience to be most prevalent. Hence the candidates who feel them, particularly, the second, are most industrious, and most successful in pursuing their object.[60]

These types of representatives, who often were in the majority, "with interested views, contrary to the interest and views of their constituents, join in a perfidious sacrifice"[61] of public interest to private interest. Then they win the reelection by masking

> base and selfish measures . . . by pretexts of public good and apparent expedience. . . . How frequently too will the honest but unenlightened representative be the dupe of a favorite leader, veiling his selfish views under the professions of public good?[62]

The hope was that the selfish interests of some legislators would be checked by conflicting interests of others. An Easterner willing to sacrifice commercial rights of the Western country would find that Westerners had other, if not less selfish, ideas. In addition, there was the safeguard of the checks and balance system that pitted various governmental agencies, representative of different interests, against each other.

Just as the people were "liable to temporary errors, thro' want of information as to their true interest . . . also, from fickleness and passion,"[63] so legislative assemblies could reach mistaken conclusions. Even assemblies

[58]Hunt, vol. 4, p. 126.
[59]Hunt, vol. 3, pp. 148–154, and 285–287.
[60]Hunt, vol. 2, p. 366.
[61]Hunt, vol. 2, p. 366.
[62]Hunt, vol. 2, p. 366.
[63]Hunt, vol. 3, p. 285.

as distinguished as the Philadelphia constitutional convention had erred in several respects. Nevertheless, those who found fault with the convention's work, or the work of any other governmental body, should hesitate in the knowledge that "They themselves are but men and ought not to assume an infallibility in rejudging the fallible opinions of others."[64] Critics of public policy must be aware of their own deficiencies in critical judgment.

In fact, it was rare when the judgment of the "unreflecting multitude"[65] was better than the opinions of their chosen political leaders. When Virginia political leaders hesitated to adopt the new national constitution while the people seemed to favor adoption, a surprised Madison wrote to Jefferson:

> It is worthy of remark that in Virginia where the mass of the people have been so much accustomed to be guided by their rulers on all new and intricate questions, they should on the present which certainly surpasses the judgment of the greater part of them, not only go before, but contrary to their most popular leaders.[66]

He ascribed the unusual situation to the fact that the political instability of the confederation had caused serious injury to the private affairs of many citizens who realized the source of their difficulties:

> I will barely observe that the case . . . seems to prove that the body of sober and steady people, even of the lower order, are tired of the vicissitudes, injustice, and follies which have so much characterized public measures, and are impatient for some change which promises stability and repose.[67]

## The Legislature as the Public's Spokesman

Had one asked Madison who spoke for the public and what constituted public opinion, he would have answered unhesitatingly that the voice of the legislature is the voice of the public. He felt that ordinarily a representative would express the opinions of his constituents, as he himself had tried to do during his years in the legislature.[68] In fact, "it may well happen that the public voice, pronounced by the representatives of the people, will be more consonant to the public good than if pronounced by the people them-

[64]*Federalist* No. 37 talks of "the fallibility to which the convention, as a body of men, were liable." Hutchins, vol. 43, p. 118.

[65]Hunt, vol. 3, p. 149.

[66]Hunt, vol. 5, pp. 66–67. See also his letter to George Washington, p. 98.

[67]Hunt, vol. 5, pp. 66–67.

[68]See, for example, Madison's letter to Joseph Jones, December 12, 1780. Hunt, vol. 1, pp. 113–114.

selves, convened for the purpose."[69] Since public opinion presumably desires the public good, whoever expresses the public good best, is expressing public opinion. Instead of contending that whatsoever the people want is good, this is the argument that whatsoever is good is wanted by the people —a significant transformation of the maxim *vox populi vox Dei*, into *vox Dei vox populi*.

Leaving aside the duty of the legislative representative to pass the voice of the public through the filter of his conscience and intelligence, Madison was also keenly aware of the impossibility of hearing the voice of the public with precision. If opinions were sampled in the towns "where there can be most despatch in such an operation," this would be merely "a partial expression of the public voice" which could easily be "misconstrued or miscalled" because opinion in the cities was likely to differ from views in the countryside.[70] On the other hand, consultation with the countryside was difficult and tedious and frequently impractical.

During the Philadelphia constitutional convention, when others spoke of the need to be guided by public opinion, Madison made the point that:

> No member of the Convention could say what the opinions of his Constituents were at this time; much less could he say what they would think if possessed of the information and lights possessed by the members here; and still less what would be their thinking 6 or 12 months hence.[71]

When representatives could not know with certainty what the public wanted, their best course was "to consider what was right and necessary in itself for the attainment of a proper Government."[72] The merit of their proposals, buttressed by their reputation for sagacity, would win the support of enlightened citizens. They would adopt the views of the representatives as their very own, making their representative's opinions public opinion in the truest sense. As an example, Madison noted that the Annapolis convention had recommended "a great and critical object, wholly foreign to their commission."[73] Nonetheless, this action was "not only justified by the public opinion, but actually carried into effect by twelve out of the thirteen states."[74] Thus there was the additional sanction that state legislatures were willing to endorse the policy by enforcing it. Likewise, the Louisiana Purchase had been legalized by *post hoc* public approval. Madison would have preferred a constitutional amendment to give greater color of legality. But even without such an amendment, obvious public approval made the action legitimate.

[69]Hutchins, vol. 43, *Federalist* No. 10, p. 52.
[70]Letter to Jefferson, April, 1798. Hunt, vol. 6, p. 314.
[71]Hunt, vol. 3, p. 149.
[72]Hunt, vol. 3, p. 149.
[73]Hutchins, vol. 43, *Federalist* No. 40, p. 131.
[74]Hutchins, vol. 43, *Federalist* No. 40, p. 131.

Madison feared that a rigid adherence to forms, rather than substance

> would render nominal and nugatory the transcendent and precious right
> of the people to "abolish or alter their governments as to them shall seem
> most likely to effect their safety and happiness," since it is impossible for
> the people spontaneously and universally to move in concert toward their
> object.[75]

Therefore, it was essential that radical changes "be instituted by some
*informal* and *unauthorized propositions,* made by some patriotic and respectable citizen or number of citizens."[76] This, then, gave a mandate to
the few, especially the President in foreign affairs, to break the law when
this appeared to them in accord with the wishes and interests of the people.
As long as the final plan was "*submitted* to the people . . . its approbation"
would "blot out antecedent errors and irregularities."[77]

Except for the Virginia and Kentucky resolutions which challenged
the right of Congress to enact the Alien and Sedition acts, Madison never
questioned the right of the legislature to speak for the public. Even when
Congress went beyond its given powers, it could claim the right to have
its actions approved by the people as long as they were for the public good.
In fact, Madison argued that the delegates to the national constitutional
convention had a duty to exceed their mandate. "They were not only warranted, but required, as the confidential servants of their country, by the
circumstances in which they were placed, to exercise the liberty which
they assumed."[78] Even if their actions "had violated both their powers
and their obligations" their work "ought nevertheless to be embraced, if it
be calculated to accomplish the views and happiness of the people of America."[79] Whether or not the Constitution accomplished "the views and happiness of the people of America" was a decision to be made, in the first
instance, by the legislature, rather than the people themselves. As justification for their action, legislators could appeal to

> the great principle of self preservation; to the transcendent law of nature
> and of nature's God, which declares that the safety and happiness of so-
> ciety are the objects at which all political institutions aim, and to which
> all such institutions must be sacrificed.[80]

The people, "enlightened . . . with regard to the nature, and interested
. . . in the effects of good government," would understand.[81]

---

[75]Hutchins, vol. 43, *Federalist* No. 40, p. 131.
[76]Hutchins, vol. 43, *Federalist* No. 40, p. 131.
[77]Hutchins, vol. 43, *Federalist* No. 40, p. 131.
[78]Hutchins, vol. 43, *Federalist* No. 40, p. 131.
[79]Hutchins, vol. 43, *Federalist* No. 40, p. 132.
[80]Hutchins, vol. 43, *Federalist* No. 43, p. 143.
[81]Hutchins, vol. 43, *Federalist* No. 37, p. 119.

The more complex public issues became, the less reliance legislators could place on guidance from the public because: "It is a misfortune, inseparable from human affairs, that public measures are rarely investigated with that spirit of moderation which is essential to a just estimate of their real tendency to advance or obstruct the public good."[82] Furthermore, the more important the measure, the more heat and the less light would be dissipated in public discussions. "This spirit [of dispassionate analysis] is more apt to be diminished than promoted by those occasions which require an unusual exercise of it."[83] Thus, on the most crucial issues, legislators were forced to rely most heavily on their own intellectual resources. Their experience, Madison believed, had made them fully aware of this need. The general public, clinging to ideal democratic theories, might be less understanding. It had not yet learned, as Madison had by the end of his career of public service, that: "Theories are the offspring of the closet; exceptions to them, the lessons of experience."[84]

## The Role of the Executive

While Madison had a high respect for the legislature's ability to express public opinion and discern the public good, he had much less confidence in the executive. The executive, being a single individual, with nothing to balance his faults and deficiencies, was as likely to go wrong as the average citizen. For instance, when Madison disagreed with the Neutrality Proclamation of 1793, he averred that President Washington had been misled by pro-British, anti-Democratic advisors to commit himself to a policy which would be harmful to the country.

Madison also questioned the President's claim that the Neutrality Proclamation expressed the wishes of the American people. The President's appraisal of public opinion was based on his political intuition and the intuition of his advisors, especially his Cabinet.[85] While this method of fathoming public opinion had often proved accurate, Madison felt that it was necessary to check Washington's statement against the facts to make certain that a President, under the influence of selfish and unpatriotic advisors, did not misrepresent the public's views.

He even suggested a method of public opinion polling. There should be public meetings in counties throughout the states so "that the real sentiments of the people here should be understood" with regard to the Revo-

[82]Hutchins, vol. 43, *Federalist* No. 37, p. 118.
[83]Hutchins, vol. 43, *Federalist* No. 37, p. 118.
[84]Quoted in Dewey, p. 6.
[85]See pp. 208–212 of this volume.

lutionary Government of France.[86] He drafted a sample resolution which might be submitted by the organizers of the meeting for discussion by the audience. If county meetings could be held "they will be respectable specimens of the principles and sensations of the Agricultural which is the commanding part of the Society." Although such a poll would be difficult, Madison believed that: "It is however of such infinite importance to our own Government as well as that of France, that the real sentiments of the people here should be understood, that something ought to be attempted on that head." Realizing the difficulties of making the necessary arrangements, except in the cities whose people he did not trust, he added that such a poll "is scarcely possible. The Country is too much uninformed, and too inert to speak for itself; and the language of the towns . . . will insidiously inflame the evil."[87]

The assumption, of course, was that the public's opinion, if it could be shown to conflict with the President's, would alter his decision. Therefore, "if the genuine sense of the people could be collected on the several points comprehended in the occasion, the calamity [neutrality policy] would be greatly alleviated if not absolutely controuled."[88] In addition, legislators, buttressed by the knowledge that the people opposed the President's policy, would and should have a strong influence in trying to change the President's opinions. As he wrote Jefferson, when he felt that the Adams administration was out of tune with public sentiments:

> I am glad to find the public opinion to be taking the turn you describe on the subject of arming. For the public opinion alone can now save us from the rash measures of our hot-headed Executive. [The majority in Congress] are ready to go as far as the controul of their constituents will permit. . . .[89]

Ever faithful to the principle of balance, Madison did not advocate complete legislative and popular supremacy over the chief executive. He was a vociferous advocate during the constitutional convention of checking legislative power by balancing it against the power of the executive. He had strongly opposed the creation of omnicompetent legislatures during the Confederacy which made of the Executive nothing but a cipher. And he did not believe that an executive should follow the advice of the public if it was foolish. Governor John Hancock of Massachusetts deserved criticism for "a dishonorable obsequiousness to popular follies" when Hancock did not oppose the influence of rebellious elements in the state with suf-

---

[86]For a description of Madison's use of similar methods, see two letters to Monroe cited in Hunt, vol. 8, pp. 397, 421–422.

[87]Hunt, vol. 6, pp. 191–193. All other quotes in this paragraph are from this source.

[88]Hunt, vol. 6, pp. 191–193.

[89]Hunt, vol. 6, p. 238.

ficient vigor.[90] How an executive could tell which popular opinions were foolish and which deserved to overrule his own sentiments Madison did not say.


## Foreign Policy as a Special Case

In policies that involved "external and internal danger" executive control would have to be greater than was desirable in other cases. Madison bemoaned the problem of "combining the requisite stability and energy in government with the desirable attention due to liberty and to the republican form."[91] In general, the principles of liberty and republicanism must be held uppermost. But in situations involving major risks to the survival of the nation, stability and energy became the paramount principles. No government could "set bounds to the exertions for its own safety" unless it could "chain the ambitions or set bounds to the exertions of all other nations."[92] Obviously, this was impossible. Hence:

> The means of security can only be regulated by the means and the danger of attack . . . it is vain to oppose constitutional barriers to the impulse of self-preservation. It is worse than in vain; because it plants in the Constitution itself necessary usurpations of power, every precedent of which is a germ of unnecessary and multiplied repetitions.[93]

The power to deal with foreign affairs must be broad and unencumbered by ordinary democratic restraints. Moreover, since "energy in government is essential to that security against external and internal danger, and to that prompt and salutary execution of the laws which enter into the very definition of good government" and "stability in government is as essential . . . to that repose and confidence in the minds of the people. . .," it was necessary in foreign affairs, that "the hands in which power is lodged should continue for a length of time the same."[94] In fact, "energy in government requires not only a certain duration of power, but the execution of it by a single hand."[95]

The exigencies of human nature and the political world dictated that foreign affairs should be relatively remote from popular and even legislative control, lodged in the hands of an executive who held office for a lengthy period of time. Madison realized that executive predominance in foreign

[90]Hunt, vol. 2, p. 354.
[91]Hutchins, vol. 43, *Federalist* No. 37, p. 118.
[92]Hutchins, vol. 43, *Federalist* No. 41, pp. 132–133.
[93]Hutchins, vol. 43, *Federalist* No. 41, pp. 132–133.
[94]Hutchins, vol. 43, *Federalist* No. 37, pp. 118–119.
[95]Hutchins, vol. 43, *Federalist* No. 37, pp. 118–119.

affairs made the conduct of foreign relations "the most susceptible of abuse of all the trusts committed to a Government, because they can be concealed or disclosed, or disclosed in such parts and at such times as will best suit particular views. . . ." Furthermore: "The body of the people are less capable of judging, and are more under the influence of prejudices, on that branch of their affairs, than of any other."[96] Nonetheless, political realities permitted no other course.

In principle, Madison believed that the public should have as much information as possible concerning the conduct of foreign policy. But how much was possible was a presidential decision, to be made in accordance with the President's appraisal of the requirements of the situation. Experience tended to show Madison, as Secretary of State and later as President, that the scope for disclosing relevant foreign policy information to the public and listening to its views is severely limited. Madison did not approve of sacrificing what seemed to him the public good for the lesser value of taking the public into his confidence in foreign policy decision making.

Foreign policy was to be judged first by its results, and only secondarily by the methods of policy formulation. If the President knew where the right course lay, it was his duty to indicate this course to Congress and, if it could safely be done, the public. It was also his duty to point out the errors of opposing views and disclose the perverting influences that had led to wrong opinions. If his own views were undecided, he should follow the advice of legislative leaders. But it was often unwise to inform the public or to heed its clamor. Public opinion on foreign affairs, even more than on domestic matters, tended to be dominated by selfish interests, misguided factions, or those who had no faith in democratic government. Madison's long public life, spanning the revolutionary period and the first third of the nineteenth century had given him ample proof that pressure groups, once they knew the trend of foreign policies, could bar their effectiveness. One need only mention the Embargo policy that he found most difficult to enforce during his term as Secretary of State and during his years as President prior to the war of 1812.

Significantly, Madison did not include the power over war and peace within the scope of foreign policy powers which were to be remote from popular control. He mistrusted the executive's capacity for self-restraint when the call of Mars beckoned:

> The executive is the department of power most distinguished by its propensity to war; hence it is the practice of all states, in proportion as they are free, to disarm this propensity of its influence.[97]

[96]Gaillard Hunt, ed., *Letters of James Madison*, vol. 2. Washington: Congressional Edition, pp. 140–141.

[97]Hunt, vol. 6, p. 174.

Besides, war and peace should not be intrusted to the decision of a single individual. "The trust . . . would be too great for the wisdom, and the temptations too strong for the virtue, of a single citizen."[98] It seemed to him that the principle of separation of powers required that:

> Those who are to *conduct a war* cannot in the nature of things, be proper or safe judges, whether a *war ought to* be *commenced, continued,* or *concluded.* They are barred from the latter functions by a great principle in free government, analogous to that which separates the sword from the purse, or the power of executing from the power of enacting laws. . . .[99]

Such views explain Madison's reluctance to make the final decision about war and peace in 1812. This decision, he believed, belonged to the legislature, buttressed by the opinions of the people:

> The right to decide the question whether the duty and interest of the U. S. require war or peace under any given circumstances, and whether their disposition be towards the one or the other seems to be essentially and exclusively involved in the right vested in the Legislature, of declaring war in time of peace. . . .[100]

Any law or treaty by which the President might commit the legislature, and thus the nation, to war would be improper because it would mean that "the people are cheated out of the best ingredients in their Government, the safeguards of peace which is the greatest of their blessings."[101] He even advocated that the legislature should adjourn before making a decision on peace or war so that legislators would have ample time to consult their constituents and "call forth the sense of the people" in the towns and countryside.[102]

### Popular Checks on Government

When legislatures or the executive or even a tyrannical majority misinterpreted or misrepresented the public good, the normal procedure was to appeal "to the recollections, the reason, and the conciliatory spirit of the majority of the people." Although there should be a "persevering hope of success," there must be an "eventual acquiescence in disappointment unless indeed oppression should reach an extremity overruling all other con-

---

[98]Hunt, vol. 6, p. 175. Also see letter to Jefferson, April 2, 1798. Hunt, vol. 6, p. 312.
[99]Hunt, vol. 6, p. 148.
[100]Hunt, vol. 6, p. 145.
[101]Hunt, vol. 6, p. 313.
[102]Hunt, vol. 6, p. 314.

sideration."[103] In that case there was a right of revolution. The political principles maintained through a justifiable revolution were the truest expressions of the public will. Nonetheless, the right of revolution was to be exercised extremely rarely, if ever.

In this respect Madison differed strongly from Jefferson. He abhorred violence and wanted to avert it at all costs. He certainly did not view revolts and insurrections as normal expressions of the public will. In fact, his inclination was to discount them in most instances as a censurable activity of a disgruntled minority that had not yet learned that "the Minority must submit to that danger of oppression as an evil infinitely less than the danger to the whole nation" when minority groups seek to enforce their own sense of right and wrong through civil disobedience and revolt.[104] In a warning that might well be heeded by twentieth century rebels against public authority, he pointed to the "general tendency of insurrections to increase the momentum of power" and lodge it in a few government officials, rather than leaving it democratically dispersed throughout the country.[105] In 1794, he wrote to Monroe that the only thing that had saved the country from disaster during the recent episodes of civil disobedience was the fact that "with a spirit truly republican, the people everywhere and of every description condemned the resistance of the will of the Majority, and obeyed with alacrity the call to vindicate the authority of the laws."[106]

While Madison felt that revolt against public authority was too dangerous an expression of adverse public opinion to be tolerated very frequently, he was willing to take his chances with written opposition by the press. However bad press opinions might be, however subversive of the public interests, it was essential to preserve "those choicest privileges of the people."[107] When he denounced the Sedition Act for its denial of freedom of the press, he declared with unabashed exaggeration, that "to the press alone, chequered as it is with abuses, the world is indebted for all the triumphs which have been gained by reason and humanity over error and oppression."[108]

As Madison knew well, the abuses were many. Adoption of the national constitution had been endangered by opposition press reports that had been written "not only with a pre-disposition to censure, but with a predetermination to condemn."[109] The country had been misled to sup-

---

[103]Quoted in Smith, p. 231.
[104]Quoted in Dewey, p. 45.
[105]Quoted in Smith, p. 212.
[106]Smith, p. 212.
[107]Hunt, vol. 5, p. 380.
[108]Hunt, vol. 5, p. 389.
[109]Hutchins, vol. 43, *Federalist* No. 37, p. 118.

port a dangerous neutrality policy through the publication of Hamilton's *Pacificus* letters in the press. The letters had been

> read with singular pleasure and applause by the foreigners and degenerate citizens among us, who hate our republican government, and the French revolution. . . .[110]

Hamilton, it had seemed to him, had expressed his selfishly motivated private views, and had done it with all the skill of the ideologue and propagandist. His efforts, which Madison had tried to counter in the *Helvidius* letters, had been successful. Nonetheless, freedom of the press, "this essential branch of liberty," must be preserved.[111] It was "better to leave a few of its noxious branches to their luxuriant growth, than, by pruning them away, to injure the vigour of those yielding the proper fruits."[112] Madison denied that it was possible to pass laws against misuse of the press while maintaining press liberty. He contended that:

> No means have ever yet been devised by which the press can be corrected without being enslaved. If opposed, freedom which admits of exceptions, alleged to be licentious, is not freedom at all.[113]

A free press must be permitted to give people a chance to express opinions and win acceptance for them, whether or not these opinions were sound, beneficial, or expressive of the desires of the majority of solid citizens.

The same reasoning held for mass meetings, memorials, and petitions. Since it was "at all times the right and at certain periods the duty of the people to declare their principles and opinions on subjects which concern the national interest," it was important to encourage such expressions of public views, even though the privilege was liable to abuse.[114] But just as the press spoke for individuals and could not be taken as the voice of public opinion, so the substance of the views and demands expressed in petitions could not be equated with the demands of the public. This was especially true since it was "the prevailing practice" to originate the bulk of petitions in the cities

> in places where the inhabitants can more easily assemble and consult than in the Country at large, and where interests, views and political opinions different from those of the great body of the people, may happen to predominate, whence there may be danger of unfair and delusive inferences concerning the true and general sense of the people.[115] .

[110]Hunt, vol. 6, p. 138.
[111]Hunt, vol. 5, p. 294.
[112]Hunt, vol. 6, pp. 388–389.
[113]Hunt, vol. 6, p. 336.
[114]Hunt, vol. 6, p. 192.
[115]Hunt, vol. 6, p. 192.

Public opinion emerged only from the clashing and amalgamation of conflicting claims and from the interaction of the demands of various petitioners and advocates. Since it required time to ripen, officials seeking the council of the public must delay decisions to give people a chance to inform themselves and then express their views:

> . . . Under the disadvantage a great proportion of the people labor in their distant and dispersed situation from the want of timely and correct knowledge of particular incidents, and the conduct of particular persons connected with public transactions, it is most prudent and safe, to wait with a decent reserve for a full and satisfactory information in relation thereto. . . .[116]

Beyond the time needed to ascertain public opinion, it was sometimes feasible and wise to delay decisions until a previously adverse public attitude had had a chance to change. For instance, Madison regarded slavery as an evil that ought to be abolished, but he felt that it must be tolerated until public views had moved to an anti-slavery position. Therefore he refused a request to introduce antislavery legislation into Congress. Like his mentor, Thomas Jefferson, he believed that "the public mind would not yet bear the proposition."[117] Since the public never became able to bear the emancipation proposition during Jefferson's and Madison's lives, both of them died as slave owners. However, both believed that the public would eventually favor abolition and that patience on the part of political leaders would be rewarded by an easier transition from a slave to a free society. Even accepting the novelty of representative government took time. Thus it was "that a sudden transition" of the people of Louisiana, after the United States had acquired the territory

> to a condition so much in contrast with that in which their ideas and habits have been formed, would be as unacceptable and as little beneficial to them as it would be difficult for the Government of the United States . . . every blessing of liberty will be extended to them as fast as they shall be prepared and disposed to receive it.[118]

On matters of greater immediacy, both Madison and Jefferson were far less willing to wait for the crystallization of favorable public sentiment. Thus Madison urged that the new national constitution should be ratified even though "the public however is certainly in the dark with regard to it." It would quickly adjust itself to a *fait accompli:*

[116]Hunt, vol. 6, p. 192.
[117]Hunt, vol. 1, pp. xxiv–xxv.
[118]Hunt, vol. 7, pp. 115–116.

> My own idea is that the public mind will now or in a very little time receive anything which promises stability to the public councils and security to private rights, and that no regard ought to be had to local prejudices or temporary considerations.[119]

Expediency was the reason for proceeding rapidly. "If the present moment be lost, it is hard to say what may be our fate. . . ."[120]

Once the action had been taken, it was the task of governmental officials to explain their reasoning to the public and seek its approval. This is what he had tried to do in the *Federalist* papers, and in his many presidential messages that explained his decisions, especially in foreign affairs. Given the basic good sense of a public whose opinions had been purified through the checks and balance of public debates, a President was sure to win approval for his policies. Later experiences seemed to bear out his theories. In an era of decline of the major opposition party, Madison never lacked the support of a sufficient number of vocal people to feel and to claim that the public followed his leadership. He watched election returns closely for elections often were "the strongest of proofs that the measures of the Executive coincided with the feelings of the Nation."[121] Continued predominance of his party was interpreted by him, as it has been by his successors, as public concurrence in his opinions.

## A Summing Up

One can distill the essence of Madison's views about the uses of public opinion from a brief article that he contributed to the *National Gazette* on December 19, 1791. At the time, he was Virginia's representative in Congress and had spent more than fifteen years in various governmental assemblies. The article begins with the observation that "Public opinion sets bounds to every government," especially to a free one. But the role of public opinion varies. At times, public opinion is fixed and the government has no choice but to obey its mandate. At other times, "where not being fixed, it may be influenced by the government."[122] Since government cannot resist a public opinion once it has become fixed, it must be concerned with all the factors and forces which affect public opinion formation. These include "Whatever facilitates a general intercourse of sentiments, as good roads, domestic commerce, a free press, and particularly *a circulation of*

[119]Hunt, vol. 4, p. 390.

[120]Hunt, vol. 4, p. 390.

[121]Hunt, vol. 8, p. 97. Madison wrote to William Pinkney on May 23, 1810, that he deemed the elections in the Eastern states as a vote of popular confidence in his policies.

[122]Hunt, vol. 6, p. 70.

*newspapers through the entire body of the people,* and *Representatives going from, and returning among every part of them.*"[123]

None of these channels for the flow and interchange of political opinions must be neglected in governmental attempts to influence opinion and ascertain it. Although "The larger a country, the less easy for its real opinion to be ascertained, and the less difficult to be counterfeited,"[124] it was worth the effort to try to discover and mold the public's views. Success would ease the task of governing well because the public would support its rulers and doubters would be won over by the evidence of public support. To be able to claim the support of the public was not only theoretically wise, and morally right, it had practical advantages as well.

[123]Hunt, vol. 6, p. 70. (Italics in original.)
[124]Hunt, vol. 6, p. 70.

# 8

# Was It "Mr. Madison's War"?

And thus the native hue of resolution
Is sicklied o'er with the pale cast of thought,
And enterprises of great pitch and moment
With this regard their currents turn awry,
And lose the name of action.
WILLIAM SHAKESPEARE, *Hamlet*

Even a nod from a person who is esteemed is of more force
than a thousand arguments or studied sentences from others.
PLUTARCH, *Lives*

# 8

## Maintaining a Precarious Peace

In 1803, England and France resumed their perennial warfare, and the United States resumed its customary trials and tribulations as a neutral power. The belligerents were eager to deny war imports to each other while the United States, as the largest neutral carrier of goods to both England and France, was equally eager to continue this profitable trade without interruption. The diplomatic maneuvers of the belligerents, the counter-maneuvers of the United States, the incidents, the near-outbreaks of war, along with the additional irritation of impressment of American sailors by the British, furnish the background of the War of 1812.

Madison knew the story first-hand from the beginning. He had been Secretary of State in the Jefferson administration when the troubles began in earnest. He, along with Jefferson, had been one of the architects of the policy of economic coercion by which the United States tried to force the belligerents, through economic rather than military measures, to respect its rights as a neutral to trade with both belligerents. Under this policy American trade was to be denied to nations which interfered with American shipping and commerce. The resulting economic hardships would, it was hoped, force them to suspend harassment of American commercial and shipping interests.

Madison realized that in essence the policy had failed, since it had won only temporary concessions from either the French or the English. When the going got rough they had never hesitated to seize and condemn American ships, to confiscate their cargoes, and to impress or imprison their crews. Possibly worse, the policies had been an economic boomerang. Interruption of trade might be painful to the English or French. But it was equally painful to their American suppliers. They lost the markets on which their economic prosperity depended, and the shipowners and merchants lost their profitable commerce.

As Madison had always contended, the economic nerves of the American public were particularly sensitive. Interruption of trade affected them like a bad toothache, and made them cross, irritable, and unwilling to bear the pain and irritation for a long period of time. A popular ditty complained:

> Th' Embargo don't answer its end.
> The PEOPLE are left in the dark yet to stumble,

> Their patience worn out, no wonder they grumble,
> While daily they see their prosperity crumble,
> And no hope their condition to mend.[1]

Discontent had mounted in the country and, at times, broken into open rebellion. Jefferson finally had been forced, as a result of public dissatisfaction and noncompliance, to rescind the embargo during the last days of his administration. Adverse public opinion had won a victory.

This was the situation that faced Madison when he took over the reins of government from Jefferson. Somehow he would have to dissuade Britain and France, locked in a deadly war, from employing measures of economic warfare that helped their struggle but injured the United States. He would have to do this with policies short of war because the United States was neither ready nor willing to fight a war at the time. Measures of economic coercion would have to be designed to inflict maximum injury on the belligerents but keep damage to the American economy to a minimum so that popular support for the policy could be retained. This was a difficult, if not impossible task. It was complicated by the fact that the administration could not take public compliance with economic coercion legislation for granted.

A number of New England legislatures had already announced their right of interposition to prevent execution of the embargo and nonimportation legislation in New England states. Several states had refused to furnish law enforcement officials to help federal collectors enforce import and export duties.[2] Bad as these difficulties were from an administrative point of view, they also had deleterious effects on foreign policy. They gave the impression, quite correctly, of a disunited nation. A President's threats of retaliation against Britain or France, even if backed by congressional legislation, certainly did not look very formidable if the public was obviously unwilling to go along with the measures.

Widespread sabotage of economic coercion policies was not the only rock thrust into Madison's policy path. He also had to fend off warhawks of various descriptions who were eager to test the nation's mettle on the battlefield. Some Westerners and South Westerners, in particular, eagerly called for war whenever news of fresh British or French outrages spread. They condemned measures of economic coercion as too weak and too dis-

[1]John B. McMaster, *History of the People of the United States from the Revolution to the Civil War*, vol. 3. New York: Appleton-Century-Crofts, 1885, p. 324.

[2]For the texts of various resolutions, see Henry Adams, *History of the United States*, Book 4. New York: Albert and Charles Boni, 1930, pp. 416–420. Also see Leonard D. White, *The Jeffersonians*. New York: The Macmillan Company, 1951, pp. 421–473, for a discussion of the administrative difficulties posed by enforcing the embargo laws in the United States.

graceful, and not consonant with the honor and dignity of a free nation. Many of them were ready and eager to take revenge into their own hands by attacking British possessions in the North, or by raiding Spanish possessions in the South on the theory that Spain, as Britain's ally, deserved to be hurt. Even some New England Federalists were working for war, although for different reasons. They advised British representatives in the United States to make no concessions to Madison's demands, for "the only way to dislodge the prevailing party from the post of power" was to stand firm and force it "to disgraceful retreat or a demonstration of wartime incompetence."[3]

Here was a real challenge for Madison's ability to control and to mold public opinion before discontents had spread far enough to endanger his policies. He had to create and maintain support for new economic coercion legislation, as well as keep the war fever in check so that it would not, through word or deed, force his hand. At the same time, he did not want to silence war talk too much (at least not officially) because he hoped that both the British and French would consider it evidence that war was a distinct possibility. The reminder that public annoyance with their conduct might raise the pressure for war to irresistible proportions could serve to soften their resistance to Madison's importunities.

For more than three years, the Madison Administration managed to keep the lid on the bubbling cauldron. In messages and answers to petitions, through articles in the country's papers, and through talks at public meetings and with opinion leaders, dissidents were kept in check. On the diplomatic front, Madison's negotiators in Paris and London pleaded, threatened, and bargained, supported by a carrot and stick policy in which the Madison Administration promised unhampered trade to cooperating nations and threatened obstructive ones with various types of restrictions harmful to their economy.

Eager to keep the peace, Madison relaxed economic coercion at the slightest indication that either France or Britain was willing to make concessions. He accepted an unofficial promise by Erskine, the British minister in Washington, that obnoxious Orders in Council, which hampered American trade, had been repealed. He believed in the authenticity of the pledge until his faith was rudely shattered by British Prime Minister Canning who recalled the indiscreet Erskine. He took as truth an equally flimsy announcement by the French that Napoleon had repealed his offensive decrees to seize and confiscate American ships as part of French economic warfare against Britain. And he clung to the belief with near desperation until contrary evidence overwhelmed him.

[3]Roger H. Brown, *The Republic in Peril: 1812.* New York: Columbia University Press, 1964, pp. 168–169.

## The Turn of the Tide: The Elections of 1811

A policy of peace-at-all-costs continued until the summer of 1811 when elections for Congress seemed to show a change in the public temper. Possibly heartened by the "Little Belt" affair in May, in which an American ship had attacked and severely mauled a British ship in a case of mistaken identity, large numbers of people responded enthusiastically to war oratory during the campaign. Although the election itself was not fought on the clear-cut issue of peace or war, when the returns were in, the balance in Congress had swung away from the old guard to new and young Republicans, many of them eager for a militant foreign policy.[4] Of the preceding period Henry Adams had written that there was "no well-defined plan." Europeans

> . . . were surprised and amused at the simplicity with which the people disputed plans of war and peace, giving many months of warning and exact information to the enemy, while they showed no sign of leadership, discipline, or union, or even a consciousness that such qualities were needed. Men like Josiah Quincy, Rufus King, John Randolph, and even Madison and Gallatin, seeing that the people themselves, like the machine of government they had invented, were incompetent to the work of war, waited with varied emotions, but equally believing or fearing that at last a fatal crisis was at hand.[5]

These days were over. From now on foreign policy would be positive. The President, sick of merely reacting to the moves of his adversaries and tired of the failure of past plans, would go along with what he deemed the mandate of the people to take the initiative and act firmly.

When Congress met for an early session on November 4, 1811, almost one-half of the membership was new. The casualties were "senile, submission men." They were replaced with young men in their twenties and early thirties—"Warhawks" and "Pepperpot Politicians" coming especially from the lower South and West, from the new states, and from the frontier regions:

> They did not remember the Revolution. . . . They lacked the caution of those who had fought and won that war and now wanted to rest rather

[4]Bradford Perkins, *Prologue to War: England and the United States, 1805–1812.* Berkeley: University of California Press, 1963, pp. 261–263, contends that the new Congress represented the customary turnover of members including the usual number of youthful ones. "It is not demonstrable that a great upsurge of public feeling flung aside Federalists and cautious Republicans in favor of avowed War Hawks. . . ." However, although the facts may be open to various interpretations, Madison interpreted the election as a mandate for the pro-war Clay faction.

[5]Adams, Book 6, p. 119.

than risk the results of victory in another battle. . . . They were representative of a new breed of nationalists.[6]

By default the leadership in Congress went to this group of young politicians who in the words of their thirty-four year old Speaker, Kentuckian Henry Clay, were tired of "the tranquil and putrescent pool of ignominious peace." The Clay forces managed to pack the crucial committees in both houses with their sympathizers. Even in the Senate, many Republicans who had not been members of the war faction in 1811 switched to the Clay camp during the 1812 session.[7]

The President's message on November 5 was stronger in tone than previous messages, or so it seemed to those eager to hear a summons of war.[8] It accused England of refusing all reasonable steps to meet American complaints. Instead of repealing its Orders in Council, the British government "at a moment when least to have been expected" had decided to enforce them more rigorously. "Indemnity and redress for other wrongs have continued to be withheld, and our coasts and the mouths of our harbors have again witnessed scenes not less derogatory to the dearest of our national rights than vexatious to the regular course of our trade."[9] Even with France, the United States had much reason to be disgruntled with "the rigorous and unexpected restriction" imposed on American trade. Then followed what many took to be an invitation to war: "I must now add that the period is arrived which claims from the legislative guardians of the national rights a system of more ample provisions for maintaining them." Because "the British cabinet perseveres not only in withholding a remedy for other wrongs, so long and so loudly calling for it," but engages in "measures which . . . have the character as well as the effect of war on our lawful commerce," counter measures had to be taken. "With this evidence of hostile inflexibility in trampling on rights which no independent nation can relinquish, Congress will feel the duty of putting the United States into an armor and an attitude demanded by the crisis, and corresponding with the national spirit and expectations."

[6]Patrick C. T. White, *A Nation on Trial: America and the War of 1812.* New York: John Wiley and Sons, Inc., 1965, pp. 87–88. Also see Reginald Horsman, *The Causes of the War of 1812.* Philadelphia: University of Pennsylvania Press, 1962, p. 226.

[7]White, p. 227; Horsman, p. 102; *Annals of Congress,* 11th Congress, 1st session, vol. 1, p. 579.

[8]Perkins, p. 296, notes that the British press considered the tone similar to previous messages.

[9]James D. Richardson, *Messages and Papers of the Presidents,* vol. 1. New York: Bureau of National Literature, 1917, pp. 492–494. All references in this paragraph are to the message of November 5, 1811.

## Slipping toward War

The message set the tone for the ensuing session. At last, the country went forward with serious preparations for war. Felix Grundy of Tennessee, a warhawk member of the House Foreign Relations Committee, minced no words when he told the House in early December of 1811, that these preparations meant that "the Rubicon is passed" and that the country must go on to war.[10] Under the leadership of Clay and his lieutenants a larger army and navy were authorized as well as new taxes to pay for them.[11] This was not done without difficulties, however. There was dissension in Congress about the size of the army, and even disagreement between the President and congressional leaders on this point. Congress eventually provided for an army larger than the President had wished. There was even more difficulty about the size of the navy. The navy had always been looked upon as a pet of the Federalist party so that voting for naval appropriations had been anathema to good Republicans. Now Republicans were asked to approve an enlargement of the number of ships and sailors. But even this, the new guard was willing to do.

The greatest difficulty sprang from the financial measures devised by Gallatin to pay for the war. Fighting was fine, but paying for it was a different matter. Madison was convinced that every generation ought to bear the expenses of its own wars. He felt that this would be a deterrent to wars that he hated so thoroughly.[12] He favored Gallatin's measures to raise taxes and duties to pay for the expenses of the military build-up. But Congress felt differently. It took much political maneuvering and oratory to steer Gallatin's war budget safely through Congress. When Congress approved paying for war measures, Madison interpreted this as "the strongest proof they could give that they do not mean to flinch from the contest to which the mad conduct of G. B. drives them."[13]

And so the winter passed, filled with Congressional debates, preparations for war, and popular and official speculations about whether and when war would break out, yet a certain air of unreality about it all. Somehow, neither the public nor even the President seemed to believe that it was really true that the nation was approaching the final climax. Business went

[10]U. S. Congress, *Annals*, 12th Congress, 1st session, p. 424.

[11]*Annals*, 12th Congress, 1st session, pp. 34–83, 131–159, 279–298, 413–427, 441–548, 595–1033, 1058–1155, 1587–1614. Even a brief glance over the legislative debates makes it clear that no President can be fully informed about the details of all viewpoints presented in Congress.

[12]See his article on "Universal Peace" in the *National Gazette*, February 2, 1792. Gaillard Hunt, ed., *The Writings of James Madison*, vol. 6. New York: G. P. Putnam's, 1910, pp. 88–91. All references to Hunt are to this work, unless noted otherwise.

surance rates did not rise, nor did prices. Negotiations with both the British and French continued in their home capitals as well as in Washington. In Washington, the French and English emissaries felt that the majority of the public favored war, but that the administration was determined to preserve the peace.

The die for war was cast in April when Congress, at the request of the President, stepped up economic warfare—relaxed since the demise of Jefferson's Embargo—by prohibiting all trade with England and France.[14] Pressured on the one side by warhawks in and out of Congress for an immediate declaration of war, annoyed on the other at the attempts of New England Federalists to wean the northeastern portion of the country away from loyalty to the government, Madison had decided that more rigorous economic measures were again in order to retaliate against attacks on American trade. He had all but despaired of winning any concessions from the British to relax their restraints on American trade with Britain's enemies. He knew that promises from Napoleon to stop interfering with American commerce, on which America's lenient policy towards France was based, were illusory. Soon it would become apparent to all that Napoleon had sold a mess of pottage to the United States and that economic retaliation against France would have to resume. Faced with these prospects, Madison had suggested a two-months stoppage of trade, preliminary to more stringent measures. Congress approved by a vote of 70 to 41 in the House, and a vote of 20 to 13 in the Senate. In the Senate, the moderate Republicans managed to extend the time limit to ninety days. Madison wrote Jefferson that there was general agreement that the measure amounted to a delayed declaration of war. For this reason, the President had been empowered to call a hundred thousand militia into service. Dissension existed only about "the time and form of entering into hostilities."[15]

But, though Madison had intended the economic rupture as a prelude to war, he was still hoping, against hope, that fate would somehow abort the war. This hope was shattered on the twenty-second of May. On that day he received a letter which became the "immediate impulse to the declaration of war."[16] The letter, a note from Lord Castlereagh to Augustus Foster, the British envoy in Washington, indicated that the Orders in Council, which closed European ports to the United States, would not be repealed, even though Prime Minister Perceval, their author, had been assassinated. Madison interpreted the note as a final British rejection of all on as usual with few financial or economic barometers indicating war. In-

[13]Hunt, vol. 8, p. 182.

[14]Hunt, vol. 8, pp. 185–186.

[15]Hunt, vol. 8, p. 188.

[16]Quoted in Abbot E. Smith, *James Madison, Builder*. New York: Wilson-Erickson, 1937, p. 302.

[17]Horsman, pp. 245, 256–257.

on Britain occurred two days later when news arrived that a French squadron had attacked an American ship. Monroe angrily complained to the French minister in Washington that when the people were psychologically ready for war, "your frigates come and burn our ships, destroy all our work, and put the Administration in the falsest and most terrible position in which a government can find itself placed."[18] The French minister was disturbed, but consoled himself with the idea that war policies had proceeded so far that neither the President nor Congress could recede.

His hunch was right, although there were some rumors that internal politics helped to tip the scales for war in the end. These rumors, ever since debated by historians, were to the effect that congressional leaders, sensing hesitation in Madison, threatened to deny him renomination for the presidency unless he declared war. The weight of historical evidence seems to be that such a threat, if it was made, was not crucial.[19] Madison knew that congressional leaders wanted war. A congressional delegation headed by Speaker Clay had told him, conceivably in connection with the threat, that the majority of Congress would vote for war if he requested it.[20] These leaders to him represented the will of the public. When a declaration of war was involved it was the President's duty, even if his own opinions were contrary, to go along with the wishes of Congress. This time compliance was easy with little desire on the part of the President to seek to persuade Congress to change its point of view. His own feelings about war were ambivalent. He had smarted under the taunts of his enemies and his own conscience about his unsuccessful policy of peaceful coercion. If Congress was willing to take its struggling President off the hook, so be it.

## War at Last

On June 1, 1812, Madison sent a message recommending war to Congress. Typically, he put the burden of final decision on the legislature:

[18]Adams, Book 6, pp. 194–195.

[19]Henry Adams, *The Life of Albert Gallatin* (hereafter cited as Adams, *The Life of*). Philadelphia: J. B. Lippincott, 1880, p. 459; Gaillard Hunt, *The Life of James Madison*. New York: Doubleday, 1902, p. 316 ff; Brown, p. 172; Edward Channing, *A History of the United States*, vol. 4. New York: The Macmillan Co., 1929, pp. 453–454. For opposing views see Sidney H. Gay, *James Madison*. Cambridge: The Riverside Press, 1884, pp. 296–297; Richard Hildreth, *The History of the United States*, vol. 6. New York: Harper and Row, 1880, p. 298; McMaster, vol. 3, p. 445; Hermann Eduard Von Holst, *The Constitutional and Political History of the United States, 1876–1892*, vol. 1, p. 230.

[20]Gaillard Hunt, "Joseph Gales on the War Manifesto of 1812," *American Historical Review*, vol. 13 (1907–1908), p. 309.

Whether the United States shall continue passive under these progressive usurpations, and their accumulating wrongs, or, opposing force to force in defence of their national rights shall commit a just cause into the hands of the Almighty Disposer of events . . . is a solemn question, which the Constitution wisely confides to the Legislative Department of the Government.[21]

Although it had been Madison's view that plans for a declaration of war should receive the widest public exposure so that those who would have to do the fighting and dying would have a chance to voice their views, Congress now went into secret session. Henry Adams commented later that "Perhaps no single act, in a hundred years of American history, showed less regard for personal and party consistency than the refusal by the Republicans of 1812 to allow society either rights or privileges in regard to the declaration of war upon England."[22]

In Henry Adams' view:

Henry Clay and his friends were weary of debate and afraid of defeat. Only a few days before, May 29, Clay forced Randolph from the floor by tactics which showed that no more discussion was to be allowed. The secret session gave the Speaker absolute power, and annihilated opposition.[23]

The House had gone along with its leadership and had rejected a motion for open debate by a vote of 76 to 46.[24] This near to victory, Clay did not want to take chances. Although a few days earlier Madison had confidently written to Jefferson that he would "throw forward the flag of the country, sure that the people would press forward and defend it," Clay was not so certain.[25] A public debate might bring to the fore the advocates of further delay, of peace, or even those who wanted to fight France and Britain simultaneously.

[21]*Annals,* 12th Congress, 1st session, p. 1629. (The entire message is found on pp. 1624–1629.)

[22]Adams, *History,* Book 6, p. 227. However, some of the congressional arguments against the war declaration were published in the press. See for example Samuel Taggart's remarks in the *Alexandria Gazette,* June 24, 1812, after war had been declared.

[23]Adams, *History,* p. 227.

[24]*Annals,* 12th Congress, 1st session, Book 6, p. 1630.

[25]Smith, p. 303. Bernard Mayo, in his study of *Henry Clay.* Boston: Houghton Mifflin Co., 1937, p. 520, quotes a speech made by Senator Calhoun nearly thirty years later in which he claimed that Clay wanted an open debate. Whe other Senators disagreed, the question was left for the President to decide. Madison allegedly favored secrecy.

On June 4, the House voted for war 79 to 49.[26] In the Senate, although debate was secret, more time was taken for deliberation. On June 18, the vote for war came, 19 to 13.[27] Like the vote in the House, it was strictly on partisan as well as sectional lines.[28] Only Republicans were for war. Except for inland Vermont, all the New England states and the eastern maritime and commercial states such as New York, New Jersey, and Delaware voted for peace. The votes of the southern and western states assured acceptance of hostilities. And so on June 19, 1812, the President proclaimed what his enemies derisively called "Mr. Madison's war."

## The Timing of the War Declaration

The declaration of war on June 19, 1812, raises two interesting questions that shed light on the role which public opinion played in the nation's war policies. Why was war declared in 1812, when it had not been declared previously; and why was war declared against Britain only, and not France?[29] Henry Adams, in his analysis of foreign policy decision making in the War of 1812, ponders the question of timing at length. He notes that even at its height, the public's war fever in 1812 seemed "somewhat intermittent and imaginary. A passion that needed to be nursed for five years before it acquired strength to break into act, could not seem genuine. . . ."[30] He doubted that: "A nation which had submitted to robbery and violence in 1805, in 1807, in 1809," could "lash itself into rage in 1811 when it had no new grievance to allege. . . ." He wondered whether the public could feel "earnest in maintaining national honor, for everyone admitted that the nation had sacrificed its honor. . . ." And then he asked: "Yet what honor was to be hoped from a war which required continual submission to one robber as the price of resistance to another?" The public, in Adams' opinion,

> could argue that Americans were not placed between desperate alternatives. They had persevered hitherto, in spite of their leaders, in the policy of peace; had suffered much injury and acute mortification, but had won

[26]*Annals*, 12th Congress, 1st session, p. 1637.

[27]*Annals*, 12th Congress, 1st session, p. 297.

[28]For the debates, see *Annals*, 12th Congress, 1st session, pp. 265–298.

[29]Various interpretations of the chief determinants which led to war are presented in Brown, especially pp. 188–189; Horsman, especially pp. 266–267; Julius W. Pratt, *The Expansionists of 1812*. New York: The Macmillan Company, 1925, p. 14; and P. C. T. White, p. 130.

[30]Adams, *History*, Book 6, p. 113. The remaining quotes in this paragraph are from the same source.

Louisiana and West Florida, had given democracy all it asked, and had remained in reasonable harmony with the liberal movement of the world. They were reaping the fruit of their patient and obstinate husbandry; for Russia and Sweden were about to fight their battles without reward. Napoleon offered them favors more or less real, and even England could not long resist the pressure of her interests. Jefferson's policy had wrought all the evil it could cause—perhaps it had cost the highest price the nation could pay; but after the nation had suffered the evil and paid the price, it had a right to profit.[31]

The moment for fighting had been in 1807 and had passed by 1809. Adams concluded, albeit without citing proof: "Not merely old Republicans, but an actual majority of the people probably held these opinions. . . ."[32]

Why, then, did Madison ask for a declaration of war in May of 1812? The answer does not lie in logic, nor even in the accumulation of irritations, although this was important, but in the coincidence and synthesis of factors which, bit by bit, relentlessly pushed Madison and Congress in the direction of war. As the preceding narrative has indicated, no single factor which propelled the country towards war would have been sufficient by itself. Rather, a combination of factors and timing turned the tide, not least of all the change in congressional complexion in 1811 that Madison interpreted as a popular mandate for war, and the pressure of impending presidential elections in 1812.

Madison was physically tired and mentally discouraged with the intransigence of his foreign and domestic opponents. More than ever, he was willing to pass the burden of decision making on to the hands of Congress rather than assuming the duties of leadership himself. Young William Preston, a house guest at the White House, noted with concern that Madison seemed "exceedingly harassed . . . his countenance was pallid and hard. . . . Indeed, he went outside but twice in seven months. At the levees and formal dinners he was taciturn . . . his manner somewhat cold and stiff. His toils and vexations were many: often he would be at his desk by candlelight in the morning."[33] According to Preston, "the opposition . . . was a source of daily annoyance . . . exciting him to petulance and querulousness. . . ."[34]

Madison hated quarrels within and among parties, and the policy of half war, half peace, was whipping factional controversy to an ugly crest. He was stunned by the insinuations that his own policy was selfishly motivated, that he was solely interested in reelection and willing to trade the country's interest for presidential votes. He despised war and all forms of physical violence. "He was a man of peace and books. . . . Nowhere

[31]Adams, *History*, Book 6, p. 114.
[32]Adams, *History*, Book 6, p. 115.
[33]Mayo, pp. 481–482.
[34]Mayo, p. 482.

in the record of his life is there a hint that he ever had a quarrel which approached culminating in a personal encounter. His blood flowed temperately. . . ."[35] Yet there were times when the clear-cut challenge of war, which silenced petty public arguments and rallied the nation around its leaders, was preferable to cantankerous, muddled peace.

One additional factor, a personnel and personality change among the President's key advisors, helps explain the declaration of war in 1812 when none had been issued in 1809. In April, 1811, Madison had dismissed Robert Smith, his ineffective, uncongenial Secretary of State. Instead, he had engaged the services of the experienced James Monroe. With the Department of State in much more capable and trusted hands, and with much less controversy about foreign policy during Cabinet meetings, Madison felt encouraged to proceed with a stronger policy than seemed feasible before.

Whether Monroe favored war when he entered the Cabinet and swayed the wavering Madison to his point of view, or whether he hoped to deflect policy into peaceful channels and was finally convinced by the President and the course of events that war was unavoidable, remains a matter of dispute. Edward Channing paints Monroe as a full-blown war hawk:

> Monroe came into office with a serious and firm conviction that the American government must resent the usage which it had received and was receiving from foreign powers, not by arguments and protests merely, but by an appeal to arms. These opinions he held forth day and night and was more responsible than any one else for the declaration of war.[36]

Julius Pratt sees him as a dove, converted to a hawk reluctantly by the force of circumstances.

> Monroe came into office desirous of seeking an accommodation with Great Britain; but when confronted with the inflexibility of the British Minister Foster in July combined with Napoleon's well-timed concessions, from this time on he, like Madison . . . set his face toward war with England.[37]

Whichever view of Monroe is correct, what matters for our purposes is that Monroe and Madison, at the crucial moment, concurred that war

---

[35]Hunt, vol. 1, pp. xxxi–xxxii.

[36]Channing, vol. 4, p. 447. Also see Thomas Hart Benton, *Thirty Years' View*, vol. 1, New York: Appleton, 1854, p. 630, that Monroe "brought Mr. Madison to the war point." Also see the evidence cited by Joseph Gales in *American Historical Review*, vol. 13 (1907–1908), pp. 306–309.

[37]Samuel F. Bemis, *The American Secretaries of State and Their Diplomacy*, vol. 3. New York: Alfred A. Knopf, 1927, pp. 218–220. Also note Henry Adams, *History*, Book 5, pp. 371 ff, in which B. Perkins, p. 271, concurs that Monroe entered the cabinet with the intention of tempering Madison's hostile policy but was converted by Madison instead.

was advisable. Apparently neither one had decided on a long-term policy when Monroe entered the Cabinet in April, 1811. In fact, Monroe had made it one of the conditions for accepting the State Department post that he should have freedom to formulate his own policies. He did not wish to enter the government "if our course is fixed and the destiny of our country dependent on arrangements already made, on measures already taken. . . ."[38] Madison assured him that no firm policy decisions had been made: "I perceive not any commitments . . . that could necessarily embarrass deliberations. . . ."[39] Furthermore, there appeared to be no basic incompatibilities in the views of the new Secretary and his President:

> With the mutual knowledge of our respective views of the foreign as well as domestic interests of our country, I see no serious obstacles on either side to an association of our labors in promoting them.[40]

## Why Peace Was Kept with France

And why was Britain, and not France, the object of war? The reasons were many. Federalists argued that the pro-French feelings of the President and his cohorts in and out of government were the sole reason. Napoleon had been treacherous and double-dealing. Between 1807 and 1812 the French had confiscated 558 American ships compared to 389 seized by the British. They had imprisoned the ships' crews which, in many ways, was worse than the impressment policy of the British. French dungeons were hardly more wholesome than the holds of British ships, however vile. Yet French crimes were not avenged. As Charles Prentiss, a contemporary poet, described what seemed like blatant favoritism:

> If England look askance, we boil with rage;
> And blood, blood only, can the wound assuage;
> Yet, whipt, robbed, kicked, and spit upon, by France,
> We treat her with the greater complaisance.[41]

What Prentiss did not say was well expressed by Nathaniel Macon when he alleged that "the Devil himself could not tell which government, England or France, is the most wicked."[42] Consistency would have dictated war with both. Calhoun favored such a "triangular" war, and so did the proponents of a motion in the Senate, which would have added a dec-

[38]Henry Adams, *The Writings of Albert Gallatin*, vol. 1. Philadelphia: J. B. Lippincott, 1879, p. 498. Also see Adams, *History*, Book 5, pp. 371–372.
[39]Adams, *History*, Book 5, p. 373.
[40]Adams, *History*, Book 5, pp. 372–373.
[41]Elizabeth B. White, *American Opinion of France*. New York: Alfred A. Knopf, 1927, p. 12.
[42]Adams, *History*, Book 6, p. 196.

laration of war against France to the declaration of war against Britain. But the motion lost by a vote of 18 to 14. Madison himself had taken a dim view of fighting two enemies simultaneously when the country was not even prepared to fight one effectively. Such a war might be long and costly, without achieving America's policy objectives in the end. Just prior to his war message he had written Jefferson that:

> To go to war ag'st both, presents a thousand difficulties. . . . it might hasten thro' a peace with G. B. or F. a termination, for a while at least, of the obstinate questions now pending with both. But even this advantage is not certain. For a prolongation of such a war might be viewed by both Belligts as desirable. . . .[43]

If triangular war was impractical, then why not war against France rather than Britain? The reasons were manifold, with considerations of public opinion dominant. The pro-French leanings of Madison and Republicans in general have already been mentioned. The President himself had cooled considerably toward Napoleon and his country, but the pro-French public had not been equally disillusioned. After all, France was an old-time ally. France had been the champion of democratic liberties, England the champion of aristocratic privileges.

But there were more compelling reasons for choosing England as the adversary. Most of England's depredations had taken place close to home, under the very noses of Americans. French assaults were less visible because they took place in far-off Europe. There were no French attacks to compare with overt British-American naval fights like the battle of the *Chesapeake* and the *Leopard* and the *Little Belt* affair, both of which stirred and fanned public hostility against the British. When American wounded and dead were carried ashore the assailants were Britishers and not Frenchmen. When American ships were searched in American waters and seamen impressed for service in the British navy, their kinfolk railed against the cruelty of the British.[44] Worse still, the atrocities of Indian warfare along the Northwest border and in the Southwest were blamed on British instigations. The Battle of Tippecanoe, on November 7, 1811, had cost the lives of nearly two hundred white settlers.[45] It was Britain that was arming the savages, Britain that allegedly was paying bounties for the scalps of American women and children. The voices of public indignation that reached the President's ears asked for British scalps in retaliation.

Moreover, as the President's military advisors and political petitioners pointed out repeatedly, it was Britain that could be attacked most easily

---

[43]U. S. Congress, *Letters and Other Writings of James Madison, 1794–1815*, vol. 2, 1865, p. 535.

[44]A presidential report on January 16, 1812, informed Congress that 6,057 Americans had been impressed by the British. Channing, vol. 4, p. 483.

[45]Bemis, vol. 3, p. 234.

by a nation lacking a navy and from whom a victorious war could exact the prizes most coveted by various sections. How easy it would be to attack sparsely settled Canada! Kentucky militia men, the President was told, thought that they could do the task single-handedly. Once taken, the area could be annexed to the United States, giving the profitable fur trade and the treasured outlets to the northern seas to Americans. In the South, a war with England would justify an attack on Spain, England's ally. In this way, the rest of Florida, which Madison and Westerners wanted, could easily be acquired. No similar prizes could be expected from war with France. Besides, to Madison and his advisors, Napoleon seemed stronger militarily than his British opponent. French victories over the British lion would make America's conquest of a weakened adversary all the easier. If a choice had to be made between enemies, Madison was well justified in selecting Britain as the victim.

## A Preference for Economic Coercion

If Madison had devised his policies toward France and England in a vacuum and without the advice or pressure of associates and the public, he probably would have chosen the same policies that he in fact adopted, with the exception of those at the very end. Judging from his personality and his writings, it seems quite likely that he would have continued the policy of procrastination and palliation in hopes that time would ultimately fight America's battles for her. He shared Jefferson's view that:

> For twenty years to come we should consider peace as the *summum bonum* of our country. At the end of that period we shall be 20,000,000 in number, and 40,000,000 in energy, when encountering the starved and rickety paupers and dwarfs of English workshops.[46]

Young America would grow into a mighty nation and would outstrip her enemies.

Measures of economic coercion were fully in accord with Madison's theories of human motivation. He believed firmly that people, individually, and in the aggregate, would yield to economic pressures. With his confidence as yet untarnished by bitter experiences, he wrote to Jefferson:

> The efficacy of an embargo cannot be doubted. Indeed, if the commercial weapon can be properly shaped for the Executive hand, it is more and more apparent to me that it can force all the nations having colonies in this quarter of the globe to respect our rights.[47]

[46]Dumas Malone, *Correspondence between Thomas Jefferson and Pierre Samuel du Pont de Nemours, 1798–1817*. Boston: Houghton Mifflin Co., 1930, pp. 172–173.

[47]Adams, *History*, Book 3, p. 75.

With Jefferson, he devised the various nonimportation, blockade, and embargo measures with the full expectation that they would be adequately supported by the public and would accomplish their purpose.

The impact of economic coercion measures was to be heightened by threatening or implying that war would follow if economic coercion failed to yield results. Madison was quite willing to arm the country to convey the impression of military strength, which would lend backbone to less militant policies. As he had told members of the Virginia constitutional convention years earlier:

> I am no friend to naval or land armaments in time of peace, but if they be necessary, the calamity must be submitted to. Weakness will invite insults. A respectable government . . . will be security against attacks and insults. . . . The best way to avoid danger, is to be in a capacity to withstand it. . . .[48]

In light of these views he often was far more willing than Congress to recommend appropriations for military forces.[49]

However, with his ingrained opposition to military forces and fighting, Madison could never bring himself to recommend forces as large as were needed, should his bluff be called.[50] Consequently, the country was poorly equipped and prepared militarily when war came in 1812. It had a navy of only 16 sea-going vessels, although these were exceedingly well-manned with expert crews. The army was small, badly staffed, and poorly administered. Since Americans disliked military service, new recruits were extremely difficult to find even after Congress had authorized them. Just before the war, John Randolph had desperately admonished Congress:

> I know that we are on the brink of some dreadful scourge, some great desolation, some awful visitation. . . . Go to war without money, without men, without a navy! Go to war when we have not the courage . . . to lay war taxes! When your whole courage is exhibited in passing Resolutions! The people will not believe it![51]

But, of course, neither Madison nor many Congressmen had expected to have to go to war. And the people who clamored the loudest for war seemed totally unconcerned about the poor state of preparations.

It seemed to Madison that war "contains so much folly, as well as wickedness, that much is to be hoped from the progress of reason."[52] It should be possible to avert it. For "if any thing is to be hoped, every

---

[48]Hunt, vol. 5, p. 169.

[49]See Adams, *The Life of,* pp. 414–415.

[50]The editor of the *Aurora* sneered that the executive prepared for war like a man who would "run a race with his legs in his pockets." Mayo, p. 468.

[51]Adams, *History,* Book 6, p. 211.

[52]Hunt, vol. 6, pp. 88–89.

thing ought to be tried."[53] War was the progenitor of armies, debts, and taxes—the favorite instruments for establishing the domination of the few over the many. It was the corroding principle of republicanism, producing inequalities of fortune, opportunities for fraud, and executive tyranny.[54] War, he feared, would upset the delicate scheme of governmental balances:

> In time of actual war, great discretionary powers are constantly given to the Executive Magistrate. Constant apprehension of war, has the same tendency to render the head too large for the body. A standing military force, with an overgrown Executive will not long be safe companions to liberty. The means of defence against foreign danger, have been always the instruments of tyranny at home.[55]

Besides, war might tear apart the Union of the States, which meant so much to Madison. He knew that the New England states might secede or that their efforts to undermine the war effort might seriously endanger victory and, in that way, result in a dismemberment of the country. What he had feared actually happened later. By mid-August of 1812, seditious opposition in New England had "so clogged the wheels of the war that I fear the campaign will not accomplish the object of it."[56] The governors of Massachusetts and Connecticut had refused to even furnish troops to defend the frontier against British incursions.[57] In addition, war might jeopardize the American position in Florida where successful interventions, abetted by the administration, were under way to detach East Florida from Spain.[58] For all these reasons Madison infinitely preferred non-military solutions to outright war.

But Madison also knew from experience that the choice of peace or war might depend on forces beyond his control; ". . . the question may be decided for us, by actual hostilities against us or by proceedings leaving no choice but between absolute disgrace and resistance by force."[59] In fact, "manifestations of patience under injuries and indignities" might "be

[53]Adams, *History*, Book 6, p. 89.

[54]Edward M. Burns, *James Madison: Philosopher of the Constitution.* New Brunswick: Rutgers University Press, 1938, p. 84.

[55]Hunt, vol. 3, p. 317.

[56]Hunt, vol. 8, pp. 210–211.

[57]Hunt, vol. 8, pp. 224–225. The tragic consequences of fighting a war when "the Presidency slept; effective power resided nowhere; an anarchy of groups reigned over the nation," is described by James S. Young, *The Washington Community, 1800–1828.* New York: Columbia University Press, 1966, pp. 183–186.

[58]Bemis, vol. 3, pp. 235–248.

[59]Hunt, vol. 8, p. 86. (From a letter written January 17, 1810 to George Joy, the American diplomatic representative in Copenhagen.)

carried so far as to invite this very dilemma. . . ."[60] By the summer of 1812, the failure of his policy of economic coercion to win substantial concessions from France and Britain indicated that the limits of patience had been reached. Widespread public resistance to congressional curbs on American trade had cut off the alternative of more vigorous economic warfare.

If the policy of economic coercion would not yield results, the only other promising alternative was a policy of war. Such a policy had many advocates among men whom Madison trusted most. He could see justification for it in the insults dealt out by Napoleon as well as the British, and he could also see the possible gains to the United States if the war should be successful. Had he not approved of the Louisiana Purchase, although the methods were irregular? Had he not ignored some of his own qualms and principles of proper procedure to acquire West Florida? If throwing aside his scruples about war would now redound to the benefit of the country, his duty to put the public welfare above all other principles justified the action. Those segments of the public who were not already with him would quickly see the merits of the action and would approve it.

### The Decision-Making Inner Circle

Like his predecessors, Madison felt duty-bound to consult his Cabinet before making foreign policy decisions. He also was in constant touch with congressional leaders. But aside from these formal sources, there is little indication that he was influenced more than casually by the advice of anyone else. A few close friends may have been the exception. He solicited Jefferson's advice throughout his presidency and he relied on Monroe's opinions even before Monroe entered the Cabinet. Madison received a volumious number of letters from friends and acquaintances throughout the country, but apparently they did not sway him in his decisions. Like Jefferson's advice, he used them largely to corroborate information that he had received from his more formal sources.

Socially, the President met and entertained hundreds of people at dinner in the White House, but apparently little official business was transacted at these events. His guests enjoyed more talking to the vivacious Mrs. Madison than to her taciturn husband. While Dolley Madison "succeeded by virtue of her gracious and amiable nature, her vivacity and abounding hospitality, in offsetting some of the stiffness of her husband"[61]

[60]Hunt, vol. 8, p. 86.
[61]Smith, p. 210.

she had little influence on his policy making. Unlike Abigail Adams who could discuss politics intelligently and help her husband in clarifying his own mind, Dolley Madison "was not a woman of much intellect."[62] Occasionally, she would relate her husband's views to some of her friends, but never with any comments of her own, which would indicate that he had discussed these views with her. In fact, Madison, mistrusting the views of single individuals, may have deemed it improper to consult his wife's opinions seriously. There is no record in his correspondence that he ever sought her advice in political matters.

Although the Cabinet was Madison's most consistent advisor on policies and the state of public opinion, its influence was limited for several reasons. Madison, on principle, preferred the advice of the legislature with its built-in checks and balances of a multitude of diverse interests to the much smaller and less well-balanced Cabinet. Second, the President thoroughly disliked and mistrusted several members of his official family and was apt to discount their advice for this reason. His personal dislike, which was heartily reciprocated, was compounded by the fact that several Cabinet members were obviously unequal to their tasks and quarrelled viciously among themselves. Henry Adams rated Madison's original Cabinet as "the least satisfactory that any President had known. . . . Gallatin alone gave it character. . . . The Secretary of State, the Secretary of War, and the Secretary of the Navy . . . stood in a position of inevitable hostility to his influence."[63] Gallatin, the most distinguished member, commented acidly that "Our Cabinet presents a novel spectacle in the political world; divided against itself, and the most deadly animosity raging between its principal members. . . ."[64]

Madison's lack of assertiveness and political skill was responsible for such a weak Cabinet. He allowed himself to be pushed around. With a certain amount of exaggeration the historian McMaster described the political scene:

> . . . All was weakness, factiousness, uncertainty, and doubt. A faction, a cabal, small in numbers, small in ability, without a leader, and without any concerted plan, completely ruled him. He was, as Randolph truly said, "President de jure." It was William Duane and Michael Leib, the brothers Robert Smith and Samuel Smith, and William Giles that determined who should sit in the Cabinet, who should sit on the Supreme Bench, who should be ministers at foreign courts, what administration measure should be passed, and what should be defeated. Madison was

[62]Smith, p. 210.
[63]Adams, *History*, Book 5, pp. 9–10.
[64]Adams, *The Life of*, p. 431.

> . . . as docile, as submissive to the dictates of the cabal, as indifferent to the ruin toward which they were driving him, as he could have been. . . .[65]

The Cabinet members, who were selected or approved by this group of politicians with an eye partly on sectional politics and partly on personal political debts, included New Englander Dr. William Eustis as Secretary of War, and South Carolinian Colonel Paul Hamilton as Secretary of the Navy.[66] Secretary Eustis had been a practicing physician and a hospital surgeon during the Revolution. He had experience in the legislature, including service as a congressman during Jefferson's Administration. The kindest comment to be made about him what that he was "mediocre."[67] Henry Adams, pointedly frank, commented: "Little could be said of the appointment, except that no other candidate was suggested who seemed better qualified for the place."[68] Paul Hamilton, the Secretary of the Navy, had been governor of South Carolina ten years earlier. Henry Adams disposed of him in one terse sentence: "No one seemed aware why he had attracted the President's attention, or what qualities fitted him for the charge of naval affairs. . . ."[69]

The least auspicious choice was the Secretary of State, Robert Smith, from Maryland. Madison had wanted to make the able and experienced Albert Gallatin, Jefferson's Secretary of the Treasury, his Secretary of State. It was an excellent selection. But Gallatin, a Pennsylvanian, had many enemies in Congress who objected to his stringent financial policies and who held his foreign birth and accent and his French background against him. Besides, the Smith clan was eager to retain a foothold in the Cabinet.[70] Madison was given to understand that the Gallatin nomination would not be approved unless a Cabinet spot was given to Robert Smith.

[65]McMaster, vol. 3, p. 399. William Duane was publisher of the *Aurora;* Michael Leib, Samuel Smith, and William Giles were senators from Pennsylvania, Maryland, and Virginia, respectively. Robert Smith was the newly appointed Secretary of State.

[66]Irving Brant, *James Madison,* vol. 5. Indianapolis: The Bobbs-Merrill Co., Inc., 1956, p. 26. Caesar Rodney, the Attorney General, served only part time, dividing his services between Washington and his private law practice in Delaware. Postmaster General Gideon Granger from Connecticut was not then considered to hold Cabinet rank.

[67]Mayo, p. 482.

[68]Adams, *History,* Book 5, p. 9. Also see Madison's letter to Henry Lee, February, 1827. Hunt, vol. 3, p. 564.

[69]Adams, *History,* Book 5, p. 9.

[70]The position of Secretary of the Navy, which Smith had held in the Jefferson Administration, was considered relatively unimportant. See Hunt, vol. 8, pp. 302–303.

A private sounding out of prospective Senatorial votes had confirmed these intimations.[71] Madison then suggested Smith for the Treasury post. Gallatin, who considered Smith incompetent and extravagant and personally objectionable, did not want the former Secretary of the Navy in the Treasury post. He feared that Smith would be little more than a bench warmer, leaving the real work of the Treasury to Gallatin, who would then be saddled with handling two Cabinet posts simultaneously. Under the circumstances Gallatin preferred to be renominated for the Treasury, leaving the State Department to Smith by default.

Madison acceded to the demands of the Smith faction, even though he felt that Robert Smith's abilities were limited. His appointment would force the President, on many occasions, to act as his own Secretary of State. Just how competent or incompetent Smith was to cope with the duties of the State Department is hard to say. His contemporaries differed in their appraisal as much as have later historians. According to some, he was "vain, talkative, wanting in discretion, ignorant of the duties of his post . . . wholly unfit for the great office. . . ."[72] Others gave him ratings of "adequate" or "mediocre" or even better.[73] John Quincy Adams bemoaned the fact that the Smith appointment placed "in the Department of State, at the most critical period of foreign affairs and against the will of the President, a person incompetent, to the exclusion of a man eminently qualified for the office."[74] Putting the responsibility for American foreign policy squarely on Smith's shoulders, he charged that the Secretary's bungling had allowed the forces for war to gain irreparable speed. "Had Mr. Gallatin been then appointed Secretary of State, it is highly probable that the war with Great Britain would not have taken place."[75]

It is possible that the able and versatile Gallatin, enjoying the trust and confidence of the President, would have been able to provide Cabinet leadership in foreign policy making. However, it is not certain in which direction he would have led, despite his eagerness to avert war so that the national debt could be paid off. But to blame the war policy solely on Smith is unfair. The President could have taken a firm lead in foreign policy making, had he desired to do so. Instead, he called his Cabinet together, listened to their divergent views and their bickering, and then, no joint conclusion having been reached, adjourned without a decision. Executive leadership was totally lacking.

[71]Brant, vol. 5, p. 24.

[72]McMaster, vol. 3, p. 339. Also see the appraisals of Hunt, *Life of Madison*; Adams, *The Life of*; Channing, vol. 4, p. 403; B. Perkins.

[73]See Brant, vol. 5; A. Smith; and C. C. Tansill's account in Bemis, vol. 3.

[74]Adams, *The Life of*, p. 391. (From J. Q. Adams' unpublished account entitled "Madison and Gallatin, 1809.")

[75]Adams, *The Life of*, p. 391.

It was Gallatin who infused new spirit into the executive branch at the end of the 11th Congress when he disgustedly tendered his resignation. His letter to the President detailed the sorry state of the Cabinet and the bad effect Cabinet conflicts were having on policy and the confidence of the American public in its government:

> New subdivisions and personal factions equally hostile to yourself and the general welfare daily acquire additional strength. Measures of vital importance have been and are defeated; every operation, even of the most simple and ordinary nature, is prevented or impeded; the embarrassments of government, great as from foreign causes they already are, are unnecessarily increased: public confidence in the public councils and in the Executive is impaired. . . . Such a state of things cannot last; a radical and speedy remedy has become absolutely necessary.[76]

Jolted by Gallatin's analysis and the impending loss of the one member of his Cabinet in whom he had confidence, Madison decided to take a firmer hand. He persuaded Gallatin to remain as Secretary of the Treasury and fired Robert Smith from the State Department. In his place he appointed a fellow Virginian, James Monroe. The appointment did not only please the President and Gallatin, but it might also help to restore public confidence if, indeed, it had been lost. As Madison wrote to Jefferson: ". . . I feel myself on firm ground, as well in the public opinion as in my own consciousness."[77] At last the Department of State was in steady, competent, experienced hands. Backed by Monroe and Gallatin and their assurances that large sections of the public favored stronger policies, Madison no longer hesitated to indicate to Congress and the country the direction of foreign policy which he deemed wisest. There would be a stronger policy of coercion by threats and economic penalties and, possibly, war.

Overall, one can probably say that the Cabinet constituted a collective mind for Madison. If this collective mind could come to no decision, Madison drifted uncertainly. With his mistrust of the views of a single person, especially in foreign affairs where no nation should "commit interests of so delicate and momentous a kind, as those which concern its intercourse with the rest of the world, to the sole disposal" of a Chief Executive, he did not wish to assert himself.[78] But if he had the support of two trusted voices, such as those of Gallatin and Monroe, he was willing to reach a decision. Had they advised him in a manner uncongenial to his own thinking he would have felt the strains of an unnerving dilemma. Whether to heed the advice or to ignore it would have been an exceedingly onerous question.

[76]Adams, *The Life of*, pp. 434–435.
[77]Hunt, vol. 8, p. 136.
[78]From a passage of Federalist No. 75 written by Hamilton and quoted with approval by Madison who claimed it expressed his own views. Hunt, vol. 6, pp. 175–176.

## The Guiding Role of Congress

For an answer Madison would undoubtedly have turned to the commands of public opinion as expressed in the voice of Congress. This was the voice that he believed must have precedence in case of conflicting advice. If the Cabinet could not agree or if the opinions of the Executive branch conflicted with the views of the people as expressed in the legislature: "the President and his Cabinet . . . were not disposed to resist. Mr. Madison would not allow his Administration to fall behind the public feeling in its assertion and maintenance of national dignity. . . ."[79]

Unfortunately, in 1811 and 1812 Congress did not speak with a united voice, which made it difficult to determine who really spoke for the bulk of the American people. There was the feeble chatter of the Federalists, always carping, criticizing, complaining. As an expression of petty and evil factionalism, that could be ignored.[80] Then there were the many voices with which Madison's own party spoke, for party discipline had all but broken down. "From 1810 to 1815, there was . . . hardly a Republican leadership. There were factions and cliques, and the consistent supporters of the administration itself could hardly be called more than a Gallatin-Madison clique."[81] The views of these factions ranged from those who seemed to have joined the Federalist chorus to the shouts of those who demanded immediate war.

Among these voices one group was outstanding—the clique headed by the Speaker of the Twelfth Congress, Henry Clay. Young, enthusiastic, and astute, he presented the triumph of a new generation over the tired old politicians who had guided the country through its early struggles. Through skilled and clever parliamentary maneuvers, Clay managed to pack the important foreign policy committees with men of his own ilk and convictions. This meant that Madison, when he communicated with the elected leadership in Congress, dealt almost exclusively with Clay's warhawk group. So did his Cabinet spokesmen, Gallatin and Monroe. Monroe especially was in almost daily contact with the Congressional foreign policy leaders.[82]

The President apparently made no effort to contact leaders of Congress aside from the chosen spokesmen. Nor did the Clay faction undertake this task. Clay and his circle were willing to listen politely and attentively to all views, but gave little evidence of serious consideration for them. Their own specific plans were a closely-kept secret. Congressmen com-

[79]Adams, *The Life of,* p. 445.

[80]B. Perkins, p. 35, claims that Federalist criticism was totally negative from 1805 to 1812.

[81]D. R. Anderson, *William Branch Giles.* Menasha, Wis.: George Banta, 1914, pp. 155–156. Also see Young, p. 183.

[82]Bemis, vol. 3, pp. 222–223.

plained that they had "little communication with the knowing ones" and that they could do little more than guess about the plans of the inner circle.[83] Although debates had taken place, there had been no real interchange of opinion—none of the balancing of opposing views that Madison considered so essential in jelling true public opinion.

Nonetheless, the President seemed satisfied with the end product. He knew that the warhawks did not mirror the opinions of all Republicans and that their advice was not a compromise solution. But he also realized that some views are incompatible and cannot be solved by a middle way. Obviously, one could not simultaneously go to war and remain at peace, fight either Britain or France or engage them both, strengthen or weaken the policy of economic coercion. In such a dilemma, when decisions had to be made the voice of congressional leaders entrusted with foreign affairs was the closest reflection of public opinion available to the President. Imperfect as it might be, there was no better, more accurate, or more widely acceptable reflection anywhere. The President acting in accordance with the wishes of the chosen leaders of the popular branch of government was playing his proper constitutional role. In Abbot Smith's words:

> For almost the first time in the history of the country the Executive played the part which the Constitution had intended it to play . . . very active in the technical business of foreign affairs. . . . On the other hand, he left strictly to Congress the determination of a course of national action: war or peace, submission or retaliation.[84]

This does not mean that the Clay spokesmen dictated to the President and that he became their puppet. Madison had his own views. He felt that his analysis and plans were sound because they were supported and approved by his trusted advisors in the Cabinet and by other political consultants throughout the country who wrote to him. Ex-President Jefferson, his long-time political mentor, concurred fully.[85] The policy alternatives pondered by Madison included the possibility of war if no concessions at all should be forthcoming from either France or Britain. The function performed by the congressional leadership was that of pointing to the one alternative among several considered by the President.

Since the congressional choice was one that the President could conceivably have adopted without any pressure at all, it is difficult to assign a precise weight to the influence of the Clay faction. Even Jefferson, prime architect of the policy of economic coercion, had come to the conclusion by the spring of 1812 that war was the only alternative and that the people favored it. However, given Madison's philosophies and his relatively close adherence to them, one is forced to guess that he would have followed con-

[83]Adams, *History*, Book 6, p. 129.
[84]Smith, p. 285.
[85]Bemis, vol. 3, pp. 222–223.

gressional directions even if they ran counter to his own preferences. The reason would not have been "passive acquiescence," as Henry Adams charged, but a firm belief that the President executes the will of the nation while the Congress establishes what that will is.[86]

While the President's official ears were primarily attentive to the "proper" mouthpieces for the expression of public opinion, he was interested in other views, too. He would often ask his associates about significant opinions which they might have heard from persons with whom the President lacked contact. William Preston, his young houseguest, observed that:

> Of his intimates he asked many questions: what had Congress done? What did John Marshall think of its doings? . . . Of Randolph he would pettishly say: "the damned rascal! I wonder how he would conduct the government. It is easy for them to make speeches."[87]

But this was largely curiosity mixed with a desire to know what sort of opposition or difficulties his enemies and some of his friends were concocting for him. Aside from subconscious reactions to these opinion tidbits and plans made to forestall or parry anticipated ill effects, the President did not receive opposition ideas as opinion suggestions that deserved a hearing. The concept of a loyal opposition, which deserved respect and consideration, had not yet made its appearance on the American political scene.

## A Snub for Papers and Petitions

Aside from heeding the advice of congressional spokesmen, trusted Cabinet members, and a few other confidants, the President was near deaf to the flood of political opinions expressed throughout the country. Nothing in the record shows that he was overtly influenced in any way by nonofficial communications or even resolutions of state legislatures, other than those which corroborated his views and his image of public opinion as formed by himself and the inner circle. But it was only *near* deafness, not complete lack of hearing and attention. The mere fact that Madison carefully read letters and petitions addressed to him and answered the arguments presented to him assured a limited degree of presidential awareness and consideration.

When petitions praised his course he would commend the senders for their patriotic sentiments, trying to strengthen their favorable attitude even further. When they complained he sympathized and chided, hoping that

[86]Adams, *The Life of*, p. 455.
[87]Mayo, p. 482.

the prestige of his office might have some effect in reversing adverse opinions. But on the whole it was a fairly sterile exchange of views, probably more valuable as catharsis for the petitioner than as information for the recipient. Thus when New England merchants had unburdened themselves about the deleterious effects which the Non-Importation Acts had on their trade, a fact that Madison knew and from which he anticipated complaints from the merchants, Madison answered blandly that "it was always the fate of the few to suffer for the good of all."[88] This was hardly a persuasive answer for injured merchants who had major grievances. Nonetheless, the fact that it came directly from the President was important. Madison knew that those who instigated the writing of the petition to him were also capable of devising obstacles that might interfere with those foreign policies that depended on public cooperation. They might not speak for many of the people whose views they claimed to represent, but they had it in their power to gather the support of like-minded citizens. He himself had instigated many petitions in hopes that they might become a focal point around which opinions and support might crystallize and, in turn, be marshalled for effective action.

When the press is as violent and vocal as it was during the early years of the country, it is easy to postulate it as a very influential force. The researcher who scans paper after paper of a given period wonders how the President reacted to this or that threat, suggestion, or well-formulated opinion. When the views expressed are those of important writers, he assumes that the President could not possibly have ignored them. But the plain fact is that no President, even in our computerized age of high-speed communication, reads or even is aware of more than a fraction of all the important opinions expressed throughout the country. Presidents take the bulk of their cues from the digests of news that they receive from their associates. These digests, both in selection of facts reported and in emphasis and interpretation, bear the editorial stamp of their human source. Most presidential advisors tell the President what he wants to hear and in the form most palatable to him. Unwelcome news is glossed over, reinterpreted to become more favorable, or denigrated to cast contempt on those connected with it. Even when the President consumes information without any intermediaries, his choice is restricted. Time, circumstances, and desires determine to what matters he will give attention. These matters are not always the most crucial ones, given human fallibility in selection and the wearying task of coping with the burdens of the presidency.

Madison's experiences are illustrative. He did not read most of the papers that supposedly carried the voice of the people to him or described the state of the public mind and temper. He was not acutely conscious of what later historians described as the "flaming words of the press,"

[88]McMaster, vol. 3, p. 424.

which "inflamed" public opinion and "editors and correspondents" who
"beseeched the new Twelfth Congress" with demands for strong action
against Britain.[89] For the most part, the man in the White House viewed
press reports with cool detachment and skepticism. He doubted that the
press mirrored public opinion or spoke the truth.

The press, as we have seen, was for Madison a hired mistress currying
favor with whoever paid the bills. There were administration papers and
anti-administration papers, each seeking to win as many adherents for their
writers' and editors' points of view as could be won, by any means—fair
or foul. If he read them, who could blame Madison for ignoring or dep-
recating as worthless newspaper accounts that referred to him as "whif-
fling Jemmy" and called him Jefferson's "political pimp."[90] When his
policies were attacked as "imbecilities" that would plunge the country into
a "bungling, quixotic war" merely to insure the reelection of "Mounseer
Madison," or when he was told that if he had any warfever "it must be a
species of *intermittent*, what is vulgarly called the *shaking ague*," he could
hardly be expected to consider this as valuable advice to be seriously considered.[91] On the other hand, if he was told that praise had been heaped
on his policies, that "*the voice of every American is FOR WAR*," that
"a spark from the altar of Seventy-Six" had united Americans behind the
government's policy, which now "must breathe our spirit, and speak our
sentiment," and write this "SECOND DECLARATION OF INDEPEN-
DENCE," who could blame him for taking such views to be as accurate
an expression of public opinion as the press was able to present?[92]

While he disparaged most press reports and rarely cited them as a
source of information or advice for his own decisions, he was fully aware
that newspaper opinions were important because they were apt to influence opinion leaders and their followers.[93] In a roundabout way, they
were likely to be reflected in the caliber of men elected to the legislature
and in the opinions that formed the basis of legislation in that body. For
the legislature, even more than Congress, was subject to petitions and press
appeals. Newspapers often addressed themselves directly to Congress, and
Congressmen found it far more difficult than the President to ignore requests by influential opinion leaders when these leaders came from their

[89]Mayo, p. 390.

[90]Mayo, p. 392, quoting the *Baltimore Federal Republican*.

[91]Mayo, pp. 392, 492, quoting *Pickering's Gazette* and the *Aurora*.

[92]Mayo, pp. 391, 393, 523, quoting the *Essex Register, Niles Register,* and the
*Lexington Reporter*. (Capitals and italics in original.)

[93] For a rare instance see his correspondence with William Pinkney in 1810.
This refers to press reports of Pinkney's conduct, which were evidently the
result of an honest misconstruction of some things, and an ignorance of others,
neither of which can be lasting." Hunt, vol. 8, pp. 119–120.

section of the country. During the war crisis of 1812, the Senate leadership reminded its passionate orators that debate for or against war had become pointless when "the National Spirit is alive and every eye is directed, every finger pointed to the same object."[94] With "the people . . . indignant to the last degree," the Senate had the "imperious duty *to act*."[95]

Moreover, political leaders in various parts of the country were apt to take their cues from the papers of their political mentors. Thus the din of the press, passed through the filter of perception of lesser political leaders, was apt to reach presidential ears through his advisors. Because evidence of public support lent prestige to policies and because newspaper accounts were commonly cited as evidence, it was useful to manufacture or solicit favorable press opinions. Although there is no direct evidence that Madison commissioned writers to present administration views in the press in order to get them circulated, it is quite probable that a number of the essays in the press that mirrored his views were inspired by him or members of his inner circle. Harriet Martineau, the perceptive English observer who had visited Madison and other government leaders and who felt that "the worship of Opinion is, at this day, the established religion of the United States," reported that the practice of opinion-planting was widespread:[96]

> It is no secret that some able personage at Washington writes letters on the politics and politicians of the general government, and sends them to the remotest corners of the Union, to appear in their newspapers; after which, they are collected in the administration newspaper at Washington, as testimonies of public opinion in the respective districts where they appear.[97]

## Wielding the Public Opinion Club

Aside from routine communications and with the possible exception of press plants, Madison did not take a very active hand in public opinion manipulation and leadership during the months leading to war. His conception of the President as a servant of Congress rather than a leader made reticence natural. His lack of leadership ability confirmed him in his decision. And his failure in his one major venture to whip up anti-Federalist sentiment hardened his inclination to keep aloof from the struggle for the minds of the American people.

[94]Hunt, vol. 8, p. 414.
[95]Hunt, vol. 8, p. 414.
[96]Harriet Martineau, *Society in America*, vol. 3. New York: Sanders and Otley, 1837, p. 7.
[97]Martineau, vol. 1, pp. 147–148.

The abortive venture was the purchase, for $50,000, of a series of reports by a British agent, John Henry. John Henry had been paid by the governor general of Canada to investigate pro-British sentiments in New England to discover whether the area was ripe for rebellion against the central government. He had talked with a number of prominent Federalists who had regaled him with stories of their distaste of the government's policies and their preference for leaving British, rather than French offenses unavenged. He offered to sell this information to Madison. Madison bought it and submitted it to Congress in March, 1812, with the idea that it would furnish ammunition against the Federalists and would discredit them as traitors in the eyes of their countrymen.[98] Unhappily for Madison, the correspondence revealed nothing that was not already public knowledge. Among those who were to be impressed with the Federalist perfidy, few could have doubted that New England Federalists were not in accord with the administration's views. The reports did not even contain the names of the persons with whom Henry had talked. He had deleted these names, and when requested to furnish them he claimed that they were "unavailable." Thus the attempt at maligning Federalists failed and even boomeranged because Federalists accused the President of spending $50,000 of public money on worthless papers.[99] Although publication of the letters did little to turn the tide against Federalists in New England, they did serve temporarily as a cause célèbre for pro-war activists. From Madison's point of view this was an undesirable side-effect because prior to the actual war decision he did not wish to inflame the war spirit too violently.[100]

Madison also used the spectre of public opinion pressure to prop up his demands to France and Britain for policy changes. In conversations with the French and British ministers in Washington, as well as in communications sent to American diplomats abroad, he frequently stressed that the U. S. public was indignant about outrages committed by their respective countries.[101] The implication was that if the President's requests were not heeded, the public would force him to sterner measures. The foreign representatives, well acquainted with the force of mob action

---

[98]For Madison's message to Congress and the text of the correspondence, as well as congressional reaction, see *Annals*, 12th Congress, 1st session, pp. 1162–1196.

[99]Although the John Henry documents disclosed no evidence of treasonable activities, other documents did. But they were not then available to Madison. See Brown, pp. 180–181.

[100]Mayo, p. 493.

[101]See for instance a letter to William Pinkney, October 30, 1810, which speaks of "public irritation . . . constant heart-burning . . . a deep and settled indignation" about British policies. Hunt, vol. 8, p. 120.

in France and Britain, took these hints seriously. However, they tried to corroborate them with their own observations. The dispatches of the diplomats of the period are full of reports about the state of public opinion in the United States, as observed by these ministers, and the state of public opinion as reported to them by the President, the Secretary of State, or other knowledgeable public figures.

For instance, the French ambassador reported to his home office a conversation he had had with Secretary of State Monroe in the fall of 1811. In this conversation, Monroe had informed him that the American people were dissatisfied with the policies of the French. Monroe had said that "the present situation was equally burdensome and intolerable to the citizens, and little suited to the dignity of the government. . . ." To this he had added the general observation that:

> The President does indeed hold the rudder of the Ship of State; he guides, but it is public opinion which makes the vessel move. On France depends the winning of public opinion; and we wish for it, as you can well conceive that in our position we should.[102]

Madison could not have expressed his theories of public opinion any better, nor used them more tellingly to try to influence a foreign power.

## The Presidential Curtain of Secrecy

Does a President who believes that "war should . . . only be declared by the authority of the people, whose toils and treasures are to support its burdens, instead of the government which is to reap its fruits. . . ." make greater efforts to keep the public informed than one who assigns to the public a lesser role?[103] A comparison of the policies leading to the War of 1812 with the policies leading to the Louisiana Purchase gives the impression that Madison was far less secretive about policy considerations than Jefferson. Time and again, Jefferson withheld important information from the public and even from Congress. Madison, with few exceptions, kept Congress and the public fully informed.

However, the record may be misleading. Secrecy to assure the Executive's freedom of negotiation seemed even more essential during the Louisiana Purchase than in the events that led to the War of 1812. Besides, secrecy was far easier to preserve in Jefferson's case than in Madison's. The assaults on American seamen and on American trade could not be hidden from the public. Americans could see for themselves when battles were fought off their shores and when dead and wounded sailors were

[102]Adams, *History*, Book 6, pp. 120–121.
[103]Hunt, vol. 6, p. 90.

brought ashore. Relatives of impressed sailors knew that their loved ones had not returned home. Merchants knew when their cargoes had been confiscated, and owners of seagoing vessels could be fairly certain when their ships did not return to port that they had been taken as prizes by either France or Britain. Thus Madison had little choice but to announce the facts.

Occasionally, when he could prevaricate he did. For example, for a long time he gave the impression that Napoleon had withdrawn objectionable limitations on American commerce. He did this even after there could no longer be any reasonable doubt that the restrictions remained in force. His purpose then was to keep the public calm and to play imaginary French concessions off against British recalcitrance. One cannot tell whether in keeping Congress and the public informed about the progress of negotiations his motive was to reassure them that proper action was being taken, or merely to inform them because they had a right to know. Both purposes were served by the same action, and both yielded the same desirable result—popular and congressional support for presidential policies.

That Madison was as willing as Jefferson to keep important negotiations secret (when this was essential to conclude them successfully) is well illustrated by his Florida policy. Here he proceeded quickly and silently by presidential fiat to acquire additional territory.[104] Nonetheless, it seems fair to say that he felt more moral compulsion to keep the public informed than did Jefferson. Jefferson's policy was to tell nothing, unless necessary; Madison's policy was to omit nothing, unless compelled to do otherwise.

Besides his principles, the pressures brought to bear on the President also made it more difficult to keep the public and Congress uninformed. A strong Congress, eager to formulate policy, continually pressured him for all the information he might have. Attacks by the press on his policies forced him to supply information in rebuttal. And the necessity to rally a divided country behind a policy of increased military expenditures, and later behind a policy of war, made it essential to present a fairly full record to the people. Although Madison felt that opposition to his policy was largely motivated by selfish considerations, especially by the cupidity of New England merchants, it was necessary to counter the opposition so that it would not paralyze governmental action. Opposition pressures were strong, including threats of secession that Madison knew full well might be carried out. If information could rally the people it had to be given—even at the risk of disclosing the hand of the government to its foreign enemies.

How successfully Madison supplied this information is another question. With his reluctance to impose his own views on others, and his belief in the importance of the interplay of varying opinions, he failed to take

[104]For details, see Adams, *History*, Book 5, p. 310 ff.

a firm hand in opinion leadership to unify the country effectively behind his policies. Aside from the Henry letters, he left opinion leadership largely to others. But without a clearcut national policy and the image of a strong President willing and able to fight for it and carry it through, none of the lesser leaders could step into the breech left by the chief executive. Not even the adversaries of the United States were convinced that the country would go to war if concessions failed to materialize and depredations continued. A firmer presidential posture might have prevented war or, if it came, might have prepared and unified public opinion to meet the military challenge more effectively.[105]

## The Wisdom of the War Decision

Would the President have done better if he had accepted opinions other than those he heeded? The question can be answered only by yet other questions: "Better for what? Better for whom?". Most of the opinions proffered to him were motivated by sectional and personal interests. From the Southerners who wanted to annex Florida, to the Northerners who wanted to seize Canada, to the New Englanders primarily interested in trade, to the relatives of sailors desperately eager for the release of their loved ones—interests varied widely and suggested policies varied equally as widely. Few people took a national point of view. But even for those who wanted to discern the national interest, broadly conceived, it was difficult to decide what this interest was and how it could best be guarded. There was no real consensus among the people or its leaders about the specific goals of the nation or the best methods for implementing various goals.

Many twentieth-century historians believe that the war could and should have been avoided and that Madison's policy of caution would have borne fruit ultimately. There are others who feel that the war was beneficial in its side effects. It rallied the nation and made it a more respected member of international society. In the future, its threats would be taken seriously and could be substituted for overt hostilities. Thus the verdict of history is split—as split as Madison's own appraisal of the advantages of various policy alternatives presented to the nation in 1812.

[105]On this point see Brown, pp. 188–189. Young, p. 186, comments: "Policy initiative thus passed to a Congress unable to mobilize itself, much less the populace, for the pursuit of any consistent policy. A nation on the brink of military disaster was thus embarked upon erratic and mutually contradictory courses of action dictated by transitory factional combinations at the seat of government."

# 9

# Monroe's Views of Political Man

Show me his friends and I the man shall know.
SILAS WEIR MITCHELL[1]

As long as several men in assembly regard themselves as a single body, they have only a single will which is concerned with their common preservation and general well-being. In this case, all the springs of the State are vigorous and simple and its rules clear and luminous; there are no embroilments or conflicts of interests; the common good is everywhere clearly apparent, and only good sense is needed to perceive it.
ROUSSEAU, *The Social Contract*

[1]Quoted in Harvey William Cushing, *The Life of Sir William Osler*, vol. 1. Oxford: Clarendon Press, 1925, p. 673.

# 9

## Outer Directedness and a Tinge of Paranoia

In the fall of 1780, Thomas Jefferson received a letter from a young friend and protégé, James Monroe. In it young Monroe in his awkward and adulatory style acknowledged extreme gratitude for Jefferson's guidance. Monroe's military career had been beset with many difficulties, few of them of his own making. Now, at twenty-two, he saw this career coming to an end, and with it his dreams for a meteoric rise to public notice. His none too robust faith in his ability to climb to the top by dint of hard work had been severely shaken:

> A variety of disappointments with respect to ye prospects of my private fortune previous to my acquaintance with your Excellency, upon which I had built as on ground which could not deceive me, which failed in a manner which could not have been expected, perplexed my plan of life and exposed to inconveniences which had nearly destroyed me.[2]

Then Jefferson had come to the rescue. "In this situation had I not formed a connection with you I should most certainly have retired from society with a resolution never to have entered on ye stage again."[3]

The letter reveals three characteristic strands of Monroe's personality and life. It intimates his strong faith and reliance on hero models. It reveals how quickly and deeply he could be disappointed if success eluded efforts that he had labeled as "perfect" to guard his self-respect. It also provides a background for understanding the life-long persecution complex of a man whose fragile ego needed scapegoats to bear the blame for his defeats. Like many other hero worshippers, Monroe saw his world in Manichaean extremes. On the good side were fellow republicans, liberty-loving benefactors of the people, and his friends. On the evil side were his enemies, selfish monarchists, interested in nothing but enslavement of the people and personal advancement for themselves. These fundamental traits go far in explaining Monroe's political decisions and philosophy.

Monroe's hero worship began early in life. He spent his youth in Westmoreland County, Virginia, which was then known as the "Athens of America." It was near Williamsburg where the Virginia legislature as well as the Virginia social elite met regularly. Monroe's uncle, Judge Joseph

---

[2]Stanislaus M. Hamilton, ed., *The Writings of James Monroe*, vol. 1. New York: G. P. Putnam's Sons, 1902, p. 8. Hereafter cited as "Monroe."
[3]Monroe, vol. 1, p. 8.

Jones, was one of them with many valuable connections. Monroe's father was a "carpenter-gentleman" and considered only a small planter by the Virginia standards of the time. Nonetheless, he and his family shared in the rich social life of the colony.

Awareness of his somewhat lower social standing may have contributed to his son's shyness, insecurity, lack of social ease, and awe and respect for the members of Virginia's "first families" with whom he came into contact. At any rate, at an early and impressionable age young Monroe, a tall, raw-boned and square-shouldered youth, became acquainted with Washington, Jefferson, Madison, the Randolphs, the Masons, the Lees, and similar luminaries. He may have felt that if he modeled himself after such people, his inordinate appetite for success would be gratified more easily. The first families of Virginia strove to follow a pattern that prepared them well for public leadership. It stressed "integrity, restraint, deference, responsibility, and honor" and "carried with it a sense of obligation to serve the state when called to public office."[4]

When a young man is ambitious, works hard, sets his sights high, and travels in good company he expects success. Yet success eluded Monroe on many occasions. His prematurely terminated military career has already been mentioned. Although General Washington characterized him as a "brave, active, and sensible officer," he was never put in charge of his own company because of recruitment difficulties.[5] He also suffered a number of electoral defeats. He lost elections to the Virginia House of Delegates, to the United States Senate, and plans to nominate him for the presidency in 1808 burst like a half-blown bubble. True enough, these defeats were paired with and topped by victories. But Monroe was apt to revel in the miseries of his defeats and to ignore the glories of his victories. With characteristic self-pity he wrote to Edmond Genêt, the former French minister, in 1800: "I too have had my day of suffering. I served with zeal the cause of liberty and my country, and was requited by every act of injustice which could be rendered me, short of imprisonment and death."[6]

The defeats that rankled him above all and gave him a jaundiced view of international intercourse were his diplomatic debacles. First among them and most traumatic, was abortive service in France during the Washington Administration. He had embarked for France with high hopes of cementing the ties between the United States and its erstwhile ally, and in the process cementing his own claim to fame. He was recalled by his su-

[4]Leonard D. White, *The Jeffersonians*. New York: The Macmillan Co., 1951, p. 550.

[5]John C. Fitzpatrick, ed., *The Writings of George Washington*, vol. 34. Washington: Government Printing Office, 1941, p. 199.

[6]Monroe, vol. 3, p. 197.

periors before completing a normal tour of duty, for acting as a partisan of France and an opponent of Britain. His recall, giving the impression of incompetency on his part, gravely damaged his reputation. At least that is what he thought and brooded about. Stuart Gerry Brown, editor of Monroe's fragmentary autobiography, contends that

> in all the long years afterward Monroe never managed to press the trau-matic experience of this ill-fated mission into the background of his con-sciousness. There is even point to the notion that his whole later career was conducted with a view to vindicating his conduct then, and fixing his reputation for wise statesmanship, to heal the spiritual wounds he had suffered.[7]

Somewhat less traumatic, although still very painful, were the failure of the mission to Spain in 1804 and the rejection of the Monroe-Pinkney Treaty of 1806. In the Spanish mission, Monroe had been sent to assist Charles Pinckney in an effort to buy East Florida from Spain and to settle various claims with respect to West Florida. After months of fruitless ne-gotiations and annoyances by the laggard Spaniards, Monroe finally left Spain in disgust.

He proceeded to London to settle a series of disputes over shipping rights and impressment with the British. His treatment in London was equally as humiliating and frustrating as had been his reception in Spain. In the end, he and Pinkney were able to conclude a treaty that they con-sidered the best obtainable under the circumstances. But President Jeffer-son declared the terms unacceptable and contrary to the instructions given to his envoys. He refused even to submit the treaty to the Senate for con-sideration. All Monroe's efforts and humiliations had been for naught:

> It was only natural that he should come home in ill humor, feeling that he had been badly used. . . . Ten years before, a Federalist Adminis-tration had repudiated him as too friendly to France. Now he found him-self repudiated by a Republican Administration as too complacent to-ward England.[8]

Monroe ascribed his major failures to the design and wickedness of others. Since he felt he had acted blamelessly, defeats did not daunt him for long, although they made him more abrasively self-righteous and caus-tic. For instance, upon his return from France in 1797 he refused to admit that the Washington Administration might have had good cause for being

---

[7]Stuart Gerry Brown, ed., *The Autobiography of James Monroe.* Syracuse: Syracuse University Press, 1959, p. 8.

[8]Julius W. Pratt, "James Monroe," in Samuel F. Bemis, ed., *The American Secretaries of State and Their Diplomacy,* vol. 3. New York: Alfred A. Knopf, 1927, p. 208.

annoyed at his fawning attitude toward the French and his failure to carry out orders to support the treaty that Jay had just concluded in England. Monroe's aspersive account of the affair, as reported by a friend, was that

> The time they chose to recall Monroe was when from his correspondence they had reason to believe that he had succeeded in allaying the resentment of the French. Then, thinking they had nothing to fear from France, and that they had used Monroe so as to obtain every service that he could render, they recalled him, with the double view of giving to another person the merit of terminating the differences and of throwing upon him [Monroe] the blame of any that had existed before.[9]

In a comment that Monroe would have fully approved, the friend, Albert Gallatin, added: "I am also pretty well convinced that the American Administration have acted with a degree of meanness only exceeded by their folly, and that they have degraded the American name throughout Europe."[10]

The rejection of the Monroe-Pinkney treaty, according to Monroe, was for "defects of so metaphysical a nature that it was impossible . . . even to remember them for any length of time."[11] Monroe suspected that "the administration had withdrawn its confidence from and really wished to get rid of me."[12] He was "ready to lend an ear to friends who whispered that Madison had plotted his downfall as a convenient way of ruining too dangerous a rival for the Presidency. For years a cloud of distrust hung between him and his former friends."[13]

At an earlier date (1787) when Governor Randolph of Virginia had not appointed him as a delegate to the Constitutional Convention in Philadelphia, Monroe typically suspected a plot against himself. He wrote Jefferson:

> The Governor, I have reason to believe is unfriendly to me and hath shewn (if I am well informed) a disposition to thwart me; Madison, upon whose friendship I have calculated, whose views I have favored, and with whom I have held the most confidential correspondence since you left the continent, is in strict league with him and hath I have reason to believe concurred in arrangements unfavorable to me; a suspicion supported by some strong circumstances that this is the case, hath given me great uneasiness—however in this I may be disappointed and I wish it may be so.[14]

It apparently never occurred to Monroe that his own qualities, age, or experience might be deemed inferior to Richard Henry Lee, George Mason,

[9]Quoted in Brown, p. 9.
[10]Brown, p. 9.
[11]Monroe, vol. 5, p. 138.
[12]Monroe, vol. 5, p. 31.
[13]Pratt, p. 208.
[14]Monroe, vol. 1, p. 174.

James Madison, and Randolph himself—the men who were appointed to represent Virginia at the Convention.

The models whom Monroe chose to emulate were the republican leaders of his period, especially Thomas Jefferson. He felt a close intellectual, moral, and personal kinship with them. "Upon political subjects we perfectly agree and particularly in the reprobation of all measures that may be calculated to elevate the government above the people, or place it in any respect without its natural boundary."[15] Such agreement was not surprising. Monroe had studied law with Jefferson and had kept in close touch with him and other friends at all times. Given Monroe's great admiration for Jefferson and his strong inclination to agree with his republican friends, it is only natural that he proved an apt pupil for the older man's political ideas. Most likely he studied the social philosophies of Locke, Sidney, Bolingbroke, Montesquieu, Rousseau, and Bacon. Their works were in Jefferson's library, and were the staple literary diet of many of his contemporaries.

Monroe's political philosophy must be distilled from his letters and miscellaneous writings. He was neither an original thinker nor a philosopher, and never composed a formal political theory of his own. His ideas were absorbed from others, particularly his associates, and from his own political experiences. By the time he reached the presidency, he had rubbed elbows with nearly all the outstanding statesmen and politicians of his time. William Cresson, one of his biographers, calls him an "inveterate office-holder" and "one of the earliest American professional statesmen," pointing to his nearly 20 years of pre-presidential service in the Virginia House of Delegates, the Virginia governorship, the Continental Congress, the U. S. Senate, miscellaneous conventions and service in the Cabinet as Secretary of State and Secretary of War.[16] In addition, he had lived and worked in the diplomatic communities of France, England, and Spain, and had traveled in other parts of Europe. Able politician that he was, Monroe used ideas and experiences to good advantage. His writings are full of aphorisms that would be serviceable in the notebook of any practicing politician.

This does not mean that he did not write any political treatises at all. In fact, he published several. He wrote a defense of his action in France in 1796, a treatise explaining the features of the Federal Constitution to his Virginia constituents, and a later treatise defending the new constitution. He also composed a long essay on the powers of the national govern-

[15]Monroe, vol. 1, p. 223.

[16]William P. Cresson, *James Monroe*. Chapel Hill: The University of North Carolina Press, 1946, p. 114. George Dangerfield, *The Era of Good Feelings*. New York: Harcourt, Brace & World, 1953, p. 97, emphasizes his desire for public service in high places. "He longed to be useful, *conspicuously* useful. . . ."

ment in connection with his veto of a bill providing for national control over roads and waterways. But none of these went beyond mere exposition. They were useful question-and-answer catechisms but lacked the philosophical depth that one finds in the writings of Adams, Jefferson, and Madison. As Professor Brown put it in a comparison of Monroe with Jefferson:

> Monroe was less well read, less perceptive, less cultivated than Jefferson had been. And his native gifts were not comparable. But he was, nevertheless, an intelligent and observant man. The political lessons he drew from his experience were sound.[17]

### An Unbounded Faith in the People

What role did a man of Monroe's personality and background assign to public opinion? Monroe recognized only two kinds of publics, thanks to his habit of seeing the world in blacks and whites with few shades of gray in between. The mass of the people were wise and good; a small minority of leaders were conniving and self-seeking. The people's compliance with sound laws was "proof of their virtue."[18] The success of the new nation was testimony to their wisdom. "Had the people of the United States been educated in different principles; had they been less intelligent, less independent, or less virtuous, can it be believed that we should have maintained the same steady and consistent career, or been blessed with the same success?"[19]

With the mass of the people on the side of the angels, the devil's side was peopled by a few aristocratic renegades. The leaders of the Federalist party, in particular, were wicked conspirators whose views were not to count for public opinion. Members of the "royalist faction," like George Washington, had deliberately "suffered our people to perish in the jails and prison ships of New York, by a pusilanimous and temporizing policy."[20] The views of the people, as represented in the Republican party, could never be united with the views of the Federalist leaders, because they were "as opposite as light and darkness."[21]

Monroe would concede that it was possible for certain sections of the public to be misled, especially when their leaders were not representative of the public. The Federalists had been able, on many occasions, to carry the public with them, mainly because "the person whose fortune is con-

[17]Brown, p. 10.
[18]Monroe, vol. 3, p. 107.
[19]Monroe, vol. 6, p. 9.
[20]Monroe, vol. 3, pp. 262–263.
[21]Monroe, vol. 3, pp. 262–263.

nected with the government has greatly the advantage" in gaining public support.[22] Even liberal leaders could, at times, turn into extremists and continue to enjoy public support beyond the period for which they deserved it. Liberty might degenerate "into licentiousness, which dishonors the name and ruins the cause it professes to espouse."[23] The "correct rational liberty" was the one which had emanated from the American Revolution. An example of the other kind could be found in the behavior of the Jacobin society in France:

> By it all those atrocities which now stain and always will stain certain stages of the revolution were committed. . . . This society was therefore the greatest enemy of the revolution . . . [it] became such only in the course of events by degenerating and losing sight of the object which gave birth to them.[24]

Monroe's category of "good people" excluded Negroes. He considered them inferior to whites and not suited to the ordinary duties of citizenship. He commended the Constitutional Convention at Philadelphia for "conceiving their natural forces inferior to those of the whites; knowing that they require free men to overlook them, and that they enfeeble the State which possesses them."[25] When Virginia's slaves engaged in an abortive revolt in 1800, he expressed surprise that "the slaves should embark in this novel and unexampled enterprise of their own accord. . . . It was natural to suspect that they were prompted to it by others who were invisible," because slaves presumably did not have the same desire for liberty as white men.[26] Monroe's proposed solution was the settlement of Negroes in separate sections of the Union or in other parts of the world.

It is not clear from Monroe's writings whether he believed that Negroes could ultimately assume full citizenship responsibilities in a democracy. However, he expressed faith that other peoples, presently unfit for self-government, could become fit in time, given an education and a good example. Prophetically, he commented on the poor chances for republican governments in Latin America:

> The great defect is the ignorance of the people, by means whereof, they are made, in the hands of military adventurers, and priests, the instruments of their own destruction. Time, however, with some internal convulsions, and the form of our example, will gradually mature them for the great trust deposited in their hands.[27]

[22]Monroe, vol. 5, p. 73.
[23]Monroe, vol. 3, p. 376.
[24]Monroe, vol. 2, pp. 207–208.
[25]Monroe, vol. 1, pp. 357–358.
[26]Monroe, vol. 3, pp. 240–241.
[27]Monroe, vol. 6, pp. 317–318.

## Disdain for Elite Guidance

Monroe made no distinction between an intelligentsia, born to lead, and a mass public, destined to follow. All free men, given enough information, were capable of making decisions about governmental policies. With Jefferson, he shared a belief in

> the supreme value of intelligence as the only reliable means of directing social change; and a conviction that such intelligence was neither safe nor effective if it was monopolized by experts. Any intelligent man who had to live with political institutions was able to form some judgment of them.[28]

Formal government was a necessary evil and was to be kept as limited as possible. Moreover, it had to be restrained from impairing the liberties of the people. This is why Monroe believed so firmly that the Constitution should not be adopted unless it contained a Bill of Rights.

Under many circumstances people could choose more wisely without guidance from political elites. For instance, during the presidential electoral campaign of 1808, Monroe pleaded that top governmental leaders should not try to influence the public in its decision whether he or Madison would be the better candidate. "My opinion is that the nation should be left perfectly at liberty to make its own election, without any of the slightest interference, on the part of those to whom the public attention may be in any degree drawn in reference to that object."[29] During the Whiskey Rebellion of 1795 he told Madison that he "was extremely happy to find that the patriotism of the people, in every quarter, left to its own voluntary impulse and without any information that was calculated to stimulate it, was sufficient to triumph over the schemes of wicked and designing men."[30] He claimed that he had always been "convinced that this was a resource to be counted on with certainty upon any emergency."[31]

On the other hand, he believed that education was a help in preparing the public for the duties of citizenship. Not only would education "give support to the principle of the government itself," but "it would draw the youth of the country into society together by means whereof they would become acquainted and form friendships . . . which would equally promote the social harmony of the State, and the comfort and happiness of the individuals who compose it."[32] Monroe believed firmly that citizens who were educated in a democratic state absorbed a common political culture

---

[28]Arthur Styron, *The Last of the Cocked Hats: James Monroe and the Virginia Dynasty*. Norman: University of Oklahoma Press, 1945, p. 90.

[29]Monroe, vol. 5, p. 22.

[30]Monroe, vol. 2, p. 207.

[31]Monroe, vol. 2, p. 207.

[32]Monroe, vol. 3, p. 309.

that was essential for governmental harmony. He was almost rhapsodic in extolling the benefits to be reaped from cultural uniformity:

> Established in the new hemisphere, descended from the same ances-tors, speaking the same language, having the same religion and universal toleration, born equal and educated in the same principles of free gov-ernment, made independent by a common struggle and menaced by the same dangers, ties existed between them [the American people] which never applied before to separate communities. They had every motive to bind them together which could operate on the interests and affections of a generous, enlightened, and virtuous people, and it affords inexpress-ible consolation to find that these motives had their merited influence.[33]

Monroe believed that the American public knew much about govern-mental affairs and that "the bulk of the people are for democracy."[34] His contacts throughout his life had been with people who were well versed in the theory and practice of government and whose conversation very fre-quently centered on governmental matters. Since it accorded with his faith that the public should know much and should be interested, he ascribed interest and knowledge to it, similar to that of his associates. Adjectives that might describe his assessment of the public mind would be impartial, just, right, perceptive, and quick.

In 1797, when the Washington Administration had recalled him from France, he wrote to Secretary of State Pickering that "I now think proper to inform you, that it is my intention to carry the subject before that en-lightened and impartial tribunal, with all the lights which I possess."[35] The people, he felt sure, would judge his case fairly. The administration would receive "from the judgment of an impartial public, the censure which their misconduct entitled them to."[36] He prepared a lengthy treatise on "A View of the Conduct of the Executive in the Foreign Affairs of the United States" to supply the people with the necessary information.

He valued the judgment of the people more than the political acumen of the Senate. In 1801 he wrote Jefferson that "I would never consider what was likely to pass the Senate, but what in itself was just and right, pursuing it with decision, and risking the consequences with the people."[37] The Senate might not know what was right or might not wish to know, but the people certainly would. In the same letter, he expressed his faith that "a wise, firm, yet moderate course" pursued by republican politicians would separate the mass of the people from the federalist leaders.[38] In an

---

[33]Monroe, vol. 6, p. 224.
[34]Monroe, vol. 1, p. 223.
[35]Monroe, vol. 3, p. 84.
[36]Monroe, vol. 3, p. 280.
[37]Monroe, vol. 3, p. 262.
[38]Monroe, vol. 3, p. 262.

earlier letter written to Jefferson in 1793 about the public's reaction to Genêt's public statements, Monroe asserted that:

> . . . the public mind will not be governed by light or trivial incidents but will take the measures of 4 or 5 years together—as the data or rule to decide by—and if upon the whole the measures of the administration partake more of evil than good, let the incident which matures the crisis be what it may, they will condemn it. This is not suggested as a mere matter of surmise. I know the principle to be at work and I am well satisfied it will produce fruit in the course of a short time.[39]

Although the public was not given to snap decisions, it could make up its mind quickly. At the start of Jefferson's first administration, Monroe advised him that: "The public opinion expects some tone to be given your administration immediately and it will not long balance before it is formed, on the subject of what they are to expect from it."[40] This should pose no difficulties for Jefferson. If one could gain public opinion approval without being in office, one could certainly retain it afterwards. "You always had the people and now have the government on your side, so that the prospect is as favorable as could be wished."[41] This was true because "the people naturally cling to their government, I speak of the great mass, and often those in office and those who wish to be in office, side with it also."[42]

Monroe was not totally oblivious to the difficulties which might obstruct the attempt to hold on to public opinion. "At the same time it must be admitted you have much trouble and difficulty to encounter. Many friends may grow cool from disappointment; the violent who have their passions too much excited, will experience mortification, in not finding them fully gratified."[43] Besides peoples' own emotions, which might get into the way of sober judgment, there were always the wiles of the opposition to fear. Although the Federalist party was "a desperate party because it knows it has lost the public confidence," it still possessed enough power and inclination to "check the popular current which runs against them."[44] This is why the issues must be clearly presented to the public so that everything "might be distinctly seen and understood by the public."[45] Any seeming compromises between Republicans and Federalists "would have confounded parties and principles, thereby bewildered the understanding and checked the ardour of the people."[46]

[39]Monroe, vol. 1, pp. 271–272.
[40]Monroe, vol. 3, p. 263.
[41]Monroe, vol. 3, p. 263.
[42]Monroe, vol. 5, p. 73.
[43]Monroe, vol. 3, p. 263.
[44]Monroe, vol. 3, p. 264.
[45]Monroe, vol. 5, p. 55.
[46]Monroe, vol. 3, p. 262.

The people were especially well qualified to perform the electoral function. Choice by one's fellow citizens was therefore a great honor, no matter how lowly the office might be. "I distinguished" wrote Monroe, "between a ministerial office, and an appointment which might be conferred by the suffrage of the people."[47] The former he would decline, the latter he would accept. Among appointive offices, he would accept none but the secretaryship of State at the time. But "with my fellow citizens I should make no such condition, but would accept the office of magistrate upon the county bench if desired by them."[48]

## A Consensus of Principles in a Classless Society

As Monroe saw it, public opinion was the opinion shared by all right-thinking people. There was only one such opinion in the country because a common public interest united all views. What kept people apart in other states were class differences. In the absence of such difference, there was no cause for quarrel. In the United States:

> There was no family dethroned among us, no banished pretender in a foreign country looking back to his connections and adherents in the hope of recall; no order of nobility whose hereditary rights in the Government had been violated; no hierarchy which had been degraded and oppressed. There was but one order, that of the people. . . .[49]

He believed that "had distinct orders existed, our fortune might and probably would have been different."[50] In that case:

> A contest would probably have arisen in the outset between the orders for the control. Had the aristocracy prevailed, the people would have been heartless. Had the people prevailed, the nobility would probably have left the country, or, remaining behind, internal divisions would have taken place in every State and a civil war broken out. . . .[51]

Thanks to "the simplicity of the elements of which our system is composed . . . every change has tended to cement the Union."[52] There might be political factions who differed with the majority on certain measures of policy. But in "all great constitutional topics" they supported the majority view.[53] This was true of Republicans as well as of Federalists because "the great body of the federalists . . . are good republicans."[54]

[47]Monroe, vol. 5, pp. 109–110.
[48]Monroe, vol. 5, p. 111.
[49]Monroe, vol. 6, pp. 224–225.
[50]Monroe, vol. 6, p. 225.
[51]Monroe, vol. 6, p. 225.
[52]Monroe, vol. 6, p. 225.
[53]Monroe, vol. 5, pp. 176–177.
[54]Monroe, vol. 5, pp. 176–177.

In fact, Monroe believed that no parties at all were necessary in a republic where consensus about basic principles prevailed.

> Surely, our government may get on and prosper without the existence of parties. I have always considered their existence as the curse of the country, of which we had sufficient proof, more especially in the late war. Besides, how keep them alive, and in action? The causes which exist in other countries do not here. We have no distinct orders.[55]

Evidence of political strife to the contrary not withstanding, the day of perfect unity was near. "We have undoubtedly reached a new epoch in our political career . . . by the general peace, and the entire absence of all cause, as to public measures, for great political excitement, and, in truth, by the real prosperity of the Union."[56] Such a state, was to be "marked by a common effort to promote the public good in every line to which the powers of the general government extended."[57] Making the wish father to the thought Monroe predicted optimistically:

> It is my fixed opinion that this will be the result after some short interval, and that the restless and disturbed state of the Commonwealth, like the rolling of the waves after a storm, tho' worse than the storm itself, will subside, and leave the ship in perfect security. Public opinion will react on this body and keep it right.[58]

The consensus on principles within a democracy was the best assurance for freedom that citizens could have. For this reason, military forces should be recruited from the general public and should form a non-professional militia, rather than a professional military force. "The militia of a free state is justly considered the bulwark of its liberty. No people are secure in the enjoyment of their rights who keep within their limits a strong military force, trained to subordination and accustomed to obey with reverence the orders of its chief."[59] In the United States, should a ruling clique attempt to use the non-professional citizens' army to suppress the people, "it is not presumable that our officers, educated like ourselves in democratic principles, would abandon those principles to turn their arms against their country."[60]

Monroe even felt that the experience of self-government would make people ideologically akin across national boundaries. When he arrived in France in 1794, he dealt with the theme of republican fraternity:

> Republics should approach near to each other. In many respects they all have the same interest. But this is more specially the case with the

[55]Monroe, vol. 6, pp. 289–290.
[56]Monroe, vol. 6, pp. 289–290.
[57]Monroe, vol. 6, pp. 289–290.
[58]Monroe, vol. 6, pp. 289–290.
[59]Monroe, vol. 3, p. 310.
[60]Monroe, vol. 3, p. 310.

American and French republics—their governments are similar; they both cherish the same principles and rest on the same basis, the equal and unalienable rights of man.[61]

Even people in Western and Eastern Europe who did not enjoy self-government but who yearned for it, shared a common view of the world and its problems. How reminiscent this is of current views that people everywhere love liberty and peace and condemn the oppressive, war-mongering policies of their rulers!

It was easy for Monroe to feel that all well-intentioned and informed people shared the same outlook on politics. His friends, whom he worshipped, saw eye to eye on most issues. The outset of his administration coincided with an era in which partisan strife in the United States was at a relatively low ebb. The Federalist party had all but disappeared in the wake of the War of 1812. "Their misconduct in the late war, and the success of that war, broke them as a party."[62] This is what happened in a democracy to all factions whose aims were hostile to the public welfare.

Monroe tried to persuade himself that the differences within his own party were mere squabbles ruffling the surface of party unity. He was baffled by serious intraparty strife when he could not ignore it, and tried to explain it as the work of a few selfish men. He confided to Madison in 1822 that "I have never known such a state of things as has existed here during the last Session [of Congress], nor have I personally ever experienced so much embarrassment and mortification."[63] Such differences might be expected "where there is an open contest with a foreign enemy, or with an internal party. . . . but we are now blessed with peace, and the success of the late war has overwhelmed the federal party, so that there is no division of that kind to rally any persons together."[64] The responsibility, he felt, rested on the shoulders of a "small portion" of the members of Congress, "by far the greater number having been spectators of the scene."[65] This small minority, in order to discredit the administration and raise its own political stock accordingly, had not hesitated to undermine important public policies:

> Every little transaction has been sifted into, in many instances under the instigation of anonymous writers, on false, or prejudiced views, and the great effort seems to have been made to pull down institutions and characters, rather than to rear them up for the support and honor of the country.[66]

[61]Monroe, vol. 2, pp. 13–15.
[62]Monroe, vol. 6, pp. 289–290.
[63]Monroe, vol. 6, p. 286.
[64]Monroe, vol. 6, p. 286.
[65]Monroe, vol. 6, p. 292.
[66]Monroe, vol. 6, p. 292.

Monroe was by no means opposed to giving free reign to divergencies, provided they did not endanger joint action in matters of mutual concern. For this reason, he always advocated leaving as many governmental matters as possible to the separate control of the states. In this way, sectional differences could be accommodated without harm to the unity of the country as a whole. He stressed these points in his special message accompanying his veto of the Cumberland Road Bill. The Constitution had left internal improvements to the jurisdiction of the states so that "ambitious men" would not hereafter "by practicing upon the sectional interests, feelings, and prejudices endeavour under various pretexts to promote" disunion.[67] Monroe averred that he had "little fear of this danger, knowing well how strong the bond which holds us together is and who the people are who are thus held together; but still it is proper to look at and to provide against."[68] Hence, his veto of a measure that might in the absence of a constitutional authorization strain the bonds of union.

Monroe also shared Calhoun's views on the principle of concurrent majorities. National laws and activities should have concurrence from a majority in each state, rather than a mere numerical majority gathered from a minority of the states. Yet he considered this no obstacle to union because of the common political interests shared by people in all of the states. If he ever had any doubts about the political loyalty of various sections of the nation, his tour of the country immediately after inauguration allayed them. His appearance along the East coast and in central and western towns

> aroused an outburst of enthusiasm which turned his tour of duty into a triumphal progress. The old prejudice against him as a Southern man, as a member of the Virginia dynasty, as a President inimicable to the interests of the North and the East, disappeared instantly. Men of both parties joined in giving him such a welcome as had never been extended to any of his predecessors.[69]

The newspaper *Columbian Centinel* christened the period as the "Era of Good Feelings" and observed that the President's visit had served "to remove the prejudices, and harmonize feelings, annihilate dissentions, and make us *one people* . . . assured that the president will be president, not of a party, but of a great and powerful nation."[70]

No wonder that the President in an address at Baltimore on June 2, 1817, pointed with pride to "the increased harmony of public opinion,

[67]Monroe, vol. 6, p. 273.

[68]Monroe, vol. 6, p. 273.

[69]John Bach McMaster, *History of the People of the United States*, vol. 4. New York: D. Appleton, 1885, p. 378.

[70]Cresson, p. 288, quoting *Niles Register*, XII, July 19, 1817. Also see Dangerfield, p. 95.

founded on the successful career of a government which has never been equalled, and which promises, by a future development of its faculties, to augment in an eminent degree the blessings of this favored people."[71] Even "the great mass of our fellow-citizens, in the Eastern States . . . who had suffered in their character by their conduct in the late war . . . are as firmly attached to the union and to republican government as I have always believed or could desire them to be."[72]

## The Democratic Leader as the Voice of the People

If there was unanimous agreement about the proper direction of governmental policies, all expressions of political opinions by sincere Republicans from every walk of life could be taken as expressions of public opinion. Since political leaders were more apt to be vocal than the general public, their views were more readily available to government officials. Hence the voice of the people was most frequently conveyed through political elites.

It did not matter whether leaders came from Congress, the executive branch, state or local governments, or from nongovernmental political and civic groups in various parts of the country. They spoke for the public, except when their words betrayed them as advocates of personal interests. When they expressed wrong opinions—with Monroe and other good Republicans the judge of what was right or wrong—this, according to Monroe's devil theory, could only happen because they were "exciters of local feelings, and interests, for selfish purposes," or because they were engaged in sinister plots.[73] Except for such self-seekers and conspirators and their willing and unwilling dupes, the opinions expressed by public leaders could be taken at face value and the substance of their remarks was bound to be in the public interest.

Accordingly, Monroe believed that the endorsement of the federal constitution by prominent men was proof that the constitution deserved and had public approval. In what sounds like an uncharacteristic appeal to the wisdom of an elite, Monroe urged acceptance of the advice of men like Dickenson, Franklin, and Washington who approved the new constitution.

> You can not for a moment suppose that such men would deceive you!
> If human nature were capable of falling at once from the height of virtue

[71]Quoted in Daniel C. Gilman, *James Monroe*. Cambridge: The Riverside Press, 1924, p. 138.
[72]Monroe, vol. 6, p. 27.
[73]Monroe, vol. 6, p. 91.

to the depth of depravity; even then you were safe—for they could construct no government which would oppress you, that would not equally oppress them, and their posterity.[74]

For Monroe this was no appeal to the knowledge of the "well-born." It was an appeal to the people to listen to their very own leaders drawn from among them and sharing their fate, because these leaders expressed the people's very own thoughts. However, if the leaders of a section opposed a major policy such as Westward expansion even though the President did not "think that the people themselves have any interest or wish of that kind," it was advisable to delay further action "until the public opinion in that quarter shall be reconciled to any future change."[75]

## Let Special Interests Speak!

Monroe was not afraid that pressure group spokesmen would receive an undue hearing. Opportunities for lobbyists were relatively scarce in the early period because lobbying had not become a well organized pressure activity as yet. Few representatives of lobby interests made their way to Washington. Even when they did, or when they found other ways to reach the attention of public officials, their influence was apt to be negligible. No leader of the public would stoop to become a tool or mouthpiece for such groups and none would be duped by them since selfish aims were readily apparent. For himself, Monroe had vowed that "I would never vote for any measure against my judgment and conscience."[76]

Far from fearing domination by special interest groups, Monroe had no hesitancy in consulting them for expert information on matters of their specific and legitimate concern. For instance, while Monroe was Secretary of State the British minister proposed a settlement of disputed claims to fishing rights in the northeast. "Before replying, Monroe consulted the fishermen of Marblehead, and Salem, and, finding that it would be more advantageous to have no eastern limit, but extending the liberty through the straits and indefinitely up the coast of Labrador, suggested such a modification."[77] When the British minister made a counter offer: "Once more the fishermen were consulted, and, as they declared that the Newfoundland coast was as little used as that of Labrador, Monroe rejected each proposition."[78]

[74] Monroe, vol. 1, p. 397.
[75] Monroe, vol. 6, pp. 127–128.
[76] Monroe, vol. 5, p. 146.
[77] McMaster, vol. 4, p. 466.
[78] McMaster, vol. 4, p. 466.

Monroe was more worried that the opinions of special interests might lack the hearing they deserved than that they might exert influence detrimental to the public welfare. His reservations about the proposed national constitution raised the question as to whether national representatives would be able to be as fully acquainted with the special interests of the various sections as they ought to be.

> Separated at the distance of near 1200 miles, suppose the disposition to do right the best that nature can infuse into the human heart, generally speaking, in the operation of the government, will the man of Georgia possess sufficient information to legislate for the local concerns of New-Hampshire? Or of New-Hampshire for those of Georgia? Or to contract it to a smaller space of New-York for those of Virginia? Will not of course most of its measures be taken upon an imperfect view of the subject?[79]

These were serious problems, since "a wise legislator should possess a precise knowledge of the situation, and interests of all the territory, and of the state of society, manners, and dispositions of the people within it committed to his care."[80]

Although he realized that sectional opinions could become a divisive influence when they pertained to matters of concern to several states, Monroe did not believe that they would ever destroy the Union or that they should be carried to the point of endangering it. Special interests, sectional or otherwise, must always be subordinated to national concerns. For instance, when "the tranquility and even the continuance of our Union" were threatened by the pro- and anti-slavery controversy, Monroe predicted confidently that national unity would prevail:[81]

> The object of those who brought it [the slavery issue] forward, was undoubtedly to acquire power, and the expedient well adapted to the end, as it enlisted in their service, the best feelings, of all that portion of our Union, in which slavery does not exist, and who are unacquainted with the condition of their Southern brethren.[82]

Nonetheless, Monroe was "satisfied that the bond of Union, is too strong for them, and that the better their views are understood, throughout the whole Union, the more certain will be their defeat in every part."[83]

Among special interest groups that were dangerous but must be allowed an untrammeled hearing, the press occupied a unique position. Some papers expressed the "right" views and hence were in tune with public opinion. But the bulk of papers were mouthpieces for a few selfish in-

[79]Monroe, vol. 1, p. 316.
[80]Monroe, vol. 1, p. 316.
[81]Monroe, vol. 6, p. 114.
[82]Monroe, vol. 6, p. 116.
[83]Monroe, vol. 6, p. 114.

dividuals intent on misleading the public. In 1797, after his recall from France, Monroe had felt their sting acutely. "There is," he complained then, "scarce a paper in any quarter of the Union thro' which I have not been and am not daily calumniated."[84] He tried to deflect such attacks with "silent contempt," but he feared their short-range impact on the public. Similarly, in 1808 he was sure that the press would put the wrong light on his unsuccessful treaty negotiations in England:

> I look with extreme concern to the violent course which is pursued in the discussion which now agitates the country and trust that it will be possible to moderate it. This sentiment is excited in a peculiar manner by what I have seen in the Enquirer of Friday last. I neither know the author of the piece or from whom he derives his information. . . .[85]

Contempt for the bulk of the press and its authors and editors did not mean that Monroe hesitated to use the press for his own political purposes, however. For instance, the story of General Jackson's controversial activities in Florida to detach the area from Spain was submitted to the *National Intelligencer* in the version which, Monroe thought, would put it into the best light for public approval. In that particular instance Attorney General Wirt was the anonymous author because the Secretary of State disapproved of Monroe's handling of publicity of this delicate national and international problem.[86]

Although the press was viewed as spokesman for special interests, rather than the public, its advice and opinions were influential on a number of occasions. It could affect the opinions of the public and its leaders, including the President. For instance, when Monroe suggested to Adams in 1818 that there might be joint British-American action to promote the independence of South America, Adams blamed the *Richmond Inquirer* for planting the idea in the President's head. He called it "the paper by which Virginia works upon the President. Its influence is much more upon him, and it is excessively impatient for the acknowledgment of Buenos Ayres."[87] He also complained that the *Inquirer* spoke arrogantly to the President "like a master to his slave."[88]

Monroe usually denied the influence of the press on his ideas because he lacked respect for the personnel and policies of newspapers. Nonetheless, Adams' analysis could well have been accurate because people often

[84]Monroe, vol. 3, p. 94.

[85]Monroe, vol. 5, p. 34.

[86]Charles Francis Adams ed., *Memoirs of John Quincy Adams*, vol. 4. Philadelphia: J. B. Lippincott, 1875, pp. 112, 114, 117–119.

[87]Adams, vol. 4, p. 118.

[88]Adams, vol. 4, p. 120. The paper may have had a special hold on the President because it was among the small number of supporters for his presidential candidacy in 1808.

accept ideas from questionable sources but then blot the identity of the source from memory. On the other hand, many papers who claimed an influence on the President because they were sent to the White House were ignored completely. As Monroe wrote Madison in 1821:

> Since I have been in this office many newspapers have been sent to me, from every part of the Union, unsought, which having neither time nor curiosity to read, are in effect thrown away. I should have stopped the practice, but from delicacy to the Editors, and expecting also that they would subject me to no charge.[89]

## Fathoming Public Opinion

It was not very difficult for a President to discover what the public thought. First of all, there were his own intellectual resources. As a man of the people, Monroe felt that he could intuitively sense what the people wished. When he was only twenty-four years old and engaged in his first job in the Virginia House of Delegates, he already felt qualified to supply to Jefferson "ye public opinion." He felt justified to give such advice gratuitously because "I am warmly interested in whatever concerns ye public interest."[90]

Monroe's correspondence throughout his life abounds with references to the public feeling, the sense of the public, and the taking of the public pulse. What he had in mind was obviously the well-known sixth sense of the politician to fathom what was publicly acceptable. For instance, while he was in Washington during the War of 1812 he wrote to General Dearborn about the public spirit which favored war. Even though he lacked direct information on the subject, he told the general that "the greatest zeal and enthusiasm prevailed throughout the whole of the western country."[91] When Jefferson expressed concern about the likely success of federalist efforts to discredit Genêt as a foreign agent who interfered unduly in the internal affairs of the host country, Monroe rebutted the argument with vigor and confidence. "Of one fact I am well assured that in case of such an appeal, the people of this State in deciding upon the merits of the controversy, would pardon the errors of the French minister, whilst they would consider those of the administration inveterate and malignant vices."[92]

Monroe's claim to speak with authority about nation-wide public opinion was more firmly grounded than similar claims of his predecessors.

[89]Monroe, vol. 6, p. 174.
[90]Monroe, vol. 1, p. 16.
[91]Monroe, vol. 5, p. 223.
[92]Monroe, vol. 1, p. 271.

Except for Washington, he was the only early President who made a tour of the country on various occasions. During the summer recess of the Continental Congress, Monroe traveled in the West, starting from Albany through the Great Lakes down the Ohio river and back to Virginia. He visited military posts to see for himself why the British were slow in evacuating them. He also wanted to ascertain the attitude of the Indians toward the new government, as well as the living conditions and views of the population in general. A few months later he made another trip to attend a pow-wow of the Shawnee Indians. He asked Madison to accompany him but Madison, leary of the expected rigors of the trip, would not go. His post-inaugural swing around the country, covering towns along the sea board and in the interior, has already been mentioned. During these journeys he made a point of talking with as many people as possible, especially about political issues.

Monroe's personal observations were supplemented by the appraisals of his friends. He drew his information deliberately from a wide range of sources. Not only did he ask questions routinely of his Cabinet and other official contacts, but he also consulted senior statesmen like Jefferson and Madison regularly. In addition, he corresponded with a host of friends and sent them copies of official documents so that they could advise him more competently. For example, during the difficulties with Britain preceding the War of 1812, he wrote to his brother Joseph that he had

> sent to several friends copies of the correspondence, as well as to yourself and Dr. Everett. I have sent them to Mr. Jefferson, Mr. Divers, Colonel Lindsey, Mr. Watson at Milton, and now send on to Colonel Yancey . . . If you think it material that I should send a copy or two more inform me, and to whom.[93]

In the answers that he received to these communications advice on policy was combined with advice on the present and future state of the public mind and what needed to be done to sustain public support. In fact, Monroe's Republican friends, like he himself, referred to public opinion approval far more frequently than had been previously customary. They had fewer qualms about admitting that changing public moods were anxiously watched by top officials. And they openly yearned for confirmation of what they thought they knew already—that the public approved fully of what they were doing.

When there was disagreement about the status of public opinion with respect to a given policy, Monroe preferred his own appraisal to that of even his most trusted advisors. His contradiction of Jefferson's appraisal of Virginia public opinion on the behavior of Genêt is one example. On another occasion, he expressed doubts that petitions and addresses sent to

[93]Monroe, vol. 5, p. 196.

the President by various groups were representative of public opinion. Accordingly, he disputed the Adams Administration's claim based on the evidence from such petitions that public opinion favored the Alien and Sedition acts. "My candid opinion is that the tone given or rather the evidence exhibited of public opinion by addresses is fallacious. The public opinion in this State is decidedly otherwise if fairly taken."[94] What a fair way of taking opinion soundings was, Monroe did not disclose.

## Congress as a Distorting Mirror

In Monroe's estimation, opinions expressed in Congress were not a true reflection of public opinion. Congressmen had their own political axes to grind. In the process they often neglected the interests and opinions of the public in favor of their own. Many congressional debates, investigations, and actions seemed like mere expressions of spite to Monroe, designed to ruin a presidential program, which, he believed, the public approved.

Monroe's chief opponent in Congress was the Speaker of the House, Henry Clay. John Quincy Adams depicted the situation in the spring of 1818:

> Clay expected himself to have been Secretary of State, and he and all his creatures were disappointed by my appointment. He is therefore coming out as the head of a new opposition in Congress to Mr. Monroe's administration, and he makes no scruples of giving the tone to all his party in running me down.[95]

Clay's objective allegedly was that in which the eccentric John Randolph had failed, "to control or overthrow the Executive by swaying the House of Representatives."[96] Capitalizing on all traces of popular opposition to the President, he had "from the time of Mr. Monroe's election . . . been constantly looking out for positions upon which to erect his batteries against the Administration."[97]

Clay and "his creatures" were just the kind of men to accomplish their mission. Adams noted regretfully that the Chairman of the Committee on Foreign Relations who had "always been considered as a member in the confidence of the Executive, and . . . acted thus at the last session" was "neither by weight of character, force of genius, nor keenness of spirit at all able to cope with Clay."[98] Even worse, he and other former sup-

[94]Monroe, vol. 3, p. 136.
[95]Adams, vol. 4, pp. 62–63.
[96]Adams, vol. 4, p. 28.
[97]Adams, vol. 4, p. 119. Clay's obstructive maneuvers during the negotiations with Spain regarding Florida are one example. See vol. 5, pp. 25–26.
[98]Adams, vol. 4, pp. 65–66.

porters of the President had been "goaded by Clay not only into disavowals of any subserviency to the views of the Executive" and into declarations that they "did not care a fig for the Administration or any member of it, but into the humor of proposing measures which the President utterly disapproves."[99] There was "no member of the House of representatives friendly to the Administration who has spirit and ability and mastery of the subject adequate to withstand" Clay and his associates.[100]

Clay himself boasted to Adams in 1821, after Monroe's reelection, that the President "had not the slightest influence in Congress" and that, as far as political effectiveness went, "his career was considered closed." To this dire forecast Adams replied that "the President must rely, as he had done, upon the public sentiment and upright intention to support him, and with these his Administration must get along as well as it could."[101] With Congress throwing down the gauntlet, Monroe had little choice but to declare himself the champion of the public and with the help of public plaudits for presidential action discredit the image of Congress as a mirror of the people's views. The circumstances of a hostile Congress, rather than a conviction that Congress was inherently unfit to speak for the public, forced him into this position, so opposed to Madison's views of the legislature.

Monroe gained support from the attitude of congressional leaders toward the public, and from the public's mounting antagonism toward Congress. Henry Adams in his *History of the United States*, with his usual perceptiveness, analyzed the problem created by congressional aspirations to policy-making leadership.

> William Pinckney, Calhoun, Lowndes, Clay, Daniel Webster, John Randolph, and their associates were not men who bowed to authority, even of the people, but rather looked on the task of government as a function of superior intellect. They proposed to correct what they considered mistaken popular tendencies.[102]

Clay bemoaned the "supineness" throughout the country which precluded overt American aid to revolutionary forces in Latin America. The public seemed to him a hindrance to wise policy making. And he lamented the fact that the House of Representatives was evidently not "a favorite with the American people."[103] His estimate of public feelings has been echoed by other observers and historians. To quote Henry Adams, for example, on public reactions to Congress:

[99]Adams, vol. 4, pp. 65–66.
[100]Adams, vol. 4, pp. 64–65.
[101]Adams, vol. 5, p. 324.
[102]Henry Adams, *History of the United States*, Book 9. New York: Albert and Charles Boni, 1930, p. 108.
[103]Adams, *History*, Book 9, p. 134.

The people . . . could not make an ideal of weakness, ignorance, or vice, even their own; . . . they revolted in their politics from whatever struck them as sordid or selfish . . . The people in truth, however jealous of power, would have liked in imagination, though they would not bear in practice, to be represented by something nobler, wiser, and purer than their own average honor, wisdom, and purity.[104]

Monroe apparently sensed this popular dissatisfaction with the legislature. He lost no opportunity to point out that the people, rather than their representatives, were the true springs of governmental power.

With us individuals count for nothing in the offices which they hold; that is, they have no right to them. They hold them as representatives, by appointment from the people, in whom the sovereignty is exclusively vested.[105]

He warned against the tendencies of those in high office "to elevate the government above the people, or to place it in any respect without its natural boundaries" and to forget that the people are "the high and pure source, from whence they respectively derived their authorities."[106] If congressional views seemed, to him, in conflict with public opinion, there was no question where Monroe would turn for policy guidance.

## The Need for Explicit Consent to War

In Monroe's case it is easy to answer the question about the scope to be allowed to public opinion in decision making. If political leaders are true surrogates of the people who drink from the same fountain of truth, then their opinion represents public opinion. In effect, public opinion rules and pervades all levels of decision making. Monroe might well have paraphrased Louis XIV whose *l'etat, c'est moi* would then become *le miroir du peuple, c'est moi*. Not only did the public guide in broad moral issues of right or wrong or in broad directions or policy, but by virtue of its ideological identity with its leaders it was represented at all levels of policy making, including the making of implementing decisions. Given truly republican leaders, a gulf between government and people was impossible. The government and the people were one and the same.

However, Monroe singled out the right to declare war as one area in which the presumption of concurrence between executive and people had to be specifically tested. The reasons were constitutional as well as practical. Like his Republican confreres, he believed in the wisdom of the

[104]Adams, *History*, Book 9, p. 135.
[105]Monroe, vol. 6, p. 223.
[106]Monroe, vol. 1, pp. 325–326.

constitutional provisions that forestall possible usurpation of the war power by a President turned tyrant. These provisions must be strictly construed to allow the people, through Congress, the final word on war and peace. Although Congress had its drawbacks, it was better to make all policies that might lead directly to war subject to the vote of a large number of representatives rather than leave them to the mercy of a single human being. Monroe complained that President Washington, whom he otherwise respected highly, had usurped the warpower when he proclaimed the country's neutrality in 1794:

> I think the position incontrovertible that if he [the President] possesses the right to say we shall be neutral, he might say we should not be. The power in both instances must be in the same hands, for if the Executive could say we should be neutral, how could the Legislature, that we should war.[107]

From such reasoning, Monroe concluded that "in truth a right to declare our neutrality, as a distinct authority, cannot exist" because, by implication, it deprives Congress of the right to declare war, an action both "unconstitutional and improper."[108]

He applied similar criteria to his own actions, although by no means consistently. For instance, in 1818 he argued that the United States had to return the Spanish forts taken by General Jackson in Florida because "holding them would amount to a declaration of war, or come so near it, that in case war followed, it would be so considered."[109] Yet he authorized General Jackson's incursions into Spanish territory without prior congressional approval even though war might have resulted. And without prior congressional sanction he repeatedly pursued policies, such as the recognition of the independence of Spain's American colonies, which might well have provoked a war against the United States. One suspects that his qualms about executive flirtation with war ebbed and crested, depending on the merits he saw in a particular policy.

Besides the thorny and yet unsettled issue of how far a President should lead a country along the path to war before seeking congressional sanction, Monroe also knew from bitter experience that war without full popular support was almost impossible to fight. During the War of 1812 troops had mutinied, governors had withdrawn militia from national service, and eastern states had traded with the enemy and talked about abandoning the war and making a separate peace. "In the American character antipathy to war ranked first among political traits."[110] Hence "If we engage in a war, it is of the greatest importance that our people be united . . .

---

[107]Monroe, vol. 1, p. 262.

[108]Monroe, vol. 1, p. 262.

[109]Monroe, vol. 6, p. 61.

[110]Adams, *History*, Book 9, p. 226.

and, above all, that the government be free from the charge of committing a breach of the Constitution."[111] For these reasons, although a President could normally be trusted to represent public wishes when he involved the nation in war, it was wise to observe the constitutional restrictions scrupulously.

## The Uses of Public Opinion

In the days of the Federalists, Monroe had talked of mobilizing public opinion to press the errant party into a change of policies. By the time he came to office this usage of public opinion had become all but unnecessary. The party of the people was in power, led by its very own spokesmen. If there was disagreement between the President and a vocal segment of the population, he could be sure that the dissidents were wrong and that the course selected by the President accorded with the true wishes of the people. There was no need to yield even to what might sound like an overwhelming public mandate. The overwhelming mandate in favor of the President's action would become obvious soon enough. Regrettably, the vacant place of the opposition party had been partially filled by congressional factions. Against such factions it continued to be useful to demonstrate public opinion approval of the policies selected by the President. Besides, it seldom hurt at election time to remind the people that their charges had been faithfully executed by their chosen representatives.

Aside from serving domestic legitimating functions, public opinion was a useful foreign policy tool. From his extensive diplomatic experience abroad, Monroe knew how important it could be to the satisfactory conduct of policy to convince foreigners that the nation was fully united behind the government. He wrote to Madison from London in June, 1804:

> It is admitted if we keep together, and prove ourselves superior to that ambitious rivalry, to the influences of those unworthy passions, which ruined the ancient republics, that we have nothing to dread from other powers. It is to the possibility of a disunion of the States that such as are unfriendly to us look for the completion of their wishes; it is to the danger of it, that the best friends of our country and of mankind turn their attention with the most anxious foreboding.[112]

With his typical optimism about the unity of the American people he predicted that:

> If we continue to gain ground at home, and to impress the world with a belief, that the American people are united, in the resolution to

[111]Monroe, vol. 6, p. 61.
[112]Monroe, vol. 4, p. 217.

support their union, and present republican government, I am convinced that we shall not only be left undisturbed, but be courted by every other power.[113]

So important was the show of unity that he brought strong pressure on the lone dissenter in Congress who opposed recognition of the South American colonies in 1822:

> It is important, as relates to the character of the measure and the public feeling that it be unanimous. The report of it to the world will produce a very strong effect everywhere, particularly with Spain, and the provinces; with the former, by announcing that if she resents it that we shall be united in meeting her resentment; with the latter, by showing the deep interest which the whole American people take in their welfare. For you to stand alone against that sentiment will deprive your country of that advantage, and without the possibility of any indemnity for it.[114]

Occasionally, a stress on disunity could be helpful, too. During his first mission to France it seemed to Monroe conducive to better Franco-American relations to stress that large numbers of Americans disagreed with their government's Anglophile policy. Another use of domestic opposition was described by Secretary of State Adams. If, during negotiations with Spain, there was evidence of public dissatisfaction with the leniency of the President's policy, "the manifestation of that very censure would strengthen the Executive in the negotiation."[115] Hence it was advantageous to announce the policy, reap public censure, and thereby convince the Spaniards that they had better accept current terms, lest future ones, due to public pressure, would be more stringent.

## The Public Information Task

Judging from his own experience of gleaning information readily from conversations with his friends and associates and from his own observations, Monroe believed that the average American had sufficient information available to judge the actions of his government. For instance, in 1789 people could observe the measures of their government to cope with British and French injuries to American interests and with dissent at home. "All these things must ultimately open the eyes of the people, if they are not the most stupid and likewise the most worthless of all people ever collected in the form of a nation."[116] The public could pay attention to congressional debates, if Congress did its job properly. "Nothing is wanting

[113]Monroe, vol. 4, p. 186.
[114]Monroe, vol. 6, p. 214.
[115]Adams, vol. 5, pp. 39, 55.
[116]Monroe, vol. 3, p. 107.

to get us right but a knowledge of our affairs among the people which nothing will so essentially contribute to diffuse as able, free and comprehensive discussion on the part of the friends of republican government in the House of Representatives."[117]

It was the President's duty, as well as the duty of every other public servant (official, and unofficial) to supply any vital missing information that would otherwise be unavailable to the public. "The want of light is the great evil which overwhelms us and this will not be remedied till more pens are put to work."[118] Monroe had done his share of informing the public in his fully documented treatise on his mission to France. Likewise, he had tried to present an impartial account of the merits and defects of the prospective federal constitution for the benefit of his Virginia constituents. His guiding maxim in these expositions was that the public, given full facts clearly and impartially presented, would be able to draw valid conclusions.

Monroe did not believe that policy alternatives had to be presented to the public. He did raise alternatives with members of his Cabinet and with advisors like Jefferson and Madison. By consulting a large number of well-informed and experienced advisors he hoped to get a representative cross section of views extant throughout the country. The final adoption of a policy course by the President could then be made with full confidence that he had consulted and acted just as the public would have done, had it been in his place. The decision, made after careful weighing of alternatives, represented "the" public opinion—the essential consensus on a single policy course to which people adhere when diversity of action is not feasible.

Information presented to the public was to be kept free from polemics or any other tactics which might unduly sway opinion. The President's influential and respected position made it incumbent upon him to maintain discreet silence in matters in which other adequate sources of information were available. This was especially true of elections, a matter in which the public was particularly competent to make its own choices:

> My opinion is that the nation should be left perfectly at liberty to make its own election, without any the slightest interference, on the part of those to whom the public attention may be in any degree drawn in reference to that object. On this principle I have acted invariably whenever I have been applied to respecting it.[119]

Attorney General Wirt confirmed Monroe's fidelity to the principle, as well as its widespread acceptance:

[117]Monroe, vol. 3, pp. 102–103.
[118]Monroe, vol. 3, p. 107.
[119]Monroe, vol. 5, p. 22.

At that time, it was not considered decorous in the Executive to make itself a partisan in a presidential or any other election. Indeed, there was a most wholesome fastidiousness exhibited on this point, which would have interpreted the attempt of a cabinet officer, or any other functionary of the Government, to influence the popular vote by speech, by writing, by favor, fear or affection, as a great political misdemeanor worthy of sharpest rebuke.[120]

When issues had to be presented to the public, Monroe had many good suggestions for effective public relations. He thought that press attacks on the government should go unanswered initially. Eventually, the opposition press would, through its own transparently false accusations, provide enough rope to hang itself with very little government assistance. It was often advisable to ignore political opponents and enemies, rather than give them free publicity. Thus he counseled Jefferson in 1801 that "the royalist faction has lost deservedly the public confidence. It will sink under its own weight if we leave it to itself."[121] At the same time, expressions by official sources must not give the impression that government and opposition saw eye to eye on important policies:

> There is no political error more to be avoided, than a step which gives cause to suspect an accommodation with that party, or coloring to an opinion it is feared or respected. Such a step would shake the republican ranks, and prove the foundation of a growing interest to its antagonist.[122]

Intraparty differences were best kept out of the public eye, lest they destroy party harmony and effectiveness. "In all parties occasional sacrifices of opinion have been found necessary and made with a view to a greater good by the most upright, independent, and honorable men."[123] Such sacrifices of the right to air differences were sweetened by the knowledge that only through party strength could the individual "hope to be instrumental to the national prosperity and happiness."[124] Moreover, public attacks on one's own party were likely to be self-defeating and fruitless:

> Repeated and violent attacks confirm the majority in error, and protect them from the public censure by presenting to view an object which is thought to have a better claim to it. If those now in power are ever to change their policy, it will be when the minority ceases to attack them.

[120]John P. Kennedy, *Memoirs of the Life of William Wirt*, vol. 2. Philadelphia: Lea and Blanchard, 1849, p. 170.

[121]Monroe, vol. 3, p. 262.

[122]Monroe, vol. 3, p. 262.

[123]Monroe, vol. 5, p. 167.

[124]Monroe, vol. 5, p. 167.

And if the blame of improvident and injudicious measures is ever to attach to them, among the people, it must be by leaving to the authors of these measures the entire responsibility belonging to them.[125]

Monroe realized that blind feelings of loyalty are aroused when hitherto respected authorities come under attack. "If the opposition does not carry with it the majority in the first attack it cannot fail to strengthen the administration, be the merits of the question between parties what they may."[126] A factional assault would also rally the administration's supporters in Congress to its side. Then "the mass of the republican party among the people would naturally follow their representatives. Thus the minority would daily lose ground in public opinion, and its advocates proportionally diminish."[127] But if faults of the administration were brought out, they should be confined "to evils already felt—such as loss of commercial capital, seamen, and so forth—not to extend it to the future."[128]

Information or symbolic action could be used to rally the public around certain policies and also to impress foreigners. For instance, Monroe advocated an impressive last-ditch peace effort directed toward Britain and France, prior to war, to unite the people behind the policy of their government. "We should enter into the war with the greatest union of which our system is capable. It has occurred that before that last Step is taken, some signal effort should be made to avert the necessity, and that a Mission to both powers should be resorted to for that purpose."[129] To produce the desired effect:

> Some solemnity should be attached to the measure by sending the person appointed in a frigate, or other public armed vessel, to secure to it the happiest effect at home and abroad. . . . Should it [the mission] fail, I think that the attempt would produce a happy effect in our interior, by uniting all parties in a common effort to meet the crisis which would be allowed by all to be inevitable.[130]

When war seemed nearly certain in the late spring of 1812, Monroe, then Secretary of State, tried one more gambit. To dispell all doubts on the part of the British and French that the United States was merely playing a game of brinkmanship and did not have to be appeased (and to prepare the public psychologically for war, should it come) Monroe published a fiery editorial in the *National Intelligencer*:

[125]Monroe, vol. 5, p. 168.
[126]Monroe, vol. 5, pp. 140–141.
[127]Monroe, vol. 5, p. 141.
[128]Monroe, vol. 5, p. 61.
[129]Monroe, vol. 5, p. 91.
[130]Monroe, vol. 5, p. 91.

Let war therefore be forthwith proclaimed against England. With her there can be no motive for delay. Any further discussion, any new attempt at negotiation, would be as fruitless as it would be dishonorable. With France we shall still be at liberty to pursue the course which circumstances may require . . . we shall always be in time to place her on the ground of her adversary.[131]

Monroe hoped that printing such an inciting editorial in a prominent paper would convey the impression that the sentiments represented a large body of influential opinion. The specter of pending war would become very real and leave its mark at home and abroad.

### Diversity of Opinions and Unity of Support

Problems of opinion evaluation were easily solved for Monroe. There was no need to balance quality against quantity. The mass of the people stood behind the government, and the government stood for quality. It did not matter which publics held strong opinions and which were noncommittal. Weak or strong, the public would rally behind its chosen leaders. Nor was there a question of yielding to strongly pressed private interests in favor of the general public interest. Thanks to mass support for popular government, the general public interest could and must prevail at all times.

Most political disagreements concerned matters of detail and could be settled by compromise, engineered by capable leaders. Monroe prided himself on his own "facility in uniting parties and drawing the country together, while principle is preserved."[132] People and leaders whose viewpoints had not prevailed, after fair discussion, would nonetheless rally behind the policies which had been adopted in the end. Their willingness to support final policy choices, regardless of content, amounted to approval of these choices.

Since the bulk of predecisional airing of differences took place within the inner circles of government, it was particularly important to keep discussion at the top free from restraint. An episode involving Monroe's Secretary of the Treasury, William Crawford, and the President, shows the length to which Monroe would go to sustain the principle. Crawford had come to the White House to urge the appointment of certain candidates to office. When Monroe disagreed with the choices, Crawford became irritated and abusive, "raised his cane as in the attitude to strike, and said, 'You damned infernal old scoundrel!' Mr. Monroe seized the tongs at the fireplace for self-defense, applied a retaliatory epithet to Crawford, and

---

[131]Quoted in Irving Brant, *James Madison: The President*. Indianapolis: Bobbs-Merrill, 1956, pp. 434–435.
[132]Monroe, vol. 5, p. 56.

told him he would immediately ring for servants himself and turn him out of the house."[133] Crawford then regained his composure and left the White House, saying he had not intended to insult the President. Even though Crawford had been an annoying critic of the President on many prior occasions, Monroe refused to use the incident to fire him. "It comported better with the principles of our government and with my own character, to permit him to remain than to remove him."[134]

Monroe was fully aware of the problem of conscience posed for a high official who disagreed with final policy decisions but felt duty-bound to support the administration. With luck, an astute politician could evade a showdown. "If he [a dissenter] is a man of great ability, acts with prudence, and enjoys the confidence of his party, he will rarely find himself reduced to the necessity of separating from it, or from the administration."[135] If a showdown did occur, "ample excuses will be made" for a dissenter with a reputation for disinterested action whose sole motivation seemed to be "to keep the Chief Magistrate in check, provided he should wish to carry improper measures."[136]

For himself, Monroe apparently had no desire to be put into such a predicament. He entered the Madison Administration as Secretary of State only after securing assurances that he would have a free hand in shaping policy as he deemed proper. He wrote to Madison that:

> it would not become me to accept a station, and to act a part in it, which my judgment and conscience did not approve, and which I did not believe would promote the public welfare and happiness. I could not do this, nor would you wish me to do it.[137]

To his friend, Colonel John Taylor, he confided that "I would never vote for any measure against my judgment and conscience to gratify any administration."[138]

Apparently Monroe's scruples were unusual. According to Professor Leonard White:

> No other correspondence involving the problem of harmony of policy between a President and a *prospective* head of a department has come to notice. Many of the men invited to this position had no strong personal views on public issues beyond the general tendencies of their party; some had no capacity for independence; those who stood on their own ground

---

[133]Adams, vol. 7, p. 81.
[134]Monroe, vol. 7, p. 39.
[135]Monroe, vol. 5, p. 146.
[136]Monroe, vol. 5, p. 146.
[137]Monroe, vol. 5, p. 182.
[138]Monroe, vol. 5, p. 146.

—Gallatin, Calhoun, Adams, for example—raised no issues when they
entered upon their duties and accommodated their views to those of the
President thereafter.[139]

This, of course, was the proper role to be played by the dissenter—predecisional diversity coupled with post-decisional support. This was the role
Monroe preached to others, although he professed reluctance to practice it
himself.


## The Presidential Prerogative to Make Final Decisions

Judging from the reports of his associates, President Monroe apparently
did not consider himself *primus inter pares*. He was more than willing to
listen to all those who had opinions to offer. He frequently accepted ideas
submitted to him or made concessions if his associates convinced him of
the merits of their suggestions. But beyond this, he did not allow himself
to be deflected from what he deemed a wise policy choice. He resented
any evidence of pressure to sway him and his friends knew that if their
requests "should in the least degree wear the aspect of threatening or
scolding, it would be ruinous."[140] After a decision had been made, the
President expected members of his administration to give it full public
support even though they retained the right to differ in private.

The same view prevailed toward public dissent. The President was
willing to listen to divergent opinions from members of the loyal public.
But he felt that it was the people's ultimate obligation to adopt the President's decisions as their own. Again, this held true only in periods when
government was truly popular. While the "royalist faction" had been in
power, he fully believed that it was the public's right and duty to object
to presidential policies which lacked the republican touch. Presidents Washington and Adams, realizing that they were out of tune with the people,
should have listened to republican voices throughout the country and
changed their policies accordingly.

Like Jefferson, Monroe had no objections to dissent which involved
physical action or even violence, provided the cause was just. People who
were suppressed by a tyrannous government had no other choice to make
themselves heard and gain control over their political institutions. The various popular revolutions in Europe and in South and North America to
which Monroe had lent physical or moral support were examples of the
value of overt action. In the case of successful revolutions the acts of the

[139]White, p. 64.
[140]White, p. 41.

rebels had been legitimated at a later date by the approval of the entire people who had been freed from the yoke of tyranny.

The situation was different if overt action took place to interfere with the actions of a popularly approved government. The activities of New England merchants during the War of 1812 to take their section of the country out of a war which they deemed disastrous and unjustified were considered little short of treason, if not treason. They were to be exposed to public condemnation and measures were to be taken to frustrate the dissenters' objectives.

But it was not necessary to silence all incitement to overt dissent out of fear that incitement would lead to deeds detrimental to popular government. Large-scale revolutionary action could not be generated through verbal pyrotechnics. It sprang solely from genuine oppression that had pushed a people beyond the limits of human tolerance. Only small-scale revolts could be the work of a few evil men who failed to submit to popular rule. Suppression of dissent could stop neither major nor minor revolt. Hence, in true Jeffersonian fashion, Monroe believed that "error of opinion may be tolerated where reason is left free to combat it."[141]

[141]Andrew Lipscomb, ed., *The Writings of Thomas Jefferson*, vol. 3. Washington: Thomas Jefferson Memorial Association, 1905, p. 319.

# 10

## An Old Doctrine
## Gets a New Name

The great man of the age is the one who can put into words
the will of his age, tell his age what its will is, and accomplish it.
HEGEL, *Philosophy of Right*

There is the moral of all human tales
'Tis but the same rehearsal of the past . . .
And History, with all her volumes vast,
Hath but one page.
BYRON, "Childe Harold's Pilgrimage"

# 10

## Britain Proposes a Joint Declaration

On October 9, 1823, President Monroe received a letter from Richard Rush, the American minister in London. The letter included a copy of a confidential message that George Canning, the British prime minister, had sent to Rush in August. Canning had asked portentous questions that Rush had not felt authorized to answer without explicit instructions from the President. Specifically, the note had inquired:

> Is not the moment come when our Governments might understand each other as to the Spanish American Colonies? And if we can arrive at such an understanding, would it not be expedient for ourselves, and beneficial for all the world, that the principles of it should be clearly settled and plainly avowed?[1]

The note had then set forth the British position with regard to the Spanish colonies in Latin America. The bulk of these colonies had declared their independence from the mother country two years before. Spain had refused to recognize the independence. But in 1823, she was under attack by France and it seemed that she would succumb. That would leave the fate of the colonies in doubt. They might be able to sustain their independence, or they might be victims of a military assault by the enemies of Spain, eager to carve up the Spanish empire among themselves.

Canning set forth the English position in five main points:

1. We conceive the recovery of the Colonies by Spain to be hopeless.
2. We conceive the question of the Recognition of them, as Independent States, to be one of time and circumstances.
3. We are, however, by no means disposed to throw any impediment in the way of an arrangement between them and the mother country by amicable negotiation.
4. We aim not at the possession of any portion of them ourselves.
5. We could not see any portion of them transferred to any other Power with indifference.[2]

---

[1]Stanislaus M. Hamilton, ed., *The Writings of James Monroe,* vol. 6. New York: G. P. Putnam's Sons, 1902, p. 365. Hereafter cited as "Monroe."

[2]Monroe, vol. 6, p. 365.

This statement of the English position concluded with the question: "If these opinions and feelings are, as I firmly believe them to be, common to your government with ours, why should we hesitate mutually to confide them to each other; and to declare them in the face of the world?"[3] A joint declaration would be a potent hands-off sign to keep European powers out of Latin America!

> If there be any European Power which cherishes other projects, which looks to a forcible enterprize for reducing the colonies to subjugation, on the behalf or in the name of Spain; or which meditates the acquisition of any part of them to itself, by cession or by conquest; such a declaration on the part of your government and ours would be at once the most effectual and the least offensive mode of intimating our joint disapprobation of such projects.[4]

On November 29, 1823, barely eight weeks after the British proposal had first been received by the President, Secretary of State Adams replied to Canning's propositions. Adams concurred with the British prime minister that the independence of the Latin American colonies seemed irrevocable, that neither the United States nor Britain wished political control over them, and that neither power could tolerate subjugation of the fledgling states by a European country other than Spain. If the United States and Britain could "move in concert" in this matter, especially if Britain would first recognize the independence of the colonies, this would be politically significant. "Never, in the history of mankind, was there a period when a stand so taken and maintained, would exhibit to present and future ages, a more glorious example of power, animated by justice and devoted to the ends of beneficence."[5]

However, while joint sentiments were praiseworthy, it would be best for each nation to act separately "for the most effectual accomplishment of the object, common to both."[6] But the door to joint action was not closed completely. Rush was instructed to inform the American government immediately, "should an emergency occur, in which a joint manifestation of opinion, by the two Governments,"[7] might become essential to preserve the liberty of South American states. In that case, after due deliberation in Washington, "we shall according to the principles of our Government, and in the forms prescribed by our Constitution, cheerfully join in any Act by which we may contribute to support the cause of human freedom, and the Independence of the South American Nations."[8]

[3]Monroe, vol. 6, p. 365.
[4]Monroe, vol. 6, pp. 365–366.
[5]Monroe, vol. 6, p. 407.
[6]Monroe, vol. 6, p. 407.
[7]Monroe, vol. 6, p. 408.
[8]Monroe, vol. 6, p. 408.

## The Monroe Doctrine Message

Three days later (December 2, 1823) President Monroe, in the course of his seventh annual message to the nation, set forth a series of policy principles for the United States which have since become known as the Monroe Doctrine. In part, these principles amounted to a unilateral U. S. declaration of a South American policy along the same lines that Canning had proposed for joint action. European powers with designs on Latin American colonies were informed that the United States would not interfere with established European colonies or dependencies. "But with the Governments who have declared their independence and maintained it," the United States warned that it

> could not view any interposition for the purpose of oppressing them, or controlling in any other manner their destiny, by any European power in any other light than as the manifestation of an unfriendly disposition toward the United States.[9]

The Monroe Administration reminded European chancelleries that "in the war between those new Governments and Spain we declared our neutrality at the time of their recognition."[10] But continued adherence to a neutrality policy was conditional on the fact that "no change shall occur which, in the judgment of the competent authorities of this Government, shall make a corresponding change on the part of the United States indispensable to their security."[11] As if to make sure that the point was fully understood in all its ramifications, Monroe restated the hands-off principle a few lines later:

> It is impossible that the allied powers should extend their political system to any portion of either continent without endangering our peace and happiness; nor can anyone believe that our southern brethren, if left to themselves, would adopt it [the European system of government] of their own accord. It is equally impossible, therefore, that we should behold such interposition in any form with indifference.[12]

To discourage any new colonial settlements by European powers in the Western hemisphere, the nonintervention doctrine was broadened beyond Canning's intentions. Monroe declared that:

> The occasion has been judged proper for asserting, as a principle in which the rights and interests of the United States are involved, that the

[9]Monroe, vol. 6, p. 340.
[10]Monroe, vol. 6, p. 340.
[11]Monroe, vol. 6, p. 340.
[12]Monroe, vol. 6, pp. 340–341.

American continents, by the free and independent condition which they have assumed and maintained, are henceforth not to be considered as subjects for future colonization by any European powers.[13]

Recent claims by Russia to portions of the West coast and future colonization attempts by England, France, and others were thus put on the *Index Prohibitorum* in hopes that such a declaration would have deterrent force.

In return for Europe's abstinence from interference in the Western hemisphere, Monroe pledged that the United States would continue its long-standing policy of nonintervention in European politics:

> Our policy in regard to Europe, which was adopted at an early stage of the wars which have so long agitated that quarter of the globe, nevertheless remains the same, which is, not to interfere in the internal concerns of any of its powers; to consider the government de facto as the legitimate government for us; to cultivate friendly relations with it, and to preserve those relations by a frank, firm, and manly policy, meeting in all instances the just claims of every power, submitting to injuries from none.[14]

## Fear of the Holy Alliance

What happened between October 9 when the Canning proposal reached Monroe and December 2, 1823 when the Monroe Doctrine was proclaimed? What policy questions faced the President, and why did he choose this occasion to make a "momentous" policy declaration in his annual message? Thanks to Monroe's habit of consulting many friends by mail, and Secretary of State Adams' very complete if somewhat egocentric diary of Cabinet meetings and conversations with visitors, an unusually full record exists to answer these questions.

In the first place, it is important to realize that the matters raised by Canning's letter were considered by the entire administration to be of utmost significance. Secretary of State Adams was not exaggerating when he assured Canning that:

> The whole subject has received the deliberate consideration of the President, under a deep impression of its general importance, a full conviction of the high interests and sacred principles involved in it, and an anxious solicitude for the cultivation of that harmony of opinions and unity of object, between the British and American Nations, upon which so much of the peace and happiness and liberty of the world obviously depend.[15]

[13]Monroe, vol. 6, p. 328.
[14]Monroe, vol. 6, p. 340.
[15]Monroe, vol. 6, p. 405.

When the President himself forwarded the Canning correspondence to Jefferson for his advice he indicated that the letters "involve interests of the highest importance."[16] In his reply Jefferson went even further:

> The question presented by the letters you have sent me, is the most momentous which has been ever offered to my contemplation since that of Independence. That made us a nation. This sets our compass and points the course which we are to steer thro' the ocean of time opening on us, and never could we embark on it under circumstances more auspicious.[17]

The reason why the matter was deemed momentous was Monroe's profound fear that attack on Spain's ex-colonies in America was imminent and might be followed by an attack on the United States. The American press, in the summer of 1823, was striking an anxious note that France's assault on Spain would bring down Spain, her former American colonies, and then the United States, domino-fashion.[18] Various reports from Europe and political pronouncements by the Tsar heightened the ominous impression that the Holy Alliance, an association of reactionary European governments, was bent on restoring monarchical government in Europe and abroad. In addition, there were rumors that a European Congress on the fate of the Latin American colonies was being planned for the near future. What such a European settlement of American questions might be Monroe could only dread. The only effective way in which a militarily weak country like the United States could stop European aggression in the Western hemisphere might be through alliance with Britain, the strongest maritime power in the world.

Observations made by Adams during Cabinet meetings give further proof that the President's concern with the intentions of the Holy Alliance was real even though the European danger signals were ambiguous and hence variously interpreted. For instance, on November 13, 1823, Adams recorded the President's attitude as follows:

> I find him . . . alarmed, far beyond anything that I could have conceived possible, with the fear that the Holy Alliance are about to restore immediately all South America to Spain . . . the news that Cadiz has surrendered to the French has so affected the President that he appeared entirely to despair of the cause of South America.[19]

[16]Monroe, vol. 6, p. 323.

[17]Monroe, vol. 6, p. 391.

[18]Edward H. Tatum, *The United States and Europe, 1815–1823.* Berkeley: University of California Press, 1936, pp. 254–255 contains excerpts from contemporary newspapers. Actually, the reactionary designs imputed to the Holy Alliance were the policies of only a few members and had nothing to do with the Holy Alliance document drawn up in 1815.

[19]Charles Francis Adams, ed., *Memoirs of John Quincy Adams,* vol. 6. Philadelphia: J. B. Lippincott, 1875, p. 185.

Confidently, Adams predicted that "he will recover from this in a few days."[20] But the mood was not transitory. Adams blamed the President's deep worries on the Secretary of War. "Calhoun is perfectly moon-struck by the surrender of Cadiz, and says the Holy Allies, with ten thousand men, will restore all Mexico and all South America to the Spanish dominion."[21] This was "the source of the President's despondency with regard to South American affairs."[22] Adams considered the fears vastly exaggerated, although not meaningless:

> I did not deny that they might make a temporary impression for three, four, or five years, but I no more believe that the Holy Allies will restore the Spanish dominion upon the American continent than that the Chimborazo will sink beneath the ocean.[23]

The fact that the administration was deeply concerned about the course of events in Europe is also apparent from diplomatic instructions given to American ministers in Europe in the summer of 1823, prior to the receipt of the Canning proposal. For instance, in mid-April the American representative in Spain had been informed that despite adherence to a neutrality policy the "essential rights" of the United States "will in all probability be deeply involved" in the war between France and Spain.[24] The United States was particularly concerned that Cuba might fall into the hands of an aggressive European successor to Spain and menace American security. Any transfer attempt would be considered "subversive" of American interests. If Cuba declared her independence to resist transfer—a course that Monroe had suggested to Cuban leaders—the United States would lend its aid.[25] Although the offer was never made, the United States even considered a joint U. S.–British guarantee of the status quo of the island. The idea was dropped because of the obstacle that a guarantee might become to the future independence of Cuba.[26]

Similar representations were made to France and Russia to warn them that the United States would not stand idly by while European states fastened the noose of reactionary government and European political control around Western hemisphere states. Gallatin, the American minister in France, informed French and Russian officials that the United States "would not suffer others to interfere against the emancipation of Amer-

[20]Adams, *Memoirs*, vol. 6, p. 185.
[21]Adams, *Memoirs*, vol. 6, p. 186.
[22]Adams, *Memoirs*, vol. 6, p. 186.
[23]Adams, *Memoirs*, vol. 6, p. 186. The Chimborazo is Ecuador's highest mountain.
[24]Monroe, vol. 6, pp. 351–352.
[25]Monroe, vol. 6, pp. 307, 312, 351, 355.
[26]Monroe, vol. 6, p. 307.

ica."[27] In case of attempts "to take possession" of Spain's colonies "or to assist her in reducing them under their former yoke . . . the United States would oppose every undertaking of this kind, and it might force them into an alliance with Great Britain."[28] The danger thus seemed extreme enough to warrant consideration of an alliance with Britain to meet it, despite the traditional American objection to European alliances in general, and to cooperation with haughty Britain in particular.

If any further proof is required of Monroe's grave concern about the aggressive intentions of the Holy Alliance, it can be found in the preliminary draft of his seventh annual message. According to Secretary Adams:

> Its introduction was in a tone of deep solemnity and of high alarm, intimating that this country is menaced by imminent and formidable dangers, such as would probably soon call for their most vigorous energies and the closest union.[29]

When Adams questioned whether the situation was really as grave as the President's tone had implied, the President, supported by Secretary Calhoun, insisted that "this was a more direct attack upon the popular principle" than any of the wars or revolutions which had taken place in Europe since 1789 [30] "Although no former message ever censured those overthrows and conquests before, yet it might be very proper to censure this now."[31] Injecting the public opinion element, Calhoun added:

> that there was great anxiety in the thinking part of the nation; that there was general expectation that the Holy Alliance would employ force against South America, and that it would be proper that the President should sound the alarm to the nation. A time was approaching when all its energies would be needed, and the public mind ought to be prepared for it.[32]

Given the dangers inherent in the situation, and his own prior toying with the idea of joint action with Britain, Monroe was immediately intrigued with the British proposal. He wrote to Jefferson:

[27]Henry Adams, ed., *The Writings of Albert Gallatin*, vol. 2. Philadelphia: J. B. Lippincott & Co., 1879, p. 271.

[28]Adams, vol. 2, p. 271.

[29]Adams, *Memoirs*, vol. 6, p. 194.

[30]Adams, *Memoirs*, vol. 6, p. 196. When it was rumored, two days after the message, that Spanish troops were on their way to subdue South America, Monroe was willing to send American troops to stop them. See Samuel F. Bemis, *John Quincy Adams and the Foundations of American Foreign Policy*. New York: Alfred A. Knopf, 1949, pp. 397–398.

[31]Adams, *Memoirs*, vol. 6, p. 196.

[32]Adams, *Memoirs*, vol. 6, p. 195.

> My own impression is that we ought to meet the proposal of the British government and to make it known, that we would view an interference on the part of the European powers, and especially an attack on the Colonies, by them, as an attack on ourselves, presuming that, if they succeeded with them, they would extend it to us.[33]

However, he realized that such a policy might embroil the United States unduly in European politics with more disadvantages than benefits. European entanglements were contrary to the tenets that Washington had expressed in his Farewell Address and that had been supported ever since by every major spokesman of the nation, including Monroe himself.[34] Before embarking on a potentially deviant policy course, Monroe therefore sought advice from his Cabinet, his ministers abroad, and a host of political associates and friends, but no attempt was made to bring the issues before the public.

## A Question of Tactics

In the course of the discussions and correspondence that ensued, the main question (with the exception of the very end) was never whether the United States should make a declaration at all opposing European intervention in the Western hemisphere.[35] Rather, most questions assumed that a declaration should be made and dealt with the form that it should take. Attorney General Wirt's query whether a declaration was advisable at all since it might incite the Holy Alliance to make war on the United States was an afterthought and quickly brushed aside. Nor was any attention directed to the question of the interventionary implications of a declaration that sought to prohibit political changes in a vast area beyond the borders of the United States.

Monroe and his associates were primarily concerned with four tactical issues. First and most hotly debated was the question whether or not a joint declaration with Britain was advisable. In the second place, there were discussions about the exact form which the declaration of policy

---

[33]Monroe, vol. 6, pp. 324–325.

[34]Excerpts from a variety of messages are quoted in Albert B. Hart and Edward Channing, *American History Leaflets*, 1–6. New York: A. Lovell & Co., 1892, pp. 3–13. See also Dexter Perkins, *A History of the Monroe Doctrine*. Boston: Little Brown, 1955, pp. 1–26; and D. A. Graber, *Crisis Diplomacy: A History of U. S. Intervention Policies and Practices*. Washington: Public Affairs Press, 1959, pp. 51–56.

[35]Edward Tatum, p. 258, contends that the British proposal forced the United States to make a declaration or by default give the impression that the United States was unconcerned about the prospective activities of the Holy Alliance. The contemporary record lends no support to this contention.

ought to take. Third, the precise contents and wording were debated and fourthly, the important issue was raised whether or not the United States should support the declaration by force of arms, if this should become necessary.

As mentioned, Monroe initially favored joint action with Britain, as did Jefferson and Madison. They agreed, as Madison phrased it, that "with the British power and navy combined with our own we have nothing to fear from the rest of the nations . . . in the great struggle of the Epoch between liberty and despotism."[36] But as discussion progressed Monroe came to feel increasingly that the British navy would be committed to the independence of the Latin American nations, regardless of any formal agreement with the United States. British commercial and political interests dictated such a policy and other European countries would make their own political appraisals accordingly, whether or not British interests were openly declared.

Moreover, there were numerous serious disadvantages militating against concerted action with Britain beyond traditional Republican Anglophobia. First, there was the dreaded specter of an entangling alliance that might draw the United States "willy-nilly" into European politics and war. A joint declaration of United States–British nonintervention in the Americas might bind the United States to refrain from taking Cuba or Texas if the occasion presented itself. Moreover, "had we moved in England, it is probable, that it would have been inferred that we acted under her influence, and at her instigation, and thus have lost credit as well with our Southern neighbors, as with the Allied powers."[37] In an alliance between a great and a small power, the United States would occupy the ignominious position of a "cock-boat in the wake of the British man-of-war."[38] South American nations would turn to the British Gulliver with thanks for their liberty and ignore the American Lilliputian.

A unilateral declaration was "more conciliatory with, and respectful to Russia, and the other powers" who might resent a joint flexing of muscles.[39] England had many enemies and the United States would avoid being tainted with the English image if she did not ally herself too closely to perfidious Albion. The mere threat of a future alliance with England might be useful to influence the policies of a power like Russia who "dreads a connection between the United States and Great Britain."[40] Such arguments persuaded Monroe that the United States should act alone.

He realized that a unilateral policy involved some risks which joint action could avoid:

[36]Monroe, vol. 6, pp. 395–396.
[37]Monroe, vol. 6, p. 345.
[38]Adams, *Memoirs*, vol. 6, p. 179.
[39]Monroe, vol. 6, p. 344.
[40]Monroe, vol. 6, p. 345.

> There is some danger that the British government, when it sees the part we have taken, may endeavour to throw the whole burden on us, and profit, in case of such interposition of the allied powers, of her neutrality, at our expense.[41]

But he considered the chances of British defection extremely slight "after what has passed on the subject."[42] If British aid was obviously not forthcoming, the United States could always retreat to a war of weasel words that did not have to be backed by military force. Besides, at Monroe's specific request the final answer to Britain had included an escape clause that allowed for the possibility of joint U. S.–British action, should this become necessary to parry the thrusts of the Holy Alliance. Since the idea of a joint declaration with Britain was shelved fairly rapidly, Monroe and his advisors did not discuss the form which such a declaration might take.[43]

With regard to unilateral action two problems concerning the form of the declaration arose. Should it be included in the President's annual message to be delivered within a month? If so, should there be separate additional declarations directed to individual foreign nations? If not, should some sort of diplomatic note to Britain be the sole reply? In addition to an answer to Canning, similar questions had been raised by recent communications received from the Tsar. In these, the Tsar had pointedly announced that he would not recognize the South American colonies and that he considered the monarchical form of government ideal. Coupled with the fact that negotiations were then under way with Russia concerning her claims to fishing rights and territory along the Pacific shores of North America, it seemed advisable to make some sort of announcement to the Russians to indicate disagreement with the Tsar's doctrines.

The foreign policy sections of the President's annual message were generally prepared by the Secretary of State and then presented to the President and the Cabinet for discussion.[44] Adams, accordingly, submitted proposals for the seventh annual message, which were combined with suggestions drafted by the President himself. A vigorous debate ensued over the contents and wording of these sections. But their inclusion in the message was not challenged, although Adams would have preferred to include only the noncolonization principle, leaving the fuller explanation of American foreign policy principles for separate diplomatic notes.[45] Monroe,

[41]Monroe, vol. 6, p. 345.

[42]Monroe, vol. 6, p. 345.

[43]Canning had suggested either a declaration, a convention, or an exchange of ministerial notes. Monroe, vol. 6, pp. 365–366.

[44]Adams, *Memoirs*, vol. 5, p. 201.

[45]Bemis, pp. 387–388, states that Adams wanted to write the notes "with an eye to spreading them before the public to justify the American position" should this become necessary. A congressional request for the documents could be used as an excuse for publishing them.

possibly with an eye to the favorable public impression that a bold presidential message might create, favored a more complete and sweeping exposition in the message.[46]

On the basis of a full and free exchange of viewpoints among Monroe and his inner circle, it was agreed that the hands-off doctrine, expressed in the form of a message to the American people, would be less likely to offend the members of the Holy Alliance than a more direct warning to them in a separate proclamation or diplomatic notes. The idea for such a proclamation or notes was shelved. Monroe and the Cabinet also decided to send notes to England and Russia which, in their essential portions, repeated the nonintervention clauses included in the annual message. The separate messages were deemed necessary for two reasons. Partly they were a warning to Russia and a courtesy to England in reply to direct communications received from these powers, and partly they were a precaution against later complaints by Congress or the public that the United States had neglected to answer important foreign messages.

The content and tone of the messages likewise represented a joint effort reflecting different ideas about the best methods to accomplish shared objectives. All agreed that the United States must openly declare opposition to foreign intervention in the Western hemisphere, especially at a time of war and suppression of liberal movements. All concurred that she must do so in a manner most likely to preserve the peace of the United States. The messages, somewhat toned down from their original drafts, seemed a suitable way of attaining these objectives.

## Sections and Factions in the Cabinet

What influence did public opinion have on decision making in the White House in the fateful winter of 1823? Since Monroe relied heavily on the advice of esteemed associates and believed firmly in compromise within ideologically homogeneous political bodies, a close look at his advisors is in order to assess the most potent influences on the President. Among advisors whose public opinion appraisals were apt to be influential his Cabinet was outstanding since he confided to them "every important circumstance occurring in our foreign concerns."[47] A sample of questions submitted to the Cabinet in October 1817 with regard to the independence of the South American colonies indicates the comprehensive foreign policy advice that Monroe expected from each Cabinet member:

[46]George Dangerfield, *The Era of Good Feelings.* New York: Harcourt, Brace and World, 1952, pp. 298–299, calls Monroe's approach "the innocence of Old Republicanism," which gave way, at least in part, before Adams' practical statesmanship.

[47]Adams, *Memoirs*, vol. 4, p. 31.

> Has the Executive power to acknowledge the independence of new States whose independence has not been acknowledged by the parent country, and between which parties a war actually exists on that account? Will the sending, or receiving a minister to a new State under such circumstances be considered an acknowledgement of its independence? Is such an acknowledgement a justifiable cause of war to the parent country? Is it a just cause of complaint to any other power?[48]

Cabinet members were expected to prepare answers to such questions so that the discussion during Cabinet meetings could proceed with dispatch and effectiveness.

Who were the men to whom Monroe directed such weighty questions? At the time under consideration John Quincy Adams of Massachusetts was Secretary of State, John C. Calhoun of South Carolina, Secretary of War, William Crawford of Georgia was Secretary of the Treasury, Samuel L. Southard of New Jersey was Secretary of the Navy, and William Wirt of Virginia held the Attorney General's office. These men had been selected with an eye to party harmony, representativeness, and appeal to public opinion in general and congressional opinion in particular.

Monroe had detailed his selection principles in a letter to General Andrew Jackson in December of 1816:

> In the formation of an Administration it appears to me that the representation principle ought to be respected, in a certain degree at least, and that a head of a Department (there being four) should be taken from the four sections of the Union, the East, the Middle, the South, and the West.[49]

Monroe conceded that:

> This principle should not be always adhered to. Great emergencies and transcendant talents would always justify a departure from it. But it would produce a good effect to attend to it when practicable. Each part of the Union would be gratified by it, and the knowledge of local details and means, which would thereby be brought into the Cabinet, would be useful.[50]

With characteristic emphasis on freedom of action Monroe added: "I am nowise compromitted in respect to anyone, but free to act, should I have to act, according to my own judgment, in which I am thankful for the opinions of my friends, and particularly for yours."[51]

Somewhat later, he explained to Jefferson why he had chosen a Secretary of State from an Eastern state:

[48]Monroe, vol. 6, p. 31.
[49]Monroe, vol. 5, p. 347.
[50]Monroe, vol. 5, p. 347.
[51]Monroe, vol. 5, pp. 347–348

Much has been said to impress a belief, on the country, north and east of this, that the citizens from Virginia, holding the Presidency, have made appointments to that department, to secure the succession, from it, to the Presidency, of the person who happens to be from that State.[52]

Although he considered the allegation of the deliberate founding of a Virginia presidential dynasty baseless, "much effect has been produced by it."[53] It had therefore become necessary to lay the suspicion at rest lest "the whole of the country, north of the Delaware, immediately, and the rest of the Potomac" later, would become opposed to the President.[54] "My wish is to prevent such a combination, the ill effect of which would be so sensibly felt, on so many important public interests."[55] Anticipating Southern disappointment with his decision, he mused that "I can hardly hope, that our Southern gentlemen, who have good pretensions, will enter fully into this view of the subject, but having formed my opinion on great consideration, I shall probably adhere to it."[56] One section might have to suffer for the sake of unity of the whole. For it was Monroe's firm belief that his duty was to the whole nation rather than to a section, faction, or party. "I will make the administration, first, for the country and its cause; secondly, to give effect to the government of the people, through me, for the term of my appointment, not for the aggrandizement, of any-one."[57]

As Monroe was to discover, a Cabinet picked to be representative of the diverse viewpoints in the country in general is not a Cabinet that works readily as a team. What made matters even worse was that Calhoun and Crawford, as well as Adams, considered themselves potential candidates to succeed Monroe. Each wanted to gain a reputation for strength and sagacity while lessening the reputation of his adversaries. The result was constant feuding, personal attacks, and often deadlock. For instance, Adams attributed Crawford's and Calhoun's suggestions that the United States should express itself in favor of Greek independence in the seventh annual message as strictly a bid for public favor. He wrote in his diary:

> In this, as in many other cases, these gentlemen have two sources of eloquence at these Cabinet meetings—one with reference to sentiment, and the other to action. Their enthusiasm for the Greeks is all sentiment, and the standard of this is the prevailing popular feeling.[58]

[52]Monroe, vol. 6, p. 3.
[53]Monroe, vol. 6, p. 3.
[54]Monroe, vol. 6, p. 3.
[55]Monroe, vol. 6, p. 3.
[56]Monroe, vol. 6, p. 4.
[57]Monroe, vol. 6, pp. 5–6.
[58]Adams, *Memoirs,* vol. 6, p. 173.

"As for action," Adams felt that "they are seldom agreed; and after two hours of discussion this day the subject was dismissed, leaving it precisely where it was—nothing determined, and nothing practicable proposed by either of them."[59]

Cabinet members expected that reports of their activities in the Cabinet would reach Congress and political leaders throughout the country via numerous much-used communication channels between Cabinet members and outsiders. For instance, Crawford was in continuous communication with Speaker Clay and Calhoun corresponded regularly with the influential General Jackson. Adams, who was less given to personal intrigues than his colleagues, bemoaned the fact that

> the only possible chance for a head of Department to attain the Presidency is by ingratiating himself personally with the members of Congress; and as many of them have objects of their own to obtain, the temptation is immense to corrupt coalitions.[60]

He alleged that "there has been intercourse of this kind, more or less explicit, between Crawford and Clay."[61] Crawford's presidential prospects depended "upon the failure of the Administration;" hence Crawford "must take care to make known his disapprobation" of presidential measures and must deviously undermine them.[62] The system "leads to a thousand corrupt cabals between the members of Congress and the heads of the Departments."[63]

The President, too, was very concerned about Cabinet intrigues and rivalries. He pleaded for unity and warned Cabinet members that their differences would be fully exploited by congressional enemies to the detriment of public policies. "A difference of opinion in the administration immediately got abroad."[64] When it did, "advantage was instantly taken of it by its enemies; other objects and other views immediately connected themselves with it and embarrassments multiplied upon the administration."[65] The President "so harassed that he scarcely knew where to set his foot" tried desperately to conceal Cabinet differences from the public eye lest they become focal points for dissent in Congress and the country.[66] When the Cabinet could not agree, despite long sessions lasting deep into the night, he often refused to take action at all on the matters under consideration. Nevertheless, he retained his original cabinet through-

[59]Adams, *Memoirs*, vol. 6, p. 173.
[60]Adams, *Memoirs*, vol. 4, p. 242.
[61]Adams, *Memoirs* vol. 4, p. 242.
[62]Adams, *Memoirs*, vol. 4, p. 242.
[63]Adams, *Memoirs*, vol. 4, p. 242.
[64]Adams, *Memoirs*, vol. 4, p. 451.
[65]Adams, *Memoirs*, vol. 4, p. 451.
[66]Adams, *Memoirs*, vol. 6, p. 367.

out his administration because he felt that his initial criteria for selection had been wise.

During Cabinet sessions concerned with foreign affairs, the dominant figure by far was John Quincy Adams. This was as much a matter of personality as a matter of his position. By personality, Adams was brilliant, tough-minded, and prickly with very definite ideas of his own about American policy. He had no hesitation at all to express these opinions, even if he formed a minority of one. By position, it was his task to prepare the basic drafts of foreign policy papers that were then submitted to the President and often to the Cabinet for discussion. By preparing the basic draft, he frequently determined which matters would receive attention and which would be ignored. He also set the initial tone for debate which often was crucial to its final outcome. For instance, without his special pleading the noncolonization principle of the Monroe Doctrine would very likely have been omitted.

The other pillar of Cabinet discussion was John C. Calhoun, a brilliant 35-year-old Southerner with a distinguished career in Congress. Even Adams, who disliked him, conceded that "Calhoun thinks for himself, independently of all the rest, with sound judgment, quick discrimination, and keen observation. He supports his opinions, too, with powerful eloquence."[67] Adams was to regret these traits when Calhoun adopted the political beliefs of General Jackson about the nefarious designs of the Holy Alliance and was able to convert the President to his point of view.

William Wirt did not participate much in the discussions of the Doctrine, except towards the very end. He was, in Adams' characterization, the President's man. Alone among the Cabinet members, he had no presidential aspirations. With unusual self-deprecation he had written of himself: "I am already higher than I had any reason to expect, and I should be light-headed indeed, because I have been placed on a knoll where I feel safe, to aspire at the mountain's pinnacle in order to be blown to atoms."[68] With no personal political ambitions to serve and with a feeling of inferiority, he was likely to follow the President's lead even though he was not afraid to make suggestions.

Crawford was ill during the Monroe Doctrine discussions. This was probably fortunate because the antipathy between him and Adams was violent. Adams appraised Crawford as a mediocre public servant:

> His talent is intrigue. And as it is in the foreign affairs that the success or failure of the Administration will be most conspicuous, and as their success would promote the reputation and influence, and their failure

[67]Adams, *Memoirs*, vol. 4, p. 36.
[68]Quoted in Arthur Styron, *The Last of the Cocked Hats: James Monroe and the Virginia Dynasty*. Norman: University of Oklahoma Press, 1945, p. 347.

would lead to the disgrace, of the Secretary of State, Crawford's personal views centre in the ill success of the Administration in its foreign relations.[69]

Since Crawford's "ambition swallows up his principle," he would place private advantage over the public welfare.[70] Although "not a worse man than the usual herd of ambitious intriguers—perhaps not so bad as many of them," he would "perhaps unconscious of his own motives . . . be impelled to throw obstacles" in the way of the administration.[71]

### Public Opinion Influence in the Cabinet

Although Adams' indictment of Crawford may have been too harsh, it was true that the personal ambitions of Cabinet members colored their beliefs and recommendations.[72] All of them were highly sensitive to the fact that the Cabinet was a fishbowl, with Congress and the public an eager audience to compare the feats and foibles of presidential contenders. Espousal of a popular cause might enhance a man's political fortunes. By contrast, any incautious remark might have the spotlight of congressional inquiry immediately thrust upon it. Thus Adams had been called to explain the position of the administration toward the Latin American colonies which were asking for recognition. Adams prepared the report for Congress, despairing of preserving his public image intact in the process:

> In this affair everything is insidious and factious. The call is made for the purpose of baiting the Administration. . . . I am walking on a rope, with a precipice on each side of me. . . . The policy pursued by the Administration in South American affairs is, in the general opinion of the public, fixed exclusively upon the Secretary of State, and, as the popular sentiment is much divided upon it, no effort is omitted to render it obnoxious.[73]

Adams knew his sensitivity to public criticism, although he tried to deny it because it did not accord with his idea of intellectual independence. But, although he criticized colleagues for what he considered undue subservience to the public mind, he appealed to this weakness when his own suggestions had run into difficulties. For instance, when President Monroe was cool to his pet project of sending a declaration of American principles to the Tsar, he used the public opinion club to prod a vulnerable Presi-

---

[69]Adams, *Memoirs*, vol. 4, pp. 241–242.
[70]Adams, *Memoirs*, vol. 4, pp. 241–242.
[71]Adams, *Memoirs*, vol. 4, pp. 241–242.
[72]For similar conclusions see Tatum, p. 198.
[73]Adams, *Memoirs*, vol. 4, p. 223.

dent. If no answer was made to the Tsar the public might wonder how his challenge to republican principles had been countered:

> If the people of our country should hereafter know, as they must, how much good advice the Emperor has been giving us in private, they would not be satisfied to be told that the only return we had made to him for it was to send him a copy of the President's Message to Congress.[74]

Monroe, with his mania for approval of his actions and his suspicion that disagreement was evidence of conspiracy and ill intent, was highly conscious of public and congressional response to his policies. In August of 1823 Adams complained that "the President is often afraid of the skittishness of mere popular prejudices" and berated him for going out of his way to avoid unfavorable reactions.[75] Adams considered the President overly cautious and concerned about the effects of distorting newspaper stories. He boasted that "I have much more confidence in the calm and deliberate judgment of the people than he has." Referring to remarks about the Holy Alliance which Monroe had asked him to delete to avoid public misunderstanding, Adams agreed that press reaction was apt to be unfavorable: "I have no doubt that the newspaper scavengers and scapegibbets, whose republicanism runs in filthy streams from the press, would have attempted to exhibit this reference to the Holy Alliance in a false and odious point of view."[76] Unlike the President, he would have risked adverse publicity because "I would have trusted to the good sense of the people to see through their sophistry and their motives. They would have seen in it what was intended."[77] What Adams apparently did not grasp was the President's desperate desire to avoid the appearance of conflict over public policies because it spoiled his image of a united people speaking with one voice through its President. In an era of nascent nationalism, this image of political unity and uniformity of principles was a vital ingredient of successful nation-building.[78]

Calhoun, too, was criticized by his colleagues for being "sensitive to the transient manifestations of momentary public opinion" and for pursuing a chauvinistic policy merely to ingratiate himself with the public.[79] True to this image, Calhoun, more than others during the Monroe Doctrine discussions, seemed concerned about public reactions. He felt that the language of the declaration should be strong and stirring to rouse the

[74]Adams, *Memoirs*, vol. 6, p. 209.
[75]Adams, *Memoirs*, vol. 6, p. 170.
[76]Adams, *Memoirs*, vol. 6, p. 170.
[77]Adams, *Memoirs*, vol. 6, p. 170.
[78]Stuart Gerry Brown, *The American Presidency: Leadership, Partisanship, and Popularity*. New York: The Macmillan Co., 1966, p. 12.
[79]Adams, *Memoirs*, vol. 5, p. 361; Adams, vol. 2, p. 242.

people to the impending dangers from the Holy Alliance and rally them around the President, should forceful resistance become necessary. Like Monroe, he felt certain that a perceptive public would support his views because they were correct: "As this was the wise course, he had no doubt it would be sustained by the people of this country, if the exigency should require it. They would always sustain the wisest course when it was properly explained to them."[80]

Secretary Wirt alluded to public opinion in the course of the debate over the risks of involving the United States in war in defense of the principles expressed in the Monroe Doctrine. Wirt said that "he did not think this country would support the Government in a war for the independence of South America."[81] Although others disagreed and pictured Americans as deeply committed to South American independence, Wirt believed that "there had never been much general excitement in their favor. Some part of the people of the interior had felt warmly for them, but it never had been general, and never had there been a moment when the people thought of supporting them by war."[82] With a lukewarm public, it would be foolish to think of war. Consequently, "to menace without intending to strike was neither consistent with the honor nor the dignity of the country."[83] Wirt also believed that public officials "ought to have regard to the popular opinion, because the credit and influence of the Administration is affected by it."[84]

There has been much scholarly dispute about the precise use Monroe made of the advice tendered to him by his Cabinet. Partisans of Adams, in particular, paint a picture of a dominant Secretary of State whose intellectual brilliance and force of character overwhelmed Monroe. "The great secretary of state was able to inspire the slow-moving and lethargic President to fling out the challenge of 1823 . . . James Monroe held the trumpet, but John Quincy Adams blew the blast."[85]

Irrespective of the intellectual paternity of various provisions of the declaration, the picture that emerges from records of discussions of Monroe with his Cabinet and from an examination of his character and interpersonal relations on other occasions shows him as no one's undiscriminating echo. Monroe consulted widely and was quite open to suggestions—espe-

[80]Adams, *Memoirs,* vol. 6, p. 206.
[81]Adams, *Memoirs,* vol. 6, p. 205.
[82]Adams, *Memoirs,* vol. 6, p. 205.
[83]Adams, *Memoirs,* vol. 6, p. 205.
[84]Adams, *Memoirs,* vol. 5, p. 371.
[85]From an address by James B. Angell quoted in William A. MacCorkle, *The Personal Genesis of the Monroe Doctrine.* New York: G. P. Putnam's, 1923, p. 8. Also see James Schouler, "The Authorship of the Monroe Doctrine," *Annual Report of the American Historical Association,* vol. 1, 1905, pp. 125–131; and Bemis, pp. 366–391, 407–408.

cially from respected colleagues—but in the end he made his own decisions. He would not yield to any suggestion no matter who the author might be unless it coincided with views which he was able to make his own. Since he was not as creative a thinker as some of his predecessors and colleagues, the germ for many of his ideas came from others. But by the time he put the powers of the presidency behind them, they had become part of his own convictions.

Nor would Adams have pressed his own views and opinions on the President over strong presidential objections. This, too, is amply clear from the record. Adams repeatedly asked the President for precise instructions about which of two opposing courses the President preferred so that Adams could draw up diplomatic papers accordingly. He deferred to the President's appraisal of public opinion even when he disagreed with it. When he differed with the President regarding the intentions of the Holy Alliance, Adams confided to his diary that "in this case, as in all others for which Mr. Monroe as the head of his administration is responsible, I submit my own judgment to his."[86] His object was "to give all the aid in my power" to the President's measures, and he "wished not one line of my writing to go forth that should not have his hearty approbation."[87] But even if Adams and other Cabinet members had tried to impose their political judgments on the President, their efforts would have been for naught. Monroe bristled at pressure. The process of persuasion to which an intelligent, experienced, public-spirited President like Monroe will yield, comes as close to the ideal of opinion-change through rational and factual appeals as seems possible in human relations.

## Advice from Foreign Policy Experts

Other advisors within the administration included members of the diplomatic corps and various officials engaged in the civilian and military public service who came to call on the President or corresponded with him. The views of Richard Rush, minister to England, were particularly important. Monroe informed Rush that his dispatches had "laid the foundation . . . of the message which I shortly afterwards presented to Congress" as well as the diplomatic notes sent to England and Russia.[88] During the Cabinet discussions Monroe also cited the views of the American minister to Spain in substantiation of his own opinion that there was a real danger of Holy Alliance intervention.

Likewise, there is a good chance that Monroe's original intention to

[86]Adams, *Memoirs*, vol. 6, p. 171.

[87]Adams, *Memoirs*, vol. 6, p. 151. Note also that Adams never claimed credit for the doctrine, except for the noncolonization principle; Bemis, p. 394.

[88]Monroe, vol. 7, pp. 184–185.

include the recommendation for recognition of Greek independence in his annual message came from a long-term public servant, Albert Gallatin. Gallatin had sponsored this idea on a number of occasions much to the dismay of Adams. On November 24, 1823, an exasperated Adams commented:

> I called at the President's, and found Mr. Gallatin with him. He still adhered to his idea of sending a naval force and a loan of money to the Greeks; and as he is neither an enthusiast nor· a fool, and knows perfectly well that no such thing will be done, I look for the motives of this strange proposal, and find them not very deeply laid.[89]

The villain was a public presumably eager for Greek independence. "Mr. Gallatin still builds castles in the air of popularity, and, being under no responsibility for consequences, patronizes the Greek cause for the sake of raising his own reputation."[90] Adams felt that "his measure will not succeed, and, even if it should, all the burden and danger of it will bear not upon him, but upon the Administration, and he will be the great champion of Grecian liberty."[91] There was formidable precedent for such irresponsible advice. " 'Tis the part of Mr. Clay towards South America acted over again."[92]

The other influential advisors who ought to be mentioned were the two ex-Presidents, Thomas Jefferson and James Madison. Monroe relied on their counsel frequently, both in personal meetings and by correspondence. He wanted their ideas to help him shape his own or give him the comfort of knowing that the great men of his age endorsed his policies. When he received Canning's proposal, as on other occasions, he forwarded the diplomatic correspondence to them so that they could be fully apprized about all happenings. Their advice included comments on the facts of the situation, as well as estimates of public reactions.

But here again, just because Jefferson and Madison advised a certain course of action did not mean that this course of action would be taken. Their advice was highly persuasive because Monroe respected their wisdom. Nonetheless, he was willing to reject it if it seemed inappropriate to him. Conversely, if action was taken corresponding to their views, this did not automatically imply a direct causal relationship between the advice and the decision. Monroe and his predecessors, ideological fraternity brothers, often reached the same policy conclusions independently. Like Monroe, both Jefferson and Madison felt initially that the British proposal ought to be accepted. Like he, they·ultimately changed their minds and concurred in the final solution of the problem, after weighing the advantages and disadvantages of various policy options.

[89]Adams, *Memoirs*, vol. 6, pp. 198–199.
[90]Adams, *Memoirs*, vol. 6, p. 199.
[91]Adams, *Memoirs*, vol. 6, p. 199.
[92]Adams, *Memoirs*, vol. 6, p. 199.

Madison, who had suggested a declaration along the lines of the Monroe Doctrine in the spring of 1822, commented four days later to the President that "One thing is certain, that the contents of the Message . . . can do nothing but good anywhere."[93] A few months afterwards his enthusiasm had increased retroactively, especially since the message was apparently a popular and diplomatic success:

> I never had a doubt that your Message proclaiming the just and lofty sentiments of ten millions, soon to become twenty, . . . would be received in the present crisis of Europe with exulting sympathies. . . . The example of the U. S. is the true antidote to the doctrines and devices of the Holy Allies; and if continued as we trust it will be, must regenerate the old world, if its regeneration be possible.[94]

## The Visible and Invisible Role of Congress

Since Canning's proposals as well as the discussions between Adams and Baron de Tuyll of Russia about Russia's attitude regarding the South American colonies had been confidential, Monroe did not feel that they should be submitted to Congress. In fact, when Congress asked for information about these negotiations a few weeks after the message, he specifically declined to give it on the grounds of secrecy.[95] Thus Congress was not directly involved in the deliberations that led to the Monroe Doctrine, either before or after its enunciation.

Even if the element of secrecy had not been involved, Monroe would have tried to by-pass Congress if at all possible. The reasons are plain. Antagonism ran high between the President and various leading members of Congress. One did not need a persecution complex to suspect that Congress was deliberately trying to wreck Monroe's political plans and programs in order to assert its own powers and control the succession to the presidency. Communication with such an obstreperous Congress was exceedingly difficult since members would try their best to misconstrue messages to accomplish their own rather than public purposes to the detriment of the President's popularly-approved program. Matters were bad enough when Congress asked for papers which could not legitimately be denied. As Adams described it:

> Papers are wanted by two classes of members in the House of Representatives—those who are panting for debate, to make fiery speeches, and those who are eager to have a thrust at the Secretary of State. . . .

[93]Monroe, vol. 6, p. 408.

[94]Gaillard Hunt, ed., *The Writings of James Madison*, vol. 9. New York: G. P. Putnam's Sons, 1910, pp. 161–162.

[95]James D. Richardson, ed., *Messages and Papers of the Presidents*, vol. 2. New York: Bureau of National Literature, 1897, p. 790.

To give all the papers now will make ample field for a month's debate, and give vent to ill humors.[96]

Why should the President then make a deliberate effort to take Congress into his confidence whenever he could avoid it?[97] Congressional cantankerousness, rather than forcing more information from a secretive Executive, as Congress intended, actually led to a distinct narrowing of the stream of information in all those areas which had not specifically attracted congressional notice.

The problem of executive-legislative friction was an old one in American politics. Federalist Presidents had solved it by asserting their own right and duty of leadership in foreign affairs. Republicans, with their deliberate emphasis on the power of the legislature as the body containing the people's representatives, had a more difficult time. Jefferson, thanks to his capacity for leadership and creative insight into problems of political manipulation, was able to build an effective organization within Congress to do the President's bidding.[98] Madison, with less ability in leadership and organization, hitched his political wagon to the star of the dominant faction in Congress and equated its voice with the voice of the people.[99] Monroe, finding no agreeable strong faction in Congress and unwilling to organize one, played the role of champion of the people who on their behalf opposed a Congress whose members had become corrupted by their lust for control of the government.

Monroe's refusal, even when the opportunity presented itself, to influence the selection of the Speaker and the Committee on Foreign Relations was heavily influenced by his belief that with intelligence, good will, and public spirit all political problems could be compromised into a single acceptable solution.[100] Such compromise required information—not persuasion. Once the President had indicated the correct policy as it had emerged from discussions, all good Americans would rally around him. Since there ought to be no need for a special organization to assure compliance, he was unwilling to create it even when the need became desperately apparent.

[96]Adams, *Memoirs*, vol. 5, p. 464. The unanimous House resolution of December 24, 1823 is contained in U. S. Congress, *Annals of Congress*, Eighteenth Congress, 1st session, pp. 867, 869.

[97]Matters requiring appropriations or involving a treaty or declaration of war could not be concealed from Congress.

[98]Leonard D. White, *The Jeffersonians*. New York: Macmillan, 1951, pp. 48–52, describes Jefferson's control over floor leaders, party caucuses, and congressional committees.

[99]White, pp. 53–55.

[100]Scruples about the separation of powers and the proper roles of President and Congress were other considerations. White, pp. 57–58; also Adams, *Memoirs*, vol. 5, pp. 428–436, 474.

The fact the Congressmen frequently were not directly consulted does not mean that their influence was slight. In the background of most decisions to be made there was always the question: "What will Congress say or do about it when it finds out?" An overt display of disunity between President and Congress, especially if the public took sides, would weaken the international prestige of the administration and sharply curtail its effectiveness. For instance, in 1818 Monroe claimed that he could not promise recognition to a new Latin American government because Congress might indicate hostility: "It was not expedient to take the step without the certainty of being supported in it by the public opinion, . . . manifested by measures of Congress."[101] The image of unity was particularly important for a weak power, like the United States, although even great power status conveys no immunity to the weakening effects of legislative-executive disunity.

There are many other examples of the distinct yet indirect influence of Congress. We have already noted Adams' argument that a specific answer must be given to Russia because Congress, in order to embarrass the administration, would surely ask what its action had been. We have also mentioned Monroe's pleadings with his Cabinet associates to reach a decision, lest Congress become impatient and question the lack of action. If the executive did not act, Congress might force its hand through measures of its own. For instance, when Speaker Clay introduced resolutions in Congress in 1820 in favor of the independence of Spain's Latin American colonies and intimated that the President was opposed, Monroe and his Cabinet felt compelled to include support for South American independence in the President's message to Congress. Although "these paragraphs [were] exotics to the proper region of the message" and, in Adams' opinion "the principal real cause of the delay of Spain to ratify the Florida Treaty," the administration considered the impression of disinterest conveyed by silence even more damaging.[102]

At times, pressures in Congress were influential by hardening the administration's resistance to the measures proposed. For instance, recognition of the Latin American colonies may actually have been delayed until 1822 because Monroe was annoyed at Speaker Clay's pressure tactics. These pressures came not only through action in Congress, but more directly through personal contacts with Cabinet members. Generally the ties between Cabinet members and congressional and other leaders were well-known. Depending on the President's and the Cabinet's reactions to the power behind the throne, the Cabinet member's influence was increased or decreased through his outside ties.

[101]Adams, *Memoirs*, vol. 4, p. 71.
[102]Adams, *Memoirs*, vol. 5, p. 200.

## The Public's Thoughts: A Synthetic Product

Monroe did not go outside of his circle of official and semiofficial advisors in seeking either factual information or appraisals about the state of public opinion as regards the advisability of a public declaration of nonintervention principles. He was not in the habit of consulting his family, especially since his wife was a chronic invalid and ill most of the time.[103] "He studied alone, far into the night, the problems confronting his administration."[104] Lacking the social graces of Jefferson, and the services of an accomplished hostess like Dolley Madison, social contacts, which might have influenced him, were at a minimum. Contemporaries report that White House dinners were "exceptionally dull."[105] In fact, "absolute silence reigned" after the formal introductions.[106]

But even without these informal contacts, which Presidents use so frequently as barometers of public opinion, the President and others considered themselves well-informed about the likely public reaction to the Monroe Doctrine. Their assurance stemmed from the fact that the issues involved in the doctrine were familiar issues of American foreign policy. Presidents presumably knew how the American public felt about American involvement in the affairs of Europe, European involvement in the affairs of the Americas in general and in the affairs of the North American continent in particular. They presumably were fully acquainted with the opposition of Americans to further colonization of the North American continent, especially if it meant interference with their right to free trade with the colonized areas. And they were certain of the public's unwillingness to act jointly with European powers since this would mean foreign entanglement.

Such visions of public opinion fit in neatly with the well known fact that American Presidents and other prominent Americans, beginning with President Washington, had repeatedly proclaimed that the Western hemisphere was different from Europe and must not become entwined with European politics. In addition to endorsements by Washington, Adams, Jefferson, Madison, and Monroe the principles had been repeatedly approved in congressional resolutions. Unanimous congressional approval of Washington's neutrality proclamation is but one famous example.[107] Since Jefferson, Madison, and Monroe, the principles had been repeatedly ap-

[103]William P. Cresson, *James Monroe*. Chapel Hill: The University of North Carolina Press, 1946, p. 360.

[104]Cresson, p. 359.

[105]Cresson, p. 364.

[106]Cresson, p. 364; also see White, p. 38.

[107]U. S. Congress, *Annals of Congress*, Second Congress, second session, pp. 17–18, 138–139.

the public evidently did not object to these declarations by prominent and seemingly popular and well-loved individuals, it was assumed that their policies had full public approval. By the peculiar alchemy of public opinion politics they became "the" public opinion.

The reasons cited for approval were always the same: the national interests of the United States, presumably plain to all people, required that the Western hemisphere should be isolated from the nefarious influence of Europe. The people were thoroughly imbued with the spirit of popular politics and wished to take no chances of coming again under the influence of authoritarian government or the control of any European power. They mistrusted European nations, especially strong ones, as neighbors. And they had a sense of mission that the entire Western hemisphere would eventually share their ideology and that large portions of the North American continent were destined to become part of the United States. With such weighty evidence at hand it is not surprising that the history books are full of statements about the overwhelming public opinion support enjoyed by the Monroe Doctrine, which "has been echoed from every American heart" and has received the applause of the "masses of the American people" because the attitudes of their leaders "corresponded very closely to those of the nation as a whole."[108]

Stirring oratory notwithstanding, the facts of public approval are not clear cut. In the first place, there is some divergency of opinion about the public feeling regarding various specific policies involved in the doctrine and concerning the manner in which the principles were proclaimed. For instance, Cabinet members disagreed about the degree of public interest in the independence of Latin American colonies and the public's willingness to fight for this independence if it were threatened. Wirt believed that the public concern was lukewarm, Adams and Monroe, that it was strong, but probably short of willingness to fight. Calhoun sensed a willingness to go to war since "the popular feeling would be jealous of every appearance of yielding to the interference of any foreign power."[109] Each was ascribing his own reasoning to the public and each undoubtedly could have located specific publics who shared his views. Wirt mirrored the disinterest of the Southerners in closer ties with territories rife with slave revolts and led by libertarians. Adams, like other New England Yankees, was keenly interested in the trade potential of the Southern hemisphere, and Monroe and Calhoun, President and Secretary of War respectively, were deeply

---

[108]U. S. Congress, *Annals of Congress*, Eighteenth Congress, first session, p. 1768; Tatum, p. 206; W. F. Reddaway, *The Monroe Doctrine*. New York: G. E. Stechert, 1924, pp. 91–93; Bradford Perkins, *Prologue to War*. Berkeley: University of California Press, 1963, pp. 53–59.

[109]Adams, *Memoirs*, vol. 5, p. 29.

occupied with security interests.[110] Calhoun, as the civilian head of the military and in close touch with Jackson and other generals, thought most strongly in terms of military solutions.

As mentioned, public approval of the nonintervention and noncolonization principles was largely deduced from lack of overt mass opposition to these principles. This lack of opposition, as concerns the Monroe Doctrine specifically, becomes less impressive when one considers the fact that the negotiations from mid-October, when the Canning and Russian messages were received, until the end of November, when the various notes in reply had been composed and Monroe's message had been written, were conducted out of the public's eye. Except for leaks, which were few because of the shortness of time, neither Congress nor the public were kept informed. By the time Monroe made the declaration, little was left to do except the proverbial shouting. Press reaction was cordial, but public reaction was relatively sparse. Historians like McMaster and Styron report that "At home the message was read with enthusiasm and pride," or that it was "received with patriotic joy."[111] But how could they tell? Neither the President's mail nor activity in Congress nor reports in the newspapers give any indication that there was more than the usual ripple of interest. Most people probably neither knew nor cared about the "calm, dull phraeseology of this message."[112]

There was some opposition also, but it was deemed to be a minority opinion. Monroe was accused of "saying things likely to bring on the country the wrath of the Holy Allies" forcing him eventually to "back down or fight."[113] "There were some cautious souls who feared it was an imperialist policy that would get us into war, and some imperialists who feared that if the policy were consistently followed it would block our territorial expansion."[114] The *Boston Advertiser* queried: "Is there anything in the Constitution which makes our Government the Guarantors of the liberties of the World? of the Wahabees? the Peruvians? the Chilese? the Mexican or Colombians?"[115] Nonetheless, press supporters of the President observed through their rose-colored glasses that "Happily, these men

[110]David N. Rowe, *A Comparative Analysis of the Historical Background of the Monroe Doctrine and the Open Door Policy in the Far East.* Chicago: Ph.D. dissertation, University of Chicago, 1935, pp. 97 ff. discusses American trade interests in detail.

[111]John B. McMaster, *History of the People of the United States,* vol. 5. New York: D. Appleton Co., 1885, p. 50; Styron, p. 406.

[112]James Schouler's phrase, as quoted in MacCorkle, p. 31. See also Dangerfield, p. 309.

[113]McMaster, vol. 5, pp. 50–51.

[114]Styron, p. 406.

[115]Quoted in Dexter Perkins, *The Monroe Doctrine, 1823–1826.* Cambridge: Harvard University Press, 1932, p. 146.

were in the minority, and in all parts of the country the approval was general."[116]

Some hint of popular reserve comes from congressional action, too. On January 20th, 1824, Speaker Clay introduced a resolution in Congress that "the people of these United States would not see, without serious inquietude, any forcible intervention by the Allied Powers of Europe, in behalf of Spain" in any war between Spain and the late colonies.[117] The resolution elicited so little enthusiasm that Clay, fearing it might harm his popularity and reduce his chances for the presidency, withdrew it. Objections came mainly from New England Congressmen who believed that their section was opposed to flirting with war, and from Southerners who were wary that proslavery interests might be hurt in the process of aiding antislavery republics.

## The Fluidity of the National Interest

The most serious doubts about the assertion that the Monroe Doctrine policies represented "the" national interest, "the" public opinion, and the unanimous judgment of American leaders, arises from the fact that these policies, popular notions to the contrary notwithstanding, had not been consistently followed by the United States. There were many instances when early statesmen had contemplated intervention in European affairs, alliances with European nations, or further European colonization in the Western hemisphere. To name but a few, during the period of the Confederation in 1785, American statesmen, including Congressman Monroe, seriously debated an alliance with Spain that would have guaranteed the possessions of each country in the Western hemisphere.[118] Jefferson weighed an international naval force to fight against the Barbary powers.[119] He was willing to "marry ourselves to the British fleet and nation" on "the day that France takes possession of New Orleans."[120] He was also prepared to guarantee West Florida to France in return for the sale of East Florida to the United States.[121]

More important, the fact that Monroe, Calhoun, Southard, and Rush were willing to accept the British offer for a joint Anglo-American declaration is proof that the idea of foreign entanglement did not seem too out-

[116]McMaster, vol. 5, p. 51.

[117]Annals of Congress, Eighteenth Congress, 1st session p. 1104; see pp. 1103–1214, passim, for debates involving the resolution.

[118]Perkins, A History, p. 9.

[119]Perkins, A History, p. 10.

[120]Paul Leicester Ford, ed., The Writings of Thomas Jefferson, vol. 8. New York: G. P. Putnam's Sons, 1894, p. 145.

[121]Perkins, A History, p. 19.

landish. In fact, as early as 1818, Monroe had raised the question in the Cabinet "whether measures shall be taken to ascertain if this [promotion of the independence of the South American provinces] be the policy of the British Government, and, if so, to establish a concert with them for the support of this policy."[122]

The questions which Monroe asked Jefferson when he solicited his advice about the British offer, dealt specifically with the problem of foreign entanglement:

> Shall we entangle ourselves, at all, in European politics, and war, on the side of any power, against others . . . If a case can exist in which a sound maxim may, and ought to be departed from, is not the present instance, precisely that case?[123]

Despite all his past protestations against entangling alliances, Jefferson answered that such alliances should be undertaken if they furthered the national interests of the United States:

> By acceding to her [England's] proposition, we detach her from the band of despots, bring her mighty weight into the scale of free government and emancipate a continent at one stroke which might otherwise linger long in doubt and difficulty. Great Britain is the nation which can do us the most harm of any one, or all, on earth; and with her on our side we need not fear the whole world.[124]

If the alliance should lead the United States into war, it would not be a British "war, but ours. Its object is to introduce and establish the American system. . . . to maintain our own principle, not to depart from it."[125]

Madison likewise felt that it was "particularly fortunate that the policy of Great Britain tho' guided by calculations different from ours, has presented a cooperation for an object the same with ours."[126] "There ought not to be any backwardness" in accepting her proposal because "with that cooperation we have nothing to fear from the rest of Europe; and with it the best reliance of success to our just and laudable views."[127] Had Monroe stuck to his original idea of accepting Canning's offer, the reasons that persuaded him as well as Jefferson and Madison that acceptance was proper would, undoubtedly, have likewise persuaded the American people. As Monroe had observed on other occasions, the people tend to follow their government as long as it moves within limits which seem to them a plausible facsimile of the public interest.

[122]Adams, *Memoirs*, vol. 4, pp. 91–92.
[123]Monroe, vol. 6, p. 324.
[124]Monroe, vol. 4, p. 391.
[125]Monroe, vol. 4, p. 392.
[126]Monroe, vol. 4, p. 394.
[127]Monroe, vol. 4, p. 394.

It is not certain which of various reasons persuaded Monroe to finally change his mind about a joint declaration. Undoubtedly, the cooling off of Canning, which came to the President's notice about two weeks after the original proposal, was part of the story. This put greater emphasis on the doubts raised by various members of the Administration about the sincerity of the British proposals and the desirability of keeping company in public with a fickle, unpopular partner. Monroe, who after his unsuccessful experience in England had no love for the snobbish British and who was always ready to believe in the duplicity of outsiders, was susceptible to such arguments.

Public opinion considerations were not in the foreground, however. There was no mention during the discussions that either the joint or unilateral solution would be easier to defend before the public opinion jury, or that popular opposition to entangling alliances or anti-British feelings was considered.[128] These may have been subconscious factors which tipped the scale towards unilateral action. If this was true, these factors were not strong enough in the face of countervailing diplomatic considerations to prevent Monroe from keeping the possibility of a British alliance open in the formal reply to Canning. If an alliance seemed advisable for diplomatic reasons, public opinion would not be a serious obstacle.

As long as culturally acceptable justifications are available for the defense of a given policy it becomes a feasible alternative from a public opinion standpoint. Monroe could have justified a joint declaration with Britain. Given sufficient support in Congress, he could have given an unequivocal guarantee to the Latin American countries that the United States would protect them against European aggression. Or he could have specifically disavowed a policy of support for Latin American nations. He could have included in his message an offer of aid to the Greeks in their struggle against Turkish domination; and he could have struck some kind of bargain with Spain in order to acquire Cuba in return for Spanish control of another American region. There would have been objections from certain quarters in Congress, in the press, and from public opinion leaders in various sections of the country. There always are. No policy wins unanimous approval. But there would have been enough supporters so that the President could claim, with the usual evidence to back him, that public opinion was with him.

It deserves to be stressed again that the options available to a President are not unlimited. Political and strategic factors and party and congressional hurdles cannot be ignored. A congressional investigation although no vote

[128]Tatum, p. 181, believes that anti-British feelings were universal. He talks of "commercial rivalry, political hostility, and virulent social antagonism." To Americans "England stood for imperialism, aristocratic rule, commercial exclusion, and the denial of the right of neutrals."

of censure has been passed can leave "a slimy track of public opinion behind."[129] There are certain limits beyond which the public cannot be pushed. For instance, it would have been inconceivable in Monroe's day to renounce the right of navigation on the Mississippi River or to cede any of the newly acquired Western territories back to their original owners. But within these dikes, public opinion—if not the other factors—allowed a fair degree of mobility.

## Ostensible and Real Motives for the Message

It is interesting as well as significant that Monroe began his seventh annual message with a long eulogy on the value of informed public opinion, especially in the conduct of foreign affairs, and then told the people nothing about the crucial negotiations and discussions which were the *raison d'être* for its most vital parts. Despite the eulogy, the message was a bid for public support, rather than counsel. It did not supply the people with sufficient information to equip them to give advice and guidance in the future. Furthermore, the impact of the message abroad received more attention than its domestic reception. Some opening passages of the message deserve to be quoted in full:

> The people being with us exclusively the sovereign, it is indispensable that full information be laid before them on all important subjects, to enable them to exercise that high power with complete effect. If kept in the dark, they must be incompetent to it. We are all liable to error, and those who are engaged in the management of public affairs are more subject to excitement and to be led astray by their particular interests and passions than the great body of our constituents, who, living at home in the pursuit of their ordinary avocations, are calm but deeply interested spectators of events and of the conduct of those who are parties to them. To the people every department of the Government and every individual in each are responsible, and the more full their information the better they can judge of the wisdom of the policy pursued and of the conduct of each in regard to it. From their dispassionate judgment much aid may always be obtained, while their approbation will form the greatest incentive and most gratifying reward for virtuous action, and the dread of their censure the best security against the abuse of their confidence. Their interests in all vital questions are the same, and the bond, by sentiment as well as by interest, will be proportionably strengthened as they are better informed of the real state of public affairs, especially in difficult conjunctures. It is by such knowledge that local prejudices and jealousies are surmounted, and that a national policy, extending its fostering care and protection to all the great interests of our Union, is formed and steadily adhered to.

[129]Adams, *Memoirs*, vol. 5, p. 46.

A precise knowledge of our relations with foreign powers as respects our negotiations and transactions with each is thought to be particularly necessary.[130]

The message then makes a brief reference to Russian-American negotiations about the Northwest coast fishery rights, a subject that had received some publicity in the press.[131] Then, without mentioning the Tsar's anti-democratic manifestos which had antagonized Adams, the message states, almost off-handedly, that the Russians "in the discussions to which this interest has given rise" were informed of the closure of the American continents for further colonization.[132] Toward the end of the message, way beyond the sections dealing with foreign affairs, come the crucial passages which form the heart of the Monroe Doctrine.

The message says nothing about the British offer, nor about Monroe's grave concern about the dangers faced by the nation from the Holy Alliance. Initially, Monroe had meant to set a more alarming tone. But Adams dissuaded him on the grounds that the nation would be frightened by the facts. The "tone of deep solemnity and of high alarm, intimating that this country is menaced by imminent and formidable dangers, such as would probably soon call for their most vigorous energies and the closest union . . . would take the nation by surprise and greatly alarm them. It would come upon them like a clap of thunder."[133]

Adams also dissuaded the President from including stirring references to the fate of Spain and her former colonies, and to the Greeks' struggle for independence in the message, even though this would probably have pleased the public. Adams felt that such passages "would be a summons to arms—to arms against all Europe, and for objects of policy exclusively European—Greece and Spain."[134] The courting of public favor was not worth taking such a chance. To Monroe's retort that Congress might express similar sentiments, if the President did not, and steal the thunder of his popularity, Adams replied that: "It was infinitely better that the impulse should come from Congress" although he doubted that Congress would act.[135] "Congress are responsible for their own acts. Foreign pow-

---

[130]Monroe, vol. 6, pp. 325–326.

[131]Cresson, pp. 414–415, states that the President was "thoroughly alarmed over the situation in the Northwest, while Congress and the public remained unconcerned over the potential loss of far-off regions."

[132]Monroe, vol. 6, p. 328.

[133]Adams, *Memoirs,* vol. 6, pp. 194–195.

[134]Adams, *Memoirs,* vol. 6, p. 195.

[135]Adams, *Memoirs,* vol. 6, p. 197. Adams once told the British minister that "the members of the legislature of this country are not only perfectly independent of the Executive, but the Executive cannot permit itself to be questioned by any foreign Minister upon anything said or done by them." Monroe concurred. Monroe, vol. 5, pp. 245, 249.

ers are apt to take less notice of them than of Executive measures, and if they put us in attitudes of hostility with the allies, be the blame upon them."[136]

Thus foreign rather than domestic considerations led to a toning down of a number of passages of a declaration that ostensibly was designed primarily for home consumption. In fact, the desire to create certain effects abroad was largely responsible for most foreign policy comments included in the message. Members of the administration thought that inclusion of these comments in the message would be the most graceful and diplomatic way of presentation to the Holy Allies:

> The message was a mere communication to our own people. Foreign powers might not feel themselves bound to notice what was said in that. It was like a family talking over subjects interesting to them by the fireside among themselves. Many things might be said there without offence, even if a stranger should come among them and overhear the conversation, which would be offensive if they went to his house to say them.[137]

By this type of internal communication the United States could set forth positions which might be deemed insulting if directly addressed to foreign powers. If Monroe had not decided to use this method to put his principles before the Holy Allies, it is doubtful whether he would have devoted so large a share of his message to foreign affairs. Although he favored public consultation, it had to be omitted if the political price seemed disproportionately high to the President.


### Presidential Silence Assures Maneuvering Room


Monroe was able to maintain silence about foreign policy making during the formulation of the doctrine because there was no immediate need for either congressional or public support. No action pended before Congress or any of its committees which might interfere with the effectiveness of the negotiations.[138] As a Senator he had chided President Washington for making a declaration which might ultimately involve the country in war, without prior consultation with Congress. But when he himself had assumed Washington's position, he felt he had the right to act without first soliciting the views of Congress.

Throughout the negotiations no public pressures were brought on the President to act in one way or another. His policy of silence had paid

[136]Adams, *Memoirs*, vol. 6, p. 197.

[137]Adams, *Memoirs*, vol. 6, p. 200.

[138]When such action pended, it was customary to clear presidential declarations with the Speaker or with the Chairman of the Committee on Foreign Relations. Adams, *Memoirs*, vol. 5, p. 34.

off. Whatever concern the public had felt about Russian activities in the Northwest had been allayed by prior reports that successful negotiations were under way. In fact, Secretary of State Adams had personally written a reassuring editorial on the negotiations for the *National Intelligencer* at the behest of Baron Tuyll, the Russian minister. The Minister had asked Adams to calm the public because the Tsar was very desirous to "stand fair in public opinion" in America.[139] Popular concern about the fate of the Latin American colonies had subsided, following American recognition of their independence in 1822. Nor was the public concerned enough about the activities of the Holy Alliance to press the President for information or action. Anxiety might have increased, as time passed, in the wake of more alarming press reports about European events. But by the winter of 1823, pressures on the President from outside the Administration were not at an acute stage.

Even after the message was delivered, the President remained largely free from requests to change it in any particular way. The explanation lies in the vagueness of the message that made it flexible enough so that all sorts of interpretations could be placed upon it. Speaker Clay believed that the message implied that the United States would give military assistance to Latin American states under European attack. Other congressmen disagreed and in 1826 Congress objected to sending delegates to the Panama conference if this would lead to an impression abroad that the United States, under the Monroe Doctrine, would automatically assist any Latin American country threatened by a European enemy.

Senator Hayne of South Carolina contended that the United States would never go to war for the independence of South America. The declaration "was intended to produce a moral effect abroad; he [Monroe] designed it for the atmosphere of Europe."[140] Its phrasing, "while it did not commit us to overt acts, . . . left foreign nations under vague dread of what we might do if the event alluded to should ever happen."[141] Calhoun, one of the participants in the Monroe Doctrine discussions, claimed at a later date that it was not a doctrine, declarative of American principles, but merely a declaration which would be a point of departure for future policies.[142]

Throughout these discussions, Monroe maintained silence. He knew full well the advantages of a policy of flexibility. While, on the one hand, it might be necessary to declare American principles in order to leave no doubt that the United States would come to the defense of certain basic national interests, on the other hand, it was not wise to predict the course

[139]Adams, *Memoirs*, vol. 6, p. 151.
[140]Quoted in McMaster, vol. 5, p. 444.
[141]McMaster, vol. 5, p. 444.
[142]As noted in Styron, p. 397.

of the nation too precisely and thereby prevent it from shifting its ground.[143] This is exactly what the Monroe Doctrine accomplished: it indicated that the United States would strongly resent intervention in the Western hemisphere, but it left the specific reaction undefined with the blanks to be filled in by later Presidents, as the necessities and circumstances might indicate. The American people, although in theory they favor a well-defined policy road, have always been content with such a pragmatic approach. American instincts in politics run towards pragmatism, even though professions and conscious preferences emphasize a policy of principle.

### The Tone Makes the Music

Vagueness was by no means the whole secret of popular and political success of the message. Most Americans judged the message far more by its tone than its substance. And Monroe, despite his dull prose and wordy sentence structure, managed to strike or elicit the right tone of patriotism so dear to Americans. The feelings that Daniel Webster professed in Congress in 1826 are probably representative of sentiments throughout the country among those who heard or read about the message:

> I look on the message of December, 1823, as forming a bright page in our history. I will help neither to erase it, nor tear it out; nor shall it be, by any act of mine, blurred or blotted. . . . It elevated the hopes, and gratified the patriotism, of the people. Over those hopes I will not bring a mildew; nor will I put that gratified patriotism to shame.[144]

Webster pictured his impression of reactions to the President's call:

> The tone . . . . found a corresponding response in the breasts of the free people of the United States. That people saw, and they rejoiced to see, that, on a fit occasion, our weight had been thrown into the right scale . . . we had done something useful, and something effectual, for the cause of civil liberty. One general glow of exultation, one universal feeling of the gratified love of liberty, one conscious and proud perception of the consideration which the country possessed, and of the respect and honor which belonged to it, pervaded all bosoms.[145]

As long as patriotism is deemed a sacred virtue, what people can resist accepting such a flattering picture of itself? The image of the great, wise public who rallies behind patriotic policies becomes a self-fulfilling prophesy. Fulfillment may come years and even decades later. But, barring debunking historians, it will surely come.

[143]On the wisdom of vagueness see Thomas C. Schelling, *Arms and Influence*. New Haven: Yale University Press, 1966, pp. 35–91.

[144]Monroe, vol. 6, p. 444.

[145]Monroe, vol. 6, p. 443.

# 11

# The Compromise between
# Idealism and Realism
# in the Opinion-Policy
# Relationship

> . . . human kind
> Cannot bear very much reality.
> T. S. ELIOT, "Four Quartets: Burnt Norton"

> Whatever the equality of political rights, so small is the share
> of total political activity performed by the great majority and
> so great that performed by the small minority, that the total
> hue and character of national political activity reflects that of
> the active minority.
> BERTRAND DE JOUVENEL[1]

---

[1] "Political Science and Prevision," *American Political Science Review*, vol. 59 (1965), p. 33.

# 11

At the start of this book three questions were posed. Why did the founding fathers deem it essential to consider public opinion in foreign policy decision making? What was the scope of influence that they assigned to public opinion? And what were the mechanics by which public officials tried to ascertain what the public wanted? The case studies and analyses of the personalities and ideologies of Adams, Jefferson, Madison, and Monroe reveal specific answers as well as broad trends. The answers and trends hold true for all four, mute testimony to the standardizing influence of a common political culture and a well-defined political role.[2] Despite divergencies in personality and political philosophy one can imagine each man in his own distinctive style arriving at the same political decisions reached by his colleagues. Each conceivably could have kept peace with France in 1799, bought Louisiana, fought the British in 1812, or announced a hands-off doctrine for the Western hemisphere in 1823.

Among the broad trends, four seem particularly significant to place public opinion theory and practice into proper perspective. They are the ever present conflict between political ideals and realities; the distinction between the advice and the veto-support function of public opinion; the uncritical acceptance of largely symbolic methods of information and opinion exchange; and the firm faith in presidential ability to ascertain public opinion and embody it so that presidential and public will become one and the same.

## Political Ideals, Myths, and Realities

Like most philosopher-politicians, the founding fathers were forever aware of the predicament of having to compromise ideals and perpetuate myths in order to cope with vexing political realities. The founding fathers believed in government by public opinion and its theoretical underpinnings. Ideally, an intelligent, moral, public-spirited people, kept fully informed by its government of public needs, *should* and *would* communicate its wishes to governmental leaders. These leaders would then carry out the wishes of their constituents. Sound policy would result.

[2]J. David Singer asserts that "the most diverse personalities will tend to converge if they are put into the same policy-making role." *Human Behavior and International Politics*. Chicago: Rand McNally, 1966, p. 154. Also see Seymour Lieberman, "The Effects of Changes in Roles on the Attitudes of Role Occupants," *Human Relations*, vol. 9 (1956), pp. 385–402.

But as experienced and practical politicians, the founders knew that the ideal conditions of the theory could be only partially realized. The public was less knowledgeable, less interested, and less public spirited than democratic value theory assumed. The means for interchange of information between government and people were rudimentary and imperfect. The requirements for effective policy formulation and execution often conflicted with the desire to proceed on the basis of wide public consultation. The most popular policy was not always the soundest.

Yet despite the obvious impossibility of rapidly changing the nature of man and society to conform to the theory's basal assumptions, the founders chose to keep the theory intact. The reasons are two-fold. In the first place, the theory served as a norm-setting ideal to which the public and its leaders could aspire. Such norms are generally set beyond expectations, reflecting the eager optimism of social reformers. In the process such norms often inspire people to reform in the direction of the high goals. The norms that tell us what men want to believe about themselves and their society and for what they intend to strive thus indicate the direction in which their society is moving. As long as the norms presented by the founders represented goals toward which American society was earnestly working, it was neither hypocritical nor meaningless to describe the opinion-policy relationship in terms of the desired pattern, rather than in terms of actual achievements on a particular occasion and at a given time and place.

Murray Edelman in his perceptive analysis of the *Symbolic Uses of Politics* points out the second reason for clinging to the ideal in the face of contrary evidence. Democratic theories "continue to be believed in spite of the lack of evidence and of the demonstrable exceptions" because "they hold men together and help maintain an orderly state."[3] Belief in the theory was practically useful because it made cooperation with government psychologically more palatable. As long as sizeable numbers of people were willing to identify themselves with their leaders and public decisions, and as long as they felt that government reflected their wishes, the political system functioned fairly smoothly in terms of public cooperation. In politics, as in other human endeavors, fantasy and symbolism are essential to blunt the harsh conflicts of life.

The agonies of fitting actual policy making into the Procrustean bed of a beloved theory are apparent throughout our case histories. Often adjustments and compromises that had to be made were uneasy ones. Discrepancies were concealed behind rationalizing language or incantations that the ritual of public opinion consultation had been observed. At times, when consultation of the public had obviously been short-circuited, the theory of post-hoc approval of policy decisions, to which both Adams and Jefferson appealed, was used to allay feelings of guilt.

[3]Urbana: University of Illinois Press, 1964, pp. 191–192.

Perpetuation of the dichotomy between theory and practice has had a number of serious consequences, some of them increasingly troublesome with the passing years. The difficulty of explaining the dichotomy is one of the drawbacks. Even worse, failure of practice to conform to the ideal has engendered disillusionment with democracy in some circles. "We become cynical about democracy because the public does not act the way the simplistic definition of democracy says that it should act. . . . The crisis here is not a crisis in democracy but a crisis in theory."[4]

Another undesirable by-product is that the ideal situation is frequently mistaken for the reality. Deductions based on the ideal are myths, but the public mistakes them for facts. Troublesome fantasies that spring from the idealized conception of the public opinion–policy relationship include the idea that a mass public exists and has well-formed views on policies, and that these views are easily discovered and clear in their instructions to governmental leaders. The fiction prevails that the single public opinion must be heeded because it reflects the public good. It thus turns opinions that have somehow captured the public opinion crown into tyrants that must be appeased by wooing or subduing them. This narrows the freedom of discussion and places an undue burden on the right of dissent because few dare to express contrary views once public opinion has allegedly spoken.

Tyranny of public opinion is further enhanced by the myth that the people will support a government that does their bidding and revolt against one that ignores them. In fact, as the cases show, the people judge a government more by the results it achieves than by its acquiescence to public pressures. If it produces popular results, as in the Louisiana Purchase, high-handed methods are forgiven. If it fails to produce advantages, as in the various embargo measures against France and Britain, prior public concurrence will not save it.

Even modern research has largely remained a prisoner of the notion that public opinion about the substance of policy deserves and receives consideration on its merits. Rosenau concludes that

> . . . despite widespread recognition that the formulation and conduct of foreign policy is sustained primarily by the opinion-making activities of national leaders and is only peripherally influenced by the views of ordinary citizens, it is the latter and not the former who have occupied the empirical spotlight.[5]

Very little attention has been paid to the limited effect that public opinion has on the substance of policy formulation. ". . . Investigators have been

[4]E. E. Schattschneider, *The Semi-Sovereign People.* New York: Holt, Rinehart and Winston, Inc., 1960, p. 134.

[5]James N. Rosenau, *National Leadership and Foreign Policy.* Princeton: Princeton University Press, 1963, p. 42.

inclined to observe mainly what the 'people' are thinking and doing and thence to bemoan the discovery that the 'people' are neither thinking nor doing."[6]

## Initiation-Advice versus Veto-Support Function

The second broad trend in the dichotomy between public opinion theory and practice relates to the functions to be performed by public opinion. Political discussions among the intellectuals during the formative years concerned themselves almost exclusively with the right of the people to be consulted about policy formulation and the public's intellectual and moral abilities to formulate or judge policy. The question to be answered was whether people were able to advise government about policy choices. The answer centered on a determination of whether people can initiate policies or merely choose among formulated policy alternatives; and whether their choices should concern general policy outlines only or extend to specific details.

Political exposition almost totally ignored the veto-support role of public opinion.[7] Little mention was made of the fact that in a democracy policy execution and even the survival of government often depend on supportive opinions or acquiescence of influential small or large publics. Despite carefully nourished myths and symbols to the contrary, governments lack power to coerce more than a tiny minority of the people at any one time. The power to govern depends on widespread acceptance and implementation of the idea that citizens ought to cooperate and acquiesce in public policies. If the public's confidence that government enjoys wide public support breaks down in the wake of vocal dissent by even small groups, government stability is in danger.

The need for the actuality or semblance of public approval presented policymakers with the problem of securing and demonstrating public opinion support for their policies to give them the seal of legitimacy. Their task was easy if policy aroused little dissent or if the views of dissenters were acceptable to the administration and could be incorporated into the policy system. But the task became delicate when vocal and powerful dissent erupted or was expected to erupt and when the wishes of the dissenters could not be accommodated within the lines of policy preferred by the administration.

The founding fathers then faced a dilemma. When opposition was strong enough so that it could obstruct policy execution directly or through its influence, or when it could destroy the appearance of mass consensus, it

[6]Rosenau, p. 46
[7]Rosenau, p. 18.

had to be stilled somehow. Methods to abort, silence, or discredit opposition could not always be used successfully. The only remaining alternative then was to make changes in the policy to appease the opponents or undermine their support. But if the President yielded to dissent, especially when the dissent came from small, special publics suspected of financial interest in the outcome, he could not admit bowing to pressure. For there also is a myth that policy must be made rationally in accord with the interests of the mass public. It cannot legitimately yield to private pressure or even large dissenting groups unless these groups can be convincingly depicted as representing the mass public. Between the Scylla of obstructive pressure and the Charybdis of a harmful display of presidential weakness, it took experienced, nimble pilotage to pass unscathed.

One question remains to be answered. How could the belief that government officials must yield to the wishes of the mass public be reconciled with the expectation of rational, unpressured policy formulation by the President? The answer lies in the myth that the mass public, in the long run, will always support rational policies presented by its political leaders. Rationality and mass support have a magnetic attraction for each other. By implication this deprives dissenters of the claim to rationality. If truly rational, their claims would win mass acceptance and their assumed minority status would be transformed into the unassailable majority position.

## Symbolic versus Actual Communication

The third broad trend that emerges from a comparison of theory with practice relates to the techniques of communication between government and people. On a few occasions the founders exhibited some awareness of the problems of adequate communication, especially between the government and the rural population. How could one be sure that messages about governmental activities and pending policies had reached responsible citizens everywhere, and how could one ascertain people's reactions when physical contacts were difficult to maintain? How could one tell which spokesmen really represented a mass public and which falsely or erroneously claimed that honor? How could one gauge the scope of support for certain ideas when there was no tally of actual support or opposition?

But on the whole, the founders revealed an almost naive faith that token communications between government and people would make Americans aware of all essential policy needs and the government aware of all important public opinions. Periodic presidential messages, often no more frequently than once a year and usually prepared for Congress rather than the public, were viewed as the chief official channel from the executive to the people. These messages traced the international situation in broad outline and sketched past steps and prospects and plans for the future. Messages were supplemented by presidential contacts with public officials, especially congressmen, and contacts with other individuals. Somehow the information disseminated in these encounters, as if by osmosis, was presumed to trickle down to the public and supply it with all essential information.

The reverse flow, from the public directly to the executive, came chiefly through petitions, letters, and word of mouth delivered by Congressmen and the small number of people who could talk to the President or to his contacts. This thin trickle of opinions, submitted expressly to the President by members of the public, was supplemented by the President's own observations and those of his advisers. Government officials would listen for opinion clues or try to estimate latent opinions from the tenor of public actions.

The early Presidents showed little concern about the extreme narrowness of these channels of communication, about the paucity of information that traveled along them, and about the restricted and haphazard spectrum of information transmitted in either direction. Government was primarily interested in keeping the accepted channels of communication free from obstruction and, aside from security inspired limitations, permitting free public discussion in the press and in the marketplace. Yet keeping a channel open and assuring its use by all those who might want or ought to use it are quite different matters.

The problem of communicating with government has been most acute at the citizens' end. Knowledge of the availability of communication channels, courage to try them, and ability to employ them effectively have always been unevenly distributed among the population. Verbal and organizational abilities and feelings of effectiveness in using communication skills occur most frequently among the economically and socially privileged. Hence the channels to the top have become predominantly a thoroughfare for ideas transmitted by various elites.[8] Some of these elites are specifically organized to communicate their views effectively to top governmental officials. Civic and academic groups and labor and ethnic organizations are in this category. While some of them mirror the views and interests of the man in the street, many others do not.

At the executive end, Presidents have had little trouble finding channels to communicate with the public. But this does not necessarily mean that citizens have been kept fully informed. Assumptions to the contrary notwithstanding, little effort has been made by various Presidents to assure systematic broad spectrum coverage of foreign policy information. Since

[8]Bernard C. Cohen, "Political Communication on the Japanese Peace Settlement," *Public Opinion Quarterly*, vol. 20 (1956), p. 28, contends that the articulate public "*is* 'public opinion,' it *represents* 'public opinion,' and it *creates* 'public opinion.'"

the veto-support criterion was uppermost, communications channels were used mainly to serve this function. Information programs were primarily consensus-building programs that moved into highest gear when a wide favorable consensus was needed or when a favorable consensus had been upset by opposition groups. At other times, the right to know and the duty to inform were subordinated to the needs of creating or maintaining consensus through disclosure or partial or complete silence. It was left to the initiative of outsiders (such as newspaper men and politicians) to ferret out information that had not been released. Depending upon executive purposes, cooperation often was less than enthusiastic.

Few students and politicians in the early years questioned the adequacy of the reception and use of information at either end of the communication channels. It was assumed that the President would be aware of all the information transmitted to him and would take it into consideration. At the citizen end, the dispatch of governmental messages was equated with their reception and absorption by the public. Rarely were doubts raised about the efficacy of written mass communications, especially lengthy and involved ones, in truly informing the public. Although messages were few and sparse and often fell on deaf ears, their mere existence became a symbol for an effective two-way communication process.

The measurement of public approval was also largely based on symbolic considerations. Evidence of group support was taken as proof that all citizens who were similarly situated concurred in the approval. For instance, a favorable memorial signed by a small number of students was considered indicative of the attitude of all their colleagues who had not specifically dissented from the petition. The possibility was ignored that lack of expression might not mean concurrence, but rather ignorance, apathy, or preoccupation with other concerns. Public silence might merely reflect an acceptance of most features of the political system even though people deemed the specific policies under consideration highly distasteful or unwise.[9] While supportive attitudes were broadly construed, opposition, by contrast, was narrowly interpreted. Given the assumption that the mass public supports the government unless there is contrary proof, allegiance to opposition groups had to be clearly demonstrated.

Similarly, supporting and opposing attitudes were symbolically evaluated. If the general tenor of a message seemed supportive, the senders were assumed to favor the entire policy or even a group of policies. Again, opposition was less broadly construed. Lest we be critical of the seeming lack of discrimination and sophistication of our forbears, we should remind our-

[9]This sort of assumption may explain the tragic surprise of leaders who are suddenly faced with overt hostility to a policy when previously silent citizens turn out to have been silent enemies rather than silent friends.

selves that modern practices are not very different. Even today's far more refined public opinion poll does not indicate adequately under what circumstances and for what groups of respondents a given answer is valid. Its uncritical citation as evidence of support or opposition amounts to the uncritical use of a symbol to stand for a crudely tested whole.

While communication with the mass public has been almost entirely symbolic, the executive branch has communicated effectively with a small number of opinion leaders who happened to be in strategic positions in the communication process. When these leaders have reflected or verbalized widely-held opinions and sentiments, the public whose spokesmen they were had effective access to the President and his advisors. If the spokesmen enjoyed high confidence and respect in decision-making circles, these publics had a good chance of having their views heard, considered, and possibly reflected in policy decisions.[10] During the early years, Westerners were particularly fortunate in having such spokesmen in the White House.

But like the direct communication link between decision makers and public, the communication link between spokesmen for the public and their clients has been largely symbolic and occasionally nonexistent. Even congressmen, who specialize in keeping in touch with the moods of their constituents, rarely communicate fully with more than a fraction of the people for whom they speak. The views expressed by people who see the President may be highly personal and shared by few others, or shared by small elites only.[11] Nonetheless, there is a very strong likelihood that their views will become symbolic for the views of their section of the country, their profession, or whatever other symbol they represent to their listeners. Generally, very little effort has been made to discover whether a spokesman has been really trying to speak for the group with whom his listeners associated him symbolically. And when he has claimed to speak for the group, little effort has been made to ascertain whether he really mirrored their views.

Commonly, attributes of capability have been uncritically transferred from one field to another. Prominent men, regardless of whether their prominence sprang from important offices held by them, from military prowess, from association with heads of government, or even from achievements in unrelated fields, were automatically presumed to be good judges

[10]For an analysis of the influence of such strategic groups see Bernard C. Cohen, *The Influence of Non-Governmental Groups on Foreign Policy Making.* Boston: World Peace Foundation, 1959, *passim.*

[11]Modern opinion studies (for example, those by Deutsch, Davison, and Edinger on Western European public opinion) concentrate on elite opinion when they desire to fathom politically important views. This is one among many signs that the political science profession is aware of the unique importance of elite views in policy making.

of the opinions of others, as well as representatives of "public" views. Conversely, opinions at times were denigrated when they were linked to people whose views were symbolic of conflict with prevailing public values.

Not only were prominent opinion submitters presumed to be spokesmen for the public, but their prominence lent additional prestige to the substance of the particular opinion and to the claim that it truly represented the public's views. Their endorsement disarmed criticism and attracted further supporters for the view, both on its merits and on the claim that it truly represented mass thinking. In this way the claim by prominent people that certain views expressed by them were shared by mass publics became a self-fulfilling prophecy. In fact, a large extent of public opinion politics has been endorsement politics of this sort. What is and what is not regarded as public opinion is not determined by any objective measurement of the views of certain publics, but by the credibility of the person who labels it as public opinion. The efforts chronicled in this book to line up endorsement by prestigious people behind controversial policies clearly indicate the importance of endorsements to make the substance of a policy acceptable and lend it the public opinion halo. Thus Monroe, long-time friend of Western expansion, became the symbol that Western viewpoints had a voice in the Louisiana negotiations, and Adams' choice of commissioners from various parts of the country symbolized a cross-sectional approach to policy toward France, reflecting the geographic differences in popular views.[12]

## Presidential Primacy

The fourth striking trait that marks the thoughts and actions of the founders about the opinion-policy relationship is the unquestioned assumption that the President is in full charge of implementing this relationship. In domestic affairs, political leaders are expected to keep their ears close to the grass roots and to listen for demands for public action. Regardless of whether political realities bear out the expectations, there is a widely-held belief that the public asks for certain policies and Congress and the executive respond to public demands.

Not so in foreign policy making. Here the President, as well as the public, have always expected that the executive branch would take the lead in initiating policy. The President would do so as the alter ego of the

[12]In fact, some political leaders have even specialized in being a "publicist of policy." Rather than originating ideas, they endorse them in the name of the public. They testify to the substantive merit of the policy. For a description of this function see Edward C. Banfield, *Political Influence*. New York: The Free Press, 1961, p. 282.

people, acting in "the public interest"—the greatest good for the greatest number of people, within the lifetime of the majority of the citizens. It was considered an ethical imperative for the President ultimately to submit prospective action for public scrutiny or to assess public reactions in other ways, and to shape policy to conform to public desires. But it was the President's prerogative and obligation to determine the best methods for public consultation and to decide when public consultation had to be delayed for practical and security reasons. So-called consensus-politics was scorned as weakness and indecision, even though it indicated presidential deference to mass views.[13]

It was assumed that an ascertainable public opinion existed with respect to basic attitudes involved in major policies, and that Presidents had the means to gauge these attitudes. Apparently there was an implicit recognition that the community of political culture of President and people, meant that each could share the other's deepest feelings and appraisals. As long as a President's decisions remained within the bounds of a common value system he could validly claim that they enjoyed public opinion support, regardless of overt proof that most people actually concurred with him. At any rate, those who might like to claim that he did not have public support faced the impossibility of proving their contention, just as the President could not fully prove his.

As we have seen, the fact that Presidents enjoyed sizeable public opinion support was rarely challenged. What was challenged was whether they had the majority of the people with them or the wisest people. This explains presidential eagerness for overt expressions or symbols of support. They were needed partly as reassurance for the President that he had indeed correctly interpreted the public views, partly as reassurance to the public that policy indeed proceeded according to popular mandate, and partly to refute critics who claimed that the President had ignored or misread public views.

The assumption that the President should lead in foreign policy formulation apparently has rested on the widespread belief that the executive branch is best qualified and equipped for the task. Analysts of public opinion formation believe that most people have recognized their inability to judge the merits of foreign policies. For this reason, they have approved of policies on the basis of the perceived merit of the endorser.[14] Under most circumstances, the President has been the most credible endorser. Whenever foreign policies have become partisan issues, identification has re-

[13]See pp. 339–343 in this volume. The differences in public attitudes toward various foreign policies, as compared to domestic policies, are discussed in James N. Rosenau, ed., *Domestic Sources of Foreign Policy*. New York: The Free Press, 1967, pp. 11–50.

[14]See pp. 342–345 in this volume.

flected party labels. Since most of the time the President's party has enjoyed majority support in the country, this could easily be construed as majority approval for presidential policy views.

Regardless of the factual situation, the Presidents we have studied assumed the effectiveness of their methods for gaining public opinion support, whether from the start or ultimately. All of them sincerely felt that their foreign policies had been formulated according to procedures which fully satisfied the democratic requirements of government guided by public opinion.

## The Comparative Worth of the "Common" Man

We have discussed theory-practice interaction and are now ready to examine the public opinion-policy relationship as expressed and practiced by Adams, Jefferson, Madison, and Monroe. While there are differences in theories as well as presidential styles, common patterns stand out. The first question posed for this study sought to discern why public opinion should be a factor in foreign policy formulation. The question was examined from three vantage points: expediency, conviction, and necessity. Turning first to expediency, we asked at the outset whether the founding fathers pleaded for public opinion consideration merely because it was fashionable and politically profitable to do so.

It is clear that Adams, Jefferson, Madison, and Monroe followed the fashions of the time when they proclaimed that the voice of the people must rule. No politician since the Age of Enlightenment and the rise of the middle classes (if he expected to remain long in politics) would have dared to do otherwise. Privately, some might share the dismal views that an American confided to an English visitor, that public opinion was

> . . . a tyrant, sitting in the dark, . . . deriving power no one knows from whom; like an Asian monarch, unapproachable, unimpeachable, undethronable, perhaps illegitimate,—but irresistible in its power to quell thought, to repress action, to silence conviction . . .[15]

But publicly most politicians felt compelled to express their faith in the wisdom and virtue of rule by public opinion.

For the founding fathers, as we have seen, the faith in public opinion was not a matter of mere expediency. Adams, Jefferson, Madison, and Monroe were true children of the Enlightenment who believed what they professed. In an environment which exuded intellectual optimism they were optimistic about human capabilities and optimistic about human intentions. Many of their experiences in politics seemed to corroborate the

[15]Quoted in Harriet Martineau, *Society in America*, vol. 3. New York: Saunders and Otley, 1837, pp. 69–70.

teachings of the time. Except in their moments of doubt, it was their sincere conviction that the average man, buttressed by education, was reasonably capable of appraising the wisdom of major public policies. They were disillusioned enough with the political decisions of eighteenth-century aristocrats to feel that the political judgment of the people was apt to be better because it certainly could not be any worse. Theirs was what Carl Friedrich calls "not so much a belief in the common man, as a disbelief in the uncommon man."[16] Their views might be expressed more absolutely than their opinions might warrant and their experiences might validate. But the distortion was one of degree and not substance.

Although the founding fathers fully believed what they said, their interpretation of what it meant substantively and how it could be implemented in practice differed from the interpretation of some of their contemporaries and later democratic theorists. None of the men whose views we have analyzed would have gone so far as to say with conviction that the collective voice of the people was always right and must be obeyed. None of them had the doctrinaire faith of later generations that the mass of people would unfailingly know their political needs as well as their wants better than any group of experts or chosen leaders. And none of them based their concept of public opinion on a mechanical counting of noses. Their public opinion was a Rousseauan general will, an often unspoken sentiment shared by decent men, who might or might not be a numerical majority.

The early Presidents were not impractical idealists. Posterity, which has stripped the backing of skepticism from their optimistic drawing of human capabilities, presents us with a mere caricature of their views. Without benefit of Freud, Pareto, or Walter Lippmann, all of them realized the narrow limits of rationality of mass publics and their susceptibility to emotional pressures. This is what lends credibility to their professed idealism. If honorable, experienced political leaders who recognized the limitations of their fellow citizens (singly or in groups) could consistently assign an important role to public opinion, probably public opinion could fill the assigned role.

Little more need be said about whether or not necessity forced Presidents to give sway to public opinion. The preceding pages are ample proof that the founding fathers had to wrestle with the practical problem of building and maintaining sufficient popular support for their policies to permit execution of these policies.[17] This meant creation of support for

[16]Carl Friedrich, *The New Image of the Common Man.* Boston: Beacon Press, 1950, p. 9.

[17]For the importance of the practical factor in modern public opinion theory see A. D. Lindsay, *The Modern Democratic State*, vol. 1. New York: Oxford University Press, 1947, pp. 272–274.

the substance of the policy as well as sustaining the image of popular consultation. If policy formulation seemed to be democratic and elective officials appeared accessible and responsive to public pressures, more than half the battle of public support was won. The substance of even an unattractive policy became more tolerable if the means of adoption conformed to the democratic image. One of the most difficult challenges in foreign policy making, throughout American history "stems from the problems of simultaneously choosing wise foreign policies and rallying a people in support of them . . . . the problem is one of enlisting consent."[18]

In addition to the danger of nonsupport for a particular policy, the founders were faced with the ever-present threat that the United States might be dissolved if a nation-wide consensus for national policies was unobtainable. If the early Presidents failed to achieve this consensus, all foreign policy would be for naught. There would be no union to protect and develop by means of well-conducted foreign policies. For these reasons, the broad outlines of policy set by the leaders reflected their appraisal of public views and reactions, as they existed and as they might be changed through opinion leadership. There was, indeed, a compelling necessity to consider public opinion.

## Variables in the Scope of Public Opinion

The second major question about the opinion-policy relationship concerns the scope to be allowed to public opinion in foreign policy formulation and the variations that differences in publics and differences in policy problems might dictate. The early Presidents distinguished between two types of publics. There was what corresponds to the modern, educated middle-class public—substantial numbers of people who had a stake in society because they owned property. These citizens had the intelligence and moral capacity to transcend their individual interest and search for the broader public interest that rational thinking could discover. These were the people whose opinions had substantive value and whose approval indicated the correctness of policies. That these were also the people most likely to concur with presidential opinions was more than a coincidence. Coming from a cultural background similar to the leadership's, their value standards for judgment were much like those of the leadership. When they disagreed, Presidents called it perverseness and even treason, not genuine and well-motivated differences of opinion. Official respect for dissent from any quarter, including the intellectual elite, was low in the early years,

[18]Kenneth Thompson, *Political Realism and the Crisis of World Politics.* New York: Harper & Row, Publishers, 1960, p. 95.

far lower even than in modern times.[19] The natural laws concept that there was only one right way and human reason could discover it narrowed tolerance for deviance from the single truth. Leaders of opposition parties were viewed as little more than power-hungry conspirators willing to sacrifice true policy to their own selfish designs.[20]

The urban masses, the selfish and uneducated rabble, interested in private advantage only, comprised the second type of public. The substance of their opinions could never be trusted, even if they were intelligibly expressed and concurred with presidential views. These people were suspect because they lacked a spirit of civic responsibility. Unlike the ideal "common man," whose individual shortcomings were neutralized in mass interactions, mobs reinforced their individual evil propensities. Nonetheless, mob opinion, too, even if barren of intrinsic merit, had to be taken into account because of the practical effect that mobs could have on policy execution.[21] Although the intellectual basis for considering mob views and the opinions of respected citizens differed in many ways, their effects on policy formulation were often quite similar. Mob views, however much they might be disdained, could force changes in policy. However, mob views were rarely quoted as a public opinion seal of approval to legitimate controversial policies.

Keeping in mind that "public" was a qualified concept, did the scope of its competence include all kinds of policies, or was its influence limited to narrow areas? Should the public be consulted about the means as well as the ends of policies? Asked in the abstract, this question would elicit answers reflecting confidence in the public's right and capacity to deal with a large variety of political questions and to determine means as well as ends. But when pressed to define the specific areas in which the public could and should make sound appraisals, the founders limited them to a fairly narrow range. There was complete confidence only in the public's ability to select public officials and to determine minor domestic matters.[22]

---

[19]In a similar vein, Kingdon's recent study of Congressmen's appraisal of their constituents notes that they consider the electorate intelligent if it elects them and misguided if it does not. Kingdon ascribes this to the reassurance function served by a Congressman's appraisal of his environment. To reassure himself of his own worth, conflicting views must be denigrated. John W. Kingdon, "Politicians' Beliefs About Voters," *American Political Science Review*, vol. 61 (1967), p. 141.

[20]James Sterling Young, *The Washington Community, 1800–1828.* New York: Columbia University Press, 1966, p. 113.

[21]For a similar distinction see Paul A. Palmer, "The Concept of Public Opinion in Political Theory" in Bernard Berelson, *A Reader in Public Opinion and Communication.* New York: The Free Press, 1950, pp. 3–13.

[22]Jefferson even doubted the capacity of the public to select good representatives and advocated a system of indirect elections for Virginia.

Broader questions, including foreign policy issues, were deemed to be beyond the public's grasp in many instances because the public had not made the necessary consistent effort to keep itself sufficiently informed. The ideal of wide popular consultation foundered and continues to founder because most major foreign policy choices are made through a series of minor, often highly technical decisions that have to be made seriatim over a prolonged period of time. Specialized decisions do not involve the broad moral judgments that the people can make effectively at those relatively rare moments in history when an aroused mass public thinks seriously about matters of state.

The practical answer to the question of the proper scope for public opinion, therefore, was an equivocal one. It varied with the predisposition of the President toward a maximum or minimum of public consultation. And it was influenced by the technical problem of reducing a given issue to simple enough terms so that the public could make a "yes" or "no" choice.

At any given time, however, the primary criterion was the need for public support. When foreign policy (like war or peace with France in 1800 or with Britain in 1812) required a great deal of public action in its execution, the founding fathers felt that they must have a sizable number of opinion leaders and their followers with them. A consensus on the general policy was essential. By contrast, a major policy like the Louisiana Purchase or the Monroe Doctrine did not require wide public support to be carried through successfully. It was therefore not necessary to solicit public support before proceeding with the policy. In fact, it was wise to withhold information from the public until the policy had been crystallized in order to keep opponents of the policy from mobilizing support against it.[23] Once the policy was irreversible, it was much easier to gain public approval since the public adjusts surprisingly quickly to the inevitable. As Adrienne Koch argues so eloquently in her essays on *Power, Morals, and the Founding Fathers*, such a flexible policy of public consultation was not political opportunism flung in the face of professed ideals. Rather, it was sound statesmanship which tempered efforts to achieve the ideal with practical considerations.[24] Given a less than ideal public and less than ideal conditions for publicity, the goal of widest public involvement had to be adapted accordingly.

[23]For a contemporary case study of how little the general public is consulted about major foreign policies which have no immediately discernible effect on the people, see Bernard C. Cohen, *The Political Process and Foreign Policy: The Making of the Japanese Peace Settlement*. Princeton: Princeton University Press, 1957. Even Congress is often kept in the dark, as failure to inform it adequately of the Berlin airlift demonstrates. See James A. Robinson, *Congress and Foreign Policy Making*. Homewood, Ill.: Dorsey Press, 1967, p. 44.

[24]Ithaca, N. Y.: Cornell University Press, 1961, p. 113.

After a general policy had been adopted, most of the Presidents felt that requests for changes in policy details could be accommodated as long as these wishes would not interfere with the main objectives of the policy. In fact, after major guidelines had been set, details were the negotiable currency of day-to-day political accommodation. Willingness to give in on lesser points demonstrated official responsiveness and therefore solidified support for the policy as a whole. For instance, Adams might decide that the nation needed to enlarge its armed forces in order to pursue a policy of strength towards France. He would not have given up his policy as long as he could continue it despite popular pressure. But when he was urged in the interests of good public relations to appoint Hamilton as Inspector General of the army, he was willing to give in because the appointment did not frustrate his overall policy. In fact, it helped to carry out the main objectives, even though Adams was opposed to the specific steps which he had to take. Likewise, after Madison had won congressional approval for an embargo on trade with Britain and France, he was willing to compromise about its precise duration. How much he yielded on this point to appease particular public officials or the people for whom they claimed to speak is difficult to say. Again, these concessions did not impair the main policy but merely changed the timetable.

Generally, there was less public concern about the details of policy than about the broader trends. Specialized publics, like shippers or manufacturers, often paid close attention to details affecting them. And their pressures, screened from public view by the public's inattention, were frequently successful in protecting their interests, although not generally at great public expense. By contrast, the mass public and most pressure groups showed little interest in details of particular policies and did not press for their disclosure.[25] Pressure to inform the public of general policy outlines rather than details thus was more frequent and stronger. Moreover, the American political culture imposes a more compelling moral mandate to inform the public about the major outlines of foreign policy than about its details. The Presidents, in accordance with their political convictions, felt bound by this mandate.

As a result, history records more instances in which Presidents informed the public about major policy decisions, rather than matters of detail. However, some distortion may arise from the fact that matters of detail are generally not as fully recorded as matters of greater substantive importance. Besides, the circle of advisors for details of policy was ordinarily broader than the high decision-making circle. "Experts" on various phases of policy, especially military and technical experts, were often drawn from a wide range extending beyond government officials. In this way a larger

[25]For a modern case that bears out this pattern, see the reports of peace negotiations between Japan and the United States in Cohen, "Political Communication," p. 30 ff.

segment of the public participated in important ancillary policy decisions, but their advice did not become a matter of record.

## Criteria for Designating Opinions as "Public"

If there are many trends of opinion among respected people, which opinion deserves to be called "public" and guide policy? The criterion of choice, as we have seen, was a very personal one and had little to do with sheer numbers of opinion holders, although the image was carefully nurtured that the opinion had mass appeal. Among the many trends of opinion expressed by spokesmen for various publics, the President would select those which, on the basis of his political experience and predilections, he deemed "public." When it was the President's prerogative to apply these criteria, it was small wonder that he selected opinions in accord with his own views of rationality and national interest. Only rarely was there acknowledgment of widespread dissenting opinions which, judged by criteria of rationality and public interest, might also claim the right to the public opinion label. The trade policy recommendations of New Englanders in Madison's day are one example. If dissenting opinions were acknowledged as legitimate public views, they were usually described as minority opinions, inferior to the correct views of the majority. Discernment of public opinion thus was considered an exercise in philosophy and logic, buttressed but not determined by arithmetic.

Since opinions that could properly be labeled as "public" were limited to those that conformed to prevailing standards of legitimacy and national interest, as interpreted by the President, early chief executives never represented themselves as mere mouthpieces for a numerical majority. Rather, they considered themselves interpreters of the people's wishes who tried to articulate public demands in a manner consistent with the national interest as the people, at their wisest, presumably saw it. Similarly, when they spoke of the role of the public they stressed that the people cooperated in policy execution and deemed the policy beneficial to their interests, or expressed confidence in the motivations of the policy-making officials. Rarely was public approval of the intellectual as opposed to practical soundness of policy mentioned as a criterion for judging the intellectual merits of a particular policy.

All the Presidents felt a very strong obligation to keep the accepted channels of communication open for submission of diverse opinions. After all, democratic ideology demanded that channels of communication between the people and their President must be free from formal obstacles. But as we have seen, the flow of communication between the general public and the President has always been symbolic rather than actual. Moreover, permitting advice and disapproval to reach the President and assuring that he listens to them or heeds them, are entirely different matters. The bulk of dissent has always been ignored or given only cursory attention.

In reality, the President's choice of the people to whom he wished to listen and accord influence was not as free as the preceding paragraphs imply. There were times when he was forced to cater to certain groups because of the political, physical, or public relations power that these groups could wield to weaken his policies.

The influence of pressure groups was diluted by the cultural aversion that the public has always had for the overt use of political pressure by small groups. Political elites and many members of the public have felt and expressed disdain for pressure tactics designed to give disproportionate emphasis to the demands of relatively small groups over the demands of the general public. In this context, numbers did assume importance. If a group could be identified or labeled as small, this designation *ipso facto* deprived it of a legitimate claim to have its pleas heeded as the demands of public opinion. At times it could be used to defeat the group's purposes.

Pressure tactics, too, had to conform to accepted standards of dissent before pressure groups could effectively claim to speak for the public. Mass demonstrations, especially when accompanied by violence, threats of political blackmail, cooperation with the nation's enemies and similar methods, when they violated widely accepted canons of fairness and propriety, could be counter-productive in winning presidential assent. Only if such tactics retained the mantle of cultural legitimacy—an easier feat in days of lusty political brawling than in calm times—could they force the President to pay heed to opinions which he would not choose in the absence of pressure.

If Presidents felt it necessary to give in to pressure groups, it was sound politics to claim that these groups represented the voice of the people. It was politically damaging to admit that the President was yielding to representatives of numerically narrow interests, and against his better judgment. Besides, the mantle of legitimacy bestowed by ostensible public opinion approval could be used to gain needed support for policies which the President felt forced to carry out. Except in minor matters, the Presidents whose actions we have examined were strong enough to resist public pressure for policies which they opposed. Although one cannot judge the seriousness of their intentions since it was never put to a test, all of them expressly or by inference had declared that they would resign in preference to acting contrary to their judgments or ideals.

There was yet another form of pressure that forced Presidents occasionally to accept as "public," opinions that they would not have freely chosen. This was the pressure to listen to influential people in their environment whose personal or political relations with the President gave them a right of access to him. Members of his family, old friends, political mentors, Cabinet officials, and congressional leaders were in this category. If they were intent on advising the President—and many were—the exigencies of human and political relations made him a virtual prisoner to the presentation of their views. Like it or not, he had to listen to their advice, including their views of the status of public opinion.

The advice was often compelling because the advisors' positions gave them access to politically significant information and because many had reputations as experts at taking the public pulse. The political prestige and contacts of secretaries of State like Pickering, Madison, Monroe, and John Quincy Adams would certainly force their chiefs to give more weight to their suggestions than they would give to the views of people not equally highly positioned. The inner circle possessed the additional advantage of face-to-face contact with the President. As modern research has demonstrated, "face-to-face contacts determine to a large degree what in fact will be transmitted most effectively. . . ."[26]

In addition, the inner circle usually contained people who could mobilize mass support or opposition and who had to be humored for that reason. As Rosenau points out: ". . . The mobilization of public opinion in support of foreign policy does not involve informing and activating the mass public so much as it requires the fashioning of a consensus within the leadership structure."[27] From the many diverse views presented to the President by spokesmen for the executive departments and Congress, he must fashion an "official" view which is broadly acceptable to most of his advisors. If associates differed markedly with their chiefs on many occasions, the sheer pressure to preserve good personal relations would make some concessions imperative. No one can perpetually say "no" to his advisors and continue to have their support and cooperation. The only alternative lies in lone decision making, in the Adams manner, or in forcing obstreperous secretaries to resign, as Madison did when he replaced Smith with Monroe.

Often the President would listen to opinions and advice from sundry sources because listening served a purpose per se. It was a way of allowing aroused people to blow off steam, to feel important, and to feel that their voice had been heeded. It was a technique that "reinforces the impression of a political system designed to translate individual wants into public policy" and that therefore serves to "quiet resentments and doubts about particular political acts," and to "reaffirm belief in the fundamental

[26]Karl Deutsch, *The Nerves of Government*. New York: The Free Press, 1966, p. 152.

[27]Rosenau, p. 27. The pressure toward consensus within decision-making groups is discussed in E. P. Hollander, "Conformity, Status, and Idiosyncrasy Credit," *Psychological Review*, vol. 65 (1958), pp. 117–127.

rationality and democratic character of the system . . ."[28] This would make it much easier to get the pleader's cooperation.

While the Presidents were not explicit in expressing these reasons for seeking advice and listening to advice, it seems from their practice that they were consciously or subconsciously aware of these considerations. The list of influential people, especially Congressmen, invited to the White House during foreign policy crises is mute testimony.[29] Anyway, it would have been politically and morally damaging to acknowledge that psychological manipulation in this or any other connection was part of the process of building public opinion support for policy choices.[30] The image that political persuasion and policy selection at the highest levels had to be conducted on a purely intellectual or political plane had to be preserved at all cost. On the other hand, who can tell with certainty whether a President who listens to an advisor merely to appease the advisor's ego is not subtly influenced by the advice, whether he knows it or not? In this way the strand of the advisor's views would be subtly woven into the public opinion tapestry.

Nor can one ignore the factor of chance in discussing to whose appraisal of public views and foreign policy needs the President will listen. To be at the right spot at the right time could be more important than having the correct answers to problems of policy formulation. As Abigail Adams was wont to remind her husband:

> There is a tide in the affairs of men
> Which, taken at the flood, leads on to fortune;
> Omitted, all the voyage of their life
> Is bound in shallows and in miseries.[31]

Gerry's and Barlow's advice, which provided a rationale for resuming diplomatic ties with France in 1799, came at a time when President Adams was groping for an answer. Hence it fell on ready ears. Had it come at another time it might not have been heeded. Adams' claim that the public desired renewal of negotiations might then have been precisely the opposite—a disclaimer of any public desire to deal with the French. Given the moot nature of the issue, either claim could have been correct. Like-

[28]Edelman, p. 17.

[29]See Rosenau, p. 333, and Robinson, pp. 51 and 104 for recent examples.

[30]Henry Kissinger is one of a handful of recent scholars who openly discusses the need for public opinion manipulation. See his *Nuclear Weapons and Foreign Policy*. New York: Harper and Row, Publishers, 1957, p. 170 ff. Kenneth Thompson describes how "complex decisions must be stated as simple choices, difficult issues reduced to a few basic propositions," and political questions asked "in a way capable of arousing emotional responses," p. 95.

[31]William Shakespeare, *Julius Caesar*, Act IV, scene 3, line 96.

wise, a message from a citizen group that might reach a receptive presidential ear on a day of political calm was often drowned out by the noise of a multitude of conflicting messages that happened to arrive simultaneously on a day of low presidential responsiveness.

What about the quality-quantity tussle? If the many asked for the "wrong" policy and the few asked for the "right" one, could the President designate minority views as "the public opinion"? Given the conceptions of the nature and role of public opinion held by the founding fathers, the answer was "yes." When the President chooses the right policy he knows that the public, given able leadership, will soon make the choice its own. The notion of public responsiveness to presidential leadership saved the founders from encountering the common dilemma of combining responsive with responsible leadership and heeding the need for expertise in policy formulation.

Another argument that made it possible to claim mass public opinion support in the face of overt dissent was the distinction between policy aims and means to carry them out. The aims required consensus, the means did not. *Federalist* No. 71 clearly makes this distinction: "The republican principle demands that the deliberate sense of the community should govern the conduct of those to whom they intrust the management of their affairs." But the people's "good sense would despise the adulator who should pretend that they always *reason right* about the *means* of promoting" the public good. "When occasions present themselves, in which the interests of the people are at variance with their inclinations, it is the duty of the persons whom they have appointed to be the guardians of those interests." Hamilton, the author of this essay, believed that

> conduct of this kind has saved the people from very fatal consequences of their own mistakes, and has procured lasting monuments of their gratitude to the men who had courage and magnanimity enough to serve them at the peril of their displeasure.[32]

Experience seemed to bear out the belief of early political leaders that they knew what views deserved the public opinion label. In every case, what appeared to be a majority came to support the decision taken by the President, regardless of earlier positions. What better proof could there be to demonstrate that leaders who lead in what seems to them to be the right direction will find the public behind them? As long as the leader is sensitive to the outer limits which the political culture imposes he enjoys great latitude in the specific decisions he makes. Resignation to the inevitable, and rationalization to make unpalatable politics more tolerable, will swing sizable opinion groups into the presidential camp.

[32]All quotes in this paragraph are from Robert M. Hutchins, ed., "The Federalist" in *Great Books of the Western World,* vol. 43, Chicago: Encyclopedia Britannica, 1952, pp. 214–215. (Italics in original.)

## The Relative Weight of the Public Opinion Component

At the beginning of this book we asked whether in any given decision public opinion should be the deciding factor, the most important single factor, or merely one of various equally important factors.[33] The answer the founding fathers gave to this question in word and deed was that public opinion is an important factor in decision making, but by no means the most important single factor. The most important decisional factors in our case histories were the "givens" as appraised by the President—factors that he could change relatively little. They included elements of national power at the particular moment in history, such as the readiness of the army and its comparative strength in relation to likely opponents, the financial soundness and resources of the country, the strategic realities, and the positions, attitudes, and policies of other relevant nations in the international community. They also included the President's conception of what the national interest required and what means were proper to achieve national goals.

Next in importance to these "givens" and partly intertwined with them were factors of personality and past policy. Past policy sets the mold into which present policy must flow because past policy shapes present conditions and outlooks. Personality provides the lens through which events are screened to become the "facts" considered by Presidents in policy making. This includes public opinion as well as other facts and interpretations. Personality also imprints itself on political style, and style is a crucial determinant in making some policies seem attractive and others repulsive.[34] A Madison would delay action, a Jefferson would forge ahead.

Just how important a factor public opinion was in the making of any particular decision depended, of course, on the President's inclinations and on the circumstances. Strong Presidents never regarded adverse public opinion as a "given" in the sense that they could not change it. They felt that their leadership capacity enabled them to persuade a sufficient portion of public opinion to be in tune with the policies which they wished to carry out. The deference to be accorded to latent or expressed adverse opinion depended on how much public support was required, how much public opposition was to be expected, and how effectively public opinion leadership could operate under the circumstances.

But public opinion influence goes beyond concern with adverse opin-

[33]For a discussion of the proper share of public opinion in decision making under various forms of democratic government see Francis G. Wilson, A Theory of Public Opinion. Chicago: H. Regnery Co., 1962, pp. 29 ff.

[34]The impact of personality on presidential style is discussed by Erwin C. Hargrove, Presidential Leadership: Personality and Political Style. New York: The Macmillan Co., 1966.

ions. Presidents want to act in conformity with public wishes if they can. In making policy decisions, even when support seemed assured, they considered the public temper in a broad sense. Likewise, through their contacts with their advisors and their environment they were exposed to the various views abroad in the land and incorporated them into their thinking. In this subtle way, which cannot be measured with any precision, the gist of public thinking became part of presidential decision making.

The appraisals of public opinion submitted to the President as part of foreign policy advice frequently concerned latent opinion—the likely reaction that would follow a given policy—as well as actual public opinion as it had already expressed itself. The appraisals of latent public opinion were apt to have a greater impact on policy formulation than the appraisals of expressed public opinion because latent opinion often involved future policies which could still be altered. The expressions of actual public opinion, by contrast, usually concerned active policies that often had become well-nigh irreversible. For instance, a forecast that the public will oppose a given war is apt to have more influence before a prospective war declaration becomes public, rather than afterwards. After the decision, reports of adverse opinions may affect public information programs, but they can hardly alter the decision. This is why information on latent public opinion ranks high as an important ingredient in policy formulation, over and above the influence of expressed public opinion.

The electoral function, too, has constituted a sizable public opinion influence on the types of decisions made in the White House. First of all, there is the ever-present threat that public displeasure with policies that cannot be made palatable will lead to defeat of the President, his associates, and other members of his party throughout the land. Its impact upon the President varies. But beyond this, elections give people a chance to select Presidents and other high officials who are in tune with prevailing public sentiments. By selecting and electing well-formed personalities the public determines its Presidents' likely preferences and style, and the type of advice and advisors who are apt to be influential. It determines which publics, through their spokesmen, will have influence in the inner circle and which will be left out. In short, it decides what publics will have a kinsman in the White House whose views will be close to theirs and what publics will be mere distant relations. When partisanship about foreign policy is at low ebb, as in the days of Monroe, the distinction matters little. But when partisanship runs at high tide, as in the days of Adams, the difference can be substantial. The "ins" have a spokesman and the "outs" have not.[35]

[35]How fear of electoral reprisal sways foreign policy decisions is discussed by Kenneth N. Waltz, "Electoral Punishment and Foreign Policy Crises" in Rosenau,

## A Time to Inform, a Time to Be Silent

The last question about the opinion-policy relationship relates to the duty of the President to take the public into his confidence. This duty was never considered absolute beyond a recognition that ultimately, in a vaguely defined future, the public had the right to know the facts. There were no issues on which the early Presidents would have said categorically "the public must know about this immediately." If major political obstacles could be avoided by keeping silent, all the Presidents felt perfectly justified in withholding news, suppressing it, labeling it as false, or discrediting it. Thus Adams kept silent about his plans to renew negotiations with France. Jefferson concealed his real estate transactions, and Monroe breathed not a word about the doctrine. If there was no special advantage or disadvantage in information release, there was neither a push to release nor a pull to withhold. Publication depended on the whims of circumstance and the personal inclinations of the Presidents toward secrecy or publicity. A Madison would disclose more and a Jefferson less. A cantankerous Congress and press could pry loose information otherwise concealed, or it could lead a President to greater exertion to maintain secrecy about his policy plans.

There could be little objection to silence in those instances in which early disclosure of policy and public airing of conflicting views could be damaging to the effective conduct of foreign policy. Secret plans, dangerous national weaknesses and uncertainties, and concessions made or about to be made to other countries had to be shielded from the gaze of foreigners, and in the process the American public as well. However, Presidents often preferred a policy of silence even when disclosure would not reveal important secrets to other countries. Disclosure of plans restrained the President's freedom to alter them, if he saw fit. It invited discussion and discussion was apt to lead to conflict, which then could interfere with policy plans and execution.[36]

Philosophically, a policy of silence to forestall disruptive dissent could be defended on the grounds that effectiveness of foreign policy involves survival of the nation and takes precedence over all other political rights. Eventually the public would be told about the policies conducted in its name, ending the temporary neglect or concealment of information. American political culture sanctions limitations of the right of public knowledge and the right of dissent where foreign affairs are concerned. Modern con-

[36]Schattschneider, p. 6, discusses the advantages of a policy of silence. Also see Roger Hilsman, "Congressional-Executive Relations and the Foreign Policy Consensus," *American Political Science Review*, vol. 52, (1958), p. 740.

cepts, such as the phrase "politics stops at the water's edge" or the notion of bipartisan foreign policy, express this feeling. However, while patriotic oratory has always urged the nation to bury its conflicts in the face of foreign dangers, serious qualms have been raised on many occasions about the wisdom of stifling dissent. Political leaders in and out of office have wondered about the exact point in time when dissent becomes too dangerous to be allowed. They have felt uncertain about the aspects of policy which presidential silence ought to place beyond the realm of discussion. Moreover, ultimate disclosure may come too late to permit a change in the policy, should it run afoul of public wishes.

There is another plausible justification for withholding or failing to call attention to foreign policy information, which is not sensitive from a security standpoint. It is impossible to call all the news to the public's attention. Choice is essential. Public officials choose to publicize those policies whose disclosure seems to them to serve public interests best. Officials in the State Department, according to one observer, make choices about the news which is to be released to the public on the basis of "estimating the extent of congressional and public participation in particular acts of policy making, and the likely direction that these involvements will take if left alone."[37] The necessity to seek public support for certain policies forces policy makers to reserve the limited time and attention span of the public for those issues on which public support is essential. Questions of war and peace, economic policies, and policies requiring congressional legislation are in this category. Public information, in so far as the policy makers have a choice, is largely limited to these instances.

The decision to release or to withhold information, to stress or to slight it, is a crucial one. The manner in which the information is released is equally crucial in determining what captures the public interest and what eludes it. When Madison proclaimed in an official message to Congress that the United States had done everything in its power to avert war and that further concessions would jeopardize the honor and safety of the nation, the official position of the author of the message and its appeal to sacred symbols were bound to assure him a large, receptive audience. Coming from a less exalted official and couched in terms of less stirring rhetoric, the same message might miss its mark entirely.

If messages are presented during a propitious time and occasion (such as an anxiously awaited address to Congress during times of crisis or a message carried from the nation's pulpits during days of public fasts and

[37]Bernard C. Cohen, *The Press and Foreign Policy*. Princeton: Princeton University Press, 1963, p. 184.

prayers) acceptance will be even wider. Many Presidents have a flair for dramatizing their messages and a highly developed sense of timing. Deliberately or intuitively they choose the time and manner of information release to control its impact on the public. Therefore, it is not enough to ask only if there is a duty of information that has been met or neglected. One must also raise questions regarding the manner in which Presidents released information.

Information released by the executive, regardless of its substance and manner of presentation, usually has had a better chance to sway the public than opposition appeals. By virtue of being "official" it usually received preferred attention and some deference from the mass public. Since official information was presented by participants in the decisions about to be made or those already made, it naturally bore the intellectual imprint of its source and supported the decision makers' views. The public, if it trusted its chief executive, was apt to agree with the policies of the decision makers since the bulk of news it received represented the same slice of reality that the policy makers had accepted. Opposing positions, with some notable exceptions, were not generally expounded favorably by people inside the executive branch. When they were, this was deemed an act of disloyalty which Presidents tolerated with annoyance or tried to discredit.

This left the statement of alternative positions to those who were outside the executive branch, most notably political opponents of the President, and the press. Yet the competitive position of outsiders, as far as credibility goes, was weakened because they lacked the persuasive force of the person who can carry out what he advocates. These disabilities weakened and occasionally discouraged the presentation of opposition arguments. By default, this made the case presented by government sources even stronger.[38]

## The Art of Measuring Opinions

What about the mechanics by which early Presidents ascertained what opinions held wide currency among the people? Political savvy, or "intuition" or "empathy" was the chief tool. There were no official observers or listeners to gauge the people's views in the manner in which American diplomats tried to assess the views of foreign people for the President. Presidential intuition was supplemented by all sorts of reports from individual or group informants and reports from the press about behavior and public expectations and reactions to past and projected policies. In addition, there were frequent attempts to read the tea leaves of election

[38]See pp. 350–352 in this volume.

results for clues to public opinion about controversial issues raised during elections.[39]

In general, Presidents favored no particular mouthpiece of opinion expression and no class of spokesman as a consistently more accurate funnel for the public voice than any other. The modern emphasis on the press as the exponent, par exellence, of mass public interest was still lacking. So was the formal public opinion poll whose importunate claims to authenticity are buttressed by the scientific paraphernalia employed in sampling and reporting. Mass petitions, more popular in earlier years than now, except for a periodic revival by academic circles, were labeled as the views of their chief sponsors rather than an expression of broad public beliefs. Depending on their contents, the sponsors' views were judged as coinciding or clashing with the views of the people. Legislative opinions were similarly appraised, according to content, as mirroring or distorting the public's opinions.

In the final analysis, each President made his decisions about the trends of public opinion on the basis of his own feelings of how his information and his informants should be evaluated. From his various sources, he picked those which, to him, seemed to have the greatest credibility. Since there is no objective standard for judging the comparative credibility of sources, the decision depends on the personality of the President and his interaction with those who submit opinions to him. Presidents relied most heavily on those few associates, regardless of official station, whose integrity and political wisdom and skill in public opinion appraisal they esteemed most highly and on those people whose advice most closely resembled presidential views.[40] In fact, when one ponders how often major decisions have been made on the basis of information that decision makers absorbed during informal consultation with their friends and associates, one shudders at the casual nature of the process. Under such circumstances confidants of the President may often toss off remarks lightly without thinking that these remarks may go into the conscious or subconscious decision making of the President. They may be unprepared to give advice on major decisions and unaware that they are, in fact, giving such advice.

[39]The difficulty of interpreting election results as a mandate for specific action is graphically discussed in Bradford Perkins' analysis of the Election of 1812. See *Prologue to War: England and the United States, 1805–1812.* Berkeley: University of California Press, 1963, p. 265 ff.

[40]A recent Detroit study reveals public support for presidential reliance on his inner circle: 71 percent of the respondents considered it proper for cabinet members to influence the President; 69 percent named Congress, and 67 percent the general public. By contrast, only 36 percent thought that past Presidents and senior statesmen should be influential; 31 percent favored an influential role for White House assistants, and 14 percent for the President's wife. Roberta S. Sigel, "Image of the American Presidency," *Midwest Journal of Political Science,* vol. 10 (1966), p. 129.

## Advice from Grass Roots Opinion

The last question asked at the outset sought to ascertain how conscientious public officials can gain access to the multitude of policy suggestions which may have been generated at the grass roots level. There is a very simple answer to this question, and the founding fathers knew it well. Policy suggestions are not generated at the grass roots level. Policy suggestions come from the top—the President and his official family, or from sources very close to the top. Public opinions cluster around these suggestions rather than the reverse. Only rarely do they come from even the very small segment of the public which Professor Almond calls the "attentive" public—people who are deeply interested in foreign affairs and pay attention to events and discussions.[41] The mass public does not know enough about "this swarming confusion" of public policy issues to have concrete suggestions for coping with them.[42] Its sentiments are cited or ignored, depending on how well they serve to support the views already held by the decision makers.

The occasional policy idea which comes to the government from the grass roots or house top levels, is generally so vague that its implementation amounts to a new policy formulation. Major innovations in existing policies and novel proposals, as Madison pointed out, come from small groups of political insiders and serve as nuclei around which public opinion crystallizes.[43] The public reacts to accomplished decisions or spelled out alternatives. It does not initiate them.

When proposals are presented to the government with enough detail to be deemed concrete policy suggestions, they generally come from policy or opinion elites who have spent much time and effort in working out these proposals.[44] These suggestions often seemed suspect to the early Presidents because they came from interest groups who had their own special axe to grind. Like the opinions submitted by modern lobby groups, they were considered essentially private rather than public opinions whose merits had to be tested carefully to make certain that they did not contravene the interest of the people as a whole.

Because workable policy suggestions came so very rarely directly from the grass roots level, Presidents made no efforts to solicit policy sugges-

[41]Gabriel Almond, *The American People and Foreign Policy*. New York: Praeger, 1960, p. 136 ff.

[42]On this point, see the conclusions reached by Robert Elder about present day public views in *The Policy Machine*. Syracuse: Syracuse University Press, 1959, p. 156. The phrase is Walter Lippmann's, *The Phantom Public*. New York: The Macmillan Co., 1927, p. 24.

[43]See pp. 171–172 in this volume.

[44]The concept of policy and opinion elites comes from Almond, p. 138.

tions from the mass public. Rather, Presidents have felt that such suggestions were their special burden and prerogative. In making decisions they
would consider public wishes as sensed by them and reported to them
by their advisors. But they would appraise public views, as Theodore Sorensen said about President Kennedy, with the realization that:

> Public opinion is often erratic, inconsistent, arbitrary, and unreason-
> able—with a compulsion to make mistakes. . . . It rarely considers the
> needs of the next generation or the history of the last. . . . It is
> frequently hampered by myths and misinformation, by stereotypes and
> shibboleths, and by an innate resistance to innovation.[45]

Given the failings of the public and the knowledge that "public opinion
and the public interest do not always agree," the President had to take
full responsibility for foreign policy formulation.[46] To quote Sorensen
once more:

> No president is obliged to abide by the dictates of public opinion. . . .
> He has a responsibility to lead public opinion as well as respect it—to
> shape it, to inform it, to woo it, and win it. It can be his sword
> as well as his compass.[47]

[45]Theodore C. Sorensen, *Decision Making in the White House.* New York:
Columbia University Press, 1963, pp. 45–46.

[46]Sorensen, pp. 45–46.

[47]Sorensen, pp. 45–46.

# 12

## Epilogue: Implications
## for Our Time

Great innovations should never be forced on slender majorities.
THOMAS JEFFERSON[1]

Personalities always matter in politics, and never have they counted for more than in our century, which has, at one and the same time, tended to collectivize the individual and to individualize collective power. . . . the man who sits at the top of the nation . . . is always "riding a tiger," but the way he rides it makes a very great difference indeed.
BERTRAND DE JOUVENEL[2]

[1] Letter to Du Pont de Nemours, May 2, 1808, Dumas Malone, *Correspondence between Thomas Jefferson and Pierre Samuel du Pont de Nemours, 1798–1817.* Boston: Houghton Mifflin, 1930. p. 102.

[2] "Political Science and Prevision," *American Political Science Review,* vol. 59 (1965), p. 35.

# 12

What do past theories and practices mean for our time? One can undoubtedly say with the French: *"Plus ça change, plus c'est la même chose."* The political world has changed greatly since the eighteenth century. But the relationship of public opinion to foreign policy decision making in the White House has remained essentially the same.[3] Key policy decisions are still made by the President, aided by a small group of advisors. That these decisions must be potentially acceptable to the public remains the heart of the public opinion impact.

## The Myths Continue

The folklore concept of the nature of public opinion in a democracy still is a myth. Presidents have not been able to discern a mass public opinion in the sense of millions of minds thinking in very similar ways about difficult policy problems and arriving at compatible conclusions. Phrases like "the President delivered a major foreign policy address to an eager public, fully in accord with his views" are nothing more than figures of speech and figments of popular and press imagination. Beyond a highly generalized sense of trust and approval, or distrust and disapproval of policy making by the executive, there apparently is no single well-structured opinion held by most people, a majority, or even a plurality.

The views which the press and polls and public opinion spokesmen and interpreters report as mass opinion are operationally useless and unstable. They do not tell the President what specific policies are acceptable and under what conditions. For instance, a report that the public favors continuance of war does not indicate what price it is willing to pay for continuance. If the President foresees the price at a high number of casualties, he may correctly estimate that the sentiment for war is really a sentiment for peace, under the circumstances. Depending on whether casualty estimates are released or not, public sentiment may swing from one policy option to a conflicting one.

[3]Accounts of foreign policy decision making during the 1950s and 1960s bear this out. See for instance, Roger Hilsman, *To Move a Nation*. Garden City, N. Y.: Doubleday, 1967, which covers policy making during the Kennedy Administration; Dwight D. Eisenhower, *The White House Years*, 2 vols. Garden City, N. Y., Doubleday, 1963–1965; and Harry S. Truman, *Memoirs*, 2 vols. Garden City, N. Y.: Doubleday, 1955–1956.

Because the myth of policy approval by a single mass public opinion has become so closel identified with democratic value theory, Presidents still must sustain and evoke it to legitimate policy in their own eyes, the eyes of the public and the eyes of other policy makers. In meeting this problem, there is a difference between modern Presidents and their pre-Jacksonian counterparts. Modern Presidents find it easier to assume that they have the masses with them. The earlier Presidents, as "governors of a nation but recently born in revolt against government . . . lacked the social acceptance that a long institutional tradition has brought to office-holders in the modern state."[4] In compensation, earlier Presidents had a stronger sense of moral rightness of their opinions and stronger aversion to the inequities of their fellow men. This made it easier for them to make decisions for the nation, even without a firm claim to mass support. "In a social environment perceived as corrupting, a regime of assertive, inner-directed righteous individualism was called for."[5]

The techniques for creating an image of wide popular support, although more refined than at an earlier day, remain essentially the same. Communication with the public, while more plentiful than in earlier days, still is largely sporadic and symbolic. The American political culture retains an aversion to institutionalized government information programs beamed at the American people. Their resemblance to totalitarian propaganda efforts is too close for democratic comfort. The public is presumed to be adequately informed through the messages passing over the ordinary channels of communication.

Lack of overt mass opposition is still counted as mass support. There is an implicit assumption that the people, who have freely elected a leader, will support his decisions throughout his incumbency. When people refuse obedience to public policies during a President's term, pejorative words like "revolt" or "insurrection" creep into the political dialogue.

Self-anointed and appointed spokesmen for large groups of people, if their views accord with the administration's, are still allowed to cast the proxies of all their presumed followers. The leader-follower opinion concurrence is detailed more carefully only if there is overt dissent within an organization or if the views of the leaders do not concur with presidential policies. A labor leader speaks for his union if his views are approving. He speaks only for himself or for a small number of union members if he expresses opposition.

By picturing supportive expressed opinions as representative symbols for unexpressed and latent opinions of the mass public, Presidents are able, most of the time, to convey the impression of mass support. Opponents

[4]James Sterling Young, *The Washington Community, 1800–1828*. New York: Columbia University Press, 1966, p. 60.
[5]Young, p. 63.

of the President in the press and elsewhere, may take a different view and claim that the mass public or its most intelligent spokesmen approve a different policy. But this is not generally fatal to the President's conclusion. As long as mass public opinion has no objective existence, it cannot be read mechanically like a stock-market report.

Modern public opinion polls are too crude to be a reliable guide to public views. They abound in often unexplained inconsistencies among results of different polls or even questions in the same poll. They do not permit reliable estimates of how people will act when faced with real rather than hypothetical choices. Worst of all for decision makers in search of guidance from the public, polls cannot get answers to complex questions. How, for instance, could one get a satisfactory answer to the question "Would you prefer limited strategic retaliation or tactical local defense in response to Soviet invasion of Western Europe?" Before such a question could be attempted a number of complicated tactics, alternatives, and possible consequences would have to be explained. Given the status of mass knowledge and analytical capacities, this would be an insurmountable problem.[6] Nor do the results collected by pollsters provide an unassailable mandate for any specific policy. For instance, what policy deductions can one make from a poll in which one-third of the respondents wish to escalate a war, one-fourth want to continue the status quo, one-fourth want to stop the war, and the rest state that they have no answer?

Harry Truman expressed the typical reluctance of American Presidents to use polls as more than an ancillary aid:

> I never paid any attention to the polls myself, because in my judgment they did not represent a true cross section of American opinion. I did not believe that the major components of our society, such as agriculture, management, and labor, were adequately sampled. I also know that the polls did not represent facts but mere speculation, and I have always placed my faith in the known facts.[7]

Although Truman's antipathy to polls was stronger than average, the fact remains that there are no objective ways to accurately measure public opinion as a guide to policy formation. When all mass opinion evaluation thus depends largely on intuitive political knowledge and deductions from it, Presidents understandably use their own insights rather than their opponents' interpretations as a basis for calculation. And they decide whose

[6]Clark C. Abt, "National Opinion and Military Security," *Journal of Conflict Resolution*, vol. 9 (1965), pp. 337–338 discusses these problems.

[7]Truman, vol. 2, p. 177. Note also the interesting observations by a special assistant to the Secretary of Defense in Adam Yarmolinsky, "Confessions of a Non-User," *Public Opinion Quarterly*, vol. 27 (1963), pp. 543–548; and E. E. Schattschneider, *The Semi-Sovereign People*. New York: Holt, Rinehart and Winston, Inc., 1960, p. 132.

reports of public opinion appraisal they deem most credible at a given moment and use them as their public opinion "facts."

If dissent arises that controverts the assumption of mass approval, old tactics to silence it are still useful. The Johnson technique to calm the ruffled waters of dissent about United States involvement in the war in Vietnam is one modern example. According to *New York Times* correspondent, James Reston, President Johnson used

> one of the oldest political techniques in the book: this is to identify the opposition with the unpopular extremists; to attack the "cussers and the doubters" and the flag burners as if they were the only opposition to the war. . . . He is still implying that loyalty to him and his policies is the path of the patriot. . . . His arguments are plain, mutton-fisted propositions—persevere; don't let the boys down; don't "tuck tail and run" before the Communists; don't abandon the weak; don't run out on our promises. The opposition argument is more complicated. . . . A defensive policy of withdrawal is not very heroic.[8]

If opposition cannot be won over, belittled or denigrated, political accommodations may be made. For instance, when Franklin D. Roosevelt received a heavily unfavorable public response to his "Quarantine the Aggressor" speech in 1937, he decided to withhold further verbal assaults on the Axis powers until the public had become more receptive.[9]

Many times policy accommodations may seem unwise. In that case, when the myth of mass public support for the President falters in the wake of widespread opposition or election returns that are interpreted as a vote of nonsupport, Presidents still resort to the theory of delayed support. They claim that the public has been temporarily misled or has been unable to see the situation clearly. Even though it briefly disagrees with action the President deems essential, it will eventually give approval. Thus Eisenhower argued that a disapproving public would ultimately support his policy of backing up the French in their losing fight in Indochina in 1954.[10]

To regain the image of mass approval, active public relations programs are still the order of the day. Presidents and their advisors and influential friends around the country are recruited for speeches, discussion programs, and quiet face-to-face contacts with opinion leaders whose assistance may help to recapture the semblance of mass support. For example, every outbreak of antiwar demonstrations on American campuses during the war in Vietnam has called forth a bevy of governmental speakers who participate in debates and teach-ins. Large numbers travel along the com-

[8]*New York Times*, June 30, 1967.

[9]Samuel I. Rosenman, *Working with Roosevelt.* New York: Harper & Row, Publishers, 1952, pp. 166–167.

[10]Sherman Adams, *First Hand Report.* New York: Harper & Row, Publishers, 1961, pp. 121–122.

mencement-speaker circuit to answer questions, still unrest, and win new friends for presidential policies.

In a modern support-building tactic, not available to earlier chief executives, the President may divert attention from criticism by putting himself and his policy into the news limelight. Lyndon Johnson's hastily summoned 1966 mid-Pacific meeting of top political and military leaders may have settled few problems in the conduct of hostilities in Vietnam. But it demonstrated that the President was hard at work seeking the best possible solutions. It also showed that a President who could summon world leaders at a moment's notice and engage in intimate conversations with them was in a better position than his critics to assess the foreign scene and to make policies.

While the image of mass support has nearly always been within the President's grasp, the reality of support beyond acquiescence has seemed shaky at times. Political observers have wondered whether vocal protests from influential citizens in public and private life reflected or foreshadowed public uneasiness and possibly unrest. It has seemed particularly difficult to maintain active consensus for policies that do not involve clear-cut major dangers and forthright quick remedies. Economic policies that aim at gradual attrition of an enemy or gradual improvement of the economic status of a friendly country, and undeclared wars in far-off lands, which keep a distant enemy in check or indirectly undermine the strength of a future adversary, are inherently unpopular. They make poor meat for red-blooded, soul-stirring oratory.[11]

Yet until methods are developed for building better mass understanding for the necessity of policies of compromise and moderation and policies that will not yield results for several generations or will do nothing but preserve a status quo, maintenance of the myth of mass approval may become increasingly difficult. Pedestrian policies that lack dramatic emotional appeal are highly vulnerable to attack by dissenters. Dissenters find it increasingly easy to create the image of mass dissent given the modern means of communication, which focus public attention on the dramatic phenomenon of active protest. Hence the need to develop more effective means of communication to sustain the loyalty of a people that is becoming better educated and more sophisticated over the years.[12]

[11]On this point see James N. Rosenau, *National Leadership and Foreign Policy*. Princeton: Princeton University Press, 1963, pp. 36–37. Also see H. Field Haviland, Jr., "Foreign Aid and the Policy Process: 1957," *American Political Science Review*, vol. 52 (1958), p. 723.

[12]Roger Hilsman contends that "there are too many participants too widely scattered to be reached by the communications resources available to . . . even the office of the President." If intragovernmental communication is already difficult, hopes for improvement on the extragovernmental scene may be slim. "Congressional-Executive Relations and the Foreign Policy Consensus," *American Political Science Review*, vol. 52 (1958), p. 738.

A change in presidential information tactics seems necessary to conform to the slowly rising level of public understanding of political complexities. Lacking such a change, Presidents may be forced into a policy of crisis publicity which exaggerates international dangers or prospective gains so as to rouse public emotions. In the process, the President may entrap himself in policies of extreme action or severely narrow his scope of maneuvering because policy must be dramatic enough to satisfy the emotions aroused by the oratory.

## The Effects of the Communications Revolution

Most of the contrasts mentioned thus far between modern and past problems of public opinion management are the results of the communication revolution. Modern mass media and means for rapid travel and information transmission have improved the President's tools for influencing public opinion and for communicating with the people. Television puts him in almost face-to-face contact with the bulk of the voting public.[13] The impact the President makes may be ephemeral, and despite nation-wide mass media coverage of his messages, mass political knowledge remains appallingly low. But a Johnson certainly can impress his image and his style and the rough outlines of his policy more readily on the public mind than could a Jefferson

> . . . in an isolated capital where reporters were rarely to be found press releases and press conferences could not be. The ability to reach the outside public and to guide opinion; the ability to appeal over the heads of Congress to their constituents; the chance to command national attention for himself and his policy objectives: these important sources of leverage were denied to the President of a nation still in the predawn of the communications revolution.[14]

Methods for appraising public opinions have greatly benefited from modern social science techniques that would have been technically impossible during the infancy of mass communication. The sophisticated methods used in the twentieth century by the State Department and other governmental agencies to gather information and to assess opinion trends had no counterpart in the early years of the nation.[15] Presidents also receive

[13]For the usefulness of television to win public support see Bernard Rubin, *Political Television*. Belmont, Calif.: Wadsworth, 1967, *passim*.

[14]Young, p. 197.

[15]State Department procedures for press and public opinion analysis are described in Robert Elder, *The Policy Machine*. Syracuse: Syracuse University Press, 1959, pp. 142–150.

more assistance from the responsible press than did their predecessors. The modern, high quality press, unlike its highly partisan ancestors, seeks to present an accurate picture of public views. Presidents are often able to rely on press coverage for their appraisals of the state of the public mind in various sections of the country and for knowledge of diverse views aired by opinion leaders throughout the nation.

But not all the advantages lie with the modern presidency. The number of issues to be considered, the wealth of opinions to be tapped, and the multitudes of people to be reached by Presidents have also grown at a rapid pace. Where John Adams would receive petitions by the dozens in the course of a month, McKinley already had to cope with over 1000 letters daily expressing views for or against a war with Spain. These figures have continued to grow in geometric progression.

In the early days the doors of the White House were open to all comers, and any citizen could carry his grievances and views directly to the President. This face-to-face contact with the public, even a self-selected one, gave an intimacy to the President's relations with the people that has never been recaptured.[16] Greater homogeneity of cultural backgrounds also eased communications and made intuitive knowledge of the public's mind a simpler task.

Aside from Congressmen and occasional visitors, early Presidents did not meet with people and reporters from all portions of the country. This isolation deprived them of valuable contacts available in the modern age. But it also insulated them against the pressures of clever lobbyists and distracting news of opposition. By the time public opposition to the Louisiana Purchase would have flowered in full force and reached Washington, the ink on the purchase treaty would have long since dried. In an age when all who were beyond riding or walking distance were beyond talking distance, the nation could more readily survive severe opinion cleavages. The rift between pro-French and pro-British Americans might have ripped apart the nation in an age of swifter communications when opponents could have organized before events had overtaken their animosities. Distance and slow communications can thus substitute for the calming effects of citizen apathy and disinterest in a more developed society.

The slower pace by which pressures traveled to the President's sphere of knowledge lessened their impact. But the greater difficulty encountered in controlling opinions and winning support in an age of slow communications acted as a counterweight. Early Presidents, even when they had their own newspapers that were mouthpieces for official propaganda, found it

[16]President Franklin Roosevelt tried to savor unexpurgated public views by dipping at random into his piles of mail and selecting letters apparently written by "simple people." Leila A. Sussman, "F. D. R. and the White House Mail," *Public Opinion Quarterly*, vol. 20 (1956), p. 12.

far more difficult to receive nation-wide coverage for their opinions. Once
opposition had arisen, it was difficult to still. By contrast, modern Presidents, with their unparalleled ability to spread their ideas before the public,
have become first-class opinion makers. They can tell the public what to
think and then cite the public echo of presidential views as evidence of
opinion concordance between the President and the people.

## Mass and Elite Advice and Support

Aside from the need to sustain the image of mass public opinion approval, Presidents still face the problem of shaping policies that are wise
in substance and that can be executed effectively. Despite greater diffusion of education and information, they still do not turn to members of
the mass public for policy advice. They believe that the issues are far too
complex to be grasped by a public which is not particularly interested or
inclined to delve deeply into the foreign relations maze. As Professor
Morgenthau remarked:

> The kind of thinking required for the successful conduct of foreign
> policy must at times be diametrically opposed to the kind of considera-
> tions by which the masses and their representatives are likely to be moved.
> The peculiar qualities of the statesman's mind are not always likely to find
> a favorable response in the popular mind.[17]

With rare exceptions, therefore, the executive branch relies on its own
intragovernmental resources for initiating policy proposals and critiques
of these proposals. Given the heterogeneity of viewpoints in Congress
and within and among various departments, a lively exchange of diverse
ideas is commonly assured. In fact, there often are full-blown battles that
may incline the President to decisions that are a compromise among the
viewpoints. Some compromises are good, others harmful. Many are unavoidable, especially when a strong Congress holds the upper hand through
its power to withhold legislative implementation of presidential proposals.
However annoying intragovernmental conflicts may be, they do enlarge
the spectrum of policy options that come to the President's attention.[18]

[17]Hans J. Morgenthau, *In Defense of the National Interest.* New York:
Alfred A. Knopf, 1951, p. 223. Also see Max Beloff's views in *Foreign Policy
and the Democratic Process.* Baltimore: Johns Hopkins University Press, 1955,
p. 158.

[18]Young, pp. 222–223 says that interdepartmental conflicts were fiercer in
the early days than now because cabinet members frequently were former congressmen and contenders for the **presidency.** This added factional political conflicts to sectional conflicts. The memoirs of recent Presidents, including Eisenhower and Truman, are filled with accounts of battles between the President and
Congress and the departments.

Presidents have not generally felt that the public is neglecting its civic obligations when it devotes itself to private pursuits in preference to public affairs. This, after all, is consistent with the concept of division of labor in complex enterprises. The average citizen, if he wishes to be well-served, cannot be his own doctor, engineer, or shoemaker. He cannot be his own economist or his own sociologist. Nor can he be his own planner of governmental policies.[19] He must be satisfied with the typical role of the client—to judge the product cursorily on those features that he understands best and to accept the rest on the strength of his faith in the integrity and acumen of his agent.

The executive branch does not even place great faith in the mass public's capacity to appraise policy proposals on their merits. Beyond judging broad trends, the public's ability to assess the comparative merits of various means to reach policy goals is considered minor. However, as we have seen, publicly expressed views and public sentiments form part of the stream of information which reaches the President during the predecisional stage. They may be reported directly or become part of the advice submitted by Congressmen and other influential spokesmen.[20] The more meritorious these views seem and the better directed toward the channels that have access to the President's attention, the better the chances that they will be subtly influential in the final decision making.

The advice that continues to have the greatest chance of gaining attention and an impact on policy making is the advice of influential elite publics. "The logic of numbers collides head on with the logic of power as the traditional power pyramid, expressing an inverse relation between power and numbers, communicates so well."[21] These are the publics who feel and successfully demonstrate that they have a culturally acceptable material or ideological stake in certain policies. Their foreign policy opinions are far more fully formed than those of the mass public.[22] While some of their suggestions may be narrowly selfish or unwise, many of their proposals have merit and receive and deserve a hearing on that score. East and West coast fishing interests, New England merchants and Western manufacturers, ethnic and religious groups, like the Irish and the

[19]For similar conclusions see Bernard Berelson, *et al., Voting.* Chicago: University of Chicago Press, 1954, p. 196.

[20]Roger Hilsman, "Congressional-Executive Relations," pp. 732–733, gives examples.

[21]Philip E. Converse, "The Nature of Belief Systems in Mass Publics, in David Apter, ed., *Ideology and Discontent.* New York: The Free Press, 1964, p. 207.

[22]H. Field Haviland, Jr., calls organized interest groups "the most influential segments of the public" (p. 717). Also see Bernard C. Cohen, *The Influence of Nongovernmental Groups on Foreign Policy Making.* Boston: World Peace Foundation, 1959, pp. 6–14.

Jews, all have been, at one time or other, among the influential opinion elites. So have a few peace societies and *ad hoc* committees set up to sponsor or oppose a particular policy like entry into World War II or recognition of Communist China.

Among the three factors that determine the success of such groups in making an impact on policy, the merits of the proposal and the group's knowledge of methods and channels of presentation generally rank below the group's political clout. The chances of opinion elites for victory on the public opinion battlefield are greatest, assuming the feasibility of their demands, if they are capable of political revenge, such as obstructing policy execution, undermining congressional implementation, or destroying the image of mass support for the policy.[23] Even then, their influence on foreign policy remains far slighter than alarmed proponents of evil elitist influence would have us believe. Presidents throughout the years have been able to successfully resist pressure groups when their demands imposed an unwanted burden on policy. In the face of pressure from protectionist groups backed by influential Congressmen, Eisenhower repeatedly refused to abandon his policy of freer trade:

> The almond growers of California, the manufacturers of band instruments from coast to coast, the members of the Bicycle Institute, the members of the Maraschino Cherry and Glace Fruit Association, fish canners, wool hat manufacturers, walnut growers—all these and hundreds of others added their voices to the powerful pleas of the producers of lead and zinc and of oil and of coal. . . . Their arguments were not a trifle. . . certain congressmen, of both major political parties, had no love for the principle of reciprocal trade agreements. . . . we had an issue where the good of the United States as a whole was pitted against the power of influential lobbies in Congress. . . . Finally we won out.[24]

Many times, successes of pressure groups are more apparent than real. The President as well as the public may share a group's predilection. Thus sympathy and support for the state of Israel in its perennial wars with the Arabs is as much testimony to Israel's political achievements as to the effectiveness of Jewish pressure groups. The effectiveness of the Jewish lobby must be judged as much by sizeable American aid to the Arab countries as by President Truman's hasty recognition of Israel in 1948.

[23]The actual size of such publics is immaterial. What matters is their estimated influence over policy execution and the opinions of wider publics. On this point see Hilsman, "Congressional-Executive Relations," p. 733.

[24]Dwight D. Eisenhower, vol. 1, pp. 209–210. The relatively small influence which pressure groups exercise on foreign policy formulation is explained by Lester Milbrath in "Interest Groups and Foreign Policy" in James N. Rosenau, ed., *Domestic Sources of Foreign Policy*. New York: The Free Press, 1967, pp. 231–251.

While the methods for dealing with lobbies have been well-developed, Presidents have had little success in systematically tapping suggestions that may originate among members of the attentive public who do not ordinarily tender their advice to the President. The polls occasionally solve this problem in a small way when they break their data down according to educational levels and when their questions attempt to probe more deeply into the intensity and dimensions of various answers. A recent study of the attitudes of professors toward the war in Vietnam is in this category.[25]

Another helpful development has been the greater use of academic and *naive* other expert advisors by the President, the State Department, and Congress.[26] Still another promising innovation has been the appointment of bipartisan nongovernmental advisory bodies to make policy suggestions to the President and to report on the state of the public mind. For instance, President Lyndon B. Johnson appointed a panel of sixteen "distinguished citizens" in 1965 to advise him on matters of foreign policy. The group contained a former Secretary of State (Dean Acheson), the former director of the CIA (Allen Dulles), and the former president of the International Bank for Reconstruction and Development (Eugene R. Black). These men were chosen by the President because he considered them "highly qualified and experienced" citizens who could help him "in finding effective courses of action in the quest for peace and the advancement of the national security."[27] But these are fairly isolated instances and the vast pool of expert citizen knowledge remains essentially untapped.

## The Demand for Policy and Opinion Leadership

Presidents still consider the role of foreign policy maker and public opinion leader as one of the official duties of the American presidency. They believe that Presidents must take the lead in policy formulation and opinion guidance, especially in dangerous times, when difficult decisions

[25]David J. Armor, *et al.*, "Professors' Attitudes toward the Vietnam War," *Public Opinion Quarterly*, vol. 31 (1967), pp. 159–175. Also see Sidney Verba, *et al.*, "Public Opinion and the War in Vietnam," *American Political Science Review*, vol. 61 (1967), pp. 317–333; and William C. Rogers, *et al.*, "A Comparison of Informed and General Public Opinion on U. S. Foreign Policy," *Public Opinion Quarterly*, vol. 31 (1967), pp. 242–252.

[26]Various nongovernmental research organizations that serve government agencies are described in Burton M. Sapin, *The Making of United States Foreign Policy*. Washington: The Brookings Institution, 1966, pp. 314–318.

[27]Lyndon B. Johnson, as quoted in the *New York Times*, Sept. 10, 1965.

must be made rapidly.[28] President Truman insisted repeatedly that the decision to drop an atomic bomb on Japan was his and his alone.[29] President McKinley, after thoroughly plumbing public opinion, would acknowledge only divine guidance as the crucial factor that finally persuaded him to add the Philippines to the American Empire.[30] Even President Eisenhower, who relied heavily on Secretary of State John Foster Dulles, insisted that policies must meet his own approval. When Dulles intimated that force might be used to free the peoples of Eastern Europe, Eisenhower rebuked him. The President subsequently reaffirmed a policy of peaceful liberation as the official American stand.[31] Speaker Sam Rayburn summed the theory up succinctly when he said: "America has either one voice or none, and that voice is the voice of the President—whether everybody agrees with him or not."[32]

Presidents cannot leave foreign policy decisions and their necessary opinion supports to a social choice process. In such a process, views and claims of various publics interact autonomously and evolve political compromises that reflect the distribution of political influence.[33] In foreign policy the country cannot enjoy the luxury of leisurely drifting, which may or may not result in a decision to act. It cannot take a chance that one strong pressure group may take the helm, even temporarily, to use public policy to satisfy its private interest. Polling data indicate that the public recognizes that major foreign policy decisions often are a matter of life or death for the individual and possibly the nation. Therefore the public, like its Presidents, has felt strongly that foreign policy decisions, even more than other decisions, must be based on deliberate and careful choices. These choices, although not completely insensitive to do-

[28]For some second thoughts on the rapidity with which foreign policy decisions must be made see James Robinson, *Congress and Foreign Policy Making* Homewood Ill.: Dorsey Press, 1967, p. 65. A chart of 22 recent foreign policy decisions shows that only two had to be made in a matter of days. Robinson also presents data on the primacy of the President in initiating foreign policy. (See pp. 174–175.)

[29]Michael Amrine, *The Great Decision.* New York: G. P. Putnam's Sons, 1959, pp. 174–175.

[30]Thomas A. Bailey, *A Diplomatic History of the American People,* 5th ed. New York: Appleton-Century-Crofts, 1955, pp. 519–520.

[31]Sherman Adams, pp. 87–89.

[32]Sherman Adams, p. 285.

[33]For a recent empirical study of role perception of leaders which substantiates the views expressed here see Norman R. Luttbeg and Harmon Zeigler, "Attitude Consensus and Conflict in an Interest Group," *American Political Science Review,* vol. 60 (1966), pp. 655–666. Also see Richard C. Snyder, *et al., Foreign Policy Decision Making.* New York: The Free Press, 1962, pp. 222–224, which deals with President Truman's views in the Korean crisis.

mestic political pressures, must be primarily grounded in expert individual appraisal of the merits of a given situation.[34]

Most American Presidents have defined their political duty to the public as Edmund Burke did in his often quoted speech to the people of Bristol: "Your representative owes you, not his industry only, but his judgment; and he betrays instead of serving you if he sacrifices it to your opinion."[35] Or as a modern politician has put it:

> We raise the question of whether it is enough in these days of danger and turmoil for our President to continue to act as a consensus politician instead of a statesman who leads. Waiting for a consensus can and often does mean ignoring little problems until they become big ones. It can and does mean inaction until the riots start—whether in Saigon or in Selma.[36]

A capable political leader does not delay necessary action while he waits for a consensus to develop. Rather, he anticipates obstacles and opposition and leads in the development of this consensus if any leadership is required. If he fails, either from lack of trying or from inept handling of his opposition, the nation suffers. Madison might have avoided the War of 1812 had he taken a firmer grasp on policy. A less stubborn Wilson could have brought the United States into the League of Nations.[37]

The necessity, feasibility, and public desire for strong opinion leadership have been substantiated by the case studies in this book, as well as other case studies of public opinion formation. For instance, a study of public opinion developments on Franklin D. Roosevelt's court-packing bill concluded:

> Public opinion in a democracy responds to leadership, and needs the stimulus of leadership in order to crystallize one way or the other on specific proposals. . . . Public opinion can indicate very powerfully the general area of its needs, but it remains for an individual or group of individuals

[34]The distinction between social choice and central decision choice is made in Edward C. Banfield, *Political Influence*. New York: The Free Press, 1961, p. 331. Banfield considers social choice decisions as preferable at the local political level.

[35]Speech to the Electors of Bristol, Nov. 3, 1774.

[36]Representative Gerald R. Ford, House Minority Leader, before the National Press Club, as reported in the *New York Times*, March 26, 1965. For the various theories underlying consensus politics on one hand and leadership politics on the other, see Charles E. Gilbert, "Operative Doctrines of Representation," *American Political Science Review*, vol. 57 (1963), pp. 604–618.

[37]Wilson's leadership difficulties are analyzed by George and Juliette Alexander, *Woodrow Wilson and Colonel House*. New York: Dover Publications, 1964.

to come forward with specific proposals toward which public opinion can display approval or disapproval.[38]

Judging from political observation and empirical data this is the type of leadership that large numbers of Americans want and expect. For example, when asked whether the President should dispatch troops abroad when most Americans opposed such action, 75 percent of the respondents in a recent poll conducted in Detroit said that the President should act in accordance with his own views rather than public opinion. The reasons given included the following: "That is his job," "That is what we elected him for," and "He knows more than the people."[39] Among qualities most desired of a President, honesty, intelligence, and independence of mind ranked first. The Detroiters asked for a President "smart enough to figure out new solutions, and honest and independent enough to pursue them no matter what the intimidation."[40] Those who would deny such a leadership role to a President as contravening the idea of popular government bear the burden of explaining why the omnicompetent people suddenly are incompetent to delegate decision making to a wisely chosen chief executive.

Psychological needs also provide an explanation for the universal popular desire for strong leadership. As the mass society theorists explain it:

> Alienation, anomie, despair of being able to chart one's own course in a complex, cold, and bewildering world have become characteristic of a large part of the population of advanced countries. As the world can be neither understood nor influenced, attachment to reassuring abstract symbols rather than to one's own efforts becomes chronic. And what symbol can be more reassuring than the incumbent of a high position who knows what to do and is willing to act, especially when others are bewildered and alone?[41]

When people cannot understand the various factors that go into the making of decisions that they recognize as vital to their welfare, they instinctively turn to a leader whose position or reputation mark him as capable of making the right choice. The President is such a reference figure.

Moreover, a government that gives proof of its willingness to act forcefully will find the public more acquiescent and less eager to listen to the

[38]Frank V. Cantwell, "Public Opinion and the Legislative Process," *American Political Science Review,* vol. 40 (1946), pp. 933–935. Also see Kenneth Thompson, *Political Realism and the Crisis of World Politics.* Princeton, N. J.: Princeton University Press, 1960, p. 214.

[39]Roberta S. Sigel, "Image of the American Presidency," *Midwest Journal of Political Science,* vol. 10 (1966), pp. 126–127.

[40]Sigel, p. 131.

[41]Murray Edelman, *The Symbolic Uses of Politics.* Urbana, Ill.: University of Illinois Press, 1964, p. 76.

apostles of doubt and dissent. Even wrong action is more likely to win public tolerance than inaction. Inaction imparts the helpless feeling that all is left to chance and drift. Reassuringly, a recent study of foreign policy decision making points out that "there are many opportunities for bold and constructive initiative in the foreign policy realm to be picked up by American political figures who understand or have discovered what imaginative leadership can do with 'public opinion'."[42]

Why should Presidents assume the full burden of this leadership? Like many other human choices, this one rests on the lesser-evil principle. Judged by the accepted criteria for competence in foreign policy decision making—factual knowledge, ability to implement decisions, and congruence with public wishes—the President scores highest. He alone is accepted as the elected representative of the entire nation who personifies it and gives it a single focus of leadership. Even in the early days of more indirect presidential nominations and elections the President came closer to a national leadership image than any other public official. Only the President can appeal to an electorate that is large enough so that he can defy the wishes of millions and still have millions to cheer him on. This gives him alone the unequalled freedom to ignore pressure groups and sectional interests and work for the broader national interest.[43] Only the President can summon opinion leaders from all walks of life throughout the nation and request their support with reasonable certainty of receiving it. Only the President thus has enough authority and power and symbolic appeal to match the grave responsibilities of foreign policy making. Whether his ideas are original or borrowed from others, they must seem to emanate from him because public trust reposes in the presidential office and its incumbent. In recognition of this fact, when foreign policies are labeled with a name, it is most commonly the President's.

If innovations are necessary in foreign policy, Presidents are in a uniquely favorable position to prepare the public to accept them. Access to the media of communication and to a responsive audience is easy. The President seldom finds it impossible to sway the public mind even when new policies are seemingly inconsistent with old ones. On one hand, President Kennedy could win approval for withholding American troops from Cuba during the anti-Communist Bay of Pigs invasion. On the other hand, President Johnson could convince the public that American marines must be sent to the Dominican Republic to support anti-Com-

[42]Bernard C. Cohen, *The Political Process and Foreign Policy.* Princeton: Princeton University Press, 1957, p. 285. See also Rosenau, *passim,* for the views of public opinion leaders about the flexibility of public attitudes.

[43]On this point, see Grant McConnell, *Private Power and American Democracy.* New York: Alfred A. Knopf, 1966, p. 8. Madison expressed similar views in *Federalist,* No. 10.

munist forces. There was no great pressure to explain why communism in Cuba deserved less rigorous measures than communism in an island more remote from the United States.

The bulk of the public rarely perceives apparent inconsistencies, even when public opinion leaders call attention to them. It rarely cares deeply enough about a particular policy to mourn its passing. Part of the reason, as psychologists point out, may be the fact that "dispositions to be friendly, to fight, and to submit coexist simultaneously inside the ordinary 'individual.' "[44] A people may want to fight a war for patriotic reasons and simultaneously long for peace. Leadership can stir a genuinely felt response by appeal to either of these conflicting moods. Thus the much condemned volatility of public sentiment is more apparent than real. Different emotional or situational stimuli bring out latent attitudes which were present all along. As long as opinion leaders in the presidency can focus public attention on those factors that will elicit the desired response, they can, in many instances, rapidly change the direction of apparent public sentiment. It made a great deal of difference in public willingness to fight Germany whether Germany was called the country of Goethe and Schiller or the homeland of Hitler and Goebbels.

Within limits, Presidents can even push back the dykes of basic public attitudes which set outer bounds to policy maneuvering.[45] Although Americans pride themselves on their great respect for the sanctity of human life and were appalled at Hitler's policies of human extermination, they sanctioned, albeit not without qualms, President Truman's use of the atomic bomb against Japan. The President was able to convince them that the vast human sacrifice was a legitimate gamble to avoid the chance of even greater casualties at a later date.

Change is easiest when there has been a visible change in world conditions, such as the altered situation in Europe prior to America's entry into World War II. Franklin Roosevelt could point to these changes in his efforts to transform a prevailing mood of isolationism into acceptance of foreign involvement. But even without external change, a sensitive leader can go far in discovering culturally acceptable and persuasive reasons to surmount the cultural limits of the past.

Presidents have the further advantage that they can act first and justify and win approval for their acts later. Approval of accomplished changes

[44]Joel T. Campbell and Leila S. Cain, "Public Opinion and the Outbreak of War," *Journal of Conflict Resolution*, vol. 9 (1965), p. 318. The ideas are based on the work of Lewis F. Richardson.

[45]For concurring opinions see Leon D. Epstein, "Democracy and Foreign Policy," in William N. Chambers and Robert H. Salisbury, *Democracy in the Mid-Twentieth Century*. St. Louis: Washington University Press, 1960, pp. 133–134 and sources cited there.

presents significantly fewer problems than winning favor for prospective policies.[46] Besides, Presidents can usually summon enough illustrious supporters for any policy that is plausibly defensible to convince the average citizen that a reasonable policy choice has been made. They have access to vital facts, opinions, and expert advice as well as the media to convey their conclusions. Opponents of the President have no such reservoir of ammunition for their psychological battles for the mass public's approval. Even congressional opposition can be overwhelmed by using the specter of an approving public. Despite the President's splendid natural advantages to carry the public with him, unpalatable policies may necessitate special public relations efforts and caution to avoid the kind of credibility gaps that opened up during the Korean and Vietnamese wars.

## Alternatives to Presidential Leadership

No other group or individual in American politics possesses the advantages for national leadership that the President has. American parties, organized on a state and local basis, with a weak national organization, cannot do the job. They are rent by sectional, factional, and ideological cleavages. Hence they cannot convincingly claim that their foreign policy suggestions represent the members' views, let alone the nation's.

Congress likewise bears the imprint of the diverse interests of the spokesmen for fifty separate states.[47] The average Congressman, even when he serves on congressional foreign affairs committees, projects the image of a local rather than a national leader. He is a haggler over petty details, while the President proposes bold programs which fire the people's imagination. The Congressman appears more sensitive to the needs of his local constituents than to the needs of the nation. Within his own bailiwick, he hearkens more to vocal pressure groups than to the silent masses. He knows that

> it is more important to appease a well-disciplined minority, which can deliver the votes on election day, than to gratify an unorganized and

---

[46]The conclusions reached by Leon Festinger in *A Theory of Cognitive Dissonance.* Evanston, Ill.: Row Peterson & Co., 1957, support this proposition.

[47]Rosenau, *National Leadership*, presents details, pp. 345–360; Gabriel A. Almond, "Public Opinion and National Security Policy," *Public Opinion Quarterly*, vol. 20 (1956), p. 373; Leonard S. Stein, "Consistency of Public Opinion on Foreign Policy" (University of Chicago, Ph.D. Dissertation, 1962), pp. 50, 51, 253–255 and sources cited there. A classical example of the dangers which representatives with national orientations face is Burke's failure to win reelection from Bristol.

casual majority, the intensity of whose convictions and the efficacy of whose action is far less likely to be decisive.[48]

As Abbot Smith, Madisons biographer, observed, Presidents who have relinquished even a portion of foreign policy leadership to Congress have "won neither the admiration nor even the approval of posterity." Madison's

> deference to Congress in time of crisis will always appear not as sturdy republicanism, but as weakness. Since the time of Andrew Jackson, at least, the country has expected to follow its Presidents, and those who have not led have been deemed feeble. That is the verdict upon Madison, and it will have to stand, not only as passed upon him, but as applying to his whole theory of the "neutral sovereign." In time of crisis the country must and will be led by someone. Pure republicanism never has been and never will be enough.[49]

Nor have Congresses, past or recent, attempted to assume opinion leadership. Just as they have largely abdicated the initiation of foreign policy to the President, so have they left the opinion leadership role to him. In both respects their function has become primarily one of "modifying, negating, or legitimating proposals that originate with the executive."[50] This does not mean that congressional power is negligible—far from it. An obstreperous Congress can mutilate or destroy the President's program. The meat-axe approach to foreign aid appropriations is a perennial example. But Congressmen do not generally mobilize nation-wide public opinion in support of their policies. Moreover, when crisis situations are involved, they often give *carte blanche* approval to any action the President might wish to undertake. The Formosa and Lebanon congressional resolutions during the Eisenhower days and the Gulf of Tonkin resolution in the Johnson Administration are illustrative.

There have been numerous proposals to increase the role of Congress in initiating foreign policies and guiding public opinion.[51] A number of them reflect the fear that presidential leadership may be prone to excessive use of force to glorify the single leader. If, for instance, President Johnson has a free hand to order the bombing of North Vietnam, to send warplanes to the Congo, or to land the marines in Santo Domingo, who will keep

[48]John C. Ranney, "Do the Polls Serve Democracy?" *Public Opinion Quarterly*, vol. 10 (1946), p. 352. How well Congressmen reflect public opinion is analyzed in Warren E. Miller and Donald Stokes, "Constituency Influence in Congress," *American Political Science Review*, vol. 57 (1963), pp. 45–56.

[49]Abbot E. Smith, *James Madison, Builder—A New Estimate of a Memorable Career*. New York: Wilson-Erickson, 1937, p. 286.

[50]Robinson, p. 180.

[51]Robinson, pp. 205–213.

him from heedlessly plunging the country into war? To quiet such fears, it may be comforting to ponder that American history lends no support to the specter of the power-drunk, reckless chief executive. The war-hawks have not usually roosted in the American presidency. More often, faceless crowds and Congressmen, egged on by their constituents, have been the ones to cry for hasty, forceful action to avenge insults or extend the national domain. Had it not been for such jingoist pressures, the United States might have avoided the war with Spain in 1898.

## Passive and Active Citizen Roles

If Presidents initiate policies and then lead the mass public to support them, what role does the individual citizen's opinion play in the opinion-policy process? Does his voice count for naught but support or opposition to the Establishment unless he joins an articulate dissenting group or becomes a member of the governing elite? Is the ideal of the public's right to be consulted about the direction of governmental policy a meaningless myth designed to keep people content?

The answer is complex. For the bulk of the citizenry, the role can only be "ritual, vicarious and ephemeral" limited to "the exchange of clichés among people who agree with each other."[52] It must be so limited for several reasons. Among them, we have already discussed the inability of the mass public to make and appraise the difficult decisions involved in foreign policy formulation. We have talked about the preoccupation of the average man with private pursuits and his disinclination to spend the necessary time to inform himself even to a small degree, about matters of public policy. Now we must mention the practical impossibility to pay attention to thousands of divergent opinions and some dangers that result when too many citizens press vigorously for the adoption of clashing policies. A look back to the eighteenth century will explain the situation.

During the eighteenth century, American politics presented a pattern of intense opinions, intensely held by a relatively large number of people who advocated incompatible policies. These people were unwilling to acquiesce in foreign policies that they deemed detrimental to their interests or the interests of the country. On more than one occasion these intense conflicts threatened to tear the nation apart. Had the Presidents not been able to gain the support or acquiescence of a large number of citizens for the policies that they preferred and had divergences of opinion not run across geographical lines, it is very doubtful that the union would have withstood the lack of consensus on foreign policy matters. One may well ask, as did

[52]Edelman, pp. 16, 18.

a recent analytical study of voting behavior, "How could a mass democracy work if all the people were deeply involved in politics?" And one may conclude as the authors of the study do:

> Extreme interest goes with extreme partisanship and might culminate in rigid fanaticism that could destroy democratic processes if generalized throughout the community. . . . Low interest provides maneuvering room for political shifts necessary for a complex society in a period of rapid change. . . . Hence, an important balance between action motivated by strong sentiments and action with little passion behind it is obtained by heterogeneity within the electorate.[53]

At this point, we do not know how much citizen interest is optimum. And we do not know whether extreme partisanship really is a concomitant of extreme interest.[54] But we do know that when a nation is sharply divided on issues, it is essential for political stability that on each issue there be a large number of people who, regardless of their convictions or lack of convictions, are willing to acquiesce in whatever decisions the government takes. Otherwise the dogmatism of the extremists may tear apart the nation. Or it may paralyze policy making because the incumbent government is fearful of tackling policies which are likely to kindle vicious controversy.

Even for those who do not participate actively in suggesting and critiquing policies, there are solid dividends to be earned from displaying an interest in foreign policy and keeping informed. The views of knowledgeable citizens, even though not directly presented to decision makers, are likely to weigh more heavily in governmental decisions than the opinions of uninformed publics. For instance, studies of constituency influence in Congress reveal that: "Congressmen who believe that their constituents are interested in and informed about issues of governmental policy are more likely to reflect constituency attitudes in their voting in Congress than those who believe that their constituents are less politically aware."[55] Similarly, Presidents tend to be more responsive to the political wishes of publics whom they perceive as politically informed and interested. Estimates of public awareness form part of the appraisals of latent opinion

---

[53]Berelson, *Voting*, pp. 314–315. See also discussion of this point by Robert A. Dahl, *A Preface to Democratic Theory*. Chicago: University of Chicago Press, 1956, pp. 90–119.

[54]For the notion that partisanship is less appropriate in regard to foreign policy matters than in domestic affairs see H. Bradford Westerfield, *Foreign Policy and Party Politics*. New Haven: Yale University Press, 1955, *passim;* and Cecil V. Crabb, Jr., *Bipartisan Foreign Policy, Myth or Reality*. Evanston, Ill.: Row Peterson Co., 1957, *passim.*

[55]John W. Kingdon, "Politicians' Beliefs About Voters", *American Political Science Review*, vol. 61 (1967), p. 137. Also Miller and Stokes, pp. 45–56.

which, as we have seen, may set bounds to what Presidents will undertake or decline to do in foreign policy in anticipation of consensus or lack of consensus. Appraisal of public awareness also influences decisions to publicize or withhold information. An alert public will be rewarded with a far fuller diet of policy news and explanation than an intellectually sluggish one. It can become a keener watchdog to guard against possible abuse of executive leadership and the bursting of culturally acceptable policy dykes.

Moreover, knowledgeable citizens are better able to judge whether policy serves them and the nation well and to perform their political functions accordingly. They can use their votes on election day to rid themselves of sponsors of unwanted policies and elect those who most closely mirror their foreign policy views.[56]

A small number of citizens can fill the role of expert advisor on technical matters or specialized economic, social, or political problems. Modern policy making requires answers to a multitude of highly technical problems. Government leaders are increasingly tapping the expertise of private citizens to cope with these problems.[57] In-as-much as broad policy hinges on the outcome of these smaller decisions, expert advice on limited issues may have a significant effect on the overall configuration of policy. For instance, advice on the feasibility of producing a specialized weapon or solving a difficult transportation problem, or estimating the economic strength of a given country, or judging the soundness of its banking practices may well determine the choice among various policy alternatives.

There also is a constructive advisory role for a small number of citizens who possess no specialized expertise but are truly well-informed and interested in major foreign policy problems.[58] However, this role is constructive only if the number of activists is limited and if their advice is well-reasoned and mindful of broad public rather than narrowly private concerns.

[56]Psychological evidence for the congruency of leader-follower views is presented in Kamla Chowdry and Theodore M. Newcomb, "The Relative Abilities of Leaders and Non-Leaders to Estimate Opinions of their Own Groups," *Journal of Abnormal and Social Psychology*, vol. 47 (1952), pp. 51–57, and George A. Talland, "The Assessment of Group Opinion by Leaders and Their Influence on Its Formation," *Journal of Abnormal and Social Psychology*, vol. 49 (1954), pp. 431–434.

[57]Rosenau, p. 18. The utility of outside experts is discussed by Sapin, pp. 324–326.

[58]A Minnesota panel of 79 "world affairs knowledgeables" selected for such characteristics included 28 teachers, mostly in social science higher education, 22 business and professional people, 12 voluntary organization leaders, 9 journalists, 5 ministers and 3 political leaders. Rogers, *et al.*, p. 243.

Several approaches are available to such interested individuals to influence the decision-making process or build public opinion pressures for their views. The individual can work through interest groups, parties, *ad hoc* citizen committees like the Citizen Committee for the Marshall Plan, or through official or unofficial sources that happen to have the ear of the executive establishment or the mass public.[59] If he has the necessary verbal and personality skills, he can join the ranks of intermediate opinion leaders —men and women who are able to get a following for their views.[60]

## Obstacles to Effective Dissent

The function of advice and dissent performed by attentive publics suffers from two major handicaps. These are unwillingness of White House occupants to tolerate dissent or take advice and the dissenters' inability to gather adequate, independent information from sources which are not linked to the Establishment. Officials at the highest level have always been sorely tempted to resent criticism and suggestions from outsiders who are not privy to all the information available to insiders and who do not have to execute policies, as well as make them. Government leaders have complained that criticism is overly generously supplied by people who present no realistic alternatives for policies which they attack. They point to the fact that government channels of communication are frequently glutted with more messages than can be handled effectively beyond a mere counting of assent and dissent for a given policy.[61]

At the same time, Presidents have frequently reaffirmed their belief that a free exchange of criticism and ideas, beyond the solicitation of expert advice, is one of the great advantages of democracy. It brings to light new ideas, calls attention to errors, and stimulates the public to pay closer heed to public affairs. Democracy presumably relies on responsive leaders whose followers question the wisdom of choices, rather than on leader charisma which carries unquestioning followers along by virtue of the leader's personal magnetism.

Since the virtues of vigorous dissent, within limits, admittedly outweigh the annoyances, receptivity to criticism should be cultivated. But it rarely is. In fact, after repeated criticisms officials may be more eager to defend a policy and cling to it to prove that it is right, than to reexamine

[59]Cohen, *Influence*, p. 19, presents opinion-submitting methods.

[60]Gabriel Almond, *The American People and Foreign Policy*. New York: Praeger, 1960, p. 140, calls "the vast number of vocational, community, and institutional 'notables'" the "most effective opinion leaders."

[61]Roger Hilsman, "The Foreign Policy Consensus," *Journal of Conflict Resolution*, vol. 3 (1959), p. 377, believes that the stream of suggestions submitted to the government is more than adequate.

the policy to test the merits of the critics' objections. Dissenters may find that they are engaged in a self-defeating venture. Under fire, officials tend to maximize successes and to minimize losses. Policies attacked as erroneous may be defended so firmly that in the end they seem more justifiable than before. Good ideas which could provide a much-needed antidote to intellectual inbreeding in the administration are lost all too often.

The other basic difficulty, the scarcity of nongovernmental sources of information, is far more onerous to resolve. Ideally, citizens ought to have ample sources of factual information that are independent of government and hence unaffected by governmental selection methods, interpretations, and possibly distortion and suppression. In practice, with some important exceptions, foreign policy data come largely from the executive branch. Individual government officials select from myriads of facts which come to their attention those which they deem important for policy formulation. These selfsame facts on which the executive bases decisions are released to various other governmental agencies, to the mass media, and then to the public. In the total of information available to the citizen, that which comes primarily from independent sources, such as special reports by newspaper foreign correspondents, is a very small proportion. Not even Congress has its own information-gathering organization, despite its many investigations and hearings on the executive's handling of foreign policy matters.[62]

Moreover, the press is not the completely independent "fourth branch" of government that idealists picture. It is also part mistress and part priest. It is a kept woman in the sense that newsmen depend on government officials for news handouts. They dare not offend the individuals and agencies supplying this news to them. Especially those newsmen who enjoy privileged access to highly placed persons find that efforts to protect these sources from embarrassment may be a highly restraining influence. Neither can responsible newsmen let the news fall where it may. Like priests, they often listen to confessions of weighty deeds, past and present, yet feel morally constrained to withhold their knowledge from the public. Their relations of confidence with their confidants and considerations of national security weigh heavily against the public's right to know. For instance, James Reston of the New York Times knew of the high altitude U-2 spy flights over Russia a year before Gary Powers' plane crashed on Soviet soil. Yet by the time the press felt free to publish the story of the U-2 flights, the nation was in the midst of a nasty diplomatic confrontation which might have led to war.[63]

[62]Robinson, pp. 188–196, recommends ways in which Congress might improve its independent intelligence collecting function.

[63]James B. Reston, "The Press, the President and Foreign Policy," *Foreign Affairs*, vol. 44 (1966), p. 558.

The practical obstacles to a substantial increase in privately secured information are vast. Independent collection or even examination of most of the data involved in foreign policy making by people outside the governmental hierarchy has become well-nigh impossible. Only a large-scale organization can assemble the data and correlate them so that they become meaningful for practical policy making. No private citizen or organization has the time or means to do a comparable job. At best, individuals and private organizations can concentrate on depth studies of single problems or policies. Despite their limited coverage, these can be highly significant in providing fresh ideas and a springboard for needed dissent.

Although the limitations under which political outsiders labor are severe, their role can nonetheless be useful, even when it is based exclusively on government-supplied data. Different interpretations based on similar information may be highly significant. They may indicate alternative courses of action that can logically be supported by government data, and that the government may have overlooked or rejected too quickly.

## A Model of Public Opinion Flow

To present the influence that public opinion has on foreign policy formulation more graphically and concisely, one can devise a multistage model. The three basic stages of the model are the information selection stage, the policy formulation stage, and the policy execution and modification stage.

Stage one, the information selection stage, can be subdivided into three parts: the information gathering phase, the information reduction phase, and the information acceptance phase. In the information gathering phase (Fig. 1), information is transmitted to the policy makers through various communications channels. Messages come from the bureaucracy, other members of government, or from outside sources. They are submitted spontaneously or following requests from decision makers. Alternatively, the information may be derived from the decision makers' own perception or the perception of their associates. In addition, decisionmakers have information recalled from memory of past events and their perception or the perception of their associates. In addition, decision from their cultural background, personality, and system of values and objectives.

The information made available to decision makers during the information gathering phase consists of factual data about relevant military, political, social, and economic factors, and frankly interpretative data that

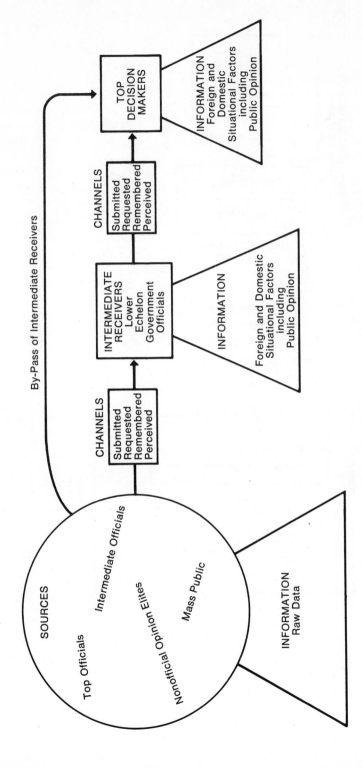

Figure 1    Information Selection Stage: Information Gathering Phase

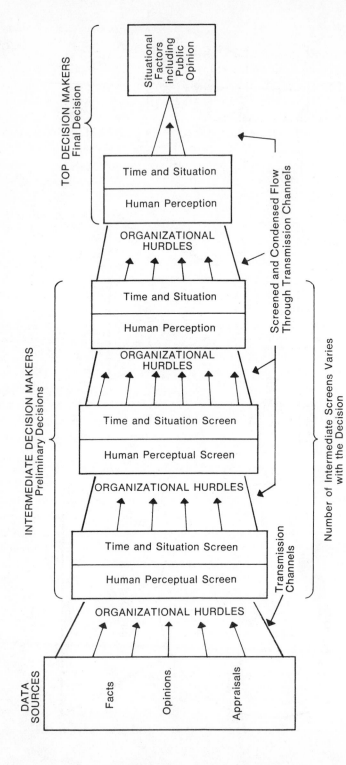

**Figure 2    Information Selection Stage: Information Reduction Phase**

assess the meaning of the "facts" and recommend certain actions.[64] The data usually include an appraisal of the public mood and the mood of various opinion leaders and their followers who are expected to respond more or less vigorously to political action in the area in which activities are contemplated. The data may also include a thin trickle of policy suggestions from nongovernmental opinion leaders. However, as the cases showed, the bulk of policy suggestions originate with the inner circle of advisors. They are, of course, influenced by the advisors' appraisal of public desires and suggestions. On relatively rare occasions there is vigorous, intelligent discussion of policy options by Congressmen and other governmental and private opinion leaders, including reactions from interested publics. At such times, these appraisals can rest more heavily on hard data rather than intuition.

During the information reduction phase (Fig. 2), the flow of information which is transmitted to policy makers, including public opinion data, narrows sharply as it is scanned and screened before reaching the final decision-making group. The process of reduction can be pictured as a series of hurdles that any given piece of information or advice must overcome. These hurdles are of three types. There are organizational hurdles in the sense that information must ordinarily pass through a series of prescribed channels. For instance, it may pass from a Public Affairs Advisor in a geographical bureau of the State Department to a higher echelon official in the Bureau of Public Affairs, to an Assistant Secretary of State, to the Secretary of State, to the President. The longer the transmission chain, the greater the chance that the message may be lost, garbled, distorted, or modified.[65]

The second type of hurdle is the human perceptual screen. Each individual who relays information in the transmission chain, except for those who merely copy data, leaves his imprint on the information. Each human source selects, omits, often rewords or rearranges and condenses information in a way that may affect its ultimate disposition by the final decision makers.[66] Information that is omitted or downgraded by intermediate interpreters may, for all practical purposes, be blotted from the communication process. As far as the decision makers are concerned, if it does not reach them, it might as well never have existed.

Lastly, there are time and situation hurdles. What happens to each

[64]The adverb "frankly" is added because all statements of fact contain an element of interpretation.

[65]Robinson, p. 126, reports that in the period studied by him the Assistant Secretary of State for Congressional relations, who had excellent access to his chief, took only 20 percent of problems presented to him directly to the top.

[66]Patterns of communication flow are discussed by Karl W. Deutsch, *The Nerves of Government*. New York: The Free Press, 1966, pp. 98–109.

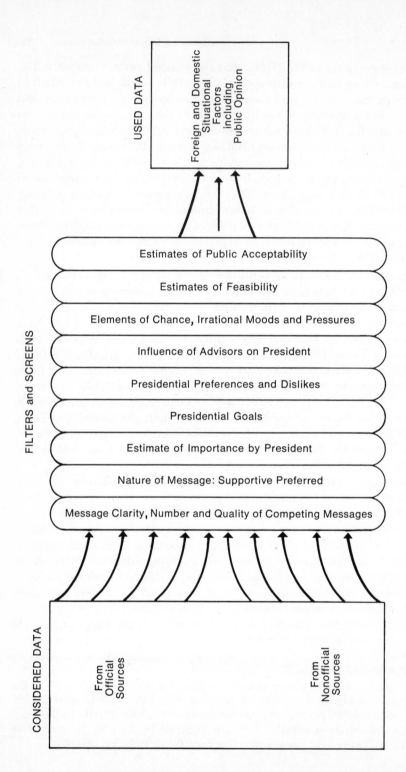

**USED DATA**

Foreign and Domestic Situational Factors including Public Opinion

**FILTERS and SCREENS**

Estimates of Public Acceptability

Estimates of Feasibility

Elements of Chance, Irrational Moods and Pressures

Influence of Advisors on President

Presidential Preferences and Dislikes

Presidential Goals

Estimate of Importance by President

Nature of Message: Supportive Preferred

Message Clarity, Number and Quality of Competing Messages

**CONSIDERED DATA**

From Official Sources

From Nonofficial Sources

**Figure 3    Information Selection Stage: Information Acceptance Phase**

discrete item of information depends very much on the overall status of the communication system at the time the information becomes available. During periods of information glut, common during crises, much is lost entirely which might pass to the top in calmer times. What seems important or unimportant also depends on the time when it is said and the events that are at the forefront of the decision makers' attention.

Whether or not a given bit of information will survive the screening processes and will reach the inner decision-making circle relatively unscathed depends largely on the number of hurdles to be passed or by-passed and the nature of the specific hurdles which it must scale. Its ultimate fate is partly a matter of formal and informal organizational procedures at a given time and partly a matter of chance.[67]

The information acceptance phase (Fig. 3), like the reduction phase, hinges on the human qualities of the links in the communication chain. The chance that a message that has managed to reach the top will be included among the information that forms the raw material for decisions, depends heavily on the source from which it emanates or through which it is transmitted. If the source scores high marks for credibility, astuteness, and access to valid data, chances for acceptance are enhanced. Since members of the President's inner circle generally rate highly on these criteria, while governmental outsiders rank comparatively low, messages initiated or transmitted by insiders stand a good chance of consideration. Because access to the inner circle greatly increases the likelihood of message acceptance, much political energy is expended by opinion submitters to rout their messages directly to the top.[68] However, one should not equate access with acceptance. A large number of messages which go all the way to the top nevertheless are rejected with or without consideration.

The reasons for rejection may lie in the nature of the message, in the perceptual background of the President, and in factors of time and situation. The President, like most human beings, often will hear and perceive only what he wants to hear and perceive, and fail to hear or perceive dissent. He will also pay attention to "important" messages and ignore those that appear to be of little significance. What is or is not "important" is a value judgment that is conditioned by his perceptual screen and that of his advisors. It also depends on the efficiency of routing procedures in the communications system.

On the whole, communications engineering in government is still at a very rudimentary stage. Aside from "fire-alarm" type messages that receive priority in attention and access to the top fairly consistently, no

---

[67]Robinson, pp. 126 ff, charts the internal communication system within the State Department. He emphasizes that personal acquaintance is the single most important factor in determining communication routes.

[68]For an example of a successful attempt see Robinson, pp. 149–150.

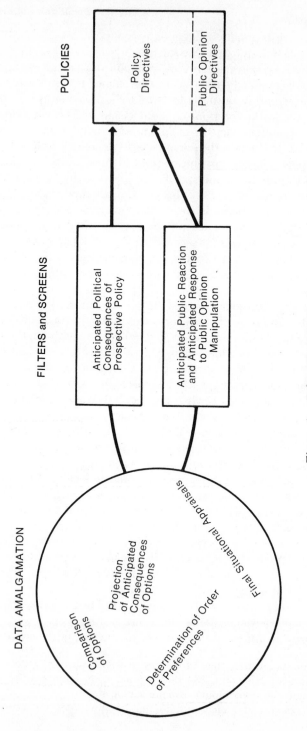

**Figure 4    Policy Formulation Stage**

effective system is available for setting up a hierarchy of importance among messages and channelling them accordingly. Decisions about what information is important enough to be sent directly to the top are made individually and impressionistically by lower echelon officials who, generally, have only very rough guidelines for their appraisals.[69] In their decisions they rely largely on their own perceptions and evaluations of the importance of data presented to them.

We have already discussed the nature of perceptual screens and time and situation screens in the information reduction phase. These same factors also operate during the acceptance phase. Whether data will be accepted or rejected by the President depends on the interplay of many factors. It is affected by the President's background and value system, his interaction with his advisors or other communicants, and the time when the information arrives. As the case studies have shown, it also depends on the value and priority he places on particular policy goals at the time the information reaches him, on what then seem to be politically relevant situational factors, and on his current estimate of available national resources including public good will for presidential policies.[70]

At the policy formulation stage (Fig. 4), the President scrutinizes and evaluates various factors that have come to his attention and the various policy options suggested to him and arrives at a policy decision. "Decision making consists in the combination of values, plus attitudes, plus information, plus perception, plus situation into the choice of a course of action."[71] The case studies have shown that presidential evaluation of public opinion factors is an important component at this point, although not the most important. The public opinion factors that are usually considered, more or less explicitly, are the anticipated reactions of mass and elite publics to various policies and the overt expressions that the reactions may take. In addition, the President examines the ways in which information release can modify the response to make it more helpful and less burdensome for carrying out a given decision.

[69]On this point, see Deutsch, pp. 94 ff.

[70]Snyder et al., pp. 130–131, distinguish between primary messages, which mean the information itself; secondary messages, which are the labels attached to information that classify it; and tertiary messages, which are the specific meanings given to the information by persons who use it during decision making.

[71]Snyder et al., p. 243. See also Delbert C. Miller and Fremont A. Shull, Jr., "The Prediction of Administrative Role Conflict Resolutions," *Administrative Science Quarterly*, vol. 7 (1962), pp. 143–160, who state that the legitimacy of claims, the power of sanction held by the claimants, and the personal orientation of decision makers are the crucial factors in the ultimate choice. The morally oriented decision maker stresses legitimacy; the expediently oriented one stresses sanctions. Many decision makers stress both.

If public opinion obstacles are expected, either because large-scale dissatisfaction fanned by elite opinion leaders will undermine the appearance of mass approval, or because opposition groups are able to bar policy execution, policy adjustments may be made accordingly. These usually involve more active opinion manipulation aimed at concealing or popularizing the policy and undermining the critics and their views, rather than a change in basic policies that otherwise seem preferable. Concessions may be made on details that are of particular interest to special publics. But there is a strong presumption that policies that seem acceptable to the major policy makers can be made palatable to the mass public, at least to the point of sustaining the image of majority consensus. On the whole, little attention is paid to policy advice that may come from intermediary opinion leaders or specially interested groups, unless it involves veto-support considerations.

In stage three (Fig. 5), steps are taken to prepare for policy execution along the needed fronts. Depending on anticipated public reactions, information is given out to gain opinion and action approval for the new policy. American political culture favors rational appeals on the assumption that doubters can and should be rationally convinced that a policy is correct and hence must be tolerated. But rational appeals have always been accompanied and supplemented by more emotional tactics of persuasion, ranging from simple flag waving and vilification of the opposition to deceptive oversimplification of issues and even outright distortion.

When acquiescence or support for a projected policy exists already, or is anticipated, simple information techniques can serve to link decision makers and the public. Official action and public opinion conform naturally, with a minimum of public relations effort. When opposition exists or is expected, the information mechanism may have to shift into high gear, straining the boundaries between impartial information and propaganda. Or there may be a total blackout in the downward flow of information in order to conceal a policy during its most vulnerable stage. If a blackout is impossible, or not indicated, information flow may be carefully tailored and curtailed to help overcome opposition and avoid arousing resistance. At the very least, if the administration can help it, information will not contain matters that are deemed harmful to the contemplated decision.

In the downward flow of messages from government to people, as in the upward flow from people to government, loss of messages is strikingly high. Much governmental information fails to reach its target or fails to make an impact and yield desired results. In a complex society, like the American, the individual is bombarded with messages from many quarters that compete for his limited attention capacity. In the melee, the majority

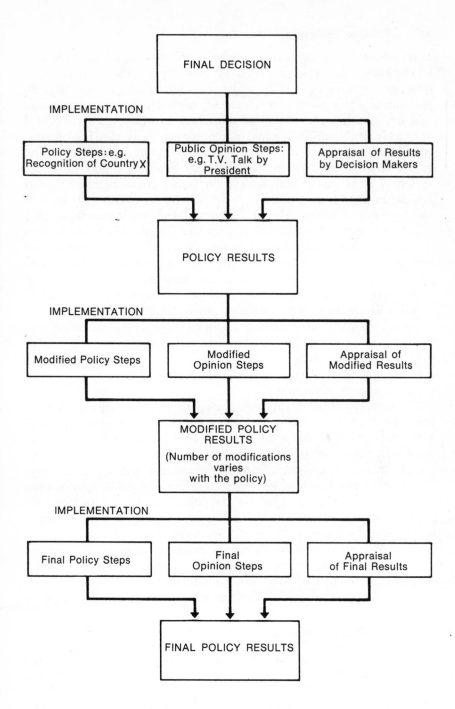

**Figure 5    Policy Execution and Modification Stage**

of governmental messages are never received. They fail to pass the various transmission hurdles, are drowned out by easily absorbed curiosity satisfying messages, or rejected by audiences who do not perceive their importance or whose intake system is already glutted with incoming messages.

If messages are received they are often misinterpreted, ignored, slighted, or quickly forgotten. The amount of information the average human being can absorb, retain, and use at any given time is paltry, indeed, compared to the flood of information that confronts him in a highly developed society. This is true of both ends of the public communication process. Neither Presidents nor ordinary people can cope simultaneously with the vast amounts of relevant data available to them to make up their minds about a given situation.[72] Much of what they presumably know, because it was available to them or called to their attention, never enters their stream of conscious thinking. However much a given item of information may impress a third party, there is no assurance that it impressed a President or a public at a given time merely because it was readily available.

Policy execution is not a unilinear process in which policy, once determined, is carried out unblinkingly. During the process of execution, continuous reassessment takes place to ascertain whether the action taken has the desired results and whether the goal needs revision. If desired results are not obtained, there may be modification of the policy or even a complete change of direction.

The appraisal of policy success includes the appraisal of public opinion reaction, elite as well as mass. Supporting views, whose origin is attributed to the public, may at this point be merely an echo of a successful government information program. At times, a policy may reach its objectives except for the public opinion front. Public relations techniques may then have to be stepped up or altered. At other times, the public opinion front may be secure but other aspects of the policy may misfire. In that case, public opinion considerations will again have to enter into the decisions to be made about policy modification or redirection.

Generally, public opinion efforts are deemed successful if there appears to be mass acquiescence or support for a policy and if no obstacles are placed in the path of policy execution by disgruntled opponents. The Establishment generally makes no attempt to encourage dissent and stimu-

---

[72]Properly programmed computers can ease this problem somewhat. How individuals cope with overloads of information is discussed by James G. Miller, "The Individual as an Information Processing System," in William S. Fields and Walter Abbott, *Information Storage and Neural Control.* Springfield, Ill.: Charles C. Thomas, 1963, pp. 301–328. The effects of overloads in crises are analyzed by John T. Lanzetta, "Group Behavior under Stress," *Human Relations,* vol. 8 (1955), pp. 29–52; and Robert L. Hamblin, "Group Integration during a Crisis," *Human Relations,* vol. 11, (1958), pp. 67–76.

late discussion to probe policy weaknesses and bring forth alternatives. Rather, the initiative for posing alternatives and finding fault is left to the political opposition and private individual and group critics.

## A Common Political Culture

The model depicts a relatively minor role for public opinion influence on foreign policy decisions. It shows that direct flow of opinions and suggestions to the apex of the governmental pyramid is but a trickle. Even the indirect flow, tainted with the interpretations of opinion transmitters, is but a small portion of the total flow of influences that go into the making of foreign policy decisions. Information from the case studies indicates that support, rather than advice, is the major concern of the decision makers and that support is sought more by finding ways to make accomplished decisions acceptable to the public than by adjusting the decisions to public tastes. Even pressure groups often find that their impact on foreign policy is slight.

But the model does not picture what is perhaps the greatest public opinion influence on governmental decision making: the sharing of a common political culture by the people and those whom they freely elect to public office. Political leaders incorporate the views of the public into their decisions because they themselves are members of the public. They have been nurtured in the same intellectual and social climate and their own reactions are in many ways akin to the reactions of the general public. Even when they differ, generally in the direction of greater liberalism and internationalism, they are no strangers to the public's moods.[73] They share what Professor Francis Graham Wilson calls the "preconditions of the existence of public opinion," namely "the sense of a community in existence, and a code for the operation of the community."[74] They also have the desire to make policy conform to the social wants and needs of the general public of which they are a vital part.

[73]Mass and elite likenesses and differences of opinion are analyzed in Herbert McClosky, "Consensus and Ideology in American Politics," *American Political Science Review,* vol. 58 (1964), pp. 361–382. Also see Sidney Verba *et al.,* "Public Opinion and the War in Vietnam," *American Political Science Review,* vol. 61 (1967), p. 331, whose survey of public opinion on the war in Vietnam concluded that "the informed and articulate do not differ from the rest of the population in their preferences or in the likelihood that they take either extreme or moderate position."

[74]Francis Graham Wilson, *A Theory of Public Opinion.* Chicago: Regnery, 1962, p. 20.

A President may be, as was said of President Truman, "the average man writ exceedingly large," but he is still an average man.[75] His selection by a large number of people indicates that he possesses the common touch and can act in accordance with the basic values of the people. Periodic presidential elections assure that Presidents keep close to the common touch. They also serve as a reminder that popular favor must be curried continuously. In electoral competition the candidate whose policies promise to be closest to popular preferences and prejudices has a decided advantage. The folksiness of a Truman or a Roosevelt that wins votes is nothing more than presidential ability to adjust behavior to environment and to be sensitive to the latent reactions of constituents.[76]

Nurtured in the ethos of American democracy, Presidents have an intuitive grasp of the broad limits of ends and means within which their policies must abide in order to be acceptable or tolerable to the public. They sense and feel, rather than measure and count, public sentiment and most of them know intuitively which combinations of publics must be heard and heeded if policy is to be executed successfully at a given time. They know, for instance, that the high regard that Americans have for the sanctity of human life precludes a policy of ruthless extermination of populations such as Hitler undertook in Europe. They know the limits set to foreign aid measures by the dread of being "the sucker" who gets nothing in return for his efforts.[77] They also know that absence of publicly acceptable motives that can be cited for a prospective policy makes it impossible to carry out the policy without sacrificing the legitimating image of mass support. As a recent study on *Foreign Policy Decision Making* notes: *"The decision to perform or not to perform a given act may be taken on the basis of the socially available answers to the question: what will be said?"*[78] Until now, American Presidents have shown no desire to adopt policies that flout the culturally imposed limitations.

Presidential advisors have been culture bearers as well:

> Their perceptions of the world scene do appear to be derived from similar frames of reference and similar sources of information. . . . their assessments of how the United States should respond to trends abroad do seem to rest on a common core of values. Behaviorly they do appear to react similarly to shared experience.[79]

[75]The phrase is from Paul P. Van Riper, *History of the United States Civil Service*. Evanston, Ill.: Row Peterson & Co., 1958, p. 405.

[76]Lewis Edinger, "Political Science and Political Biography," *Journal of Politics*, vol. 26 (1964), p. 665.

[77]Almond, *The American People*, pp. 61–62, discusses this attitude.

[78]Snyder *et al.*, p. 146. (Italics in original.)

[79]Rosenau, p. 331, speaking of national opinion makers in foreign policy.

As long as American political culture prepares public officials to act as true surrogates of the people, executive initiative in policy formulation and strong public opinion leadership to rally mass support behind policies are compatible with the belief that public policy reflects public opinion. In the final analysis, it is the general climate of democratic life in the United States that makes public opinion an important ingredient in foreign policy decisions.

The most immediate danger in the public opinion-policy relationship is not that the people's views will lack consideration or that public opinion will place undue restraints on imaginative policies. Rather, the greatest danger is that a noisy minority, ably led, will be mistaken for a majority and will be allowed to be unduly influential by a President who feels that he must defer to the commands of an imperious public. Modern Presidents share with their predecessors an inherent aversion to noisy pressure groups employing flamboyant tactics to call attention to their views. Nonetheless, they may find it more difficult in the mass communication age than ever before to resist the pressure to accommodate the demands of such groups. Protest demonstrations receive instant, wide publicity. The very fact of publicity tends to exaggerate the size of objecting groups. This magnified image of the strength of such groups may put the government into a defensive posture. It may choose to accommodate the objectors to preserve what it considers a waning popularity. If this occurs, and regardless of the merit or lack of merit of the altered policies, a dangerous divorce of decision-making authority and responsibility takes place.

Conflicting views on specific policies are unavoidable and are a sign of political vigor, rather than decay. But when a choice must be made among conflicting versions of what constitutes "the public interest" to be served by foreign policy decisions, the constitutionally designated final judge is and must continue to be the President. That is the lesson of the past—one that Americans cannot ignore lest it imperil the welfare of the nation.

# Bibliographical Note

This book owes a profound intellectual debt to a vast variety of printed sources. Philosophically, the book is grounded on the extensive literature relating to the democratic process. Particularly relevant are studies that explore the extent to which policy making must be based on the will of the people and studies of the obligations of elected representatives to lead and follow their constituents. To cite all these studies here would be an unnecessary encumbrance. They range from Plato's *Republic* and Aristotle's *Politics* to studies by twentieth century political theorists. A few recent works that provide an introduction to this vast intellectual domain are Peter Bachrach, *The Theory of Democratic Elitism*. Boston: Little Brown, 1967; John Plamenatz, *Man and Society*. New York: McGraw-Hill, 1963; Leslie Lipson, *The Democratic Civilization*. New York: Oxford University Press, 1964; Henry B. Mayo, *An Introduction to Democratic Theory*. New York: Oxford University Press, 1960; and Giovanni Sartori, *Democratic Theory*. Detroit: Wayne State University Press, 1962.

Literature on decision making and on the impact of the personality of political leaders on the nature of their decisions has also been used extensively in writing this book. The footnotes in Chapters 1, 11, and 12 are guides to such works. Additional sources are listed in recent collections of readings on foreign policy making, such as R. Barry Farrell, ed., *Approaches to Comparative and International Politics*. Evanston: Northwestern University Press, 1966; Herbert C. Kelman, ed., *International Behavior*. New York: Holt, Rinehart and Winston, Inc., 1966; James N. Rosenau, ed., *Domestic Sources of Foreign Policy*. New York: The Free Press, 1967; and J. David Singer, ed., *Human Behavior and International Politics*. Chicago: Rand McNally, 1966.

Methodological problems in public opinion research are discussed by a number of recent texts, including Harwood L. Childs, *Public Opinion:*

*Nature, Formation, and Role.* Princeton, N.J.: D. Van Nostrand Co., 1965; Bernard C. Hennessy, *Public Opinion,* Belmont, Calif.: Wadsworth Publishing Co., 1965; and James N. Rosenau, *Public Opinion and Foreign Policy.* New York: Random House, 1961. The entire Winter 1967–1968 issue of the *Public Opinion Quarterly* is devoted to "The Historical Study of Public Opinion" and contains a weatlh of references to recent methodological investigations. Problems of tracing linkage of public opinion to public policy are discussed in a series of readings edited by Norman Luttbeg entitled *Public Opinion and Public Policy.* Homewood, Ill.: The Dorsey Press, 1968.

The reader interested in a particular case or in the political theories and backgrounds of the Presidents discussed in this book should use the respective chapter footnotes as a bibliographical source. There may be some raised eyebrows, especially among historians, about the inclusion of many older and seemingly outdated works and about the exclusion of some recent, highly esteemed sources. These omissions and inclusions result from the focus of concern of the book: public opinion as seen and interpreted by the *President* and his closest advisors. Many old sources, such as the McMaster and Henry Adams histories, dwell at much greater length on expressions of public reaction and on the daily personal contacts of the Presidents than do more recent histories. Since individuals personally involved in a political event are more apt to capture the nuances of what seemed important at the time and what was ignored, special emphasis has been placed on the accounts and biographies of participants in the decision-making process. Likewise, the works of historians who had personal acquaintance with the period in question or personal access to Presidents or their associates have been given preference. Although observer-participants and close-range observers are often deficient in objectivity, they excel in reporting subjective phenomena, such as tensions or feelings of relief and good-will that often pervade a meeting or the personal interactions of participants in a decision. Those flavors of life largely elude outsiders and writers after the fact who then are forced to substitute synthetic reasons for the feel of reality.

It was, of course, impossible to determine a priori which works would be helpful and which would be barren in terms of the objectives of the present study. For this reason, a very inclusive research policy was followed. All works with any promise of relevance were checked. Undoubtedly, there have been some inadvertent omissions; but, on the whole, the reader can safely assume that omission of certain works from the footnotes means that they contained no materials relevant to the impact of public opinion or that other works, cited in the footnotes, presented more suitable accounts.

# Index of Authors

# Index of Subjects

Adams, John, 39–103; advisors to, 57, 72–73, 89–91, 94; on alliance policies, 80–81; and Cabinet, 67, 73–75, 77, 85–89; on campaign oratory, 54; and civil disobedience, 102; and Congress, 67–69, 70, 71, 93–94; on congressional capabilities, 48–49; and decision making, 82–84; on dissent, 82; on education, 46; on electoral competence of people, 54; on elites in government, 58–59; on equality, 59; foreign policy of, 65–79; on human nature, 41, 45, 47, 53; on legislature's role, 55–56, missions to France, 66–68, 74, 78–79; on mob rule, 50; and neutrality policy, 65–66, 71, 80–81; on partisanship, 53; and party politics, 83–84, 98; personality of, 41–44, 47, 58, 60–61, 79; on political competence of people, 43–45, 47–48, 50, 53–54; on political debates, 44; and political meetings, 91–92, 99–100; on political recruitment, 86; political socialization of, 42–45; on presidential role, 35, 58–60; and the press, 27, 55, 76, 92, 99; and Preston defense, 60; on property ownership and politics, 50–53; and public information, 61–62, 96–97; and public opinion, 47–48, competence of, 54, consultation of, 56–57, management of, 94–101, measurement of, 55, 75–76, 91–92, submission channels 54–56, submission to, 56–57; and public service, 8, 43, 48–49; and religion and politics, 100; on representation, 45; social origins of, 42; speeches and messages, 100–101; on war spirit, 48; writings of, 45–46, 61; and XYZ dispatches, 68–70

Adams, John Quincy, 24, 85, 211, 245, 273–275, 276, 291n; and Monroe Doctrine, 275, 278–279
Advisors to Presidents, 38, 57, 72–73, 89–91, 94, 149–150, 208–209, 215, 279–281, 284, 312–316, 323, 336, 339, 349
Alliance policies, 80–82, 267–269, 288–289
Ames, Fisher, 90–91

Britain, relations with U.S., 28, 191–200, 203–205, 261–265; sympathy for, 19, 21, 68–71

Cabinet, and Congress, 276, 283; and foreign policy, 67, 73–75, 77, 85–89, 141, 146–147, 208–212, 270–276; and President (see names of Presidents); and public opinion, 87, 276–279; selection methods, 85–87, 146–147, 209–212, 272–276
Cabot, George, 98–99
Calhoun, John C., 266–267, 275, 277–278, 293
Canning, George, 261–265
Censorship (see Press, censorship of)
Chance as political factor, 316–317, 355–357
Channels of communication (see Communication channels)
Checks and balances system, 41n, 168–170, 179–180
China, relations with U. S., 11
Churches and politics, 22, 43, 100, 129
Citizen, role of, 347–350; see also Political competence of people
Civil disobedience, 47, 55, 102, 120–121, 183, 256–257